Thinking Like a Researcher

Thinking Like a Researcher

An Engaged Introduction to Communication Research Methods

Jake Harwood

University of Arizona

Bassim Hamadeh, CEO and Publisher
Todd R. Armstrong, Publisher
Tony Paese, Project Editor
Abbey Hastings, Associate Production Editor
Jess Estrella, Senior Graphic Designer
Alexa Lucido, Licensing Manager
Natalie Piccotti, Director of Marketing
Kassie Graves, Vice President of Editorial
Jamie Giganti, Director of Academic Publishing

Printed in the United States of America.

Brief Contents

Table of Contents

Preface

Teaching research methods can be a frustrating experience. There is a lot of terminology, much of which takes everyday words (e.g., "random") and uses them in ways that students find counterintuitive (who knew how hard it is to be truly "random?!"). There are obscure processes to test hypotheses that even their daily users admit are backward ("We have to disprove the negative?!"). These issues can make it difficult to lose track of the simple goal: to ask a question and answer it using observations of the world. This book tries to refocus students toward that simple process by using the following, hopefully somewhat novel, techniques.

1. Organization of the text around extended examples that frame pairs of chapters: The first chapter in each pair deals with methods (what would you do to gather data to answer the question?) and the second with analysis (what would you do with the data?). The problem is front and center, so students know *why* they are learning certain techniques.

2. A personalized approach: Each problem is encountered by a student or recent graduate in a context that most students can relate to.

3. Active student engagement: Students reading the book will repeatedly be asked to fill in the blanks, provide responses, and guess at the answer to a question. These prompts (assuming students use them!) will keep the student engaged in the material and in most cases will reinforce the idea that much of the practice of doing research is fairly intuitive once you are thinking like a researcher.

4. Jumping right in: The book starts with a research problem. There is minimal introductory material; instead, readers are encouraged to start thinking like a researcher from the first paragraph of the book.

5. Writing the research: Each chapter includes a model of how to write the research, so students see an "end product" at each step of the way.

6. Real tools: The book describes free and familiar tools (e.g., Google Sheets) that will allow students to run analyses on real data and get real results.

Students will learn the technical vocabulary typical of a research methods class in the course of reading the book, but they will do so in the context of engaging examples. It is my hope that this will get them ... Thinking Like Researchers!

I would like to acknowledge the people who read earlier drafts of this work and provided invaluable feedback: Bradley J. Bond (University of San Diego), Jon Nussbaum (Penn State University), Rick Olsen (University of North Carolina Wilmington), Maggie Pitts (University of Arizona), and Kylene J. Wesner (Texas A&M University). I would also like to thank the hundreds of students who have taken my research methods classes over the years. It is their questions, confusions, and corrections of *my* mistakes that shaped the content of this book. Thanks also to my fantastic colleagues and students at the University of Arizona who make researching (and writing about researching) such a pleasure on a daily basis.

Introduction for the Student

Welcome to research!

In this book, you're going to meet some people who are busy doing communication research in their daily lives.

- **Cassandra:** She works at the student newspaper and has a rather demanding boss who keeps asking her to find stuff out.
- **Francisco:** He is doing an internship at a city government health agency, trying to find out whether a social media campaign getting kids to exercise is reaching its audience and having any effects.
- **Andre:** He is interning with a political campaign, helping the candidate understand whether appearing on social media is good or bad for her image.
- **Aaliyah:** She is a recent college graduate working at a public relations firm. The firm is helping a company that has gotten into hot water over leaking private information. Aaliyah is helping them figure out who should be their spokesperson.

These are all situations in which research is important. Having an opinion about the answers to questions is fine, but social science research offers the opportunity to find out the *correct* answer to certain questions. Through the experiences of our four budding researchers, this book will help you learn how to do research right.

Each section of the book (except the last) contains two chapters. The first ("Doing the Research") describes how to gather data. Research almost always involves observing the world to get information to answer a question, and there are good and bad ways to make these observations. The second chapter in each section ("Reporting the Research") describes how to analyze the data. Once you have observed the world and gathered information, there are best practices for examining the data to answer your question. Both sections will tell you how to write about your research in ways that are accurate and clear.

Learning how to be a researcher is a process—one that is never finished. But this book will give you a tool kit that will allow you to actually perform real research studies from start to finish.

Imagine your dream job. It can be as far-fetched as you'd like. Now, can you imagine one way in which you might need to either do or at least understand social science research as part of that job? Perhaps it's not obvious to you yet. I'll ask you the same question at the end of the book, and I suspect you'll have an answer by then.

SECTION 1

Using Measurement to Answer an Empirical Question: How Much Are People Reading the Campus Newspaper?

By the end of this section, you will be able to:

- ✔ Measure the frequency of a communication behavior
- ✔ Distinguish between a conceptual and operational definition, and understand how the two are related
- ✔ Appreciate when a question requires the gathering of data
- ✔ Understand the difference between self-report, observational, and archival data analysis
- ✔ Report the results of a basic statistical analysis of data

CHAPTER 1

Doing the Research: Measuring a Single Variable

Cassandra works for the *Daily Centurion*, the campus newspaper at Middle State University. Her editor has asked her to "find out how much students are reading the student newspaper." The editor is asking for *information* and wants an answer (as opposed to a guess or an opinion). In this case, the answer will involve numbers—an answer in hours per week or something similar would help Cassandra answer the question. Where will she start?

Measurement: Turning Social Behavior Into Numbers

Cassandra needs to **measure** something. Let's call it *Centurion* reading. And she is assuming that *Centurion* reading *varies*—some students read the paper a lot and some don't ever read it. It would be weird if everyone on campus read the newspaper exactly the same amount, right? Anything that varies is called a **variable.** How should Cassandra measure the variable *Centurion* reading? Before proceeding, think about how *you* would go about measuring this variable. In the space below, write a brief description of how you would measure it.

Using reader response boxes

There are reader response boxes throughout this book. Taking a couple of minutes to respond in these areas will be valuable for helping you engage with the content and in subsequent review for exams. Go ahead—scribble away!

There are a few different approaches to this sort of measurement problem. In your earlier response, you probably described something like one of the following:

a) **Self-report:** Maybe you decided that you could ask people how much they read the newspaper. Whether or not you went this route, think now in a little more detail about how you might do that. And yes—just asking people "How much do you read the newspaper?" is an option here, but think about the vague responses you might get if you just asked that. ("A lot!" "I dunno." "Once a week or so." "Whenever I get around to it.") Think about how to ask the question in a way that you'll get answers that are meaningful.

   Write a question or questions here and think about the answer options people might have. Are people allowed to respond in any way they want, or will you give them a limited set of options?

b) **Observation:** Maybe you decided you could watch people in a location where newspapers are available and see what they do. For example, you could observe a newspaper stand and see how many people pick the paper up (versus don't), or you could observe classrooms before classes start to see how many students are flipping through the paper before the professors begin talking. Think about what *you* could observe that would let you get *numbers* from observations of people's newspaper consumption. Write two to three sentences describing what observations you might make if you were trying to measure newspaper reading by observation.

c) **Existing data ("archives")**: Sometimes you get lucky and data already exist that measure what you are interested in. In the newspaper-reading example, for instance, perhaps at the end of each day, a university truck drives around campus picking up all the unread papers from the distribution stands and sends them to a recycling agency. If the university or the recycler keeps track of the volume of papers, then you could get a decent idea of how many people are taking a paper with a simple subtraction calculation:

[total number of papers printed] – [total sent to recyclers] = total "read"

How might *you* measure readership using information that already exists? [Hint: Think about new technology here—readership includes online reading, so are there data that exist there That might help you?]

Before continuing, look back at your initial strategy for measuring *Centurion* reading. Did it use self-report, observation, or existing data? After having thought about those three types of data collection, which one would you go with now?

Cassandra's First Measurement Plan

Cassandra went through the same process you did in terms of brainstorming some different ways to answer this question. She realized that to do good observations would take a lot of time—she didn't have enough time in her schedule, and her research project (like many such projects!) has a very limited budget. Similarly, it was a nice idea to look at how many papers get recycled, but it turns out that on her campus, nobody keeps track of that, so she couldn't use such information. She also thought about using website views (that was my earlier hint about technology), but her information technology department couldn't help her get that information. Sigh. So, Cassandra decided to go with self-report measurement.

Cassandra asked a group of students at the university library the following question:

How often do you read the newspaper (select one option)?

- ☐ Almost every day
- ☐ A couple of times a week
- ☐ Once a week
- ☐ Once a month
- ☐ Never

This question is called an **operational definition**: an operational definition is a description of *how* something is measured—the *operations* you have to perform to get the data. An operational definition for taking someone's temperature might be something like "Take a thermometer, stick it in the person's ear, read off the number."

In the boxes that follow, describe three pros and three cons of Cassandra's operational definition and her broader research strategy. Think carefully about the way her question is worded, the response options she provides, and the people whom she is asking the question.

Pros	Cons

Hopefully, you identified some of the following points:

Question wording: Doing social science research can make you obsessive about wording. When writing questions like the one Cassandra wrote, you should think about *every word* in the question. Notice, for instance, that her question asks how often people read the newspaper, not how much they read it. So, someone who just glances at the front page headline each day might technically count as having "read" the newspaper every day; while someone who reads it in depth once a week would score lower. Think about the word read in her question. For one student, glancing at the headline might count as "reading," while for another student it might not; Cassandra should think about how her respondents may interpret the wording of her question. Perhaps most critically, Cassandra's question asks about the newspaper—a term that may imply *any* newspaper. But actually, she is only interested in the *Daily Centurion*. A critical error that researchers sometimes make is to imagine that their respondents are psychic!

KEY POINT

Conceptual definitions. If you don't know precisely what you mean by "*Centurion* reading," your measurement will not be clear. Before thinking about how to measure *Centurion* reading, Cassandra should have carefully defined what she meant by the term. For example:

> *Centurion* reading is the number of minutes per day that a student spends reading or looking at pictures in the *Centurion* newspaper.

This is called a **conceptual definition**—a verbal definition of what your variable *is*. A conceptual definition is a little like a dictionary definition. This definition should guide your measurement—if the conceptual definition says minutes per day, then you must measure reading in minutes per day. In other words, *your conceptual and operational definitions must match*—they must be consistent with one another.

Response options: In much social science measurement, respondents must select from a series of choices. The choices offered determine the data that you get, and sometimes the choices you offer can cause problems. In Cassandra's example, for instance, people who read the newspaper four times a week are stuck "between" two options (do they check "almost every day" or "a couple of times a week"?). That's not good—these people may just skip the question, or answer haphazardly, or just get pissed that they are not "represented" in the answer options. The "never" option here also may be problematic: How many students on a university campus will literally *never* have read the campus newspaper? It isn't good to include options that apply to no one, so almost never or very rarely would probably be a better option here. Most importantly, if Cassandra really wants to know about *Centurion* reading in *minutes per day* (look back at the conceptual definition), she needs to ask about *that!* When writing this sort of question, you must think carefully about the response options you provide. We will explore how to write this kind of question much more later in the book.

Female or male (check only one option)!?

Even when the response options for a particular question seem "obvious," they may need careful consideration. A few years ago, "male" and "female" seemed like the only and obvious options to a question asking people their gender (or "sex"). In recent years, we have become more aware of complexities in gender identity and the need to allow people more options than just male/female. The Human Rights Campaign (HRC) suggests wording like the following for asking about gender (and it is always worth checking with resources like the HRC for this sort of wording because opinions on what is appropriate change over time). This suggestion is for a workplace survey:

Our company does not discriminate on the basis of gender identity or expression. In order to track the effectiveness of our recruiting efforts and to ensure that we consider the needs of all our employees, please consider the following optional question. What is your gender?

- ☐ Female
- ☐ Male
- ☐ Nonbinary/third gender
- ☐ Prefer to self-describe ____________________
- ☐ Prefer not to say

Source: Human Rights Campaign: http://bit.ly/2NxwCjd

The people: Remember that Cassandra's editor asked her how much students are reading the newspaper. Presumably, the editor meant *students in general* or *average students*. Are students at the library "average" students? Probably not. Next, write *three* ways that students in the library may differ from students in general.

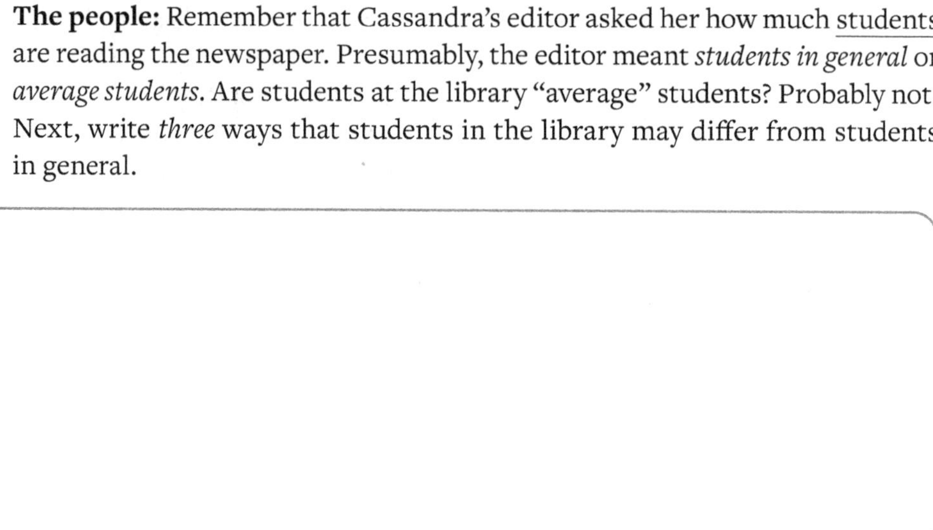

You probably guessed that students at the library might be more studious than students not at the library. Studious students might also be more serious and more likely to read the newspaper, so that difference really matters for the question the editor is asking. If Cassandra only asks students at the library, she might get an estimate of students' newspaper reading that is higher than it really is. Her estimate would be **biased.**

Students in the library might also be unusual in other ways. They might be older students (students who are parents might use the library as a refuge from their kids), or lower income students (if you can't afford broadband at home, the university library is a good place to do research), or history students (if the library has rare old books, perhaps you need to be in the library to study them—biology students are more likely to be in the lab). So the students in the library might not be the best way to go.

Subjects/respondents/participants

The people in a study are variously called **respondents**, **subjects**, or **participants**. Those terms all mean the same thing. The group of *all* the respondents is called the **sample**, and the process of creating a sample (selecting the respondents) is called **sampling**. A sample that reflects a larger group of people is called a **representative sample.** The larger group of people is called a **population**. Cassandra's sample of students from the library is a **nonrepresentative** sample—it doesn't represent all students for the reasons described.

Cassandra's Final Plan

Cassandra's editor wants to know how much an average student reads the newspaper. Cassandra has now carefully defined what she (and the editor) mean by "reading the newspaper" (i.e., in the conceptual definition from earlier, it is minutes per day of reading or looking at the newspaper). Adopting this definition, Cassandra's measurement must be in minutes per day—her **operational definition** must match her **conceptual definition**. We also know that she wants to measure this variable with a group of students who are similar to the entire student body (not a group of particularly studious students, or students from only one major, etc.). She needs a **representative sample.**

To get a representative sample, Cassandra asks the campus registrar for a **random sample** of 50 student cell phone numbers. Random? That doesn't sound very scientific! Random actually has a very specific scientific meaning in this context. It means that every student on campus has an **equal chance** of being in Cassandra's sample of 50. This assures Cassandra that there can't be any **bias** toward more (or less) studious students, or one major over another, or any other characteristic. For communication researchers, random does *not* mean haphazard, hit or miss, or slipshod. To be truly random actually requires quite a bit of care—something we will return to later in the book.

KEY POINT

Sampling error and bias. Samples can go wrong (fail to represent a population perfectly) because of two things: **bias** and **error**. A **biased** sample will *always* tend to feature a certain type of person. If you want a sample representing the entire U.S. population, you shouldn't sample outside an elementary school (you'll get ridiculous numbers of soccer moms and dads) or a movie theater (you'll get too many dating couples). On the other hand, *all* samples have **error**—error just means that the sample doesn't *perfectly* represent the population. Just due to chance factors, Cassandra's random sample of 50 cell phone numbers might turn out to contain a larger proportion of history majors than in the entire student population, or a smaller proportion. But it won't be **biased**—if you took a whole bunch of samples, on average, they'd have just the right number of history majors.

To get her data, Cassandra texts each student on the list and asks them to answer the following question:

In minutes, how much time did you spend yesterday reading the *Daily Centurion*?

_______________ *minute(s) (please respond with a whole number; if you did not read the newspaper at all, respond with zero)*

Why do you think Cassandra asked specifically about yesterday? What are two pros and two cons of that strategy?

Pros	Cons

Asking about a very recent time period is a common strategy used by researchers. By asking about yesterday, Cassandra ensures that students are responding about a time period that they can fairly accurately recall. Our ability to remember what happened yesterday is much better than our ability to remember what happened 3 weeks ago. This strategy will mean Cassandra gets more accurate (valid) data.

The downside, of course, is that yesterday might not have been a normal day for some respondents. If it was a weekend day, or a day when they didn't have class, some respondents would report zero, even though on other days they read the newspaper a lot. Cassandra should send out the texts on a variety of days so as to capture students' reading across the entire week, not just on one day. It's OK if she captures a few students on unusual days—unusual days happen, so it's OK to measure them. Most students Cassandra measures will be captured on typical days because ... most days are typical (indeed, that's pretty much the definition of typical!).

Cassandra's strategy also relies on students responding accurately and indeed remembering accurately. The students' responses will not be perfect, obviously—they might misremember whether they spent 5 or 10 minutes with the newspaper. But they are unlikely to think they spent 2 hours with the newspaper when in fact they didn't look at it. This is what I mean by a "good enough" solution: Cassandra's data will reflect students' broad patterns of newspaper reading, even if they are not accurate to the nearest millisecond.

Assuming Cassandra's respondents answer her text, she will end up with 50 students' estimates of their previous day *Centurion* reading. Data! In the next chapter, you will see some things that Cassandra can do with these data.

Research ethics. It is important to consider whether your research might have harmful effects before you do it. Of course, a researcher might not be the best judge of whether her research may be harmful, so most research institutions (universities as well as private research companies) have their own ethics boards, often called Institutional Review Boards (IRBs). These boards decide whether it's "OK" for the researcher to do a study based on a description submitted by the researcher. Throughout this book, we'll see some things a researcher might need to do to make sure they get the "thumbs up" from the IRB.

Writing the Report

Throughout the book, I'll be giving you examples of how to write reports of research. Gathering data is great, but it's typically not just for your own benefit. If you are working for a business, you will probably have to write a report for your boss about the data, and if you are an academic researcher, you will want to publish your findings. When you gather data, you need to explain what you *did* so that other people can judge what your findings *mean*. Report 1.1 is an example of what Cassandra might write to her editor to explain *how* she gathered her data. In the next chapter, you'll learn how she might report *what she discovered*.

REPORT 1.1 Methods for Measuring a Variable

I randomly selected 50 Middle State students from a list of all students' phone numbers. They were sent a question via text message asking them to report their readership of the campus newspaper. Response rate was 100%.

The sample was 70% female (26% male, 4% nonbinary/third gender) and was of typical college student age (M = 20.32 years, SD = 4.27). It was diverse in terms of race and ethnicity (62% white, 35% Latino/a/x, 28% black/African American, 14% Asian American, 6% Native American; numbers do not total to 100% because respondents could select more than one option).

Newspaper readership was assessed with a single question that asked the students to report in minutes how much time they spent "yesterday reading the *Daily Centurion*."

NOTES: The "*SD*" in this report represents standard deviation, a statistic you will learn more about in the next chapter. Typically, when reporting scientific research, you let your reader know basic information about your sample like the demographic information described here. This helps us understand the nature of the sample, even if you are not examining those factors in any detail. Most questionnaires, therefore, include questions about this demographic information. When doing research on any sample, reporting the response rate is also important (see the end of the first paragraph). This tells your reader how many of the people you *asked* to participate actually *did* participate. A response rate of 100% is, as I'm sure you can imagine, very rare!

Qualitative, quantitative, and nonscientific questions

Research involving numbers is called **quantitative** research—quantitative research involves counting, or rating, or scoring things. In contrast, some research is **qualitative**. Qualitative research explores questions that can't be fully answered with numbers. An important question like "*Why* do people read the newspaper?" doesn't have a purely numerical answer. Finally, some questions can't be answered with quantitative *or* qualitative information. If you want to figure out whether God exists, whether the death penalty is morally right or wrong, or *Star Wars* vs. *Star Trek*, you need the help of a philosophy or a film theory. Those are not *scientific* questions. This entire book is about questions that can be answered using facts about the world: **empirical questions** or **scientific questions.** Empirical questions can be answered with quantitative or qualitative information. The book will deal first with quantitative questions and then discuss qualitative questions later.

Other Applications

You've been working through a fairly standard research problem in this chapter. Cassandra was trying to measure a single variable (time spent reading the newspaper) with a well-defined population (her school's student body). A strategy like hers would be useful with lots of other research questions involving measuring how much time people spend on specific tasks. Can you think of a couple of communication activities that you might be interested in measuring in a similar way?

I would use a strategy like Cassandra's if my research involved finding out things like the following:

- In an organization, how much time do employees spend checking and responding to e-mail?
- On basketball teams, how much time do players spend talking to one another about rebounding?
- In marriages, how much time do the spouses spend talking to each other face-to-face? How much time do they spend texting each other?
- In college classes, how much time do students spend checking their cell phones?

The strategy might not work as well in other contexts. If you were interested in how much time preschool children spend playing with tablet computers, you would need to ask the parents or teachers, not the kids. Young children (and some other groups) can't respond to typical self-report measures because of reading ability, and young children also have a fairly loose idea of time. If you were interested in how much time prisoners were spending planning their escapes, using a cell phone or e-mail would not be a good idea, both because prisoners have limited access to electronic devices and because those devices *identify* the prisoners. When asking about sensitive information, you need to ensure respondent **anonymity**, both to get accurate responses and to protect your respondents. If you were studying the prisoners, you might use an anonymous paper and pencil questionnaire that is put in a locked drop box with many other responses.

Your Turn

Each chapter in this book has a "Your Turn" section for you to practice what you've learned in the chapter and to develop a real research project over the course of the book.

For this first chapter, pick one of the variables you thought of in the last response box (or another variable if you have since thought of something else that is more interesting to you). If you are having trouble thinking of a variable, consider aspects of people's communication in relationships, or their uses of media or technology, or communication phenomena that happen in their workplaces. Pick something that you find interesting.

Write a single sentence conceptual definition of your variable: define it like a dictionary would define it. Then describe in detail how you would *measure* the variable, including the exact wording of the question(s), and the response options you would give to people responding (i.e., create an operational definition for the variable). It is useful when doing this to put yourself in the position of the person responding—imagine you were answering the question as a naïve respondent, and make sure your question or questions make sense.

When you are happy with your question, you might want to create it in a free online survey creation tool—two good options are SurveyMonkey (www.surveymonkey.com) and Google Forms (www.docs.google.com/forms). An advantage of Google Forms is that it connects directly to Google Sheets, so if you actually collect data, you can move it easily from Forms to Sheets to do your analysis. A Google Forms version of Cassandra's question is at this link: http://bit.ly/2gtVclL.

Write your question down and have a friend respond to it to make sure it works. Ask your friend if s/he had any trouble understanding your question. Remember this information for the next chapter!

Wrap Up

This chapter has introduced some important concepts that you will use throughout the book. You may want to review the "key words" that follow to make sure that all the terms look familiar and that you understand the basics of each. More broadly, the chapter introduced the research process—how to go from a question to a plan for answering the question using observations of the world.

If you get nothing else from this chapter, remember the following:

1. You need to carefully define any variable that you want to measure (a conceptual definition).
2. Your measurement technique (operational definition) should be consistent with your conceptual definition.
3. Doing a research study is a process of making choices—choices about your sample, and your conceptual/operational definitions, and your research technique. Often, there is no "best" choice, but there *are* better and worse choices; the rest of this book is about helping you make good choices.

Key Chapter Concepts

Archives: Yes, "archives" sounds like some dusty library in the basement of a museum, but an archive is just any existing set of resources (information, data) that you might use to answer a question. If you downloaded all of President Trump's Twitter account you would have an archive, just as if you accessed the completion statistics for National Football League (NFL) quarterbacks over the past decade. Notice in the Twitter example that "data" doesn't have to mean numbers. Communication researchers use language as data all the time.

Bias (in sampling): Systematic (regular, predictable) ways in which a sample doesn't represent a population. A sample of Olympic athletes taken from right outside the swimming pool will include a lot more swimmers than the entire population of Olympic athletes. See also **Error.**

Conceptual definition: A verbal "dictionary" definition of a variable. See also **Operational definition**.

Data: Recorded information about the world that can be analyzed to answer scientific questions. Data are often numbers, but they can be many other things—videos, texts, audio recordings, etc. The word "recorded" is important here. All the texts you sent in 2014 would count as data, but only if you have some magical way of recovering them!

Empirical questions: Questions that can be answered using observations of the world, including questions that can be answered using scientific research. A question like "What color is Julie's shirt?" is an empirical question but doesn't really require scientific research!

Error (in sampling): Haphazard ways in which a sample doesn't perfectly represent a population. A random sample of Olympic athletes might include a few more swimmers than the entire population of Olympic athletes, just due to chance. That is called sampling error. See also **Bias.**

Nonrepresentative sample: A sample that does not represent a larger population. If you are trying to predict the results of a presidential election, a group of students is a nonrepresentative sample. Students vote differently than the population as a whole, and so their voting plans won't help you in predicting the election outcome. Students differ in *systematic ways* from the rest of the population. See also **Representative sample.**

Observation: Gathering data by watching what goes on, but typically without intervening. If you want to find out whether certain types of people drink Pepsi versus Coke, you could hang out near a vending machine and see who buys what.

Operational definition: The precise method you will use to measure a variable—how you get numbers that represent a given person's "score." The operational definition must be consistent with the **conceptual definition.**

Population: The entire group of people that a researcher wants to understand. If you were studying attitudes toward gay marriage in America, then all Americans would be your population of interest. If you are studying the effect of a breast cancer detection program among low-income women in Minneapolis, then the population would be all low-income women in Minneapolis.

Random sample: Same thing as a **representative sample.** Random does not mean the same thing as "haphazard." True statistically random processes are designed to guarantee no bias in the selection of a sample.

Representative sample: A smaller group of people (the sample) that can be treated as representing an entire population; a representative sample is not biased—meaning it does not deviate in *systematic* ways from the characteristics of the population. The average of a random sample will probably be different from the population average, but it will not be predictably different: it might be higher or lower. If a sampling method is *biased,* then samples you take using that method will differ from the population in predictable ways (e.g., every sample you take in the student library will yield a set of students who are more studious than your average student). A representative sample means that every member of the population has an *equal* chance of being in the sample. Representative samples are often also called random samples because they are selected using statistically random techniques. See also **Nonrepresentative sample.**

Self-report measurement: A measurement in which the respondent provides data about him or herself. An easy way for you to find out if I prefer Pepsi or Coke is to ask me.

■ CHAPTER 2

Reporting the Research: Descriptive Statistics

Cassandra did a great job of measuring newspaper reading. She now has her raw data—scores for newspaper reading in minutes per day for 50 students. Her data might look a little like Table 2.1. The first person in the data set read the newspaper for 0 minutes a day, the second for 9 minutes, the third for 10 minutes, and so on. There are a total of 50 scores representing 50 people's newspaper reading. Just from scanning the data, you can see a few things: There are several people who don't read the paper at all and a handful who read it quite a bit; the big numbers are fairly easy to spot (e.g., at least one person reads the paper for a full 30 minutes a day). However, Table 2.1 is not hugely informative: Our brains process this sort of information better when it is organized and summarized. This chapter will focus on those two activities: organizing and summarizing.

TABLE 2.1 Raw Data

0	9	10	5	15
9	7	10	0	7
10	3	5	5	0
0	0	15	20	6
4	15	0	0	20
4	15	7	10	0
10	9	3	7	30
3	0	20	2	4
10	5	18	8	9
5	15	10	0	30

Describing Data 1: Distributions

The simplest form of organization with a set of numbers is just to put them in order (see Table 2.2). Now it is suddenly very easy to see that there are 10 people (20% of the sample) who don't read the newspaper at all and two people who read it for 30 minutes a day. Other patterns in the data become much clearer (e.g., there are more single-digit numbers than two-digit numbers). If you know that there are 10 scores per column, you can quickly see that 32 people read for less than 10 minutes a day: that's 64% of the sample [32/50*100 = 64]. Taking a set of numbers and arranging it in order creates a **distribution.** Table 2.2 is a distribution, while Table 2.1 is not.

TABLE 2.2 Data Arranged in Order: A Distribution

0	2	5	9	15
0	3	5	9	15
0	3	6	10	15
0	3	7	10	15
0	4	7	10	18
0	4	7	10	20
0	4	7	10	20
0	5	8	10	20
0	5	9	10	30
0	5	9	15	30

Google Sheets

For the rest of this book, you will be doing quite a bit of work in Google Sheets (www.google.com/sheets). There are more sophisticated statistical software packages out there, including some others that are free (e.g., R Project: https://www.r-project.org/; JASP: www.jasp-stats.org). However, Google Sheets is the easiest free option available, so it is what we will be using for all the basics in this book. Google Sheets will work best if you create a Google account (if you don't already have one) and if you use Sheets in the **Chrome** browser. In other browsers, it looks pretty funky and works slowly. To create your own Google Sheet, just go to www.google.com/sheets and click on "Blank" on the top left of the page. To edit any of my Google Sheets, go to "File—Make a copy" to create your own version of my sheet. You'll see a set of menus at the top of the screen: File, Edit, View, etc. As the book progresses, some of the "Going Further" sections will also introduce you to running some statistics in JASP—a more sophisticated, but also more complicated, statistical software.

Creating a distribution is very easy. Open a new Google Sheet (see sidebar) and enter a few numbers in the first column (don't enter them in order). Then just go to "Data—Sort Sheet by Column A," and your numbers will now be in order. Fantastic.

You can see Cassandra's data distribution at the following link: http://bit.ly/2vcJ0gT. We'll be using this spreadsheet quite a bit in this chapter, so go ahead and open it. If you want to experiment with the data on your own, you can go to "File—Make a Copy" to create your own version, which you can edit however you want. Cassandra's data are in Column B of that spreadsheet (first tab). In Column A, I put a few names just to remind you that each score belongs to a person; there are 50 rows of data corresponding to the 50 people who told Cassandra about their newspaper reading. Each cell is identified by a column letter and a row number. So, for instance, cell B9 contains Alison's newspaper reading score (Alison doesn't read the newspaper, so her score is a zero).

Describing Data 2: Using Graphs

One excellent way to summarize a data set like this is with a **histogram**. A histogram represents the scores of a variable along the x-axis (in our case, minutes per day of newspaper reading will be on that horizontal axis). The number of times that a particular score appears is represented on the vertical or y-axis. These are called frequencies.

The chart that follows is the first attempt to create a histogram for Cassandra's data. The Google Sheet contains instructions for you on how to create this chart. From Figure 2.1, it is very easy to see the 10 people who don't read the newspaper—they are the first column in the chart, showing a frequency of 10 for the score of 0 minutes per day. You can also see that seven people read the newspaper for 10 minutes a day, and three people read it for 20 minutes a day. Figure 2.2 matches some of the data to the histogram to make this clearer.

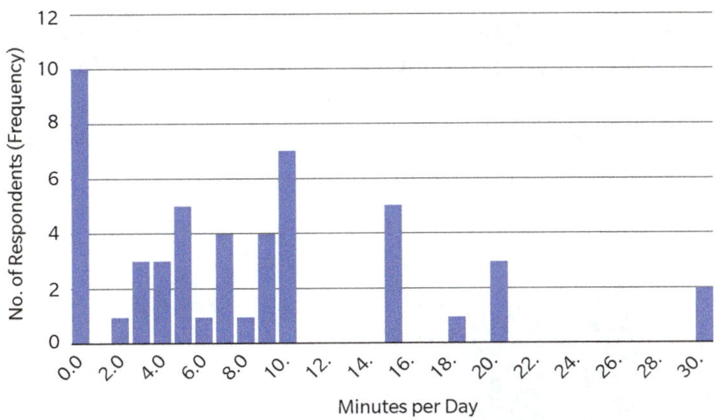

FIGURE 2.1 Histogram of minutes per day of *Centurion* reading

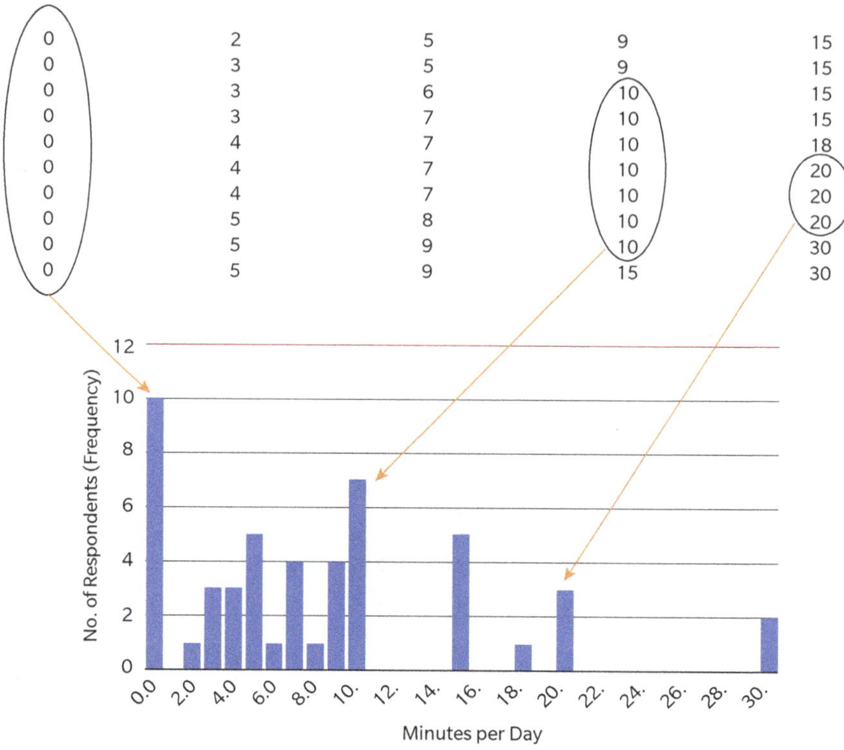

FIGURE 2.2 Connecting raw data to a histogram

If this histogram contains too much detail, you can "collapse" the x-axis into bigger ranges of minutes per day. Figure 2.3 uses "bins" of 5 minutes. So the first column represents people who read the newspaper for 0–4 minutes a day, then 5–9 minutes, etc. So you should be able to see that six people read the newspaper for between 15 and 19 minutes a day (the fourth bar in the chart). The Google Sheet (http://bit.ly/2vcJ0gT) gives you instructions for modifying these aspects of a chart presentation—practice a little so you are comfortable and appreciate how some charts provide more useful information than others.

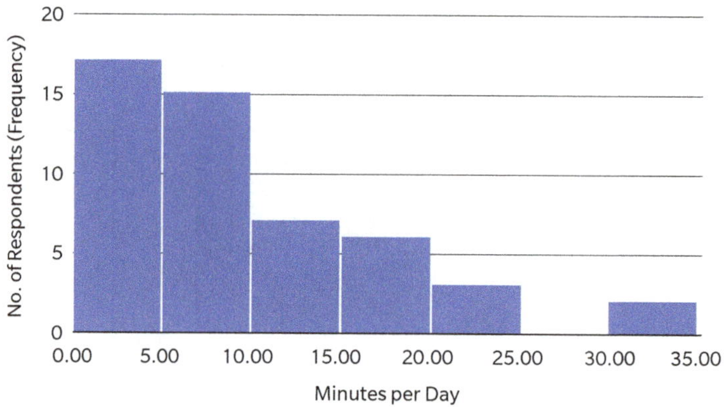

FIGURE 2.3 Histogram of the same data arranged in larger bins

Histograms provide a visual image of the "**shapes of distributions.**" Figure 2.1 shows visually that the majority of people score fairly low, with fewer people scoring high. This shaped distribution is called a **positively skewed** distribution. In contrast, you might imagine other variables where scores are distributed in the opposite manner. An easy exam, for instance, might yield a distribution that looks more like Figure 2.4. This sort of distribution is called **negatively skewed.** Relatively few people got scores below 80, and most people scored in the 90s on this particular test. In a negatively skewed distribution, most scores are on the right-hand side of the histogram.

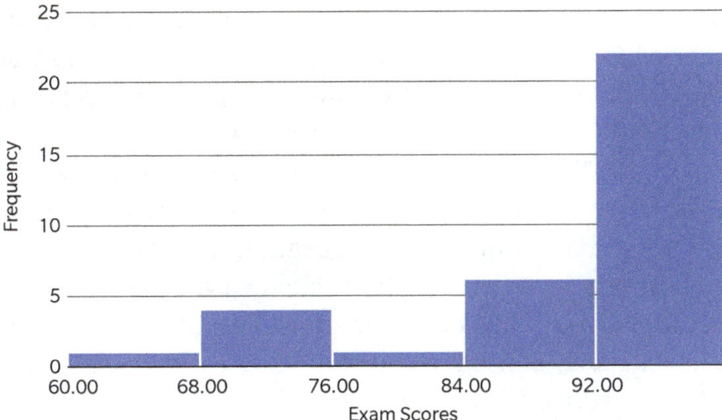

FIGURE 2.4 A negatively skewed distribution

Meanwhile, a lot of variables have a more symmetrical distribution. If you ask people how many text messages they sent in a day, you might see something a little like Figure 2.5: Some people send a lot of text messages, while others send none at all (if the numbers seem low overall, then you've learned something about how often I send texts!). This shape is often called a **normal distribution.**

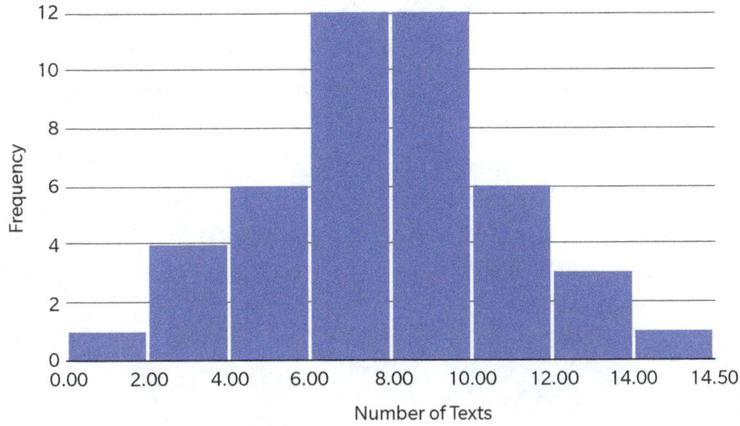

FIGURE 2.5 A normal distribution

The general shapes of these distributions tell you something interesting about how people score. Are people bunched up at one "end" of the distribution, or are most people in the middle? These distributions also illustrate that the "middle" of a distribution is not always where most people score. We tend to think that the middle also equals "average," but that is not always the case, as the next section will show.

Describing Data 3: Using Central Tendency Statistics

Cassandra's initial report and the histograms in Figures 2.1–2.3 are quite informative. There are other statistics she could provide about her data, however, that would help her editor understand what is going on with the readership of the newspaper. He might ask her how much time the "average" reader spends with the paper. You are probably familiar with how to calculate an average (also called a "**mean**")—just add all the scores and divide by however many scores there are. You can see this calculation at the bottom of the 50 scores in the Google Sheet (http://bit.ly/2vcJ0gT: the numbers in red, beginning with cell B52). The "sum" is all the scores added together: All 50 people read the paper for a total of 409 minutes a day. The Google Sheet gives you the formula you can use to calculate this for your own data. The next cell down tells you that there are 50 scores. So the mean is 409/50 = 8.18; as the spreadsheet shows, you can also calculate this directly using a formula (see the formula in cell B55).

Cassandra can tell her editor that the average person reads the paper for 8.18 minutes a day.

The mean is not the only measure of the "middle" of a distribution, however. There are two other measures of "**central tendency**" that Cassandra might want to explain. First, the **median** is the "middle" score: half of the distribution scores at or above the median and half of the scores at or below it. For Cassandra's data, the median is 7. For a distribution with an odd number of scores, the median is literally the middle score; for a distribution with an even number of scores (like Cassandra's), you take the average of the two middle scores (which in Cassandra's case are both 7). Notice that the *average* of the distribution is not the same as the *middle* score—there's over a minute's difference between them.

The third measure of central tendency is the **mode**. The mode is the most frequent individual score in a distribution. In a histogram, it's easy to spot the mode: it's the tallest column. In Cassandra's numbers, more people scored a zero than any other score, so the mode is zero. You can see this visually in Figure 2.2 from earlier in the chapter.

Can you think of one important reason why we have these three different measures of central tendency rather than just having a single measure?

Why do we have three different measures of central tendency? There are two main reasons. First, not all measures of central tendency work with all types of data. If you ask people their religion, for instance, it doesn't make sense to calculate the "average" (or even the median religion). Calculating an average requires having "scores," but your membership in a religion isn't a score. For something like religion, the only sensible measure of central tendency is the mode. It is perfectly sensible to calculate the most *common* faith in whatever group of people you are studying. We'll discuss this issue of "types of data" more in the next chapter.

The second reason is that the relative size of the mean, median, and mode tell you something about the shape of the distribution. Typically, if the mean of the distribution is higher than the median and mode, the distribution is positively skewed. Likewise, if the mean is lower than the median and mode, the distribution is negatively skewed. You can see this even with very simple distributions. Calculate the measures of central tendency for the following two distributions and draw a histogram of each. You can do this by hand or in a spreadsheet.

Distribution A: 1, 1, 1, 2, 2, 5

Mean =

Median =

Mode =

Distribution B: 1, 4, 4, 5, 5, 5

Mean =

Median =

Mode =

Either just from looking at the numbers or from drawing the histogram, you should be able to see that Distribution A is positively skewed, while Distribution B is negatively skewed. And the measures of central tendency reflect that. The mean is larger than the median and mode for Distribution A, but smaller for Distribution B. Details on working through these calculations are provided in Figure 2.6. The histograms clearly indicate the skew, with scores bunched on the left side for Distribution A (positive skew) and to the right for Distribution B (negative skew).

Distribution A: 1, 1, 1, 2, 2, 5

Mean = (1+1+1+2+2+5)/6 = 12/6 = 2
Median = (1+2)/2 = 3/2 = 1.5 [Remember, with an even number of scores there isn't a "middle" score, so we take the average of the two scores nearest the middle of the distribution; the third score is a 1, and the fourth score is a 2, so the median is the average of 1 and 2.]
Mode = 1

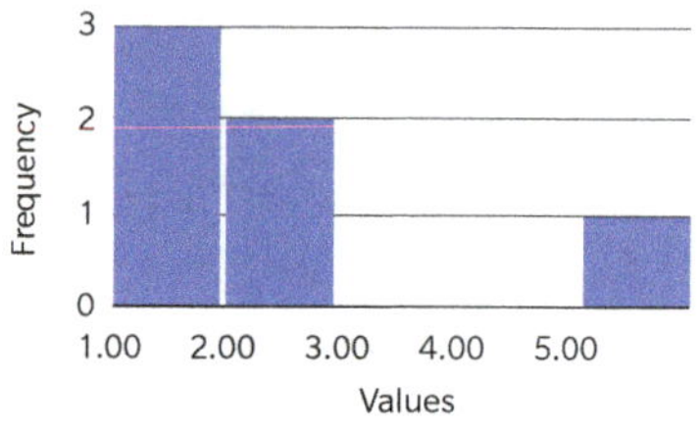

Distribution B: 1, 4, 4, 5, 5, 5

Mean = (1+4+4+5+5+5)/6 = 24/6 = 4
Median = (4+5)/2 = 4.5
Mode = 5

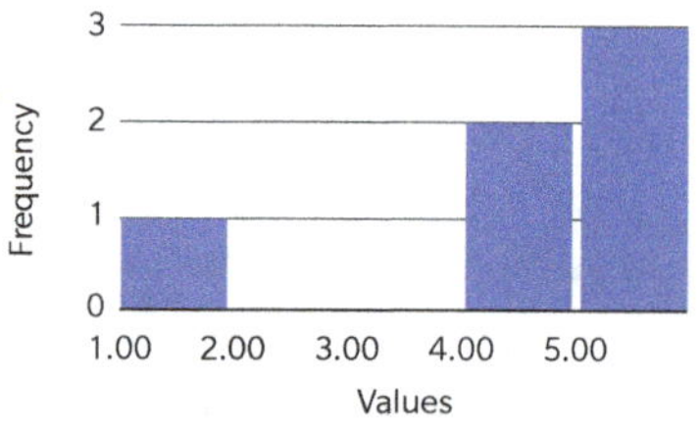

FIGURE 2.6 Descriptive statistics and histograms for distributions A and B

Using this information, Cassandra could have figured out that her distribution was positively skewed just from looking at her measures of central tendency. Remember that her mode (0) and her median (7) were both smaller than her mean (8.18), which reflects the typical pattern in a positively skewed distribution.

Describing Data 4: Using Variability Statistics

In addition to the "middle" of a distribution, it can also be very helpful to get an idea of how "spread out" scores are. Consider the following scores from two exams taken by six people:

Exam 1: 80, 80, 80, 80, 80, 80

Exam 2: 60, 70, 80, 80, 90, 100

The mean (average) score of both exams is 80 (as is the median and the mode). But clearly, there are radical differences between the two exams. One of them doesn't seem to differentiate between students at all, while the other has very substantial differences between the high and the low score, and the students are spread out across that range.

These two exams are very different statistically, but the measures of central tendency don't help us understand those differences. This is where measures of variability or dispersion come in handy.

The simplest measure of dispersion is called the **range**, and it simply tells you how far apart the high and low score in a distribution are. You can report the range either by reporting both the high and low scores for a distribution or by reporting the difference between them. So the range for the first distribution noted earlier might be reported as [80, 80] or simply as 0. The range for the second distribution is either [60, 100] or simply 40 (the difference between 60 and 100). A range is always positive, so subtract the smaller number from the bigger number (100–60, not 60–100).

If Cassandra was interested in the range of her distribution, she would find the smallest number (0) and the largest (30) and report her range as [0, 30] or just 30—there is a 30-minutes-a-day difference between the least and the most avid newspaper readers in her sample.

The second (and more complex) measure of variation is called the standard deviation. The standard deviation tells us how much all the scores in a distribution deviate from the mean—on average, how different is each person's score from the average of all the scores? You can easily see that in our first exam (80, 80, 80, 80, 80, 80), the average person doesn't deviate from the mean at all: everyone scored exactly at the mean. The standard deviation here will, therefore, be 0. Each deviation (difference between a score and the mean) is 0, and so the standard deviation is 0.

It's more difficult to think about what a standard deviation means when all the scores are not the same, but let's try. Remember the scores from Exam 2:

Exam 2: 60, 70, 80, 80, 90, 100

The average is 80, and so the two people who scored 80 don't differ at all from the mean—their "deviation scores" are 0. The most extreme people (60 and 100) both scored 20 points away from the mean—their deviation scores are 20 (it doesn't matter for these purposes whether they scored above or below the mean). So you should expect that the standard deviation should be somewhere between 0 and 20.

In fact, the standard deviation of this set of scores is around 14, so our guess was not too far away (details on calculating the standard deviation are provided in the "Going Further" section of this chapter and the Google Sheet's "Calculating SD Manually" tab: http://bit.ly/2vcJ0gT). This bit of guesswork illustrates an important fact: The standard deviation will always be somewhere between 0 and the largest difference between any individual score and the mean, and it will often be somewhere around halfway between those two numbers. If in a given distribution the most extreme individual in a distribution scores 70 points away from the mean, your standard deviation might well be somewhere around 35, and it *must* be somewhere between 0 and 70. This can be a useful reality check when you do a standard deviation calculation. Notice that the standard deviation can't *ever* be negative. If all the scores are the same, it can be 0 (see Exam 1 example), but *there is no such thing as negative variation.*

So what might Cassandra's standard deviation be? We know the mean of her distribution is 8.18 and that the range is between 0 and 30. The difference between her lowest score (0) and the mean is 8.18. The difference between her highest score (30) and the mean is 21.82 (30–8.18) (notice, again, that we are just concerned with the size of the difference, we're not interested in whether it's positive or negative). We know that the standard deviation in Cassandra's data must be somewhere between 0 and 21.82 (the highest deviation). We actually also know that it can't be 0 because we know there is variation in her data—not everyone read the newspaper for the same amount of time each day. If you had to guess her standard deviation, you might guess somewhere around 10—about halfway between 0 and the largest deviation score (21.82). In fact, her standard deviation is 7.32; our guess wasn't perfect, but it also wasn't crazy.

If you had a distribution with a mean of 20 and a range between 14 and 29, what might be a good guess of the standard deviation?

Your first step here should be to look at the difference between the mean and the highest and lowest scores in the distribution. The difference between the mean and the lowest score is 6 (the difference between 20 and 14), while the difference between the mean and the highest score is 9 (the difference between 20 and 29). A reasonable guess for the standard deviation here would be somewhere around halfway between 0 and 9: If you guessed 4.5, then you are on your way to understanding the standard deviation. Just remember, this is a guess, a reality check, an intuition. You would need the data to actually calculate the real standard deviation.

Can you think of a key advantage of using the range and of using the standard deviation (relative to each other) as measures of variation?

Advantage of the Range	Advantage of the Standard Deviation

A key advantage of the range is that it is easy to calculate and easy for a reader to understand. Pretty much everyone can understand what you mean when you tell them the lowest score and the highest score in a set of numbers. The standard deviation, on the other hand, is only useful information if your audience has taken a statistics class (or read a book like this one).

A key advantage of the standard deviation is that it uses **all** the information in the distribution. Consider the following set of scores:

7, 7, 7, 7, 7, 7, 7, 7, 7, 7, 7, 7, 7, 7, 7, 7, 7, 7, 7, 7, 7, 7, 7, 7, 7, 7, 7, 99

The range is [7, 99] or 92—there is a difference of 92 between the lowest and highest score in the distribution. That 92 clearly doesn't represent the fact that *all the scores except one are the same!* The standard deviation calculation uses *all* the numbers and so contains *more information* about the distribution as a whole.

Why Is the Standard Deviation Useful?

The standard deviation is an incredibly useful statistic for communication researchers. Here's a brief introduction to why we care about it.

It allows you to compare different groups of people or distributions of numbers. Cassandra only studied one group of newspaper readers but imagine that she had a friend working for a different campus newspaper (Bob) who collected similar data. By comparing standard deviations, Cassandra and Bob could learn whether there is more *diversity* in newspaper readership across their two campuses. Do students at one campus all tend to read the newspaper the same amount (low standard deviation) while there's a lot of variation in how much students read the news at another campus (high standard deviation). If Cassandra's campus has a higher standard deviation than Bob's, that means people on Cassandra's campus *vary* more in their newspaper readership.

Using standard deviations to understand variation within individuals

Imagine two people (Kim and Jim) both watch an average of 1.5 hours of Netflix per day. It looks like they're "the same" in terms of their viewing. However, Jim has a much higher standard deviation than Kim in his viewing from day-to-day. That super-high standard deviation means that Jim's daily viewing is sometimes very high and sometimes very low—it is *fluctuating* dramatically. Kim's viewing is much more stable—she watches about the same number of hours every day. Even though both people have the same *average*, it's clear that Jim is a binge-viewer while Kim is not. The important difference between them is in the standard deviation, not the mean.

Standard deviations can also help you understand how *individuals* score *within* distributions (i.e., where individual people fall *relative to their peers*). Think again about Cassandra's friend Bob who collected data about newspaper readership on a different college campus. Cassandra and Bob might be interested in identifying some people who are similar in their readership *relative to their own campus*. This is straightforward in terms of the average: Someone who scores at the average on one campus would be similar to someone who scores at the average on the other campus. But what about someone who scores well above (or below) the average? His or her position relative to peers can be understood using something called a **z-score**.

The *z*-score tells you *how far an individual score is from the mean* in *standard deviation units*. So for a distribution with a mean of 78 and a standard deviation of 2, someone who scored an 80 would have a *z*-score of +1: The person scored "one standard deviation above the mean." Note that positive and negative matters here: a positive *z*-score tells you that the person scored *above* the mean, while a negative *z*-score tells you that the person scored *below* the mean. What do you think the *z*-score would be for someone who scored a 74 on that same distribution?

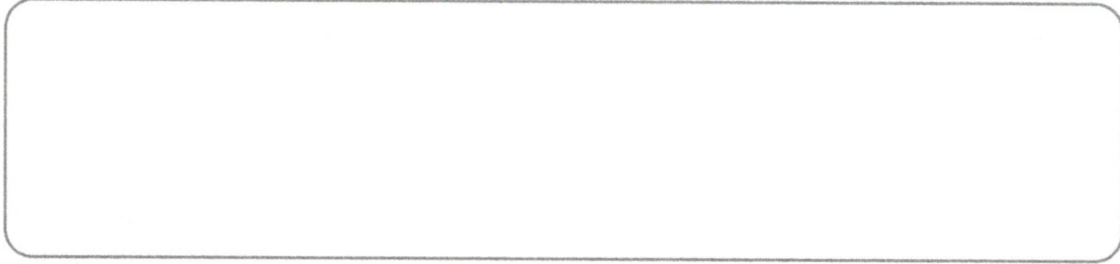

To figure this out, you would just think about how many "standard deviation units" that person is away from the mean and in what direction (see Figure 2.7 if you find it easier to think about this visually).

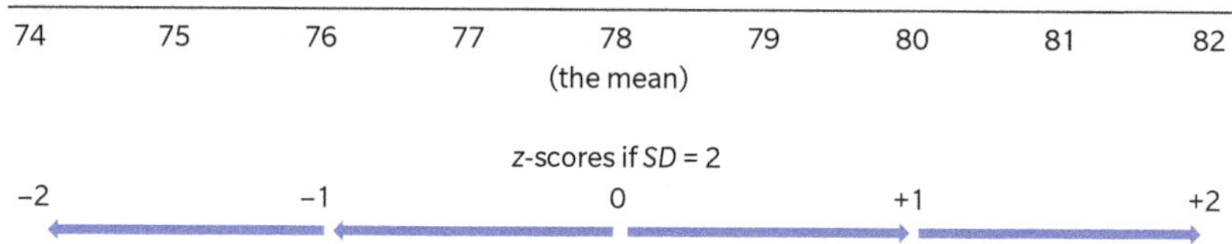

FIGURE 2.7 Illustration of *z*-scores

A score of 74 is 4 *points* below the mean. The standard deviation is 2, so 4 points is equal to 2 *standard deviations* below the mean (each blue arrow in Figure 2.7 represents one standard deviation). Therefore, a score of 74 equals a *z*-score of −2. In these examples, it is quite easy to simply "see" what a *z*-score is. However, when the numbers are less tidy, it is also useful to know the formula for calculating a *z*-score:

$z = (X - M)/SD$, where X = an individual score,
M = the mean of all the scores,
SD = the standard deviation of all the scores.

For our example of someone who scored a 74, we could use the following formula:

$$\begin{aligned} z &= (X - M)/SD \\ &= (74 - 78)/2 \\ &= -4/2 \\ &= -2 \end{aligned}$$

OK, so let's get back to Cassandra and Bob who were trying to find students with similar *z*-scores on their two campuses. Cassandra has some people who read the newspaper for 30 minutes a day. What is the *z*-score for those people?

Remember that the mean of Cassandra's group was 8.18, and the standard deviation was 7.32.

To calculate the *z*-score for someone with a score of 30, you'd do the following:

$$\begin{aligned} z &= (30 - 8.18)/7.32 \\ &= 21.82/7.32 \\ &= \mathbf{2.98} \end{aligned}$$

So, these people scored almost exactly 3 standard deviations above the mean. If on Bob's campus the mean was 14 and the standard deviation was 4, how many minutes per day would someone need to read on Bob's campus to have a *z*-score of around 3?

Figure 2.8 provides an illustration of this problem. If you are looking for the "minutes per day" score, you simply count standard deviation units equivalent to the z-score. For someone to get a z of 3 on Bob's campus, the person would need to read the average (14) plus 3 standard deviation units. With the standard deviation of 4, then that's

$$= (14 + (3 \times 4))$$

$$= (14 + 12)$$

$$= 26 \text{ minutes a day.}$$

Someone who reads 26 minutes a day on Bob's campus (3 standard deviations above the mean) is thus very similar, relative to his or her peers, to someone who reads 30 minutes a day (also +3 standard deviations) on Cassandra's campus.

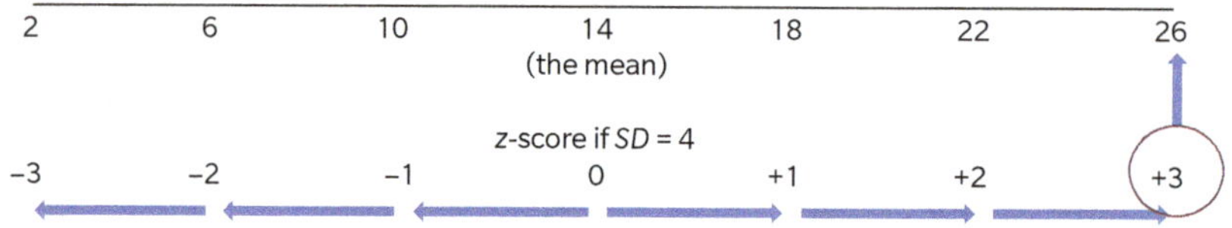

FIGURE 2.8 Illustration of going from z-score to raw score

The "z-scores" tab in the Google Sheet (http://bit.ly/2vcJ0gT) shows you the z-scores for everyone in Cassandra's distribution. You can see that people below the mean have negative z-scores, and those above the mean have positive z-scores. Notice that with real data, the numbers start to get messy—there are lots of decimals flying around!

Why are z-scores useful? They can help you compare individuals from different distributions or data sets. They help you understand where people stand relative to their peers.

Writing the Report

Being able to write about your analysis is just as important as being able to do the analysis. Report 2.1 is an example of what Cassandra might write to her editor about her analysis; remember that she would also already have written the information in Report 1.1 (previous chapter), so the editor knew what she did to get these results. Notice that Cassandra reports the median and the mode, as well as the mean. People don't often do that, but with a skewed distribution like this one, it is useful to do so.

Copying charts

If you create your charts in Google Sheets, you may want to move them into a Microsoft Word or Google Docs document to present your report. To do that, you can click on the three dots in the upper right of your chart and click "Save Image." The chart will save as a .PNG file, and you can then insert that image file into a Word document using "Insert—Pictures." In Google Docs, you would use "Insert—Image."

REPORT 2.1 Results for Descriptive Statistical Analysis

Our random sample of Middle State students read the newspaper for about 8 minutes a day on average (*M* = 8.18, *SD* = 7.32, Mdn = 7, Mode = 0). As shown in Figure 1, the distribution is positively skewed, with most people (64%) reading the newspaper for less than 10 minutes a day, including 20% who don't read it at all. Reading for 20 minutes a day or more is relatively rare—only 10% of the sample read this much.

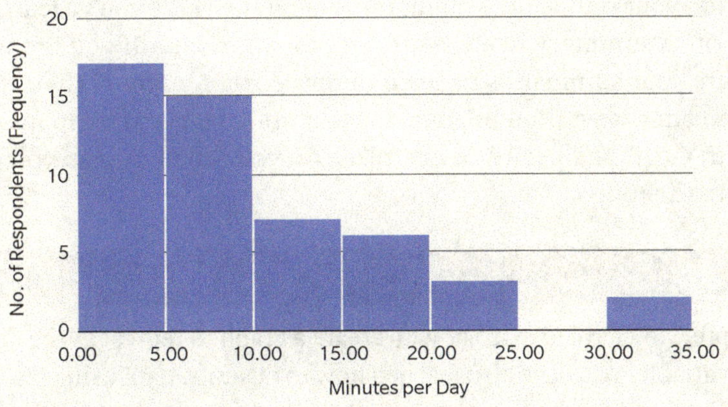

FIGURE 1 Frequency of *Daily Centurion* reading in minutes per day

Other Applications

Whenever you have a data set, being able to represent the data graphically and calculate central tendency and variability statistics is going to be very useful. The statistics described in this chapter are used in almost all quantitative research studies. They are also used in society more broadly. Trends in the real estate market are tracked using the median home price (the distribution of home prices tends to be positively skewed, so the median is often a better indicator of central tendency than the mean). The quality of a football running back is assessed (among other things) by average yards per rush (the role of statistics in sports could fill multiple books!). For communication researchers, these descriptive statistics and graphical representations are often the starting point for examining more complicated questions. For example, an examination of whether men or women send more texts to their romantic partners would begin with a calculation of the average "texts per day" by men and by women.

Your Turn

Remember the "Your Turn" section from the previous chapter? Go back and look at that to remind yourself of what you've done so far. Now imagine that you had a number of people respond to your question. If you are working in a class, you could have some of your classmates actually fill out your questionnaire either using paper and pencil or by sharing your online survey with them. The more of them there are, the more you will appreciate an online survey tool—it will save you from having to enter their responses manually! If you don't have people available to fill out your questionnaire, you can make up responses; using online tools, you can pretend to be multiple respondents and enter responses for yourself, or you can just make up numbers.

Once you have some responses, enter them in a new Google Sheet (or export the data from your online questionnaire). Using the skills you've learned in this chapter, write a summary like Cassandra's for your data. If you are working in a class, share your summaries to see if other people presented the data in more or less interesting ways. You might want to start saving your responses to all of these "Your Turn" challenges in one place on your computer so you can easily refer back to them.

Wrap Up

In this chapter, you have learned how to create a graph to represent the distribution of a single variable. You have also learned how to describe data using statistics. The mean, median, and mode are measures of central tendency: What is the middle of the distribution? The range and standard deviation are measures of variability: How spread out are the numbers in a distribution? Using graphs and descriptive statistics you can concisely provide someone with a lot of information about your data without having to show him or her very many numbers.

If you get nothing else from this chapter, remember the following:

1. The mean, median, and mode provide different information about a distribution, and when looked at together, they can tell you whether a distribution is skewed.
2. The standard deviation conveys information about variation in a distribution and must always be positive (there is no such thing as negative variation).
3. A *z*-score tells you how far from the mean a particular score is in standard deviation units; a negative *z*-score means that the score is below the mean.

Key Chapter Concepts

Central tendency: The "central tendency" of a distribution is another way of saying the "middle" of that distribution. The chapter covers three measures of central tendency: the mean, median, and mode.

Distribution: An arrangement of a set of scores in order; more generally, a name for a set of scores (data) that are to be examined and analyzed.

Histogram: A chart that illustrates the frequency of specific values (or sets of values) in a distribution. High bars in a histogram indicate that there are a lot of scores of that value.

Mean: The arithmetic average of a set of scores—add all the scores and divide by how many scores there are.

Median: The middle score, the 50th percentile. The point in a distribution where half the scores are above that number and half are below.

Mode: The most frequent or common score in a distribution. More people have this score than any other score.

Normal distribution: See **Shapes of distributions.**

Range: The difference between the lowest and highest score in a distribution; a measure of **variability.**

Shapes of distributions (normal, skewed): A normal distribution is symmetrical—scores below the middle of the distribution are arranged similarly to those above the middle, and there is an equal number of scores below and above the middle. The mean, median, and mode are all in the same place, and the distribution has a bell shape. In a skewed distribution, more scores are bunched together at one end of the distribution than the other—the distribution is not symmetrical. Positively skewed distributions have more scores on the left side of the distribution; negatively skewed distributions have more scores toward the right-hand end.

Skewed distribution: See **Shapes of distributions.**

Standard deviation (*SD*): A measure of variation or **variability** in a distribution.

Variability: How much heterogeneity there is among scores in a distribution. In distributions with low variability, most people have quite similar scores; in high variability distributions, people have dramatically different scores from one another. See also **Standard deviation.**

z-score: A measure of how much a score deviates from the mean, expressed in **standard deviation** units. A z-score of +3 means that a score is 3 standard deviation units above the mean.

Section Wrap

Section Summary

Section 1 has introduced the process of collecting data and analyzing it. Most research follows this same pattern. It begins with a question or a problem (how much are people reading the newspaper?), and a method is developed to gather data that can answer that question (e.g., asking people how much they read the newspaper). Once the data have been collected, they are then analyzed to answer the question (e.g., calculating an average score for newspaper reading in minutes per day). As you can imagine, the types of questions, types of data, and types of analysis will get more complicated as we proceed through this book, but the basic process will remain the same.

Going Further

For some classes, it might be enough to understand generally what the standard deviation represents (variability in a set of scores). Other classes may want you to calculate the standard deviation. If so, Figure 2.9 provides an example of doing the calculation, and the "Calculating *SD* Manually" tab on the Google Sheet provides the same information on a larger scale (for all of Cassandra's data). If you are hand calculating the standard deviation, there are formulas that are quicker to use than the method in Figure 2.9. I show this method because it illustrates what the standard deviation *means* in ways that other formulas don't. Of course, you can always calculate the standard deviation automatically using your computer—cell B58 of Cassandra's data spreadsheet shows how to get the computer to do the hard work for you! Don't freak out if your instructor wants you to calculate the standard deviation a different way—all the formulas give the same result. *Except* ... the formula I showed you is for the "sample standard deviation" (*s* or *SD*), which is what is used for most social science research. There is a slightly different formula to calculate the "population standard deviation" (generally called σ or sigma). Your instructor may want you to learn that one as well.

As you look at the calculation, consider what it is accomplishing. Each deviation score represents how much the particular score differs from the average of all the scores. Squaring this number gets rid of all the negatives (for scores below the mean), providing a simple way to get the overall *size* of the difference from the mean, independent of direction. When all those scores are added together, the total (the sum of squares) is not very useful because it will be big if you have lots of observations and small if you don't have many observations. Dividing the sum of squares by the sample size (actually N–1) fixes this problem. It gives us the *average squared deviation from the mean*. This is the variance, which is also sometimes called the mean square (short for mean (or average) squared deviation). Taking the square root of that in a sense "gets rid of" the earlier squaring that we did. You can think of that number (the standard deviation) as telling you something like how much the "average" score deviates from the mean. The bigger this number, the more the scores as a group differ from the mean. The standard deviation is expressed in *the same units as the original measure*. If you measured the height of a group of 10 people (in inches) and found a standard deviation of 4, that would mean that among those 10 people, the typical person's height was about 4 inches away from the mean.

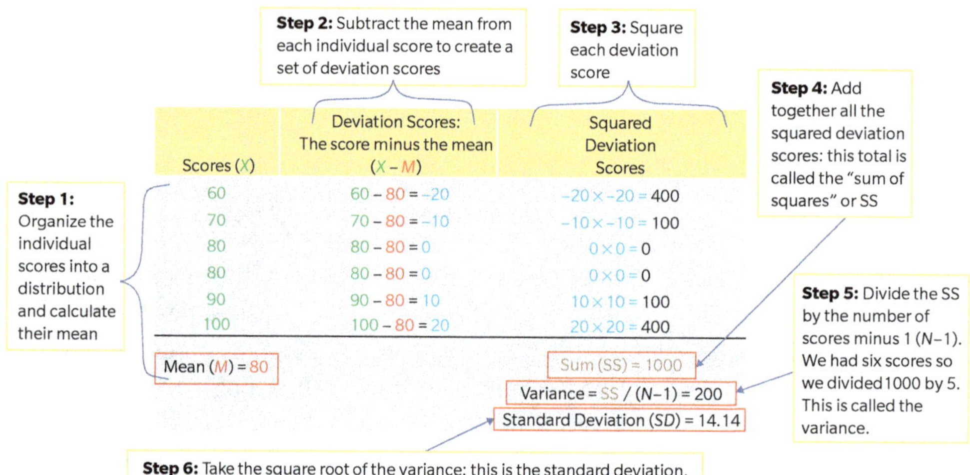

FIGURE 2.9 Manual calculation of standard deviation

SECTION 2

Examining Associations Between Variables: Do Liberals Read the Campus Newspaper More Than Conservatives?

By the end of this section, you will be able to:

- ✔ Understand the difference between a hypothesis and a research question
- ✔ Distinguish between directional, nondirectional, and null hypotheses
- ✔ Distinguish between categorical, ordinal, and interval levels of measurement
- ✔ Understand why using existing measurement tools is a good idea
- ✔ Understand what distinguishes an association between variables from a causal effect between variables
- ✔ Understand the role of theory in social science research
- ✔ Calculate a correlation coefficient
- ✔ Create a scatterplot
- ✔ Report the results of an analysis involving two interval-level variables

CHAPTER 3

Doing the Research: Measuring Multiple Variables

Cassandra's first foray into research turned out pretty well, and so her editor has given her a new assignment. The newspaper is doing some market research to understand more about the demographics of their readers: advertisers are easier to recruit if you can tell them more about the audience they will reach. Cassandra's editor has asked her to investigate this issue. She'll be exploring a number of characteristics of the readers, but here we are just going to focus on one: the political orientation of *Centurion* readers.

When you start a research project, it can be very helpful to state a question in clear and specific form to guide your research. This question provides clarity for your reader, and indeed for *you*, about the goals of the project and what we all might know when the project is done. This type of question is called a research question (RQ). Here's Cassandra's question:

> RQ1: Is there an association between political ideology and readership of the *Daily Centurion*?

An alternative to an RQ is a hypothesis. A hypothesis states an explicit prediction about what the research project is expected to find. For instance, Cassandra may have a suspicion that liberals read the paper more than conservatives, and so she might hypothesize the following:

> H1: Students with more liberal political ideology will read the *Daily Centurion* more frequently than students with a more conservative political ideology.

Underlying the RQ and the hypothesis is the same fundamental question concerning an association between two variables. A lot of social science research begins at this level: Is variable A associated with Variable B? What are the two variables that Cassandra is examining?

If you decided that she is studying (a) newspaper readership and (b) political ideology, then you are following along.

What is the difference between an RQ and a hypothesis? As you can see from the earlier examples, a hypothesis is a statement that makes a prediction. To formally state a hypothesis, you have to go out on a limb and make a claim about your data before you have actually collected it. Notice that the earlier example (H1) includes a *direction* for the association: It says liberals will read the paper *more than* conservatives. It is possible to write a hypothesis that doesn't include the direction of the association—this is (appropriately!) called a nondirectional hypothesis:

> H2: Political ideology will be associated with *Daily Centurion* readership.

Notice how this hypothesis makes a prediction (that ideology and readership are associated) but doesn't say in what direction (maybe liberals read the paper more, or maybe conservatives read it more). A directional hypothesis is good if you have a clear prediction for what you expect to find. If you just expect to find "something" but are not sure what, a nondirectional hypothesis or an RQ is a better choice. An RQ is (of course) a question: It *asks* whether something is true rather than specifically predicting it.

One final note on language. When you have an RQ, your research is then aiming to *answer* the question. When you have a hypothesis, the research will aim to *test* the hypothesis. You can't test a question or answer a hypothesis. The rest of the chapter is going to focus on how Cassandra can test her directional hypothesis:

> H1: Students with a more liberal political ideology will read the *Daily Centurion* more frequently than students with a more conservative political ideology.

How to Test a Hypothesis

As you may guess, you test a hypothesis by doing research. One common mistake people make is trying to test a hypothesis simply by *asking people whether they think the hypothesis is true*. For Cassandra's H1, she might be tempted to go out and just ask people, "Do you think that liberals read the newspaper more than conservatives?" Provide one clear explanation of why that might be a bad way to test the hypothesis:

Think about a pharmaceutical company testing a new type of flu vaccine. Would they test it by asking people whether they *think* the vaccine will stop people from getting the flu? No! They would study people who receive the vaccine and people who don't receive the vaccine, and see whether the people who've been vaccinated actually get the flu less. The same is true for social science hypothesis testing. When a hypothesis makes a prediction about the association between two variables, the researcher measures how people score on both those variables and looks to see whether the predicted association is present. Let's explore the idea of measurement a little more.

Conceptualizing and Operationalizing a Variable: Levels of Measurement

Cassandra is fortunate in that she already knows how to measure one of her variables (newspaper readership)—Chapter 1 described the process of developing that measurement in some detail. All she needs to do now is figure out how to measure political ideology.

In Chapter 1, Cassandra learned the importance of defining her variables conceptually before trying to figure out how to measure them. That becomes even more important with a more complex variable like political ideology. People can mean a lot of different things when they talk about political ideology. Consider just the following three definitions:

1. Political party: Your political ideology is the political party to which you belong: Democrat, Republican, Green, Libertarian, Communist, Socialist, Modern Whig (yes, there's really a Modern Whig party), etc.
2. Ordered political category: Your political ideology is defined by whether you call yourself liberal, moderate, or conservative.
3. Political continuum: Your political ideology is your position on a scale from extremely liberal to extremely conservative.

These are all fairly reasonable definitions of political ideology, but they represent different types of variables. The first represents a set of categories, and they are categories without much order to them—they are much like a set of "bins," and people fit into one or another of the bins. The bins aren't arranged in any meaningful order—people just fit into one category more than they fit into any of the others. It might look a little like Figure 3.1.

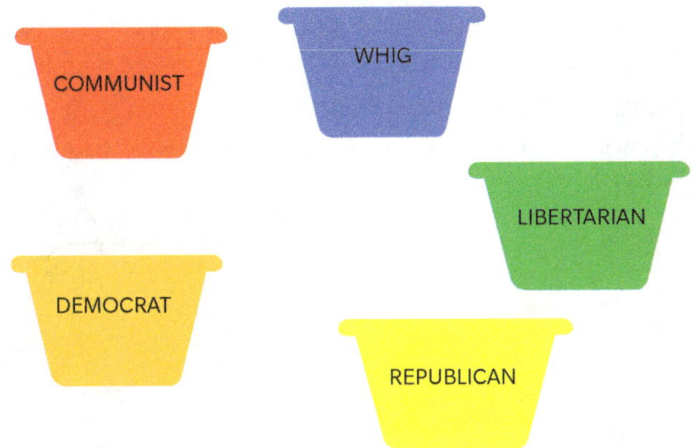

FIGURE 3.1 Categorical data

This type of variable is called a **categorical** variable. Categorical variables are defined by a number of categories that are not arranged in any meaningful order. Other examples include religion (if you are Buddhist, Muslim, Catholic, Jewish, atheist, etc.) or nationality (whether you are American, Mexican, Nigerian, Pakistani, etc.). Of course, categorical variables can get complicated if someone falls into multiple categories—someone with dual citizenship, for instance. But for now, we'll keep things simple and imagine that everyone fits neatly into one and only one bin.

The second definition just involves three bins, and now the bins do have some sort of order to them: the "moderate" bin clearly fits in between the other two. See Figure 3.2.

FIGURE 3.2 Ordinal data

This kind of variable is called an **ordinal** variable. The word "ordinal" comes from the idea that these bins (categories) have an *order* to them—they make sense in one order but not in other orders. A lot of measures of socioeconomic status are ordinal (lower class, middle class, upper class), as are measures of university class standing (freshman, sophomore, junior, senior). One common characteristic of ordinal measures is that there are a very limited number of bins, and there is a lot of variation within the bins. For instance, at the University of Arizona, you are a sophomore if you have anywhere between 30 and 59 credit hours. If all I know about a student is that she is a sophomore, I am still missing a lot of information about how far advanced she is in her studies.

The third definition involves lots more bins—and they are arranged in a long line from one extreme to the other. See Figure 3.3.

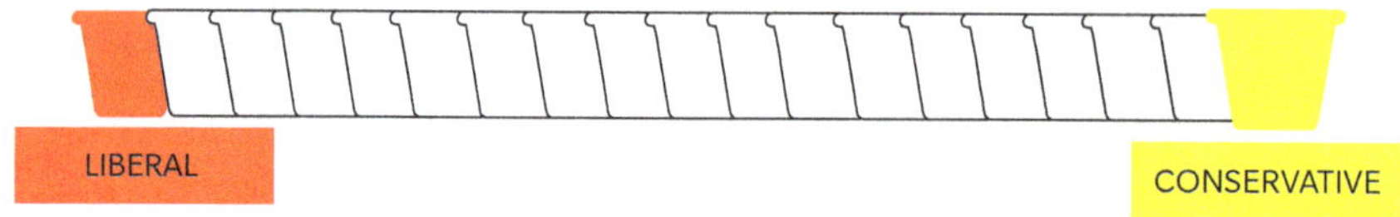

FIGURE 3.3 Interval data

This type of measure is called an **interval** variable. The measurement of someone's degree of liberalism/conservatism is much more detailed, and the people who fall into the same bin will be very similar to each other. This is more like measuring academic progress using "credit hours completed" rather than class standing. Most variables that involve some sort of "score" are interval-level variables (your height, your SAT results). In the social sciences, a lot of measures of traits and attitudes are also measured this way (e.g., how extraverted you are, how high your self-esteem is, how much you love your spouse).

Take a moment to check your understanding of the different levels of measurement.

Which of the following are categorical-, ordinal-, or interval-level variables?

Biological sex ______________________________

Time taken to run 100 meters ______________________________

Type of computer operating system (Mac OS, Windows, Linux)

____

How you feel today (unhappy, meh, happy) ______________________________

Your level of support for increased defense spending (very low, low, medium, high, very high) ______________________________

In order, those examples are

- categorical (assuming we are just dealing with male and female, those are just two categories with no order associated with them),
- interval (time is a continuous scale),
- categorical (again, operating systems are just types of things with no order),
- ordinal, and
- ordinal. (However, it's worth noting with this one that there's no strict rule for how many options (bins) it takes for an ordinal scale to become an interval scale. If you weren't absolutely sure whether to call the last one ordinal or interval, then you are in good company—experienced researchers might treat it both ways depending on the circumstances.)

Understanding whether your variable is measured at the categorical, ordinal, or interval level is crucial to knowing what sorts of statistics you can use. You can only calculate a mean with interval-level data: It makes no sense to ask what the "average religion" is in a group of people. On the other hand, you can certainly calculate a mode with categorical-level data (the most common religious affiliation in a particular group of people). The following represents which measures of central tendency are appropriate with which types of data:

Level of Measurement	**Measure of Central Tendency**
Interval data	Mean, median, and mode
Ordinal data	Median and mode
Categorical data	Mode

The fact that you can't calculate a mean with categorical data, for instance, also means that you can't calculate a standard deviation or a *z*-score. A lot of statistics in the social sciences are based on means, standard deviations, and *z*-scores; if you have a choice, it can be very helpful to try to measure things at the interval level so you can use those statistics.

Before Cassandra can start testing her hypothesis, she needs to decide on a *conceptual* definition of political ideology (remember Chapter 1). Based on her hypothesis (which asks about people who are "more liberal" or "more conservative") she decides that it is most appropriate to use an interval-level conceptualization of political ideology. However, she knows she is dealing with busy undergraduates and that she doesn't have any compensation to offer them for helping her, so she wants to use a measure that will be really quick for the students to fill out.

Cassandra knows that other people have probably measured political ideology, so she starts looking through scientific research articles to see how they measured it. In her college library, she finds an article called "The Secret Lives of Liberals and Conservatives" (Carney, Jost, Gosling, & Potter, 2008). In it, the researchers measured political ideology with the following item:

On the following scale, rate your own political views:

1	2	3	4	5	6	7	8	9
Extremely Conservative				*Moderate*				*Extremely Liberal*

This looks perfect for Cassandra's needs, but she wants to make sure it is a good measure. First, she asks around about the journal the measure is published in (*Political Psychology*), and her professors tell her it's a good journal. Second, she reads the article she found it in and notices that the authors say that the measure has "good **test-retest reliability**" (p. 818). Test-retest reliability means that if someone fills the measure out at two points in time, it tends to give similar results. Somebody responding to this measure and saying that they are a "2" (very conservative) will not come back the next week and tell you that they are a "9" (extremely liberal). Test-retest reliability is one way to tell that a measurement instrument is OK to use. Imagine taking your temperature, and it says you are at 98.6 degrees, and then you come back 10 minutes later, and it says you are at 104. That would be poor test-retest reliability, and (unless you have suddenly become very sick very quickly!), you should buy a new thermometer!

By using an existing measurement instrument, Cassandra can be relatively sure that it is good quality and will measure what she needs. What is the level of measurement of this measure of political ideology—is it categorical, ordinal, or interval?

This is definitely not a categorical measure, and the best answer here is that it is an interval-level measure. Researchers might argue about whether it's an ordinal measure—and it wouldn't be wrong to say that it's ordinal.

Cassandra is ready to gather her data—she has measurement tools to assess both of her variables. She will get a sample in a similar manner to that described in Chapter 1—and for simplicity, let's imagine she again uses 50 people. As in Chapter 1, the sample will be asked how much they read the newspaper, and now they will also be asked to report their political ideology using the question shown earlier. Cassandra will then have all the information she needs to test her hypothesis. Chapter 4 will discuss what Cassandra's data will look like and how she might analyze the data.

Cassandra's Curiosity, Causality, and Scientific Theory

Through her data collection, Cassandra will learn the demographic profile of *Centurion* readers—which was her goal. She will be able to tell her editor whether there is an *association* between newspaper reading and political ideology. Her editor, in turn, will be able to tell advertisers what sort of readership they will reach if they advertise in the *Centurion*. This research project will meet the immediate needs of the paper.

In the course of gathering the data, Cassandra may get curious about *why* these two variables are associated. If liberals in fact read the newspaper more than conservatives, why might that be? Try to think of some different explanations for the association between these variables and write at least two of them here:

You probably thought of ideas like the following:

- Something about the newspaper causes liberals to read it more (e.g., that the paper is biased toward liberal viewpoints).
- Something about liberals makes them read the newspaper more (e.g., liberals are more interested in politics)

- An *effect* of reading the newspaper (i.e., reading the newspaper is *causing* people to become more liberal)
- Some other factor that causes the association between liberalism and news reading to happen (e.g., if liberals tend to enroll in easier majors, maybe they just have more time available to lounge around catching up on the news)

In a number of cases, these are causal (**cause-and-effect**) relationships: they describe how one variable (e.g., liberalism) causes changes in another (e.g., newspaper reading).

Causal Relationships Between Independent and Dependent Variables

You may have heard the phrase "correlation does not equal causality." Just because you observe that two variables are associated does not mean that one of them is causing the other. The association between the two variables is a **fact**. The interpretation of that fact can vary quite dramatically. Cassandra has found some *support* for all of the earlier bullet points, but she is a long way from *proving* any of them. When we do research, we need to understand the difference between what our data definitively say, as opposed to things that the data "suggest." Sometimes (as in the bulleted list), it can be quite fun to think up lots of possible reasons why two variables might be associated with one another.

Problems in knowing whether one variable *causes* another are inherent in **cross-sectional** survey research designs like Cassandra's. A cross-sectional design involves measuring a group of people on whatever variables you are interested in at one point in time. One key requirement in demonstrating causality is **time order:** a cause needs to occur *before* an effect. If I think that high quality social support causes improved mental health, I need to study whether mental health improves *after* people receive social support. This is one reason why cross-sectional research designs have trouble demonstrating causality. You can't show time order if you measure everything at the same time.

An additional requirement for cause-and-effect relations is a clear **mechanism** by which the effect happens—*how* A influences B shouldn't be a mystery. Can you think of a mechanism leading from social support to better mental health? How does it happen?

Sensible explanations for social support improving mental health might include the following:

a) Social support provides useful information to people (e.g., about seeking medical help for a mental health issue—which would improve mental health).

b) Social support provides logistical help (e.g., watching someone's kids so he or she can get a break from caregiving or catch up on schoolwork—this would reduce stress, which would improve mental health).

c) Social support provides emotional assistance (e.g., letting people talk through their problems and sympathizing with them, which would make them feel that they have a supportive "ear" when they need it, which improves mental health).

If you see that two variables are associated but have no sensible explanation for *why*, you are limited in your ability to claim that one causes the other.

While we are talking about cause-and-effect relationships, it's worth learning a couple of new terms. If variable X causes changes in variable Y, then X is called the **independent variable**—the variable that *does the causing*. Variable Y is called the **dependent variable**—the variable that is affected by X.

$$X \rightarrow Y$$

Independent variable → Dependent variable

Identify the independent and dependent variables for each of the following RQs (answers are on the next page):

	Independent Variable	Dependent Variable
Does engaging in synchronized behavior with someone (e.g., playing catch) make you like that person more?		
Is the quality of decision a small group makes influenced by the diversity of people within that group?		
Are physicians more satisfied when patients look up health information on the Internet before a visit or when patients do not look up health information?		
Does playing "racing" video games make people more likely to drive aggressively?		
Do people who consume more snacks have a higher body mass index?		

Answers:

	Independent Variable	Dependent Variable
Does engaging in synchronized behavior with someone (e.g., playing catch) make you like that person more than if you don't do the synchronized behavior?	Engaging in synchronized behavior versus not	Liking for the other person
Is the quality of a small group's decision influenced by the diversity of people within that group?	Diversity of group	Quality of decision made by group
Are physicians more satisfied when patients look up health information on the Internet before a visit, or when patients do not look up health information?	Looking up health information (versus not)	Physician satisfaction
Does playing "racing" video games make people more likely to drive aggressively?	Playing racing video games (versus not) or maybe the number of games you play	Aggressive driving
Do people who consume more snacks have a higher body mass index?	Snack consumption*	Body mass index

*This is probably the most obvious ordering—eating snacks makes you overweight. However, the way the question is worded doesn't actually specify that order, so it wouldn't be wrong to infer the reverse for this one—it's plausible that being overweight may cause you to eat more snacks for some reason. When trying to identify independent and dependent variables, look for language like "causes," "influences," or "makes" (as in X *makes* you do Y) but also think logically about what might plausibly influence what.

Theory

Cassandra's project is aiming to answer a very specific question for a very specific purpose: to address her editor's desire to describe the readership of the paper. To that extent, her research project is not particularly theoretical. However, theory is central to most communication research. Researchers are not trying to answer one specific question in one specific context, but instead are trying to understand something more general about human communication. Theory helps us frame questions at that more general level. Indeed, even Cassandra's project can be understood as theoretically interesting, as hinted at in the previous section on causation. Once Cassandra gets interested in *why* the two variables are associated, she is starting to get interested in theory.

Here are some theoretical ideas that may be informed by Cassandra's research:

- Liberals are more interested in current affairs than conservatives.
- Newspapers are biased toward a liberal point of view.
- Liberals read more than conservatives.
- Liberals are lazier or less ambitious than conservatives.

Each of these represents an idea with broader implications for our social worlds than Cassandra's rather narrow question. If Cassandra wanted her work to become part of a broader theoretical discussion, she would need to decide which "angle" she wanted to take on her data. Then she should look at previous research and theory about her particular angle, understanding not only the claim but also the *processes* underlying that claim. A theory involves a detailed explanation of an entire process, not just a bullet point.

For example, if Cassandra is interested in the idea that the media have a liberal bias, that might lead her to some analysis of the *content* of her newspaper: does it actually lean liberal in terms of the stories it covers or the tone of the editorials? Using careful scientific procedures (see Section 7), she could examine media bias as an empirical question. She might also discuss with her editor whether they could increase conservative readership by increasing the number of conservative editorials in the paper. Again, this is an empirical question that could be investigated by manipulating the content of the paper over time and measuring how much the readership changed. Notice here that there are practical implications of theories. If your theory suggests liberal bias in the media, your scientific research should incorporate an examination of the content of the paper, and your practical solutions might involve adjusting the content. Alternatively, if your theory suggests that conservatives are just less interested in current affairs, you might be more interested in scientific research that measures interest in those issues among liberals and conservatives, and perhaps practical interventions designed to increase involvement in politics across the political spectrum.

Figure 3.4 illustrates the place of theory in the research process. Theory serves two fundamental functions. First, a theory can generate RQs or hypotheses—as in the earlier examples, a theory provides ideas for what observations of the world need to be done to test the theory. Second, a theory is a "repository" for research. Once a research study (or a series of studies) is complete, the results from those studies will contribute either to building new theories or adjusting existing theories. Cassandra was really just interested in her specific readers and her newspaper. But her research findings could become part of a much broader discussion about who reads newspapers and why, with implications for understanding what makes someone "liberal" or "conservative," and what counts as "news." Those are important questions that have implications beyond any specific study: That's what theory is.

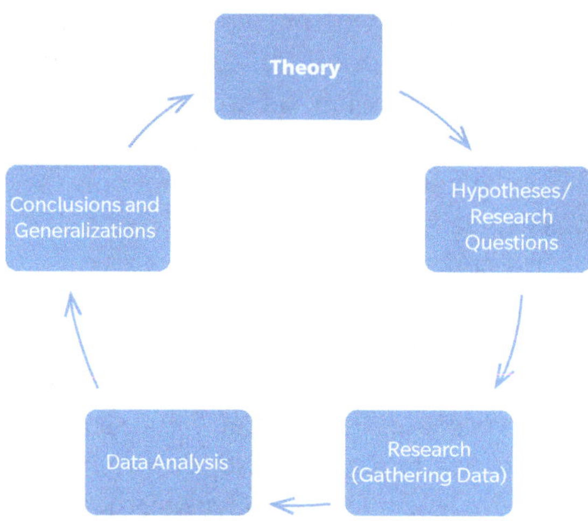

FIGURE 3.4 The connections between theory and research

Writing the Report

If you remember Report 1.1 (Chapter 1), then some of the following will seem quite familiar. A lot of Cassandra's description of her methods for the current project would closely resemble what she did in her first study. The only addition would be the description of how she measured the political ideology question.

NOTES: It is important that if you use a measure taken from someone else's research that you cite the source—note how Carney et al. (2008) is cited in the section on measurement of political ideology. It's also important to describe the potential scores a measure can have and what high scores mean. On the political ideology measure, for instance, the description makes it clear that the scale can range from 1 to 9, and higher scores indicate more liberal ideologies, lower scores indicate more conservative.

REPORT 3.1 Methods for Measuring Multiple Variables

I randomly selected 50 Middle State students from a list of all students' phone numbers. They were sent a link via text message asking them to respond to a brief questionnaire. Response rate was 100%.

The sample was 70% female, 26% male, and 4% nonbinary/third gender, and was of typical college student age (M = 20.32 years, SD = 4.27). It was diverse in terms of race and ethnicity (62% white, 35% Latino/a/x, 28% black/

continues on next page

continues from previous page

African American, 14% Asian American, 6% Native American; numbers do not total to 100% because respondents could select more than one option).

Newspaper readership was assessed with a single question, asking the student to report in minutes how much time they spent "yesterday reading the *Daily Centurion*?"

Political ideology was assessed with a single question, asking for the respondents' political views on a 9-point scale (1 = extremely conservative, 9 = extremely liberal; item from Carney et al., 2008).

Other Applications

Many research situations use the issues raised in this chapter: situations where the researcher is interested in the association between two interval-level variables. An advertising researcher interested in whether a campaign has been effective might measure how much people were exposed to the campaign and their feelings about the product. A relationships expert might be interested in whether the number of times couples say they love each other is associated with the longevity of their relationship. A political communication researcher might be interested in whether people who talk about politics more with their families also tend to vote more regularly. All those questions could be answered using the kinds of methods described in this chapter. Can you think of something that a new technology researcher might be interested in that could be addressed using a strategy like what was described in this chapter? Write an RQ and try to identify the independent and dependent variables.

RQ	Independent Variable	Dependent Variable

There are infinite questions that you may have thought of here. Is the number of texts sent during class associated with class grades? Is time spent using social media associated with low self-esteem? Does frequently checking your phone correlate with your attention span? Perhaps you thought of one of those ideas!

Your Turn

Remember the "Your Turn" sections from the previous chapters? Go back and look at those to remind yourself of what you've done so far. For this chapter's activity, add another variable to your questionnaire. Think about the variable you already measured in Chapter 1 and consider what other things might be associated with it. For instance, if you were interested in how much people watch sports programs on television, you might think about whether viewing sports is associated with actively playing sports. **Important:** For this second variable to work with where we are going in Chapter 4, you should try to think of a variable you can measure at the **interval level**.

Once you have picked your variable, think about how you might measure it. To help you with this, you might do some library research to find out whether someone else has already measured the variable and simply copy their measurement. Alternatively, you can create your own questionnaire if you want. Think about the things you learned in Chapter 1 in terms of how to write your question or questions if you are going to write the questionnaire yourself. Create a questionnaire (pencil and paper, or online) so you know exactly how you might ask the questions of a set of respondents. Write a report like Report 3.1 to describe for an audience how your variable is measured.

Wrap Up

In this chapter, you have read about a more extensive research project involving measuring two variables to examine the association between them. Most social science research projects involve at least two variables, as researchers attempt to understand how different social phenomena are associated with each other. You have learned the difference between categorical, ordinal, and interval levels of measurement, and the importance of understanding level of measurement before you start calculating statistics. You have also learned why it's a good idea to use an existing measurement tool when one is available rather than trying to create your own—don't reinvent the wheel! Finally, you should have started to get an idea of how theory and research interrelate. Most academic communication research aims to answer general questions about the world, not just a specific question in a single specific context. Applied research may be more oriented toward getting a single question answered for a single purpose ("did our advertising campaign work?"); however, applied research may also have theoretical implications.

If you get nothing else from this chapter, remember the following:

1. To answer any RQ about two variables, you must measure both variables (not just ask people if they think the two things are associated).

2. Understanding the level of measurement of a variable (categorical, ordinal, interval) is critical to knowing how to measure it and analyze those measurements.
3. Correlation is not causality—showing that two things are associated may be an important step in understanding a causal relationship but be cautious in making a causal claim from a correlation.

Key Chapter Concepts

Categorical measurement: Measurement where scores represent membership in categories, with no order assigned to the categories. Examples include religious denomination membership or preferred flavor of ice cream.

Cause-and-effect: When variable A causes changes in variable B, it means that changes in A will reliably result in changes in variable B, because of something that A is doing to B.

Cross-sectional research design: In cross-sectional research designs, variables are measured in a group of people at the same point in time. Cross-sectional studies are useful for understanding whether certain variables are correlated; they are not good for uncovering *causal* relationships.

Dependent variable: see **Independent and dependent variables**.

Hypothesis: A hypothesis is a statement of the expected association between variables. An example might be "people with stronger social skills will be less lonely than those with weaker social skills."

Independent and dependent variables: These variables are defined by their (either real or hypothesized) causal relationships. An independent variable is expected or shown to cause changes in a dependent variable. In the relationship between exercise and physical health, exercise is the independent variable in that it has been shown to cause changes in physical health (the dependent variable).

Interval measurement: Measurement where the scores represent values on a continuous scale, with even intervals between numbers. Examples would include scores on an intelligence test or the frequency with which someone discloses personal information (measured in number of times in a week). See also **Ordinal measurement and categorical measurement**.

Ordinal measurement: Measurement in which scores represent membership in categories that are arranged in order; distances between categories may not be equal. An example might be an airline frequent flyer program that categorizes members as "regular," "gold," or "platinum" based on how many miles they have flown (the actual number of miles flown would be an **interval**-level measure). See also **Categorical measurement** and **Interval measurement**.

Research question: A question that can be answered by gathering data.

Test-retest reliability: An indicator of the quality of a measurement tool. If you measure a variable at two points in time among the same group of people, the greater the association between the scores at the two times, the better test-retest reliability the measure has.

CHAPTER 4

Reporting the Research: Correlation and Hypothesis Testing

To revisit the previous chapter, Cassandra has measured a group of 50 people on (a) how much they read the newspaper and (b) their political ideology. You can see what Cassandra's raw data look like here: http://bit.ly/2wXQDu1. Notice that the political ideology variable is now called "liberalism" because high numbers (scores) on this variable reflect increasing liberalism. This is an arbitrary decision, and we could just as easily have written the question the other way around so that high scores indicate conservatism. Given that high scores represent more liberal ideology, however, it is good to label the variable so that readers can immediately understand what it means. If we called it "political ideology," readers would have to constantly be checking whether high scores mean more liberal or more conservative.

This is now starting to look like a real data set. Data in communication research are typically organized in this way, with rows representing "cases" (which normally means people) and columns representing variables. We measured two variables, so we have two columns of data, the first representing newspaper reading and the second representing political ideology. Because a row represents a person, each person's scores on the two variables are next to each other: Roberto (the first line of data) does not read the newspaper at all (0 minutes per day) and has a moderate political ideology (5—remember that ideology goes from 1 to 9). If you scroll down to the bottom of the spreadsheet, you'll see that we now have descriptive information (means and standard deviations) for both variables.

Describing Data 1: Using Scatterplots to Visualize

The classic way to visualize this sort of data set is using a **scatterplot**. The second tab of the Google Sheet (http://bit.ly/2wXQDu1) displays a scatterplot and shows instructions for creating one of your own; the scatterplot is also shown in Figure 4.1.

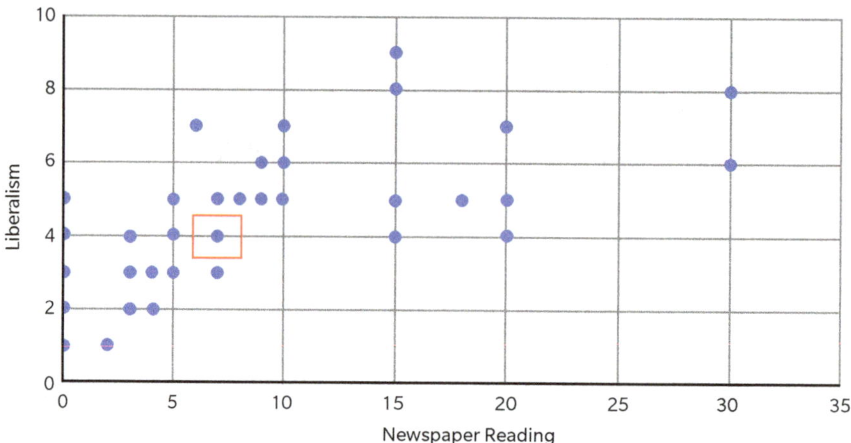

FIGURE 4.1 Scatterplot of the association between newspaper reading and liberalism

Each dot on the scatterplot represents at least one person—there aren't 50 dots because sometimes two people have the same scores on both variables, and so their "dots" end up in the same place. For instance, in the scatterplot in Figure 4.1, the dot outlined with a red square represents two people in the data set, both of whom read the newspaper for 7 minutes a day and score a 4 on political ideology (they are both slightly conservative). You can see those same people in lines 26 and 27 of the raw data in the Google Sheet.

Looking at the scatterplot gives you lots of useful information about your data. You can see that most people are clustered on the left side of the chart, reflecting (as we already know) that most people read the newspaper just a few minutes a day. More important, you can start to see a trend in terms of the association between reading the newspaper and liberalism. Across the chart, the dots appear to move upward as they go toward the right. This is our first indication that there is an **association** between political ideology and newspaper reading; an upward trend here suggests that people who are more liberal also tend to read the newspaper more.

This association is more obvious if we add a "**trendline**." A trendline is a line that "summarizes" the left-to-right "movement" in a scatterplot. It is sometimes called a "**line of best fit**" or a "regression line." The trendline is the straight line that comes closest to all the points in the scatterplot—it is the line that minimizes the average distance between all the points and the line. Any other line would be, on average, farther away from the points in the scatterplot than the line shown. The trendline for Cassandra's data is shown in Figure 4.2. Instructions for creating a trendline are given in the Google Sheet (http://bit.ly/2wXQDu1).

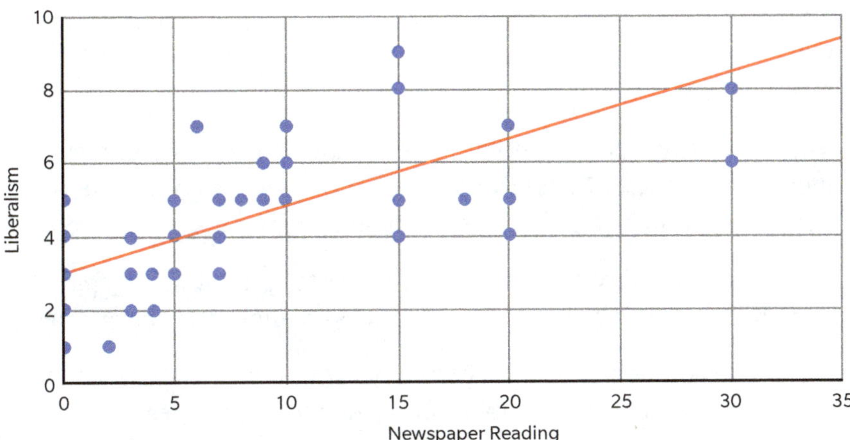

FIGURE 4.2 Trendline for the positive association between newspaper reading and liberalism

This upward trend from left to right is called a positive association. As scores on one variable (newspaper reading) increase, the scores on the other variable also increase. Can you think of two other variables that are positively associated? Write the names of the variables and draw a chart representing their association.

Easy options here are simple physical variables—people's height and weight, for instance, are positively associated (tall people tend to also be heavier). You might also think about the political ideology variable we have been talking about. Being more liberal is positively associated with things like favoring gun control legislation, opposing regressive taxes, and voting for Democrats. Your income is positively associated with the size of your home, and your GPA is positively associated with the number of hours you spend studying. In the field of communication, we often study positive associations such as the following:

- The association between social support and strength of relationships: Relational partners who exchange more social support typically have better relationships
- The association between watching television and beliefs about law enforcement employment: People who watch more television believe that more people are employed in law enforcement occupations
- The association between income and access to technology: People who earn more have better Internet access and access to more and better tech devices

Pick one of these associations and draw what you think a scatterplot and trendline would look like for these variables. Be sure to label the axes.

Most associations are not perfect!

When you think about two variables being associated with one another, it is important to remember that those associations are typically not perfect. So while height and weight are positively associated (tall people tend to be heavier), there are clearly short people who are quite heavy and tall people who are super skinny and hence not particularly heavy. In a perfect association, if you drew a trendline, all the points would be on that line—everybody who was 5′6″ would weigh the same amount and everyone who was 5′9″ would be the same amount heavier. Most associations don't look like that; hence, when we look at a scatterplot and draw a trendline, there are lots of dots that are not right on that line. While liberals tend to favor gun control legislation, for instance, there are liberals who vigorously support the right to bear arms, and there are conservatives who favor more gun regulation. On a scatterplot, those people would be dots that are not on the trendline.

Of course, positive associations are not the only kinds of associations. Figure 4.3 shows what it would look like if liberalism and newspaper reading had a **negative** association. As you go from left to right (increasing newspaper readership), the dots are lower on the chart (meaning decreasing liberalism or increasing conservatism). Cassandra's data would look like this if conservatives read the newspaper more than liberals—the trendline would slope downward. In communication research, we examine negative associations such as the following:

- The association between using technology in class and grades: The more you check your Facebook in class, the worse your grades
- The association between watching television and physical fitness: People who spend more hours watching TV tend to be less physically fit
- The association between expressing affection and loneliness: People who are better able and more willing to express affection to others tend to be less lonely

Pick one of these associations. Draw a scatterplot and trendline for the variables, making sure to label the axes.

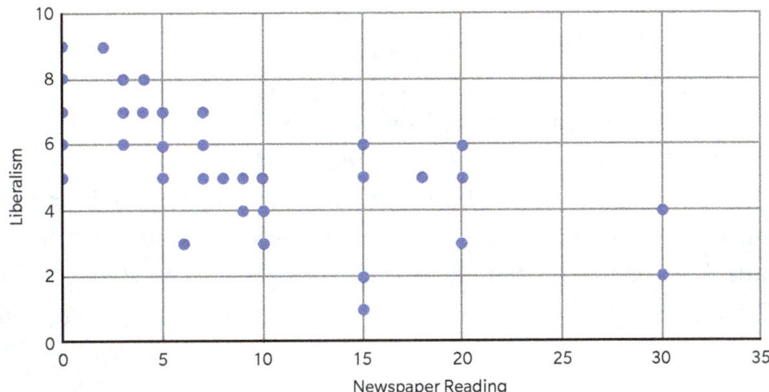

FIGURE 4.3 Scatterplot for a negative association between newspaper reading and liberalism

Describing Data 2: Using the Correlation Statistic

Looking at scatterplots and drawing trendlines helps Cassandra understand what her data look like (literally!). But it is difficult to look at lots of scatterplots and trendlines and figure out how *strong* the association is between variables or whether the association in one scatterplot is stronger or weaker than in another one. For this, Cassandra needs to use a statistic. The appropriate statistic for this situation is the correlation coefficient.

You have probably heard of a **correlation** before; the word is often used interchangeably with "association" or "relationship" to mean that one variable is associated with another one. However, the correlation is also a specific statistic that is used to figure out precisely how strongly associated two variables are. Correlations range from −1 to +1, and as you can see from Figure 4.4, higher absolute values (positive or negative) indicate stronger correlations. A correlation of zero indicates the two variables are completely unrelated to one another.

Stronger correlations are useful to researchers because they mean we have more predictive ability. Imagine finding a correlation of 1.0 between political ideology and newspaper reading. In that situation, if I knew your political ideology score, I could *perfectly* predict how much you read the newspaper. If there was a weak association between the two variables (r = .10, say), then knowing your political ideology might give me a *vague* idea of your score on the other. I would know that being liberal means you're *slightly* more likely to read the newspaper, but my guess would be a very loose estimate—more like a guesstimate. The strength of association between two variables is sometimes called an **effect size.**

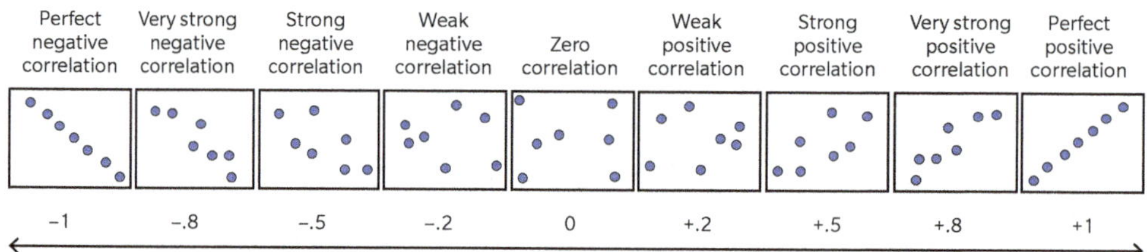

FIGURE 4.4 The range of the correlation coefficient (r)

The easiest way to calculate a correlation is to let the computer do it for you. In the Google Sheet (http://bit.ly/2wXQDu1), if you scroll to the bottom of the "correlation/scatterplot" tab, you will see that Cassandra's correlation is already calculated—it's .67. It is listed as "r" because that's how statisticians refer to a correlation coefficient. If you double-click on the highlighted cell containing the correlation, you will see the code for getting Google to calculate it. The correlation contains two useful pieces of information. First, note that the number is positive. This is telling you the same information as observing the upward trend in the scatterplot. It is critical to pay attention to whether a correlation is positive or negative. Second, the size of the correlation tells you about the strength of the association. If you refer back to Figure 4.4, you can see that a correlation of .67 is a strong correlation—newspaper reading and liberalism are pretty *tightly* associated with one another.

Estimating the Population Correlation

A sample does not perfectly estimate the true correlation value in the population. If you were to estimate the average height of the student population from just 50 students, you wouldn't expect to get a perfect estimate, right? You might end up with a sample a little taller than the population as a whole, or a little shorter. This is called **sampling error**: Samples don't perfectly represent populations. We actually already encountered this concept in Chapter 1.

In the same way that a sample mean doesn't exactly reflect a population mean (the earlier height example), a sample *correlation* doesn't exactly reflect the population correlation. If you calculate a correlation in a sample, the true population correlation will probably be somewhat smaller or larger.

If Cassandra is trying to estimate the correlation in the population, her best *estimate* is the correlation in her sample. This is called a **point estimate:** your best single numerical estimate of the population value. Even though Cassandra knows that her sample correlation value is probably not exactly correct, it is the best guess she has available.

However, Cassandra could give her editor a better idea of the value in the population if she could give him a range. It would be cool if she could tell him, for instance, that she is 95% sure that the correlation in the population is somewhere between a correlation of .48 and .80. Guess what? She can tell him exactly that by using something called a confidence interval. Here's how.

A **confidence interval** is a range of values *around* the observed (sample) value. With Cassandra's correlation of .67, it might be a range from .64 to .70 or .59 to .75: It must contain her point estimate (i.e., her sample correlation). A key term associated with the confidence interval is the **confidence level**. Your confidence level is the likelihood that the true population correlation coefficient is somewhere inside your confidence interval.

So in a statement like, "There is a 90% chance that the population correlation is between .30 and .50," what is your confidence level, and what is your confidence interval?

Confidence level: ______________________________

Confidence interval: ______________________________

Your level of confidence is expressed in the percentage term—it is the estimate of how sure you are (confidence level = 90%). Your confidence interval is the range of possible values (confidence interval = .30–.50).

Confidence intervals are critically important because they give you a solid idea of how accurate your estimates are. Which is more useful to you as a confidence interval for a correlation of .35—a confidence interval of .15–.55 or .33–.37? Why?

The first confidence interval indicates that your .35 estimate for the correlation is potentially very inaccurate—perhaps almost to the point of being useless. The true population correlation could actually be anywhere from a pretty small correlation (.15) to a very large one (.55). On the other hand, a confidence interval from .33 to .37 indicates a high level of accuracy. You can be very confident here that the true population correlation is very similar to your estimate.

You probably won't be surprised to learn that larger samples result in smaller (more accurate) confidence intervals. The size of the confidence interval reflects the amount of sampling error in the data, and sampling error gets smaller when sample sizes are bigger. You probably also won't be surprised that there is a relationship between confidence level and the size of the confidence interval. You can have a very high level of confidence about big confidence intervals (you can be 100% sure that a correlation is between −1 and +1!), but if you want a narrower confidence interval, you will end up being less certain about that interval. The *wider* your confidence interval, the *higher* your confidence level.

KEY POINT

These facts about confidence intervals are represented in Figure 4.5. Confidence intervals get wider as your desired confidence level gets higher and as your sample size gets smaller. If you want to be 90% sure about your confidence interval containing the population value, and you only have a sample of 10 people, you are going to have a very large confidence interval! Remember that a large confidence interval is ***not*** a good thing: that means that your estimate is less precise—it is closer to a guesstimate! **Narrow confidence intervals combined with high confidence levels are the best.**

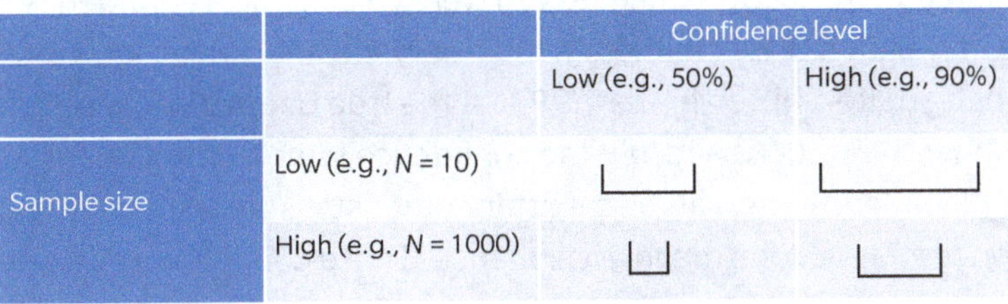

FIGURE 4.5 The relationships between sample size, confidence level, and width of confidence interval

Calculating a confidence interval is not that difficult but has a couple of tricky elements that this book is not going to get into. Computers can do the calculation just fine. If you go to the "confidence interval" tab for this chapter's Google Sheet (http://bit.ly/2wXQDu1), you can see the result for a 95% confidence interval around Cassandra's correlation. Cassandra can tell her editor, "I am 95% sure that the correlation between newspaper reading and liberalism in the student population is between .48 and .80."

Make a copy of that confidence interval spreadsheet so that you can edit it ("File—Make a Copy"). Experiment a little.

Keep the correlation at .67 but change the sample size to 100. Enter your confidence interval below:

Lower end of the confidence interval: ____________________

Upper end of the confidence interval: ____________________

What happened to the confidence interval? You should have observed that it got "narrower"—Cassandra could make a more precise estimate of the true population value if she gathered data from 100 people rather than just 50. Try changing the sample to 1,000.

Lower end of the confidence interval: ____________________

Upper end of the confidence interval: ____________________

With a really big sample, your estimate becomes *very* precise.

Why isn't the confidence interval symmetrical?

You might expect that an estimate of the correlation could be equally wrong in both directions. That is, that the true population correlation could equally be .20 bigger than Cassandra's or .20 smaller. Confidence intervals for correlations don't quite work that way. As you can see from Cassandra's 95% confidence interval, the calculator tells us that the true population value is somewhere between .19 below Cassandra's sample value and .13 higher than her sample value. To understand this, you just have to remember that a correlation can't *ever* be higher than 1.0. So—imagine you were calculating a confidence interval around a correlation of .99. In theory, the true population value for the correlation might be quite a bit lower than .99, but the true population value couldn't be any higher than 1.0. As a result, the confidence interval can't be fully symmetrical. Confidence intervals also exist for other statistics—you can calculate a confidence interval for a mean, for instance. Those confidence intervals *are* typically symmetrical.

Notice that the Google Sheet also includes calculations for a 90% confidence interval (directly below the 95% confidence interval). This confidence interval, of course, tells Cassandra that she can be 90% sure where the population correlation lies. Notice the trade-off here; she is *less* confident that the true value lies in that region (only 90% rather than 95%), but the interval itself is more precise (narrower). Typically, social scientists use 95% confidence intervals.

But Is the Correlation Real? Statistical Significance

In addition to understanding the size of the correlation, whether it is positive or negative and what the population correlation might be, Cassandra has one more important task. While her correlation is an impressive size, it is possible that it might have occurred *by chance*. That is, she *happened* to study a weird group of students for whom reading the newspaper and liberalism were positively associated, but in the student population overall, the two variables are actually unrelated. Even random samples can sometimes be weird. How can she defend herself against this possibility? Cassandra's best defense is to find out whether her correlation meets the requirements for what we call **statistical significance.** If a correlation is statistically significant, it means that it is *very unlikely that the true population value of the correlation is zero.*

Another way of describing statistical significance is that it is *very unlikely that the null hypothesis is true.* What is a **null hypothesis?** The null hypothesis says that there is no association between two variables—that the correlation between them is zero. You remember Cassandra's original hypothesis:

> H1: Students with a more liberal political ideology will read the *Daily Centurion* more frequently than students with a more conservative political ideology.

Can you write the null hypothesis that says there is no association between her variables?

Your null hypothesis should express the idea that newspaper reading and liberalism have nothing to do with one another, so wording something like "students with a more liberal political ideology will read the *Daily Centurion* at the same rate as students with a more conservative political ideology" would work very nicely. Or, since you are hopefully now getting comfortable with "correlation" language, you could write a null hypothesis that states, "There is no correlation between political ideology and *Daily Centurion* readership."

If Cassandra wants to claim that the correlation she observed is *real*, she needs to reject this null hypothesis. She needs to demonstrate that it is very *un*likely that there is *no* association between political ideology and *Centurion* reading in the population. Yes—that is a very awkward double negative, but one that you will need to get used to. To claim confidently that a correlation is true, social scientists try to prove that the *lack* of a correlation is *un*likely!

KEY POINT

Most quantitative social science is built around the process of statistical null hypothesis testing:

- You expect to find an association between two variables; you state that association as a hypothesis.
- You collect data.
- Using your data, you estimate the likelihood that there is *no* association between the two variables in the population.
- If that likelihood is very low, you reject the null hypothesis, thus supporting your original hypothesis. If no association is unlikely, then your prediction that there is an association is more sensible.

Now for the good news: Cassandra has *already shown* that it is very unlikely that the null hypothesis is true. Remember her confidence interval from the previous section? The confidence interval said that she was 95% sure that the true population correlation was between .48 and .80. That means that there is only a 5% chance that the true population correlation is some value other than between .48 and .80. Guess what? Zero is one of those values *outside* of the confidence interval, and hence a value that we can say is very unlikely.

Specifically, we can say that because there is a 95% chance that the true population value is between .48 and .80, there is, therefore, less than a 5% chance that the true population value is zero. There is less than a 5% chance that the null hypothesis is true. This is typically written as "$p < .05$." The "p" indicates "probability of the null hypothesis being true," and the .05 indicates 5% expressed as a probability: probabilities range from 0 to 1, while percentages range from 0 to 100, so a probability of .05 is the same as 5%.

There are other ways to test the null hypothesis, but they will always give the same answer as using the confidence interval. The confidence interval thus provides two useful bits of information simultaneously. It gives you a good idea of how precise your estimate of the correlation is (via the width of the confidence interval—a narrower interval is better), *and* it tells you whether the null hypothesis is likely to be true (by looking for whether the confidence interval includes zero). **If a confidence interval doesn't include zero, then a correlation is statistically significant**.

Degrees of freedom (df)

The statistical significance of statistics like the correlation coefficient is determined based on the size of the statistic and the sample size. Remember that confidence intervals get narrower (more precise) when sample sizes are larger. This means that the same correlation might be significant (confidence interval doesn't include zero) when your sample is large but nonsignificant (confidence interval does include zero) when your sample is small. If you want to experiment with this, just play around with a correlation of .20 and sample sizes of either 20 or 200 in the Google Sheet. When you report a correlation, you typically don't report your sample size; instead, you report "degrees of freedom" (df) which is $N - 2$. The reasons for this will become a little clearer as the book progresses. For now, all you need to know is that df represents sample size. With more complicated statistics, df also represents some other things (e.g., in comparisons of multiple groups, df represents how many groups are being compared).

Writing the Report

As in the previous chapters, it is not enough to do the research—you need to tell people about it. Here's how Cassandra would write up her report (Report 4.1). Notice that there are no prizes for length—if you can report a statistical result in a sentence or two, feel free to do so! The "48" in parentheses after the "*r*" is the df (df = $N - 2$): see the sidebar earlier. The statement "$p < .05$" and the confidence interval are somewhat repetitive—you now know that if the confidence interval doesn't include zero, then *p* must be less than .05. For audiences familiar with statistical reasoning, you may not need to include both; other readers may want to see them both, so I've included both in this example. Pay attention to details. Statistics (e.g., *r*) are typically italicized, as is *p* when it represents the statistical significance level. Confidence intervals (CI) are always presented in square brackets and separated by a comma. Figures should always have a number and a title, and for something like a scatterplot, you should make sure both axes are labeled.

KEY POINT

Distinguishing statistical significance from effect size. One consequence of how we test for statistical significance might be apparent at this point. Larger samples give us smaller confidence intervals and therefore increase the chances of saying that any given effect is statistical significance. This means that, perhaps confusingly, a "bigger effect" might be nonsignificant, and a "smaller effect" might be significant if measured with different samples. For instance, look at the following examples:

Example 1: $r = .20$, $N = 200$, 95% CI [.06, .33], $p < .05$

Example 2: $r = .40$, $N = 20$, 95% CI [-.05, .72], $p > .05$

The first example says that with a sample of 200 people and a correlation of .20, there is a 95% chance that the population correlation is between .06 and .33. Therefore, we are pretty sure that the population value is not zero, and we can reject the null hypothesis.

In the second example, with a correlation of .40 from a sample of 20 people, there's a 95% chance that the population correlation is between −.05 and .72; zero **is** in that range, so we cannot reject the null hypothesis—there is too much of a chance that the true population value might be zero. Even though a correlation of .40 is bigger than a correlation of .20, we are more convinced that the correlation of .20 is "real."

Our chances of finding statistical significance are thus influenced by both sample size and effect size. Figure 4.6 illustrates this relationship: As effect size and sample size increase, chances of statistical significance increase. With very large samples, even *tiny* effect sizes can sometimes be significant. If you had a sample of 20,000 people, a correlation of .02 would be significant! Remember that "significant" just means that you are confident the effect is not zero. When you hear that a statistic is "significant," you should always pause a moment and ask "OK, but is it *important*?" That question about importance is a question about **effect size.** In the case of that correlation of .02, the effect is probably unimportant, even though it is significant, because the correlation is tiny.

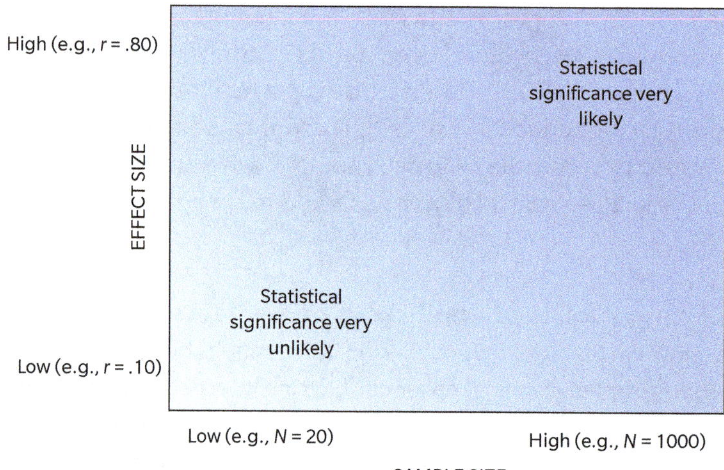

FIGURE 4.6 The relationships between sample size, effect size, and statistical significance

REPORT 4.1 Results for Correlation Analysis

Liberalism and *Daily Centurion* reading are significantly positively correlated, $r(48) = .67$, $p < .05$, 95% CI [.48, .80]. A scatterplot depicting the effect is shown in Figure 1. Liberals tend to read the newspaper more than conservatives.

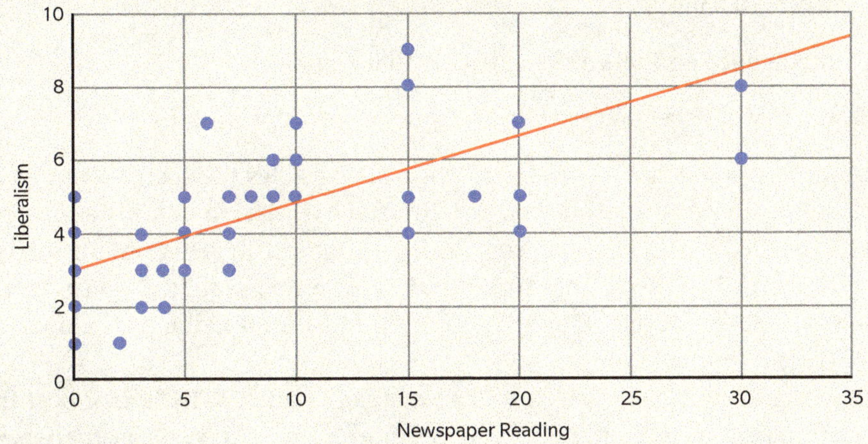

FIGURE 1 Scatterplot and line of best fit depicting the association between *Daily Centurion* newspaper reading and political liberalism

Other Applications

The correlation coefficient is a useful statistic whenever you have two interval-level measures—two sets of scores. Can you think of some situations in which you might use a correlation coefficient to gauge the strength of association between two variables?

If you thought about other variables with numerical scores and how they are associated with each other, then you are thinking along the right lines. As a communication researcher, I might use the correlation to look at associations between

- time spent reading novels and level of personal empathy,
- time spent playing team sports and degree of teamwork skills in the classroom,
- intelligence and interpersonal sensitivity, and
- number of Facebook friends and number of "real" friends.

The correlation is not useful for categorical variables. If you have categorical variables with only two levels, you can use the correlation, but it has a special name (it's called a point-biserial correlation—that's probably more information than you want). But if you were interested in examining religion—a categorical variable with lots of levels (Christian, Jewish, Muslim, Buddhist, Hindu, etc.)—you'd need a different statistic.

The correlation also only assesses *linear* relationships. The line of best fit in the scatterplot is a *straight* line. If you are interested in an association between two variables that may not be a straight line, you would need a different statistic. Consider the amount of practice required to give a good speech. Not practicing at all is bad, of course. But maybe people who practice "*too much*" also perform worse. They "overpractice." That association would look something like the following, with very low and very high amounts of practice (the x-axis) resulting in worse performance (the y-axis) than moderate amounts of practice.

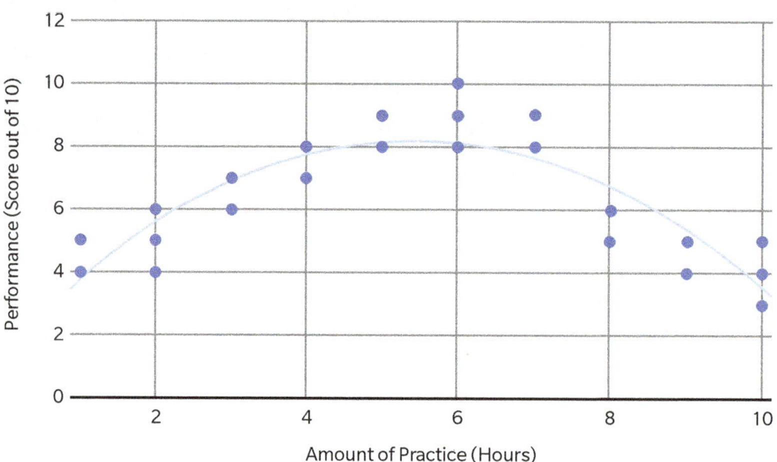

FIGURE 4.7 Performance as a function of amount of practice

If you calculated a correlation for the data in the scatterplot, it would tell you that there is *zero* association. However, you can clearly see that there is an association; it's simply not a *straight-line* association. There are statistics that would help you check for a curvilinear association like this, but they are beyond the scope of this book.

Many associations in the real world are curvilinear—this is sometimes called the Goldilocks principle. Things are best when they are not too extreme (too much or too little) but instead fall in a sweet spot somewhere in the middle. A little "sex" might help get people's attention to an advertising campaign, but too much and you will offend a lot of your audience. Disclosing some personal information to a casual acquaintance might help build your relationship with that person but telling the person a lot of deeply personal information might creep him or her out. Using social media efficiently to connect with your friend network will help you maintain a good social life. FOMO-driven checking of Instagram every two minutes will make you nuts.

Your Turn

Remember the "Your Turn" section from Chapter 3? You decided on a second variable to measure for your research study. Go back and look at that to remind yourself. If the variable you picked can't be measured at the **interval level,** now would be a good time to pick a new variable and figure out how you would measure that variable.

You should now have a questionnaire that assesses two variables—the one from Chapter 1 and the one from Chapter 3. If you are working in a class, have some of your classmates respond to your questionnaire. If you don't have people available to fill out your questionnaire, you can make up responses. Using online tools, you can pretend to be multiple respondents and enter responses for yourself, or you can just make up numbers.

Once you have responses, enter them in a new Google Sheet (or export the data from your online questionnaire). Using the skills you've learned in this chapter, write a summary like Cassandra's for your data. Be sure to include a scatterplot and a report of the correlation, and make sure to interpret the data: Tell your reader exactly what the data *mean.*

Wrap Up

In this chapter, you have learned how to draw a scatterplot and calculate a correlation. These are two key ways in which you would communicate the relationship between two interval-level variables to a reader. You have learned what a confidence interval is—it represents a range of values within which you are pretty sure the true population value lies. You have also learned how to use a confidence interval to test for statistical significance: If a confidence interval does not contain the null hypothesis value (typically zero), then the researcher can *reject* the null hypothesis. Rejecting the null hypothesis is written as $p < .05$ (assuming you are working with a 95% confidence interval).

If you get nothing else from this chapter, remember the following:

1. A correlation's absolute size represents how strong the effect is, while the sign (positive or negative) tells you the nature of the effect.
2. Larger sample sizes reduce sampling error, resulting in narrower (more precise) confidence intervals, and a greater likelihood of statistical significance.
3. It is always important to pay attention to effect size: A statistically significant effect can be trivially small (if, for instance, you have a very large sample size).

Key Chapter Concepts

Correlation: A statistical measure of association between two variables. Correlations range from −1 to +1; their absolute size indicates their strength. A positive correlation indicates that as one variable increases, so does the other. A negative correlation indicates that as one variable increases, the other decreases.

Confidence interval: A statement of the range within which the researcher is confident that the population value of a statistic lies. See also **Confidence level.**

Confidence level: The degree of confidence that a researcher has in the confidence interval (typically 95%). See also **Confidence interval.**

Effect size: The strength of a statistical association. Stronger effect sizes indicate that one variable is more closely tied to another one and that you can more accurately predict scores on one variable from scores on the other variable.

Line of best fit: A line on a **scatterplot** indicating the trend in the points. Typically, a best fit line minimizes the vertical distances between points in the scatterplot and the line. Also called a trendline. See also **Scatterplot.**

Null hypothesis: A statement that two variables are *not* related to one another, that there is no statistical effect. Typically, researchers try to *disprove* the null hypothesis in order to show that there *is* an association.

$p < .05$: The most common way **statistical significance** is referenced. If you see this phrase, it means that your data would be very unlikely (occur less than 5% of the time) if the null hypothesis was true. Or put more simply, there is less than a 5% chance that the null hypothesis is true. Saying "$p < .05$" is the same as saying "statistically significant."

Scatterplot: A visual representation of the association between two variables, with one variable represented on the x-axis and the other on the y-axis. A **line of best fit** is often overlaid on a scatterplot.

Statistical significance: A statement of confidence that the effect being examined is not zero. The statement "$p < .05$" indicates statistical significance; it literally means that there is less than a 5% chance that the null hypothesis is true.

Trendline: See **Line of best fit.**

Section Wrap

Section Summary

Section 2 has expanded the research enterprise to include multiple variables. It has shown some ways that researchers investigate associations between variables and use those associations to test hypotheses. When researchers examine associations between variables, they are typically interested in issues such as whether it is possible to predict people's scores on one variable from their scores on the other or whether one variable is causing changes in the other variable. Of course, just finding an association doesn't mean that there is a causal effect occurring. The section has introduced the important idea of statistical significance: Communication researchers rely on tests of statistical significance to determine whether a particular statistical effect is "real."

Going Further

This section introduces some additional free software that has features beyond what Google Sheets can do. It also provides some detail on how to calculate the correlation coefficient manually.

Introducing JASP Software

Google Sheets does everything required in the core of this book. However, other statistical software is helpful for doing more advanced statistics or providing additional information on the Google Sheets analyses. One great option is JASP, which is also free, works on PCs and Macs, and contains more powerful tools than Google Sheets. I highly recommend it if you want to go beyond the tools in Google Sheets and use something more like a freestanding professional statistics program. It is easiest to use if you install it, so it requires you to have access to a computer that you can install programs on. To install, go to https://jasp-stats.org/, click on "Download Now" and follow the normal procedures for installation of a new program. You can also (as of time of writing) use JASP online without having to install it on your computer—access is at https://www.rollapp.com/app/jasp. This is trickier to use than the freestanding program.

The data for this chapter in JASP format are located here: https://bit.ly/2JnXcbm. You can download this data file (don't worry that it looks like multiple files: when you download it, it will be a single file) and open it in JASP. To open, go to "File—Open Computer" within JASP and navigate to wherever you have saved the file or just double-click on the "Section 2" JASP file, and it should open in JASP automatically. You'll see a spreadsheet similar to the Google Sheet with labels for the variables at the top. To run the Chapter 4 analysis, click on "Regression" in the top bar and select "Correlation Matrix." Select our two variables (minutes per day and liberalism) and move them into the right-hand box (you can click the arrow or "drag and drop"). Figure 4.8 illustrates what this should look like.

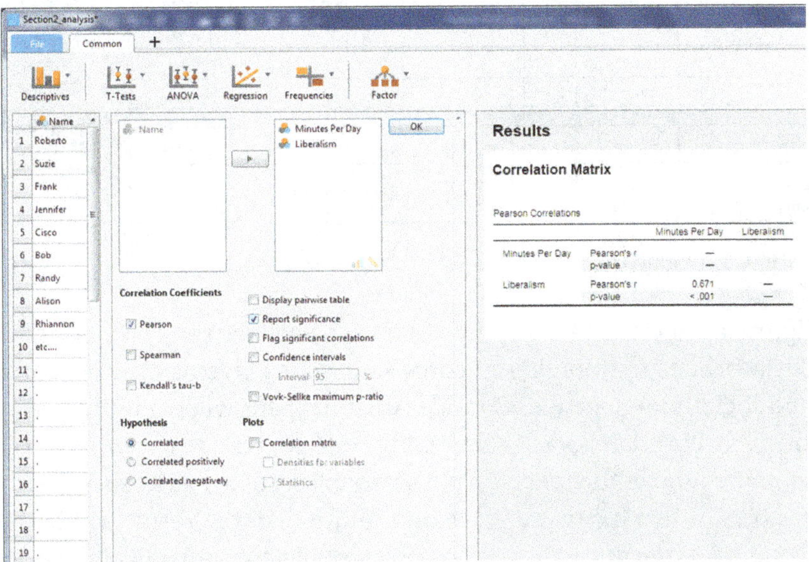

FIGURE 4.8 Calculating a correlation in JASP

You will immediately see a preview of the output on the right side of the screen. You can experiment with some of the options underneath (e.g., you might want to select the "Confidence Interval" option—it will provide the confidence interval without the extra steps needed in the Google Sheet). Click "OK." You will then have the output that you requested: If everything is working smoothly, these results will look exactly like the results from the Google Sheet. As the book progresses, in this "Going Further" section, we will explore some possibilities with JASP that are not possible in Google Sheets.

Calculating the Correlation Coefficient by Hand

For the more adventurous, Figure 4.9 shows one way to compute a correlation manually for a small data set. This should give you some idea of how a correlation "works." The same method for calculating a correlation is also illustrated with Cassandra's data in the "calculating correlation" tab of this chapter's Google Sheet (http://bit.ly/2wXQDu1). The logic behind this calculation is described in more detail next. There are other ways to calculate a correlation that are easier to use, but this method illustrates the logic of the test more clearly.

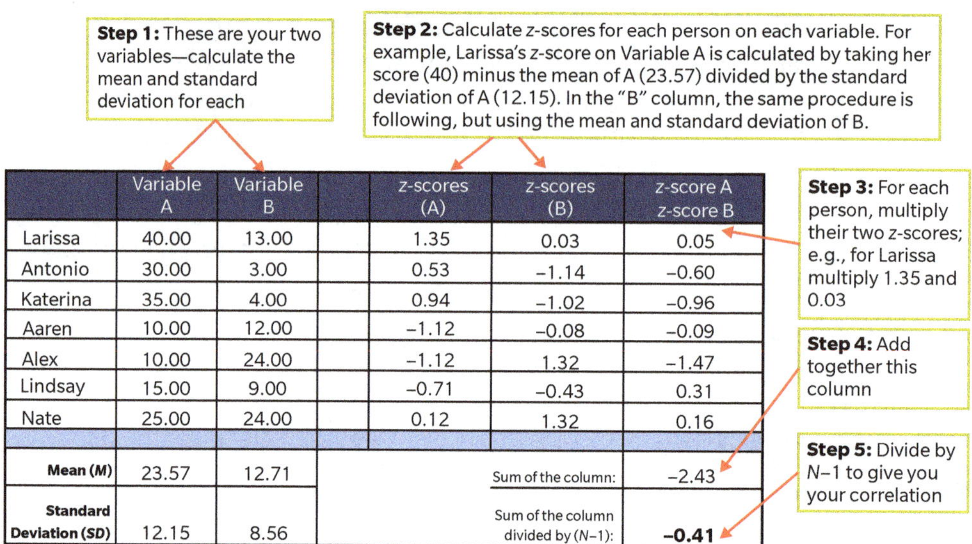

	Variable A	Variable B		z-scores (A)	z-scores (B)	z-score A z-score B
Larissa	40.00	13.00		1.35	0.03	0.05
Antonio	30.00	3.00		0.53	−1.14	−0.60
Katerina	35.00	4.00		0.94	−1.02	−0.96
Aaren	10.00	12.00		−1.12	−0.08	−0.09
Alex	10.00	24.00		−1.12	1.32	−1.47
Lindsay	15.00	9.00		−0.71	−0.43	0.31
Nate	25.00	24.00		0.12	1.32	0.16
Mean (*M*)	23.57	12.71			Sum of the column:	−2.43
Standard Deviation (*SD*)	12.15	8.56			Sum of the column divided by (*N*−1):	**−0.41**

FIGURE 4.9 Calculating the correlation using a *z*-score method

In Figure 4.9 and the Google Sheet, you can see *how* the correlation is calculated. But *why* does multiplying *z*-scores sometimes give us positive correlation values and sometimes negative? Consider what happens when multiplying *z*-scores from positively correlated variables. In Figure 4.10, you can see that Jordan, for instance, scores above the mean on both variables, so he has positive *z*-scores on both variables. When his two *z*-scores are multiplied, the result will be positive. Maria scores *below* the mean on both variables, so her *z*-scores will both be negative; when multiplied, those two negatives will also make a positive number. Consider all the other points on this scatterplot of a positive association: All the multiplied *z*-scores will give a positive result, and so summing them will give a positive outcome; it's this that determines the sign (positive or negative) of the correlation.

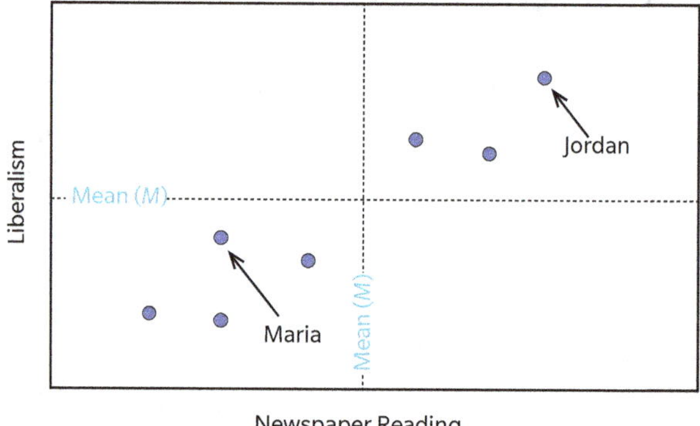

FIGURE 4.10 Positive correlation

In Figure 4.11, you can see the same process but with two negatively correlated variables. Jordan scores above the mean on newspaper reading, but *below* the mean on liberalism (he is a conservative who reads the newspaper a lot). He will have one positive z-score and one negative z-score. When his two z-scores are multiplied, the result will be negative. Maria scores below the mean on newspaper reading, but above the mean on Liberalism; she will also have one positive and one negative z-score, and so the product of the two z-scores will also be negative. Consider all the other points on this scatterplot of a negative association: all the multiplied z-scores will give a negative result, and so summing them will give a negative number and hence a negative correlation.

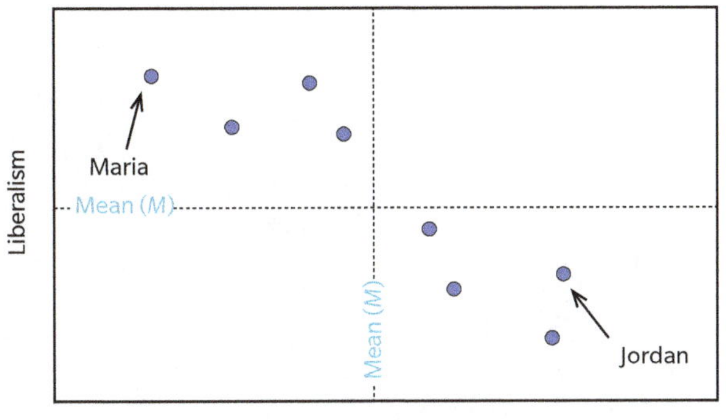

FIGURE 4.11 Negative correlation

Finally, consider what happens when there is no association between variables (see Figure 4.12). You will have a wide variety of people with different combinations of positive and negative z-scores, and so some of the z-score products will be positive (Jordan and Alba) and some will be negative (Maria and Abou). When you add a bunch of positive and negative numbers, you end up with a total close to zero and hence a correlation close to zero. Calculating statistics can get complicated, but sometimes it's comforting to know that there is some sensible logic underlying the calculations!

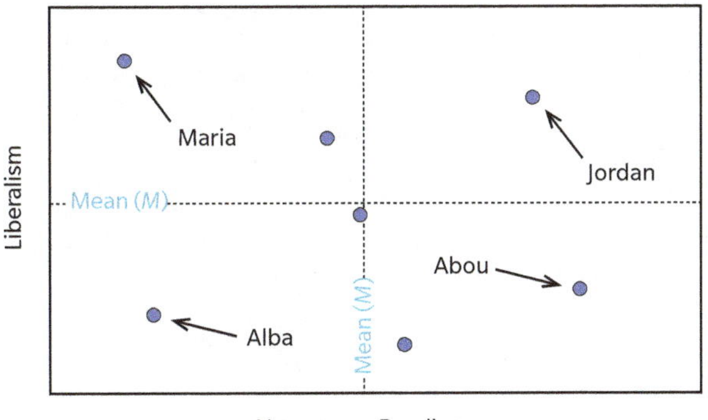

FIGURE 4.12 Zero correlation

Credit

Fig. 4.8: Copyright © by The JASP Team.

SECTION 3

Social Science Experiments: Does Appearing on a Social Media Site Make a Politician Appear Less Credible?

By the end of this section, you will be able to:

- ✔ Describe the defining features of an experiment
- ✔ Explain what random assignment does
- ✔ Describe the difference between measuring and manipulating a variable
- ✔ Explain the meaning of experimental control
- ✔ Calculate a *t*-test using Google Sheets
- ✔ Calculate a *t*-test by hand
- ✔ Write a report of the results of a simple experiment

CHAPTER 5

Doing the Research: Introduction to Experiments

Cassandra's friend Andre is a student interning with a political campaign. The campaign wants to know whether having their candidate appear on BuzzFeed would hurt the candidate's credibility. Or, put differently, they have the following hypothesis:

> H1: A political candidate who appears on BuzzFeed will be perceived as less credible than a candidate who does not appear on BuzzFeed.

They have tasked Andre with figuring out the answer to this question. Before we begin, imagine you are Andre: What sort of research would you do to figure out whether BuzzFeed appearances are good or bad for a political candidate? Try to think of a couple of details for your strategy.

You probably thought about using some of the techniques already discussed in the book. A self-report approach might just involve asking people what they'd think of a political candidate who did a BuzzFeed interview. Or think back to Chapter 1 where we discussed doing archival research: You could do an analysis of previous political campaigns in which candidates appeared on social media and see what happened to their bids. But Andre has a different idea.

Andre's Experiment

Andre chooses to do an **experiment** to answer the question. Andre knows a critical fact about experiments: Experiments are the best research strategy for uncovering cause-and-effect relationships, and he is specifically interested in a causal effect. He wants to know whether appearing on BuzzFeed *causes* a politician to appear less credible. Remember from Chapter 3 that the independent variable is the "causing" variable. If X → Y, then X is the independent variable.

Appearing on BuzzFeed (or Not) → Perceived Credibility of Politician

Independent Variable → Dependent Variable

A lot of people think that "experiment" is just another word for a scientific study, and indeed a lot of scientific studies are experiments. But a social science experiment is a specific type of research study with certain characteristics (see Figure 5.1). The research studies Cassandra did in the first few chapters were *not* experiments. Experiments involve three essential features: manipulation of the independent variable, random assignment to conditions, and experimental control. The next three sections describe each of these in detail.

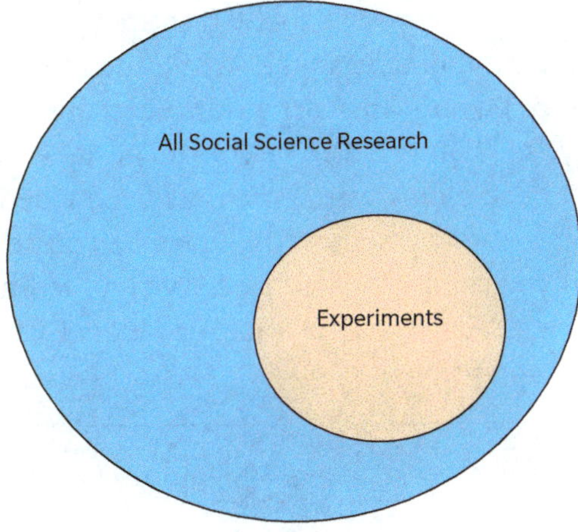

FIGURE 5.1 Not all research studies are experiments!

Communication researchers do experiments to demonstrate *cause-and-effect relationships*. The features that define experiments described in this chapter are all aimed at this goal.

KEY POINT

Essential Features of an Experiment 1: Manipulation of the Independent Variable

Manipulation of a variable means that you, the researcher, are in control of the variable. For Andre, rather than just waiting for some political candidate to appear on BuzzFeed, he "makes it happen" (within his experiment, at least). He is lucky in that, because he works for the campaign, he has access to the actual politician. To manipulate his variable, he video records a short interview with the politician.

Then he uses his computer to insert a "BuzzFeed politics" logo in the bottom corner of the screen (the "BuzzFeed video" condition). He also keeps a copy of the video without the logo (the "**control group**" condition). Andre now has two versions of the same interview that he can show to research subjects: one that looks like a BuzzFeed video and one that is just an interview without any apparent source. These two videos represent his manipulation. Of course, even if he didn't have access to a real politician, he could achieve something similar by using any interview of a politician he could find and editing it to include (or not) a BuzzFeed logo. Note, he has two videos, but just *one variable*. The variable here might be called "*source of video*," and it has two conditions: BuzzFeed versus control. What you *do* to a group of research subjects (e.g., showing them a particular video) is sometimes called a **treatment**.

This manipulation of the video is useful, because now Andre can show the different videos to different groups of people. If the people who see the BuzzFeed video all think that the candidate is a joke (while the folks who see the control interview don't), Andre has his answer: a BuzzFeed appearance will hurt the candidate's credibility (see Figure 5.2). The control group is important to provide a clear comparison: If people only watch the BuzzFeed video, there's nothing to compare them against to know whether that video had any effect. With the control group included, if you see any difference between the BuzzFeed and control conditions, you know it's because of the BuzzFeed logo: Everything else was the same across those two conditions.

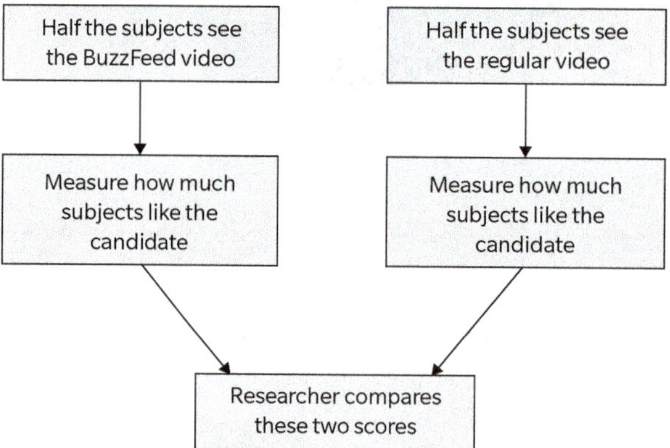

FIGURE 5.2 Manipulating an independent variable: The starting point for an experiment

Research ethics: debriefing

A "**debriefing**" occurs when you explain something about your research study to your research subjects after they are done with the study. Debriefings are particularly important if there has been any sort of deception in a research study. Deception is sometimes necessary to maintain a "cover story" for a study—you tell research subjects you are studying X, so they are less likely to figure out that you are actually studying Y! If you lie to people, afterward you need to apologize and explain to them a little about why the lie was necessary. Andre's study doesn't really include deception, but he does present a video as if it was from BuzzFeed, whereas in fact it is not. At the end of his study, he should explain to the research subjects in the BuzzFeed condition that in fact the video was created for this particular study, and it is not available on the BuzzFeed website. Any explanation or additional information about an experiment provided *after the study is over* is called a **debriefing**.

There are some other aspects of experiments to discuss that we'll get to in a moment. First, though, let's practice manipulating variables. Imagine you were a communication researcher interested in the effects of background music on conversation in restaurants (e.g., do people talk more in a restaurant when fast-paced versus slow-paced music is playing?). Your study would look something like the following:

Pace of Music → Amount of Conversation

Independent Variable → Dependent Variable

Assuming you had a friendly restaurant owner to help you, how would you manipulate your independent variable?

This one is fairly simple. If I were doing this study, I would play fast music some nights in the restaurant and slow music on other nights. Or I might alternate fast and slow music in the playlist on any given night. Then I could observe people in the restaurant and see whether their level of conversation varied along with the music.

Now let's do something a bit more complicated. Imagine you were studying romantic relationships and were interested in whether self-disclosure by one partner influenced the *other* partner's relational satisfaction.

Self-Disclosure by Person A → Relational Satisfaction for Person B

Independent Variable → Dependent Variable

How would you manipulate your independent variable?

If you wanted to manipulate this variable, you would need to recruit romantic couples to help in the study. For half of the couples, you would give one partner instructions to do lots of disclosure ("tell your partner more personal information about yourself, share your emotions, etc."). The other couples wouldn't receive any special instructions (they are the control group). Then you would measure the relational satisfaction of the partners at some later point in time.

This is a complicated manipulation in terms of getting it to work. You can *tell* people to disclose things to their partners, but whether they do or not is another question! If you could assess whether they actually *did* self-disclose more as a result of your instruction, that would be very helpful to you—that kind of test is called a **manipulation check**. Andre could include a manipulation check in his study just by asking people whether they remembered seeing a logo on the video and if so what the logo was.

The self-disclosure manipulation is also complicated in terms of research ethics. You would be trying to intervene in people's relationships, which has the risk of causing harm to an important aspect of your participants' lives. This "interfering" aspect of experiments is why research ethics issues arise with experiments more than with other forms of research. Observing people or asking them questions can cause harm but has less potential to do so than when you actively *intervene* in people's lives. As noted in Chapter 1, all research studies involving human subjects require ethical approval, but experiments often receive the most scrutiny.

Hopefully by now, you have a good idea of what a manipulation consists of: the researcher intervening to create different levels of an independent variable for different groups of subjects. There are a couple of other important things that an experiment has to include; let's talk about those now.

Essential Features of an Experiment 2: Random Assignment to Conditions

What does "**random assignment**" mean? When you randomly assign people to groups, you are placing them into those groups in a way that is left purely up to chance. And "chance" here means true *mathematical* random chance. A coin flip. A randomly generated number on a computer. Chance doesn't mean that Andre just picks people to be in one condition or another based on a whim or that people get to pick what condition they are in. Andre has two experimental conditions: the BuzzFeed video and the regular video. To randomly assign his research subjects to his conditions, he can just flip a coin. If it comes up heads, then the subject sees the BuzzFeed video, and if it comes up tails, the subject will see the regular video.

Why the coin flip? Why not show the BuzzFeed video to everyone whose last name ends with letters A–M, and the regular video to all the N–Z last names? Or why doesn't Andre show the BuzzFeed video to folks who come to his lab in the morning, while everyone who comes in the afternoon watches the non-BuzzFeed video? Think a little about why these solutions might be bad. Provide at least one reason for why each of these two strategies might be a bad choice.

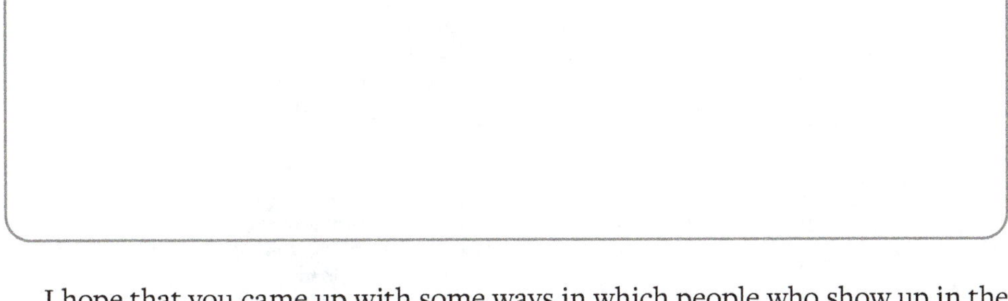

I hope that you came up with some ways in which people who show up in the morning might be different from those who show up in the afternoon. Afternoon attendees might be more likely to have been partying the night before, or they might be people who don't need to pick up their kids from school (they are too young to have kids or old enough that their kids are driving). Morning attendees are probably not in the party crowd and might be parents rushing from dropping their kids at school to their workplace. In all sorts of ways (some of which we probably can't even guess), people who show up in the morning are almost certainly different from those who show up later in the day.

The same might be true of last names. People with last names near the end of the alphabet might include more people of Eastern European origin (Zbikowski, Zelinski, Vukovich), while those at the start of the alphabet might include more

Middle Easterners (Abbas, Khan, Hussein). That could be critically important if the political candidate was of Eastern European or Middle Eastern origin! There might be other differences between the two ends of the alphabet that we can't even think of—perhaps people at the back end of the alphabet feel bitter because they are always at the end of alphabetical lists!

Here's the problem: If the BuzzFeed group and the control group people are different from one another *before they even watch the video*, then finding out that they have different perceptions of the politician *after* watching the video doesn't tell us much. Let's briefly imagine (probably not true, but humor me here) that people who get up early tend to like politicians (any politicians!) more than those who don't get up early. And imagine that you did Andre's study, showing the BuzzFeed video to morning attendees and the control video to afternoon attendees (see Figure 5.3). What is the problem here?

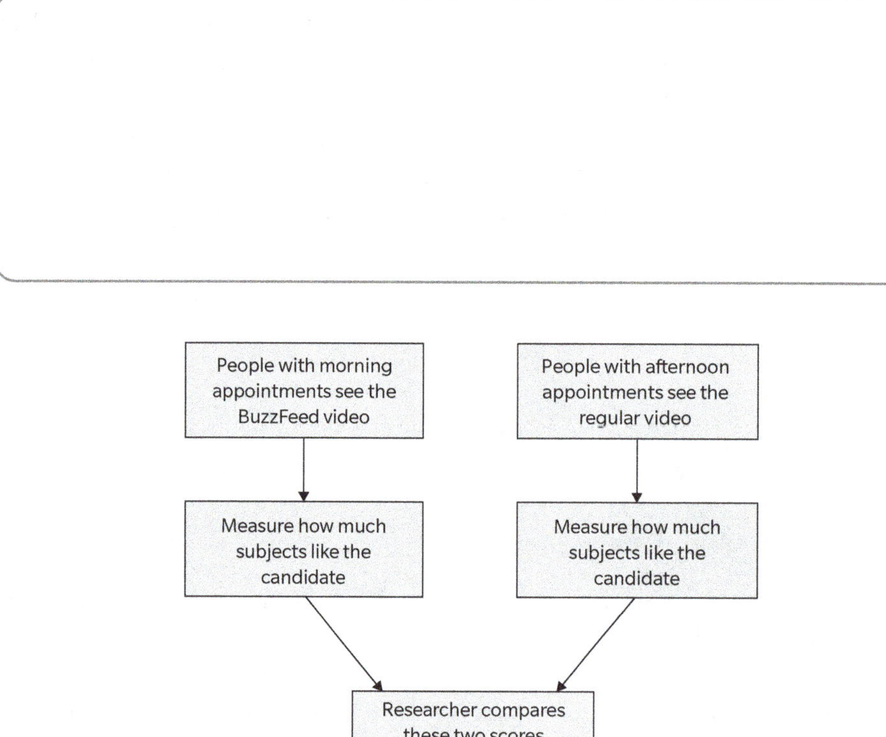

FIGURE 5.3 What is the problem with this research design?

From this study, a researcher might conclude that the BuzzFeed video is *improving* the candidate's image—subjects in that condition generally liked the candidate, while those in the regular video condition didn't like the candidate. But, unfortunately, and unknown to the researcher, this "effect" had nothing to do with the video. The people with morning appointments just tend to like politicians more than the afternoon folks. The researcher will draw an incorrect conclusion about the effect of the video. The problem is a lack of random assignment.

Random assignment gets around this problem. We know that there are no *systematic* differences between people whose coin flip comes up heads and people whose coin flip comes up tails, so we can be confident that differences in those people *after* they watch the video are *because of* the video and not because of some difference that existed before they saw the video (see Figure 5.4).

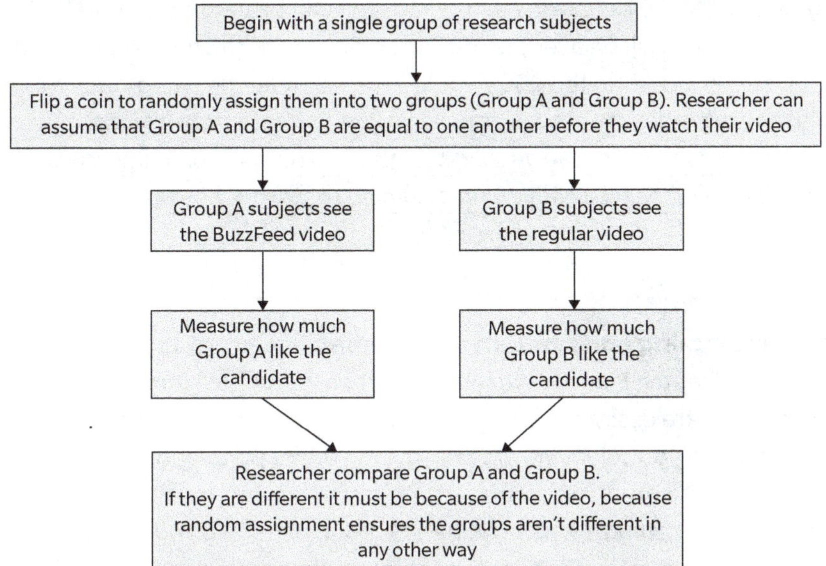

FIGURE 5.4 Random assignment to conditions: A true experimental design

The power of large numbers

The effectiveness of random assignment varies depending on sample size. Imagine having four people and flipping a coin to randomly assign them into two "groups" with two people in each group (see Figure 5.5).

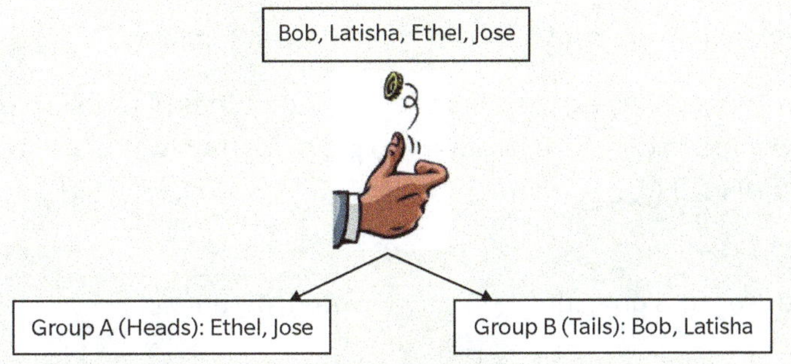

FIGURE 5.5 Randomly assigning four people to two groups

continues on next page

continues from previous page

How confident are you that the people in Group A will be similar to people in Group B? I hope you answered, "not very confident"! A sample of four people is simply too small for random assignment to *work*. For example, if there are three women and one man, there is literally no way that you can end up with two groups that have a similar makeup in terms of subject sex.

On the other hand, if you have 200 people and you randomly assign them to two groups with 100 people in each group, you can be very confident that those two groups will, on average, be extremely similar to one another. Whatever the sex ratio among the 200 people in the sample, the two groups will end up with a very similar sex ratio. *Bottom line: Random assignment tends to "work" pretty well once you get above about 40 subjects in each experimental group; below that number you should be cautious in assuming equivalence between groups.*

KEY POINT

Random sampling and random assignment. You heard about random sampling in Chapter 1, and we're talking about random assignment in this chapter. These are easily confused concepts. Remember: You do ***random sampling*** when you select individuals from an entire population with the goal of creating a small group of people who *represent* the entire population. You do ***random assignment*** when you have a group of people and you want to split them into two equivalent groups to test an experimental manipulation. The concept of randomness is the same across both: You are either selecting or assigning people in a way that eliminates bias and is truly mathematically random: a random number generator or a coin flip. But your goals are different: In one case, your goal is generalization to a population, and in the other case, your goal is creating two groups that are equivalent to each other.

Imagine you were doing a survey about the use of mobile gaming apps, and you wanted to be able to draw a conclusion about *all* cell phone users. Which would you probably be using?

Random assignment *Random sampling*

Imagine you were studying the effects of different types of mobile gaming apps and wanted to compare people who played 15 minutes of *Flappy Bird* with people who played 15 minutes of *Clash Royale*. Which would you probably be using?

Random assignment *Random sampling*

In the first case, you are aiming to generalize about a population, and so you should be using random sampling: You will ask the questions about mobile gaming apps to a random sample of mobile phone users so as to be able to make a projection about *all* mobile phone users. In the second case, you would be using random assignment. Your goal would be to have two groups of people who were equivalent to one another *before* they played one of the games so that any differences you observe *after* they play the game must be because of the game. In this case, it probably doesn't matter too much whether you have a random sample—you are just interested in the effects of the game but don't care particularly whether you can generalize those effects to the entire population.

Essential Features of an Experiment 3: Experimental Control

The last component of a strong experimental design is experimental control. Experimental control means that the researcher controls the situation as much as possible, in particular ensuring that everything *except* the manipulation is held constant across the groups. Consider a situation where Andre did not have access to the politician to video record an interview, and he didn't have video editing skills. He might consider going on BuzzFeed and downloading a video of a politician and then searching the Internet for a non-BuzzFeed video of a politician. He could then do everything in Figure 5.4, but his study would have some significant problems. Can you think of a key problem with this procedure?

The two videos are probably completely different, right? He might have found videos that feature different politicians, or that are about different topics, or that involve friendly versus unfriendly interviewers. Any of these aspects of the video might influence perceptions of the politician and so make it impossible to reach any conclusion about the influence of the video being from BuzzFeed. When you go to the trouble to manipulate an independent variable, you need to make sure that the manipulated independent variable is the *only difference between conditions*. Ensuring this is the core of **internal validity** (see Key Point).

KEY POINT

Internal validity. Internal validity is your *level of confidence that your independent variable caused any differences you observe in your dependent variable.* As the discussion in this chapter should have made clear (see Figure 5.4), you will have good internal validity if you randomly assign subjects to conditions, manipulate an independent variable, and keep everything else constant between experimental conditions. Sometimes it's impossible to do all of these things and studies end up with less good internal validity. Here are two important examples:

- **Lack of random assignment:** If you want to compare the effects of a new educational program, you might not be able to randomly assign elementary school kids to classrooms. The school might tell you to work with the class groupings that already exist in the school. Your study would be *like* an experiment, but without random assignment. Often, studies like this that are similar to (but not quite) an experiment are called **quasi-experiments**. You couldn't have complete confidence in your findings because two different classrooms of children might be different on an important variable that you aren't aware of.
- **Confounded variables:** A **confound** occurs when the manipulation of the independent variable also involves manipulating some other variable. For example, if Andre had a video of a male politician in the BuzzFeed condition and a female politician in the control condition, he would have confounded his main independent variable (source of the video) with another one (politician sex). It would be impossible to know whether differences he observed were because of the video source or the politician's sex. A confounded variable can also exist if you fail to control the *environment* in a study. If all the BuzzFeed condition subjects watched the video while sitting on a comfortable couch, while the control condition subjects watched it while sitting on an uncomfortable chair, that would be a confounded variable and might affect Andre's results. The source of the video would be confounded with the comfort level of seating.

Measuring the Dependent Variable Using an Existing Multi-Item Scale

Remember the starting point for Andre's project. The campaign wants to know whether having their candidate appear on BuzzFeed would hurt the candidate's *credibility*. Up to this point, we've just been assuming that Andre will measure something about his candidate's credibility. We haven't talked about how that will happen. From the earlier chapters in this book, it should be clear that there are good and bad ways to measure things, and measuring things in an experiment is no different. Once you have manipulated your independent variable, you need to measure the dependent variable to see if the independent variable affected it.

Using Existing Measurement Tools

One option for Andre would be for him to create his own questionnaire. He could start thinking about questions he could ask to get at perceptions of a political candidate's credibility. This would be the way to go if Andre was the first person ever interested in measuring perceptions of credibility. As you might guess, however, other people have also studied credibility over the years, so by creating his own questionnaire, Andre would be reinventing the wheel. Critical research lesson: Don't reinvent the wheel!

Using other people's measurement tools

People often wonder if they are "allowed" to use a measure that already exists. The answer is almost always "yes." Most research measures from published research are fair game to be reused in other studies. Occasionally, researchers may copyright their scale and insist that people who want to use it pay for the privilege. But one of the basic principles of science is that it should be public, so unless you see explicit warnings that you are violating copyright by using a measure, you can go ahead and use it. If someone wants you to pay them to use their measure, just look for a different measure—there's almost certainly a good one out there that you can use without paying

Rather than inventing his own questionnaire to measure perceived credibility, Andre could start with a computer search of his college library or Google Scholar (scholar.google.com) for other researchers who have measured credibility. Alternatively, he could look in a book that summarizes many research measures—for instance, Rubin, Rubin, Graham, Perse, & Seibold's (2011) book *Communication Research Measures II*. If he looked in that book, he would find a measure of source credibility created by McCroskey and Teven (1999). There are two key advantages for Andre in using this existing measure:

- Save time: Andre doesn't need to spend the time writing his own measure—one already exists
- Indicators of quality: When a measure has been used in published research, that research will contain information about the quality of the measure. Chapter 7 will discuss the details of assessing measurement quality, but

the key point here is that existing measures will provide that information. (Of course, sometimes published research might reveal that the measure is *not* good quality; in which case, you should move on and look for an alternate measure!)

This is like the difference between you buying a thermometer at your local hardware store versus trying to handcraft one out of a vial of mercury and a glass tube. Purchasing one from the store will save you a lot of time and effort, *and it* will be more accurate than your homemade attempt!

A part of McCroskey and Teven's scale is reproduced here in Figure 5.6, along with instructions for the researcher on how to create scores from the scale. This section of the scale measures perceptions of *trustworthiness*—one component of credibility. McCroskey and Teven's full scale also measures other perceptions related to credibility, but we'll just look at trustworthiness. Teven and McCroskey's scale is an example of **semantic differential** measurement. A semantic differential scale involves antonyms (opposite meaning terms) at each end of a numerical scale (trustworthy-untrustworthy, for instance). We will run into other types of scales throughout the book.

Please indicate your impressions of the politician by circling the appropriate number between the pairs of adjectives below. The closer the number is to an adjective, the more certain you are of your evaluation.

Honest	1	2	3	4	5	6	7	Dishonest
Untrustworthy	1	2	3	4	5	6	7	Trustworthy
Honorable	1	2	3	4	5	6	7	Dishonorable
Moral	1	2	3	4	5	6	7	Immoral
Unethical	1	2	3	4	5	6	7	Ethical
Phony	1	2	3	4	5	6	7	Genuine

For researcher: Items Honest-Dishonest, Honorable-Dishonorable, and Moral-Immoral should be re-scored: change 1→7, 2→6, 3→5, 5→3, 6→2, and 7→1 (4s remain unchanged). This is done so that high scores always mean more trustworthy. Then average scores across all six items to get a score for trustworthiness.

FIGURE 5.6 An existing measurement instrument to assess credibility

KEY POINT

Conceptual definition before operational definition. Using other people's measurement instruments is almost always a good idea. However, don't forget the importance of conceptually defining your variables. Before you measure something, you should always be clear in your head about what you *mean* by that thing. Before Andre commits to using McCroskey and Teven's measure of source credibility, he needs to make sure that their definition of that concept matches his own. Using their measurement wouldn't make sense if they mean something different by "source credibility" than he does. Always be clear on the conceptual definition before thinking about measurement.

Figuring out just how credible a politician is perceived to be from this questionnaire can be challenging. There are six different questions, but as a researcher, you just want one number that represents perceptions of credibility. Imagine that Andre receives one questionnaire when a research subject has circled the numbers in Figure 5.7. What score should this research subject get on the questionnaire? *Be sure to read the "For Researcher" note* in Figure 5.6 before trying. The answer is in Figure 5.8.

Honest	1	2	3	4	5	6	7	Dishonest
Untrustworthy	1	2	3	4	5	6	7	Trustworthy
Honorable	1	2	3	4	5	6	7	Dishonorable
Moral	1	2	3	4	5	6	7	Immoral
Unethical	1	2	3	4	5	6	7	Ethical
Phony	1	2	3	4	5	6	7	Genuine

FIGURE 5.7 Responses

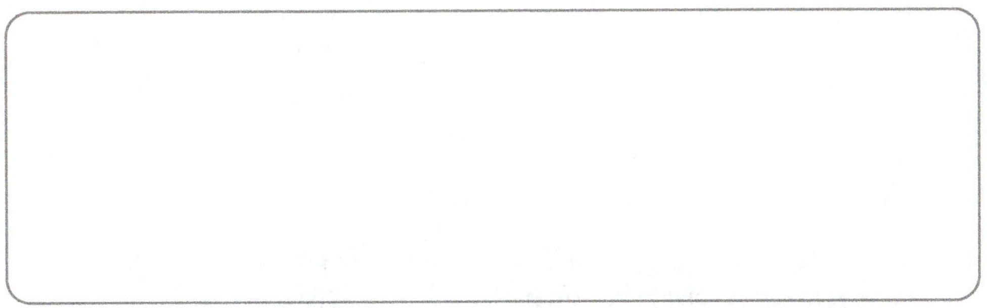

To score this, first remember that some items are re-scored so that high scores mean more credible for all the items (again, see the "For researcher" note in Figure 5.4). In the table below, the original scores are still in blue, but the scores you would actually *use for the calculation* are circled in red. For instance, the "3" on the honest-dishonest scale means that the politician is perceived towards the "honest" end of the scale. If we want high scores to mean "better" (in terms of credibility), then we need to change that 3 to a 5 to make it mean "more honest" and hence "more credible." We don't need to change the "7" on the "unethical-ethical" scale, because that score means very ethical, so the high score already fits with being more credible.

Honest	1	2	3	4	5	6	7	Dishonest
Untrustworthy	1	2	3	4	5	6	7	Trustworthy
Honorable	1	2	3	4	5	6	7	Dishonorable
Moral	1	2	3	4	5	6	7	Immoral
Unethical	1	2	3	4	5	6	7	Ethical
Phony	1	2	3	4	5	6	7	Genuine

To calculate this person's score on the credibility measure you would add all the red-circled scores together (5+4+5+6+7+6=33) and divide by six (there are six items in the scale). This subject's score on the measure of credibility is 33/6 which equals 5.50. This is, of course, quite labor intensive to do manually. If you used this measure in an actual research study with many respondents, you would get the computer to do the math for you automatically. You can see this process and an example of these calculations in a larger data set in this Google Sheet: https://bit.ly/2Kedqrq

FIGURE 5.8 Calculating a score from multiple items

Features of Multi-Item Scales

McCroskey and Teven's scale resembles many communication measures in a couple of important ways. It contains more than one item to ask about a single topic, and it includes some items where high scores mean the opposite of other items. Let's talk a little more about those two features.

Multiple Items

First, why do you think this scale asks six questions instead of just one? Why does it have questions concerning how "moral" and how "ethical" and how "honest" the politician is when in the end what emerges is a single number that the scale's authors say measures "trustworthiness"? Think a little about this and try to come up with at least two reasons for including multiple items in a measurement instrument.

Incorporating multiple items in a measurement tool to assess a single variable is very common social science research practice. This type of measurement instrument is often called a **multi-item scale**. Multi-item scales are generally regarded as better than single-item scales (just asking people one question to get their score) for the following reasons.

Precision: If there was only one question on this scale, the potential scores could only be whole numbers from 1 to 7. By using six items and averaging them, a much larger number of possible scores are available (someone can score 1.00, or 1.17, or 1.33, or 1.5, etc.). Imagine someone telling you tomorrow's temperature, but only being able to tell you in multiples of 10—it will be 20, or 30, or 40 degrees. You'd probably prefer that they be able to report the temperature as 27, or 44: more precise is better. Highly related to this point, scales with more items are less likely to be "ordinal" and more likely to be clearly "interval" (see levels of measurement in Chapter 3).

Consistency of responding/attention checks: By having multiple items, it is possible to see if people are responding in vaguely consistent ways. If somebody says the politician is highly trustworthy, but entirely unethical, that is a pretty good sign that the person isn't really reading the questions! Checking for consistency across items can also help you understand whether these items really do measure the same thing: If lots of people differ widely in how they rate the politician on "trustworthy" and "genuine," then the researcher may need to consider whether in fact trustworthiness and genuineness don't belong on the same scale. See Chapter 7's discussion of reliability for more information about this issue.

Measuring complex ideas: Many ideas addressed in communication research are complex. Seeing a politician as "trustworthy" involves a set of perceptions that probably shouldn't be boiled down to a single question. For sure, you want to ask about "trustworthiness," but perceptions of trustworthiness also involve the other concepts on the scale—being ethical and honorable and the like. If you were asked to assess someone's "health," you probably wouldn't *just* want to know his or her cholesterol level, or weight, or muscle mass. You would need multiple bits of information to get an overall picture of how "healthy" someone is. Multi-item scales allow you to assess the full *breadth* of a concept you are attempting to assess.

Where possible, it is good practice to use multiple items when measuring a concept.

Reverse-Scored Items

A second interesting feature of the trustworthiness scale is the way that some of the items flip between the positive word on the right-hand side (e.g., ethical) or the left-hand side of the scale (e.g., moral). This caused us some hassle in scoring the questionnaire (remember how we had to change 3s to 5s, and 2s to 6s, for instance). Why do we create work for ourselves in this way? What are the benefits of wording questions in opposite ways? Try to think of at least two.

This type of item is often called "**reverse-scored**." Reverse-scored items have some benefits:

a) These items are *particularly* useful for identifying people who are not carefully reading your questionnaire—if somebody circles all 6s on the trustworthiness questionnaire, you know that person is not paying attention!

b) These questions capture subtle differences in responses to questions worded positively and negatively. If you ask people how much they "love" certain foods, most will say that they don't "love" rice very much. On the other hand, most people also don't "hate" rice very much. If you asked them their love and hate for oysters, on the other hand, you might get different responses: People who don't "love" oysters may actually "hate" them. If you only asked about levels of "love," then you would miss the detail in levels of dislike. This is true of many concepts—a low score on one concept doesn't necessarily imply a high score on the opposite, and so asking the "same" question in a reversed way will provide more detail on people's feelings.

c) There are differences between people in terms of their general tendencies in using rating scales. Some people tend to "agree" a lot, or "disagree" a lot, or use the right (or left) end of the rating scale a lot, or prefer to keep near the middle of the scale. Reverse-scored items help control for some of these tendencies by "forcing" people to use the entire scale and to think carefully about their responses.

For these reasons, a lot of researchers like to include reverse-scored items in their measurement tools. However, there are some potential downsides to these types of instruments (see sidebar). You should always think carefully about how reverse-scored items are worded so that they do not confuse respondents. The debate over whether reverse-scored items are good or bad is ongoing among researchers.

The dark-side of reverse-scored items

For some respondents, switching back and forth between items asking apparently opposite things can be confusing. This is particularly the case when items include negatives. Imagine responding to the following two Likert-type items (Likert items are ones where respondents are asked how much they agree or disagree with certain statements).

I enjoy dancing to electronic dance music.

Strongly disagree	1	2	3	4	5	*Strongly agree*

I do not enjoy dancing to electronic dance music.

Strongly disagree	1	2	3	4	5	*Strongly agree*

I am guessing that you found the first item pretty easy to respond to. The second was probably a bit more challenging—you might have had to read the question a couple of times, and even then, figuring out whether you *"disagree"* with a "not" statement is mentally taxing: it's effectively a double negative. If you want your research participants to respond sensibly and carefully to your questionnaire, confusing them is a bad idea! For some researchers, at least with some kinds of questions, the potential for confusion created with reverse-scored items is too great.

Writing the Report

Andre's study is more complicated than the ones we read about in earlier chapters. As a result, his description of his methods is more complicated. Notice that you can make the report easier to read by creating sections describing separate elements of the methods, such as *who* you studied (*participants*), what *happened* to them (*procedures*), and how you *measured* things (*measures*). This makes it easier for your reader to follow what went on in the study. Report 5.1 includes a description of recruiting a sample in a public location rather than on a campus.

REPORT 5.1 Methods for Experiment

Participants. A convenience sample of 100 people was recruited at a suburban midwestern shopping mall. Shoppers were approached, shown a form featuring information about the study, and asked if they would participate in exchange for $10. Volunteers were 55% female, 38% male, and 7% nonbinary/third gender, and diverse in terms of age (M = 42.32 years, SD = 8.27, Range = 18–73). The sample was also diverse in terms of race and ethnicity (42% white, 25% Latino/a/x, 33% black/African American, 15% Asian American; numbers do not total to 100% because respondents could select more than one option).

Procedures. Participants who agreed to participate were escorted to a private area to complete the study. They sat in front of a computer and were asked to watch a video of a middle-aged female political candidate being interviewed about state and national political issues. Participants were instructed to "try to get an impression of the candidate" while watching the video. The participants were randomly assigned to see either a version of the video featuring the logo of a social media website (BuzzFeed), or a version with no logo. All other aspects of the video were identical. After watching the video, respondents completed a computer-based questionnaire assessing perceptions of the candidate's trustworthiness (described next). The entire procedure took approximately 15 minutes, after which respondents were debriefed and paid $10.

Measures. We measured perceptions of the candidate's trustworthiness using McCroskey and Teven's (1999) trustworthiness scale (one component of their ethos/credibility measure). Six semantic differential items tapped perceptions of the candidate as dishonest, trustworthy, dishonorable, immoral, ethical, and genuine using a 1–7 scale. After recoding reverse-scored items, scores were averaged to yield the measure of perceived trustworthiness (M = 3.54, SD = 1.27).

KEY POINT

Doing the three things described in this chapter is the strongest way to demonstrate that changes in one variable cause changes in another: cause-and-effect relationships. Random assignment means that you begin with groups that are equal to each other. Careful manipulation of an independent variable ensures that one group of people experience one level or condition of the independent variable while another group experiences a different condition. Experimental control guarantees that the *only* way the groups differ is the independent variable—other than the independent variable, the groups are treated in an identical manner. If the groups differ at the end of an experiment, it *must* be because of the independent variable. Any alternate explanation has been controlled through the experimental procedure.

Other Applications

Andre was interested in how one variable (appearing on BuzzFeed) influenced another variable (perceptions of a politician's credibility). A strategy like his would be useful with lots of other research questions involving the **causal effect** of one variable on another. Can you think of a couple of similar questions that could be answered with experiments?

I would use a strategy like Andre's if my research involved finding out things like the following:

- Does listening to a woman providing commentary on a sporting event result in different levels of interest compared to listening to a man providing commentary? (Independent variable = Sex of commentator; Dependent variable = Level of interest in sporting event.)
- Does providing a written agenda cause small groups to make decisions quicker? (Independent variable = Providing a written agenda [versus not]; Dependent variable = Speed to reach a decision.)

- Does watching a video about the value of intercultural experiences increase students' desire to study abroad? (Independent variable = Exposure to the video [versus no exposure]; Dependent variable = Desire to study abroad.)
- Does using anatomical diagrams improve patient comprehension of a physician's explanation? (Independent variable = Physician showing anatomical diagrams [versus not]; Dependent variable = Patient comprehension of their illness.)
- Are men more (or less) sexually attracted to their partners after watching a pornographic video? (Independent variable = Exposure to pornography [versus no exposure]; Dependent variable = Sexual attraction to partner.)
- Do cell phone bans increase test scores in college classes? (Independent variable = Presence versus absence of cell phone ban; Dependent variable = Test scores.)

The strategy might not work as well in other contexts. There are lots of things that you can't manipulate. Perhaps you are interested in whether having a romantic partner who smokes causes people to take up smoking. You're out of luck if you want to investigate that question with an experiment. It is both logistically and *ethically* impossible to manipulate the independent variable here. You would have to either (a) randomly assign people to have a romantic partner who smokes versus one who doesn't or (b) you would have to take existing couples and randomly assign some members of those couples to start smoking. Very few people would agree to be in such a study. And even if you found people willing to participate, your campus ethical review board almost certainly wouldn't allow it. It's similarly difficult to randomly assign people to live in new locations, or to experience highly traumatic personal events, or to have cosmetic surgery or get a divorce. So, some topics require you to seek out alternative research methods. But if you *can* manipulate your independent variable, experiments provide a very powerful demonstration of the causal influence of one variable on another.

For situations where you are interested in causality but cannot use an experiment, **longitudinal research designs** can be useful. In a longitudinal design, you measure the variables of interest at multiple points in time and look for relative changes over those time periods. For instance, if you want to look at whether having a romantic partner who smokes causes people to take up smoking, you might study people over time and observe when they enter new romantic relationships and whether their new romantic partners smoke. If entering a new relationship with someone who smokes is associated with starting to smoke in the subsequent weeks or months, that is strong evidence of a causal relationship.

Your Turn

Consider one of the variables you measured in the previous "Your Turn" sections. Write that variable's name here: ______________________________. This is your dependent variable.

Now, try to think of something that might *influence* that variable and that you could *manipulate*. For instance, if your dependent variable was online news consumption, you might think about whether having news alerts on your phone increases news consumption. (If it seems obvious that it would, sometimes obvious things don't work out—news alerts might annoy people and make them consume less news!). Phone alerts are an easy thing to manipulate: You could just randomly assign people to either having news alerts turned on or off on their phones. So, what variable could *you* manipulate that might influence your dependent variable? ____________________. This is your independent variable.

Now think in detail how you would manipulate it. Write a report like the one Andre wrote describing the process of your study; divide it into participants, procedures, and measures. Your manipulation should be described in the "procedures" section and the measurement of your dependent variable put in the "measures" section. Remember to mention random assignment and experimental control.

Wrap Up

In this chapter, you have learned the important characteristics of an experiment: random assignment, manipulation of an independent variable, and control of everything else. You also learned some processes for working with multi-item scales, including how to reverse-score items and calculate a single score for a person from the multiple items.

If you get nothing else from this chapter, remember the following:

1. An experiment is the best way to demonstrate a causal relationship between two variables. Not all scientific research studies are experiments.
2. Experiments require you to randomly assign subjects to experimental conditions, to manipulate an independent variable, and to hold as much constant between conditions as you can.
3. Measuring variables using multiple items is typically better than measuring them with a single item.

Key Chapter Concepts

Confounded variable: If an experimental manipulation manipulates two independent variables in a way that makes it impossible to distinguish the effects of each, the two variables are said to be confounded. If one group sees a super-scary antismoking *video* while another group sees a *not-very-scary* antismoking *print* ad, the scariness of the message (scary versus not) and the medium it's presented in (video versus print) are confounded, and so it would be impossible to know whether any effects were because of the scariness or the medium. Scariness and medium are confounded.

Control group: A control group is a group of people in an experiment who either receive no **treatment** at all or who receive a "default" treatment; the control group provides the relevant comparison for an experimental treatment. If you were studying the effects of a public health campaign message, the control group would be people who you don't show the message to. If you were looking at the effects of a new fourth-grade math curriculum, you couldn't have a group of kids who got zero math instruction for a year, however. So, in this case, your control group would be a group of children who get the "regular" or default math curriculum.

Debriefing (ethics): Any explanation about a study given to research participants after the study has been completed. A debriefing often includes an explanation of any deception that occurred in the study. If a study might have caused any distress for research subjects, a debriefing will also include information about where to seek assistance for that distress (e.g., information about the campus counseling center).

Experimental control: In an experiment, you need to hold everything constant, *except* for your manipulation.

Internal validity: A global assessment of the quality of a research study in terms of its ability to conclude that the independent variable caused changes in the dependent variable. Experiments with good internal validity include random assignment, a clear and nonconfounded manipulation of the independent variable, and control of all other factors in the environment and procedure.

Longitudinal design: A research design in which variables are measured at multiple points in time. This is useful for examining causality when experiments are not possible.

Manipulation check: A test to make sure your manipulation operated in the intended way. For example, Andre could ask people whether they saw a logo on the screen; if people correctly remembered seeing a BuzzFeed logo (in the BuzzFeed condition) or not seeing a logo (in the control condition), that would be evidence that his manipulation was implemented appropriately. If nobody remembered seeing the BuzzFeed logo, then the manipulation "failed" and probably the study would need to be redone ("we're going to need a bigger logo").

Manipulation of the independent variable: A defining feature of an experiment. The researcher must be able to change some aspect of the independent variable to create different "conditions" or "levels" of that variable.

Multi-item scale: A measurement instrument in which responses to more than one question are combined (typically averaged) to yield a single score.

Quasi-experiment: A study that appears to be an experiment but is lacking random assignment to conditions.

Random assignment: The process of putting research subjects into two or more experimental conditions without any bias. The process of assigning respondents to conditions purely by chance processes reduces the possibility that the experimental groups will be different from one another. Works well with relatively large samples (i.e., more than 40 per condition).

Reverse-score: In a **multi-item scale,** some items may be worded in an opposite manner from other items. These are reverse-scored items, and before calculating the final score for the multi-item scale, scores on those items must be reordered so that high scores on all items mean the same thing.

Semantic differential: A type of response scale where the extremes on a dimension are indicated by antonyms: Happy-Sad, Good-Bad, Strong-Weak, and the like.

Treatment: An experimental treatment is what gets "done" to participants in an experiment to manipulate the independent variable. A treatment might be exposure to a video, or giving people a set of instructions ("disclose a lot to your partner"), or intervening in a situation (e.g., changing a thermostat setting in a room).

Credit

CHAPTER 6

Reporting the Research: Comparing Means Using the *t*-Test

Ande has collected his data and is now ready to find out the answer to his question: Does appearing on BuzzFeed really hurt a politician's credibility? Here's a reminder of Andre's hypothesis:

> H1: A political candidate who appears on BuzzFeed will be perceived as less credible than a candidate who does not appear on BuzzFeed.

The previous chapter described how Andre collected data from 50 people who saw a "BuzzFeed" video and 50 who saw a non-BuzzFeed video. Each person rated the credibility of the candidate using the measurement tool described in the previous chapter, and so Andre has ended up with 100 scores. The Google Sheet (https://bit.ly/2G3VGto) shows what the data look like in the first tab (scroll down to see all the data).

In Chapter 4, we learned about the correlation test. You can probably see that the current data are different from the data we were looking at in Chapter 4. There we had a whole bunch of different scores on two variables. Here we have two different groups of people with scores on a single variable. A correlation test won't work here. We are going to learn a new statistic called the **independent samples *t*-test** that is appropriate for our situation. How do I know that this is the right test, however?

Deciding Which Statistical Test to Use

One of the most critical decisions to make when using statistics is figuring out *which* statistic to use. The most important information in making this decision is understanding the level of measurement of your variables, and to do that, you have to be able to identify your variables. What do you think Andre's variables are?

If you have a good memory, you might remember this from the previous chapter:

BuzzFeed Appearance (Appearing versus Not Appearing) → Perceived Credibility of Politician

Independent Variable (IV) → Dependent Variable (DV)

This tells you what Andre's variables are. However, if you thought that Andre had three variables (appearing on BuzzFeed, not appearing on BuzzFeed, credibility) then you are not alone. People often think that "categories" are the same as "variables," and so they think that different groups in an experiment are different variables. To get over this, it can be useful to think about categories that we deal with on a daily basis. "Protestant" is not a variable but "religion" is. The variable "religion" encompasses lots of categories, including "Protestant" as one of those possible categories. Likewise, "female" is not a variable but "sex" (or "gender") is. The variable "sex" encompasses the categories male and female (and sometimes other options too). When labeling variables, such as "BuzzFeed appearance," it is sometimes useful to name the categories afterward in parentheses just so you're sure that what you are talking about is a variable: BuzzFeed appearance (appearing vs. not).

So now, think back to Chapter 3 and what we learned about **levels of measurement**. What is the level of measurement for the following two variables (**categorical, ordinal,** or **interval**)?

	Level of Measurement
IV: BuzzFeed appearance (appearing vs. not)	
DV: Perceived credibility of politician	

The independent variable (appearing on BuzzFeed vs. not) just has two categories. The credibility variable, on the other hand, has many possible values, ranging along a continuum (from not at all credible to highly credible). So you should have identified the independent variable as **categorical** but the dependent variable as **interval** level.

Now, remember the hypothesis from Chapter 3:

> H1: Students with a more liberal political ideology will read the *Daily Centurion* more frequently than students with a more conservative political ideology.

Political ideology → *Daily Centurion* Readership

Independent Variable (IV) → Dependent Variable (DV)

If you remember, political ideology was measured on a 1–9 scale, and *Daily Centurion* readership was measured in minutes per day. What is the level of measurement for these two variables (categorical, ordinal, or interval)?

	Level of Measurement
IV: Political ideology	
DV: *Daily Centurion* readership	

Since both variables are measured on a numerical scale with a lot of possible values, we called both **interval**-level measures.

To decide which statistical test is appropriate to test a particular hypothesis, you can use the simple flowchart in Figure 6.1.

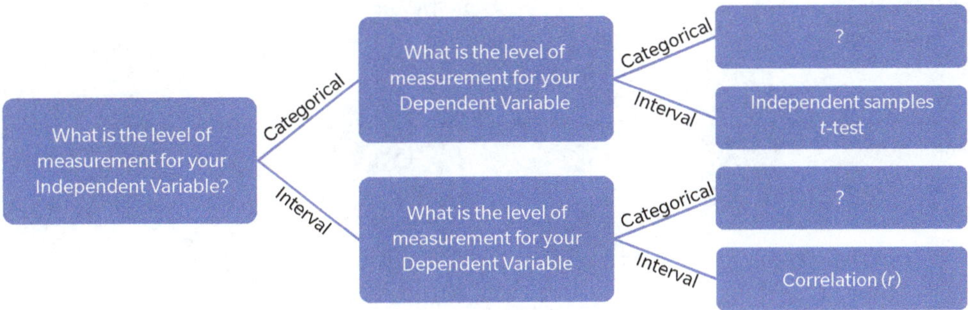

FIGURE 6.1 Flowchart for deciding which statistical test to use

You can see that the flowchart in Figure 6.1 is incomplete. This flowchart will grow as we move through the book, but it will always follow a similar structure. You will need to identify the level of measurement for your variables and understand which are independent and which are dependent variables, and then just follow the flowchart to make the decision about which test to use. You can see in the current flowchart that if you have an interval-level independent variable and an interval-level dependent variable, you should calculate a correlation. However, if you have a *categorical*-level independent variable and an interval-level dependent variable, you should calculate an **independent samples *t*-test**. Let's practice using this flowchart. Identify the variables and their level of measurement for the following problems and decide which statistical test you would use. The first one is done for you.

Research Problem or Hypothesis	Independent Variable (IV)	Level of Measurement for IV	Dependent Variable (DV)	Level of Measurement for DV	Statistical Test
Investigating whether people who smoke cigarettes are rated as less attractive than those who do not smoke cigarettes	Smoking (versus not smoking)	Categorical	Attractiveness ratings	Interval	Independent samples *t*-test
Seeing whether people's height influences their communication competence level					
Understanding whether high school grade point average (GPA) predicts income after graduation					
Comparing a group of people who watch a violent video and a group who do not watch the video in terms of their levels of aggression					
Seeing whether married couples who go to therapy are happier than those who don't go to therapy					

continues on next page

continues from previous page

Research Problem or Hypothesis	Independent Variable (IV)	Level of Measurement for IV	Dependent Variable (DV)	Level of Measurement for DV	Statistical Test
Seeing whether people who drink different levels of alcohol (from zero to 30 drinks a week) have different amounts of social interaction in their lives (e.g., the number of conversations they have in a week)					
Comparing men and women in terms of their levels of self-disclosure					

For each of the problems, you should think about what the independent and dependent variable are, and their level of measurement. Answers in a little while. First, though, notice that Figure 6.1 includes some question marks. Right now, we won't be learning any tests for situations where you are examining categorical dependent variables. Such tests do exist, but they will come later. You will also notice that there aren't any tests for ordinal data in Figure 6.1; again, such tests exist, but for the most part, they won't be covered in this book. So, while Figure 6.1 looks simple, it is just a starting point for something that will get more complicated. Get comfortable with the general idea.

OK, so here are the answers:

Research Problem or Hypothesis	Independent Variable (IV)	Level of Measurement for IV	Dependent Variable (DV)	Level of Measurement for DV	Statistical Test
Investigating whether people who smoke cigarettes are rated as less attractive than those who do not smoke cigarettes	Smoking (versus not smoking)	Categorical	Attractiveness ratings	Interval	Independent samples *t*-test

continues on next page

continues from previous page

Research Problem or Hypothesis	Independent Variable (IV)	Level of Measurement for IV	Dependent Variable (DV)	Level of Measurement for DV	Statistical Test
Seeing whether people's height influences their communication competence level	Height	Interval	Communication competence rating	Interval	Correlation
Understanding whether high school GPA predicts income after graduation	High school GPA	Interval	Income	Interval	Correlation
Comparing a group of people who watch a violent video and a group who do not watch the video in terms of their levels of aggression	Video exposure (watching video vs. not)	Categorical	Aggression	Interval	Independent samples *t*-test
Seeing whether married couples who go to therapy are happier than those who don't go to therapy	Therapy attendance (going to therapy vs. not)	Categorical	Happiness ratings	Interval	Independent samples *t*-test
Seeing whether people who drink different levels of alcohol (from zero to 30 drinks a week) have different amounts of social interaction in their lives (e.g., the number of conversations they have in a week)	Alcohol consumption level	Interval	Social interaction level	Interval	Correlation
Comparing men and women in terms of their levels of self-disclosure	Sex (male vs. female)	Categorical	Self-disclosure	Interval	Independent samples *t*-test

Calculating the Independent Samples t-Test

You will remember in Chapter 3 that we learned the basics of testing for statistical significance. For any statistic, a "significant" effect tells us that whatever effect we observed in our data is likely to be "real" (i.e., not zero) in the population. We indicate such "real" or statistically significant effects with the marker "$p < .05$," which means that the *probability of observing our data if the null hypothesis was true* is less than 5%. You don't have to use the 5% level, but this is the norm in social sciences right now. If you want to be surer that you really can reject the null hypothesis, you could use the 1% level, for instance. This level is called the "**alpha level**" of a statistical test. For this book, we will be using an alpha of .05 pretty much exclusively.

The independent samples *t*-test uses the same logic as was described in Chapter 3 for the correlation, but with a different null hypothesis. Do you remember what the null hypothesis was for a correlation? What correlation do you expect if the null hypothesis is true?

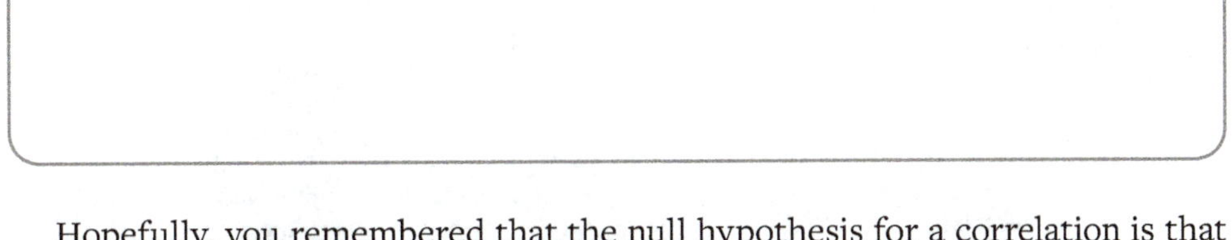

Hopefully, you remembered that the null hypothesis for a correlation is that the correlation is zero—that r in the population equals zero. With a *t*-test, the null hypothesis is that the *difference between the two groups in the population is zero.*

Add features to your Google Sheets

For some of the analysis in the rest of the book, you need to add capability to Google Sheets using what's called the XLMiner Analysis ToolPak. To add this (it's free), go to the "Add-Ons" menu in Google Sheets, and click "get Add-Ons." Search the add-ons for "XLMiner" and then click the "+" or "Install" button. Once it has installed, click on "Add-Ons" and by "XLMiner ToolPak," click "Start." You should see a new sidebar pop up.

Let's look at how Andre will go about calculating the *t*-test for his data using Google Sheets. Figure 6.2 illustrates what the data looks like in the Google Sheet, and Figure 6.3 illustrates the process using the XL Miner ToolPak. See the sidebar for how to install the XL Miner add-on and start it running.

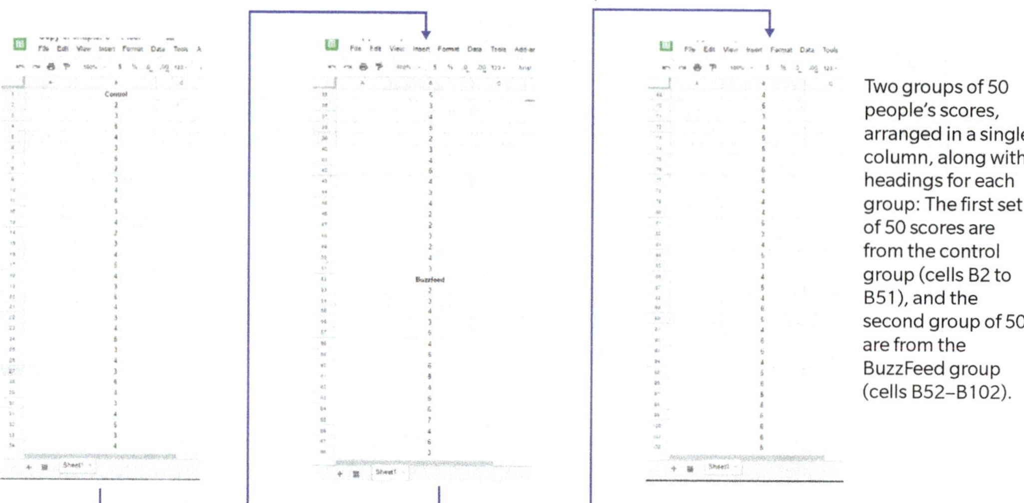

FIGURE 6.2 Organizing data for an independent samples *t*-test

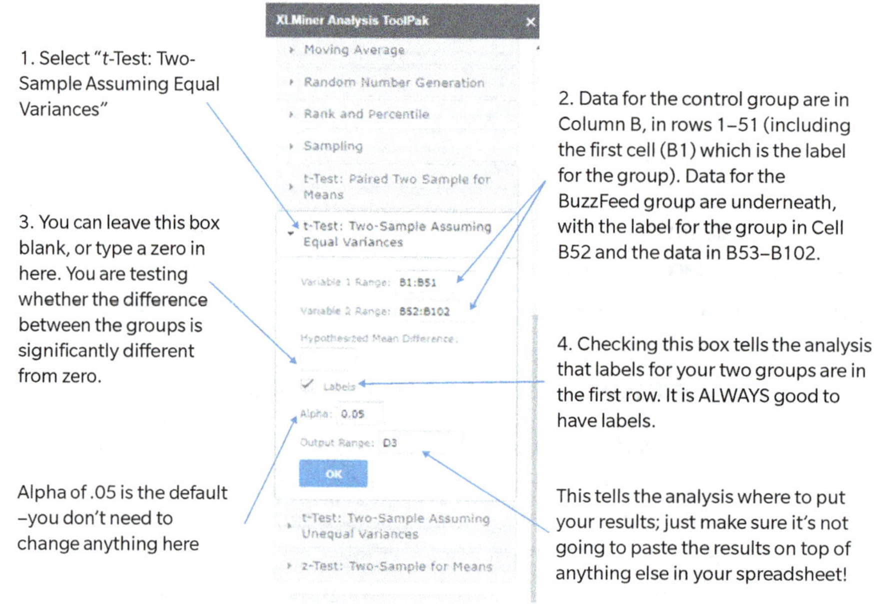

FIGURE 6.3 Using XLMiner to run the independent samples *t*-test

To calculate the *t*-test, Andre selects the "*t*-Test: Two Sample Assuming Equal Variances" option and enters the ranges in which his two groups' data are present. There are a few other elements to enter, which are described in Figure 6.3. However, most of the default settings in Google Sheets work fine. Once this is all entered, Andre clicks "OK," and the output appears in the same sheet. You can see

Andre's output in the Google Sheet (https://bit.ly/2G3VGto: independent samples *t*-test tab) and in Figure 6.4.

t-test: Two-Sample Assuming Equal Variances		
	Control	*BuzzFeed*
Mean	3.62	4.64
Variance	0.98	1.13
Observations	50	50
Pooled Variance	1.05	
Hypothesized Mean Difference	0.00	
df	98	
t Stat	–4.97	
P(T<=t) one-tail	0.00	
t Critical one-tail	1.66	
P(T<=t) two-tail	0.000003	
t Critical two-tail	1.98	

FIGURE 6.4 Independent samples *t*-test output

The most important elements are highlighted. First, pay attention to the means for the two groups, highlighted in yellow. This is critical information for understanding the results. You can see right away that credibility scores in the BuzzFeed group are *higher* than credibility scores in the control group. So, in a sense, Andre doesn't need to look any further—he can go back to the campaign and tell them not to worry: BuzzFeed exposure is definitely not *hurting* his candidate's credibility.

However, given this information, the campaign is likely to ask whether BuzzFeed might actually be *helping*. Just looking at the means is not enough information to make a claim that BuzzFeed is helping. We know from our earlier discussions that means in samples vary due to chance factors: sampling error. This BuzzFeed group might just score a little higher than the control group because of chance rather than because of the manipulation. To check for this possibility, we need to look at a test for statistical significance—the *t*-test in this case.

The *t*-statistic is highlighted in blue in the Google sheet output (independent samples *t*-test tab, t Stat: $t = -4.97$). Where does this number come from? The *t*-statistic is a ratio of two things:

$$\frac{\text{The Difference Between the Groups}}{\text{Differences Within the Groups}}$$

To understand why this ratio is important, consider the pictures in Figure 6.5.

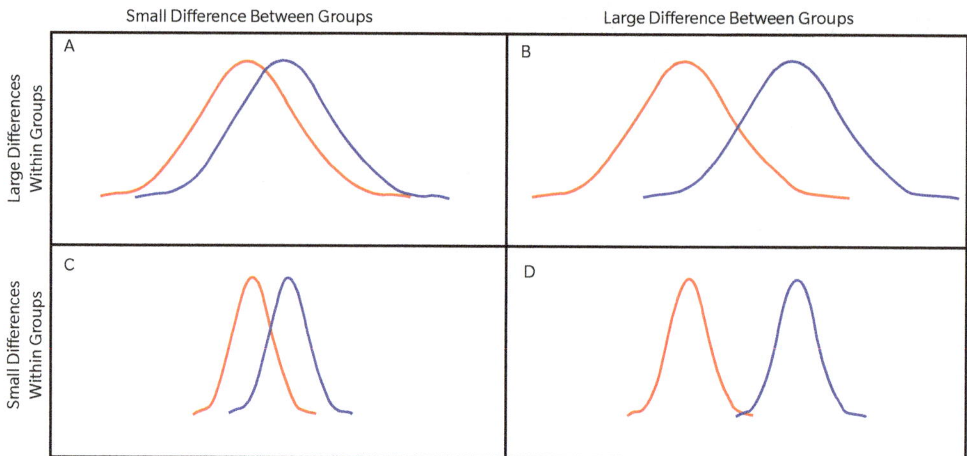

FIGURE 6.5 Differences between and within groups

Each picture represents the frequency distribution for two groups of people: the x-axis represents scores on some variable, and the y-axis represents the frequencies with which people scored. The means of each group are represented by the "peaks" in the curve, and variation within each group is represented by the "spread" or width of the curve. The two pictures in the top row (A and B) represent scenarios with fairly large variation in scores within groups (large standard deviations). The bottom row (pictures C and D) represent comparisons of groups with small standard deviations. The left column (pictures A and C) represents scenarios with fairly small **between group differences** (small differences between the two group means), and the right column (B and D) represents scenarios with larger differences between means.

As you look at pictures A–D, which scenario is the one where you are *most* confident that the two groups are really different from one another? Where are you *least* confident?

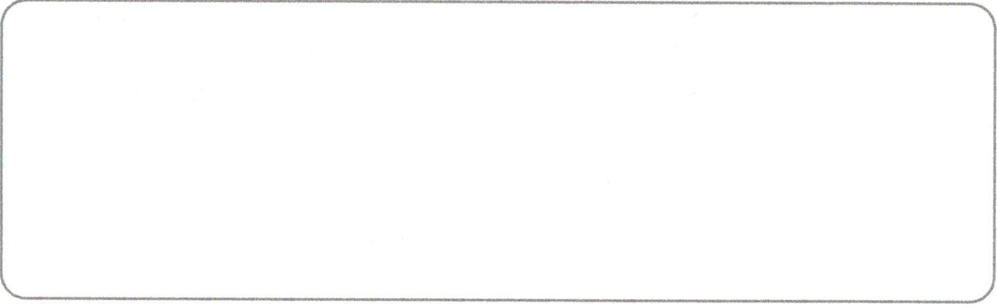

If you are like most people, you are *least* confident that the difference between the groups is real in scenario A. In that scenario, the two groups are close together and they overlap a lot. On the other hand, in scenario D, the two groups are very clearly distinct—there is virtually no overlap between them. Scenarios B and C represent the middle ground—there is a moderate amount of overlap between the groups. What you just did visually is what the formula for the *t*-test does statistically. The *t*-statistic is bigger when the differences between group means are bigger, and the standard deviations of the groups (their **within groups differences**) are smaller. That calculation is where the "**t-Stat**" box in Figure 6.4 comes from. We are not going to worry about the actual math here.

Beyond that *t*-Stat box, the "**P (T<=t) two-tail**" number is perhaps the first thing Andre will look at. This number is the significance level of his effect—his *p*-value. Remember that an effect is statistically significant if *p* is less than .05. So, if this number is smaller than .05, then the effect is significant. In this case, it *is* a *lot* smaller than .05, so Andre can conclude that the BuzzFeed group is significantly different from the control group.

The only other number that you should pay attention to right now is the "df" box. This abbreviation stands for "**degrees of freedom**" (**df**)—**df** is a statistical term that is related to sample size. For the independent samples *t*-test, the degrees of freedom are always *N* – 2: the total sample size minus two. In this case, the total sample is 100 (50 in each group), so the degrees of freedom are 98. You don't need to worry about degrees of freedom, but it is important to *report* them, so always include them if you are reporting results of statistical analyses.

Andre is now ready to report the results of his analysis. He would write something like the following:

> Counter to our expectations, BuzzFeed group participants (M = 4.64, SD = 1.06) rated the candidate significantly more credible than the control group (M = 3.62, SD = 0.99), $t(98) = -4.97$, $p < .05$.

If you are not sure about where any of those numbers come from, or why the report is worded in a particular way, take a look at Figure 6.6.

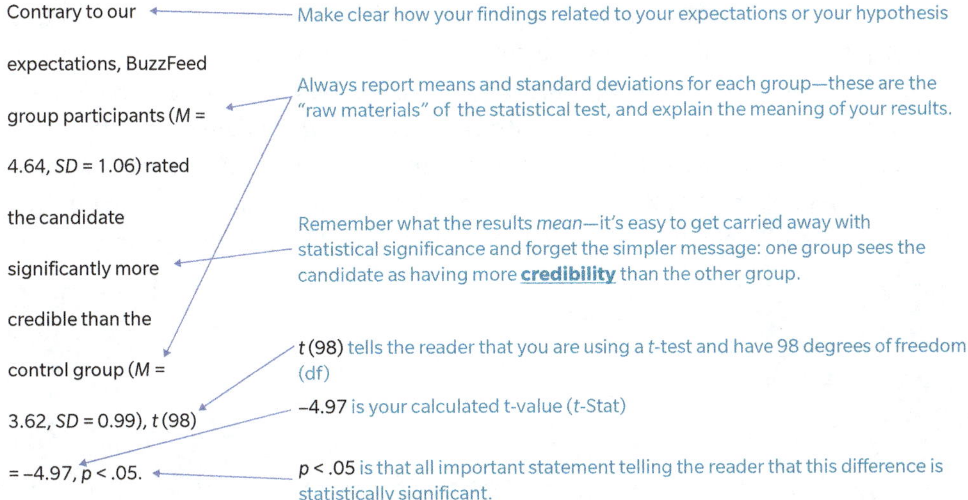

FIGURE 6.6 Writing the independent samples *t*-test

Finally, a word about the positive/negative sign in the *t*-statistic. As described earlier, the *t*-test involves a ratio of differences between groups and differences within groups; the numerator of the calculation (differences between groups) is simply the difference between the two group means: the average of one group minus the average of the other group. Whether the *t*-statistic ends up positive or negative is simply a result of what order the means are included in the subtraction. The reason that the *t*-statistic in Andre's calculation is negative is because it was calculated as

Control group mean – BuzzFeed group mean.

If instead it had been calculated as

BuzzFeed group mean – Control group mean,

all the results would have been identical, but the *t*-statistic would have been positive (4.97, instead of −4.97). So, in a sense, the "sign" of the *t*-test doesn't matter, so long as you pay attention to the means once you have the results.

Cohen's d*: A Measure of Effect Size for* t

The *t*-statistic is one of the most widely used statistics in all of the social sciences. However, it has one substantial disadvantage compared to the *r*-statistic from Chapter 4. It is not possible to compare one *t*-statistic against another one or to get any idea of the true *size* of an effect just from looking at the *t*. In fact, the size of the *t* is substantially influenced by the sample size: big sample sizes tend to give big *t*-statistics, even if the actual difference between the groups is fairly small. So, we need to have a measure of the *size* of the effect. One commonly used option for this is called Cohen's *d*.

The *d* statistic tells you the difference between the two means, expressed in standard deviation units. In the second tab of the Google Sheet for this chapter (https://bit.ly/2G3VGto), you will see *d* calculated for Andre's data. You can use this with your own data: just create a copy of the sheet and enter the relevant information from your own *t*-test output as illustrated with the color coding. This *d* statistic (−.99) tells us that there is almost a full standard deviation difference between the two groups. That is a very large effect in social science terms. To give you some context, the difference between men and women in terms of height has a *d* of about 1.40. Typically, we use the following rule of thumb for interpreting *d*:

d	Effect
<.20	Very small, perhaps trivial
.20	Small
.50	Medium
.80+	Large

When you report a *t*, it is good practice to also report a *d* so that your reader understands the *size* of your effect as well as whether it's significant. Andre's report has grown a little:

> Counter to our expectations, BuzzFeed group participants ($M = 4.64$, $SD = 1.06$) rated the candidate as significantly more credible than the control group ($M = 3.62$, $SD = 0.99$), $t(98) = -4.97$, $p < .05$, Cohen's $d = .99$.

A Confidence Interval for t

A final element that you might remember from Chapter 4 is the confidence interval (**CI**). Remember, this was where Cassandra figured out the likely range for her correlation in the population as a whole, based on the correlation in her sample.

A confidence interval for the *t*-statistic isn't very interesting, given that the *t* on its own doesn't tell us very much. However, what can be useful is to calculate a confidence interval for the *difference* between the means. In the population as a whole, how big of a perceived credibility difference would we anticipate between politicians seen on BuzzFeed versus a control condition?

The second tab in the chapter Google Sheet (https://bit.ly/2G3VGto) has a calculator for this confidence interval. If you want to use this with your own data, create a copy of the sheet, and copy the relevant information from your *t*-test output as illustrated with the color coding; the confidence interval will be calculated for you. In Andre's case, the resulting 95% confidence interval is [−1.4275, −0.6125]. This tells us that the *true* difference between the two groups is somewhere between a difference of −1.43, and −0.61. Notice that this range does *not* include zero. Thus, much like with the correlation, calculating the confidence interval is one way of testing the null hypothesis. We are 95% sure that the true value of the difference is between −1.43 and −.61, and thus we are at least 95% sure that the true value of the difference is not zero. Therefore, we are at least 95% sure that the null hypothesis is not true.

Andre is now in a position to write a more comprehensive report of the results that includes the effect size and the confidence interval.

> Counter to our expectations, BuzzFeed group participants ($M = 4.64$, $SD = 1.06$) rated the candidate as significantly more credible than the control group ($M = 3.62$, $SD = 0.99$), $t(98) = -4.97$, $p < .05$, Cohen's $d = .99$, 95% CI for difference between means [−1.43, −0.61].

You should now be able to replicate this same analysis and write it up using your own data; remember, you can copy the spreadsheets so as to use them to calculate your own confidence intervals, *d*-statistics, and the like. Just go to "File—Make a Copy."

When the null hypothesis isn't zero

You might wonder why there's a box in the XLMiner to enter the "hypothesized mean difference" under the null hypothesis. Isn't this always zero? Most of the time, the answer to that is "yes"—typically, the null hypothesis is that there is no difference between two groups. In rare cases, however, you might be interested in a nonzero null hypothesis. Imagine, for instance, that you were comparing the vocabulary skills of 7-year-olds and 10-year-olds after the 7-year-olds have done some intensive vocabulary training. The null hypothesis here is that the vocabulary training had *no* effect. If it had no effect, you wouldn't expect zero difference between the vocabulary skills of the 7-year-olds and 10-year-olds. You'd expect the *normal* difference between those groups—10-year-olds naturally have a larger vocabulary than 7-year-olds. So, if you knew that the normal difference was that the 10-year-olds know 300 more words than the 7-year-olds, then your null hypothesis would be a difference of 300 words between the two groups, and your hypothesis test would be to see if the special vocabulary training had narrowed that gap. In XLMiner, you would enter 300 as the "hypothesized mean difference." Again, this is a fairly unusual scenario, and most of the time, you will be safe in entering zero in that box or leaving it blank.

Writing the Report

The report of the *t*-test was already been described in some detail earlier. The only remaining items that Andre has to remember in the write-up are to remind the reader what the hypothesis is and include a summary of what analysis he is using. As will be discussed in a little bit, there is more than one type of *t*-test, so his readers will want to know specifics.

REPORT 6.1 Results for an Independent Samples *t*-Test

We predicted that people exposed to a politician on a BuzzFeed video would perceive that politician as less credible than those exposed to a politician on a non-BuzzFeed video. We compared credibility scores for the two groups (BuzzFeed video versus control video) using an independent samples *t*-test. Counter to our expectations, BuzzFeed group participants ($M = 4.64$, $SD = 1.06$) rated the candidate as significantly *more* credible than the control group ($M = 3.62$, $SD = 0.99$), $t(98) = -4.97$, $p < .05$, Cohen's $d = .99$, 95% CI for difference between means [−1.43, −0.61].

Note that Andre's results were the *opposite* of what he predicted. When reporting the results, it is good to alert the reader to this—for instance, where he writes "counter to our predictions." However, the report of the results isn't where you would get into talking about *why* the results were different from your expectations. You would do that in the "Discussion" section of your research paper.

Other Applications

As you saw in some of the earlier examples, the *t*-test is useful for a wide variety of situations. The idea of comparing two groups of people is a fairly fundamental scientific goal. Even outside of the social sciences, a *t*-test might be used for comparing two groups of plants grown under different conditions (in terms of how fast they grow, for instance) or comparing two groups of astronomical objects (e.g., comparing the estimated mass of neutron stars versus quasars ... yes, I know nothing about astronomy!). And in the social sciences, it is not just groups of *people* that we might compare using the independent samples *t*-test. In communication, you might use a *t*-test for

- comparing levels of intraorganizational communication in large versus small businesses,
- comparing numbers of ethnic minority characters in broadcast versus cable television shows,
- comparing column inches devoted to violent crime in newspapers versus news magazines,
- comparing the length of tweets from Republican versus Democrat political candidates, or
- comparing the amount of time between a first and a second date among high school versus college students.

While this is a very useful test, there are a few cases that *seem* like they would be good for an independent samples *t*-test, but that actually are not appropriate. For the most part, these exceptions relate to the term "independent samples." This particular *t*-test assumes that the groups you are comparing are separate groups of people (or other objects) who don't have any particular connection to one another. It is perfect for comparing unrelated men and women or groups of people randomly assigned to experimental conditions. However, it does not apply to the following:

- Cases where the *same* group of people are measured at multiple points in time. If you measured a group of people, then exposed them to a BuzzFeed video, and then measured them *again*, you could not use the independent samples *t*-test for comparing the scores before and after the video. Those scores are from the *same* sample of people, and hence these are not *independent samples.*

- Comparing pairs of people who are related to one another. For instance, imagine you were interested in whether husbands or wives in heterosexual marriages do more romantic talk. If you gathered data from husbands and wives who were *married to each other*, you could not use the independent samples *t*-test because those people are not independent of one another. The amount of romantic talk a husband does might be influenced by (*dependent on*) the amount his wife does (and vice versa), and the *independent* samples *t* can't take that dependence into account.

The appropriate test for situations like these examples is called a **paired** or **dependent samples** (those terms both mean the same thing) ***t*-test**. Let's check that you understand this difference. Which of the following uses an independent *t*-test and which uses a paired *t*-test? Circle the correct answer.

1.	Comparing older and younger siblings from the same family in terms of their amount of talk during family dinners	Independent *or* Paired?
2.	Comparing male and female college students in terms of their number of close friends	Independent *or* Paired?
3.	Comparing males and females who are dating each other in terms of their use of social media for maintaining the relationship	Independent *or* Paired?
4.	Comparing the amount of roommate conflict experienced by freshmen with the amount of roommate conflict those *same* students experience as seniors	Independent *or* Paired?

The paired samples test would be used for cases 1, 3, and 4, and the independent samples test for case 2. The "Going Further" section of this chapter shows you how to calculate a paired *t*-test.

Your Turn

In Chapter 5, you developed an idea for a manipulation of an independent variable that would influence a dependent variable. Go back to the "Your Turn" section of Chapter 5 to remind yourself of your variables. Your independent variable should have had just *two* categories (conditions) associated with it (e.g., an experimental and control condition). If it had more than two categories, then for the purposes of this section, just use two of the conditions.

Your independent variable: ______________________________

Its two levels: ______________________________

Your dependent variable: ______________________________

Either have classmates respond to your study or make up data in a Google Sheet. Using the skills you've learned in this chapter, analyze your data using an independent samples *t*-test and write a summary like Andre's for your results. Be sure to include an explanation of exactly what the data *mean*.

Wrap Up

In this chapter, you have learned how to calculate an independent samples *t*-test in Google Sheets and when it is appropriate to use this statistical test. You have also learned the appropriate measure of effect size for this *t*-test (Cohen's *d*) and how to compute a confidence interval for the size of the difference between two means. You should also have reminded yourself of the meaning of the term $p < .05$: if your statistical test indicates that you should reject the null hypothesis, you will say $p < .05$.

If you get nothing else from this chapter, remember the following:

1. The term $p < .05$ tells you that you are rejecting the null hypothesis and that your test is statistically significant.
2. The independent samples *t*-test is widely used for comparing two means, but it can't be used if the means both come from the same group of people or from people who are connected to one another (e.g., siblings, dating partners)—for that, you need to use the dependent samples (paired) *t*-test.
3. To know which statistical test to use, it's critical to understand levels of measurement and to be able to identify the levels of measurement for all of your variables.

Key Chapter Concepts

Alpha level: The probability level at which you are confident in rejecting the null hypothesis. In the social sciences, the norm is to set alpha at .05. This means that to reject a null hypothesis, you need to find $p < .05$, indicating less than a 5% chance of the null hypothesis being true based on your data. But alpha can be set at other levels—this is discussed more later in the book. See also ***p***.

Between groups differences: Differences between the average score (mean) in different groups. Often considered relative to **within groups differences**. Many statistical calculations, including the *t*-test, involve a ratio of between and within group differences. When between group differences are large and within group differences are small, statistics like *t* are large and the null hypothesis is typically rejected.

d: A measure of effect size for *t*-tests; also called Cohen's *d*.

Dependent samples: Separate samples of data where observations in one sample are *connected to* observations in another sample. This can be because of relationships between people in the samples (e.g., husbands and wives) or because the two sets of data are from the *same* people (e.g., with repeated measurement over time). Data from dependent samples are analyzed using different statistical tests (e.g., the **paired** or **dependent samples t-test**).

Dependent samples t-test: A *t*-test for comparing **dependent samples**. The same thing as a **paired t-test**.

Effect size: A measure of how big an effect is, independent of sample size. Some statistics (e.g., *t*) can appear large because of a large sample size; in such cases, a separate measure of effect size is required. For the *t*-test, **d** is a commonly used measure of effect size.

Independent samples: Samples of data where the observations in one sample are completely unrelated to the observations in the other sample. See also **Dependent samples.**

Independent samples t-test: A *t*-test for comparing **independent samples**; contrast this with the **dependent samples t-test.**

p: Shorthand used in reports of statistical hypothesis testing. The term "*p*" can be read as short for "the probability that the null hypothesis is true"; when *p* is small (less than .05), then researchers can reject the null hypothesis and conclude that whatever association they are observing between variables is "real." This is the same thing as statistical significance and is typically reported as $p < .05$. If an effect is *not* statistically significant, it is reported as $p > .05$.

Paired t-test: See **Dependent samples t-test.**

Within groups differences: Differences between individual observations *within* groups of people (e.g., within an experimental condition or among people of the same sex, religion, etc.). The most commonly used measure of within group differences is the standard deviation. Measures of within group differences are typically in the denominator in calculations of statistical tests like the **t-test.** See **Between groups differences.**

Section Wrap

Section Summary

Section 3 introduced the idea of an experiment. Experiments have three key features: random assignment to conditions, manipulation of an independent variable, and control. These features allow researchers to make definitive statements about causality. If you successfully manipulate an experimental variable with randomly assigned groups while controlling everything else, any differences you observe in a dependent variable must be because of the manipulation. The section introduced the independent samples *t*-test as a commonly used statistical test for examining the results of a two-group experiment.

Going Further

The focus of Section 3 was on a situation in which the two groups you are working with are separate people. However, as described in the "Other Applications" section of Chapter 6, there are also situations in which you want to compare two means from the same group of people (or from people who are related to one another, e.g., spouses). This requires using a different sort of *t*-test called a *paired t*-test (also sometimes called a dependent samples *t*-test).

The "Going Further" tab for this section's Google Sheet (https://bit.ly/2G3VGto) illustrates this analysis with a very small data set (see Figure 6.7). Imagine measuring just nine people at two points in time (T1 and T2). Each row in the data set now represents a single person, measured *twice*. Andre might be interested in this sort of analysis if he measured perceptions of a candidate's credibility *before* and then again *after* viewing the BuzzFeed video, for instance. The critical pieces of information here are highlighted in green. Notice that the average at T2 is smaller than the average at T1, and the effect is significant (you need to look at the two-tail *p*-value for reasons we don't need to get into here). So, if the data looked like this, it would indicate that perceptions of credibility significantly *decline* between T1 and T2, suggesting negative effects of viewing the BuzzFeed video (thus supporting Andre's hypothesis).

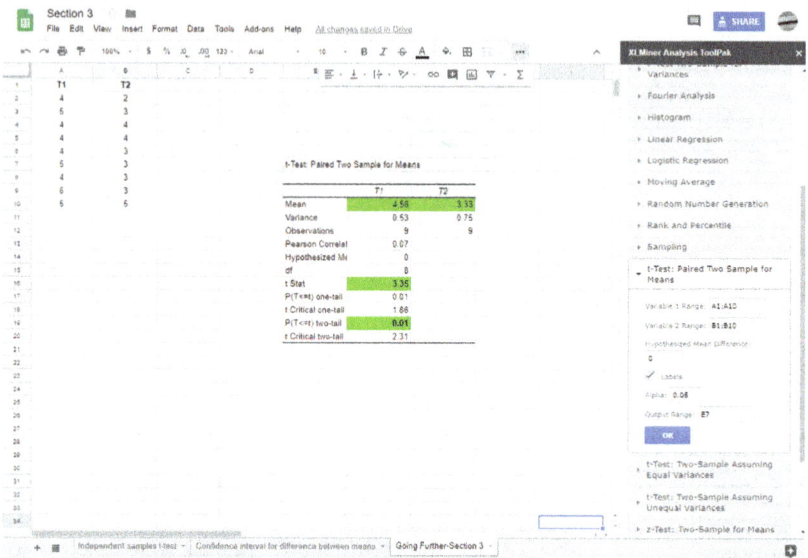

FIGURE 6.7 Data and analysis for paired *t*-test

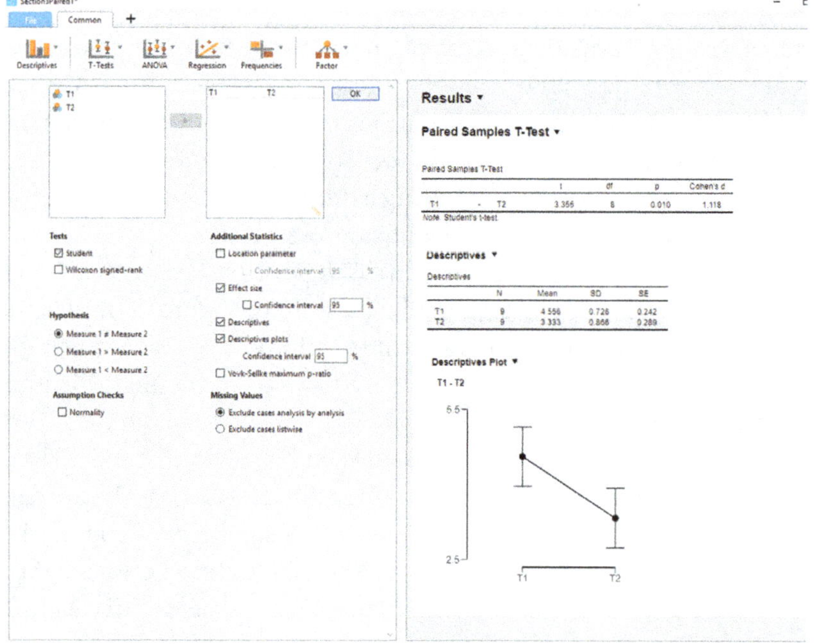

FIGURE 6.8 Paired *t*-Test output from JASP

The same analysis can be done in JASP (see Chapter 4 for information on JASP). You can download the JASP data file at https://bit.ly/2KJOiG0 and see the output in Figure 6.8. To recreate this output with your own data, just go to "T-Tests-Paired Samples T-Test" and move both variables into the box on the right-hand side. This output is a little more nicely organized than the Google Sheets results and includes some additional information. By checking particular options (see Figure 6.8), JASP will give you the measure of effect size (*d*—see Chapter 6 for interpreting *d*), the standard deviation (Google Sheets just gives the variance), and a nice plot of the means.

Notice the vertical bars in the plot of the means. These indicate a 95% confidence interval around each mean, thus helping the reader understand not only what each mean is in the data but also the likely range in which the "true" population mean might fall. The write-up for this analysis might look something like the following.

> Perceived credibility after watching the BuzzFeed video ($M = 3.33$, $SD = 0.87$) was significantly lower than before watching ($M = 4.56$, $SD = 0.73$), paired $t(8) = 3.36$, $p < .05$, $d = 1.12$.

This analysis is just to illustrate how JASP calculates this test. In a real research situation, you should avoid running analyses with an *N* this small!

Credit

SECTION 4

Advanced Measurement: Measuring Perceptions of "Spin" in Delivering a Public Relations Message

By the end of this section, you will be able to:

- ✔ Design a new measurement instrument
- ✔ Distinguish between validity and reliability in judging the quality of a measurement instrument
- ✔ Calculate reliability and validity statistics
- ✔ Compare the average scores in the three groups using a one-way ANOVA analysis in Google Sheets and write a report of this analysis
- ✔ Compute the effect size of a one-way ANOVA

■ CHAPTER 7

Doing the Research: Developing a New Measuring Instrument

Aaliyah recently graduated and has started work at a public relations (PR) firm. Her agency is giving advice to Tumblrgram—a social media company that has been hacked. The key question right now is *who* in the organization should be the public "face" providing information to the public about the hacking. The PR firm knows that Aaliyah took an undergraduate research methods course, so the company has asked her to investigate the question of whether it is better to have the company CEO, a company spokesperson, or the company attorney present information at press conferences. Tumblrgram is particularly concerned about being perceived as "spinning" the event and wants the agency to see whether one of these people is perceived as less of a spin doctor. If the company is seen to be putting "spin agents" out to face the press, that might hurt Tumblrgram's image. Here is Aaliyah's preliminary research question.

> RQ: Which source (CEO, company attorney, company spokesperson) is seen as engaging in the most spin?

Before reading on, try to figure out what Aaliyah's independent and dependent variables are, and what their level of measurement is.

	Name of Variable	Level of Measurement
Independent Variable:		
Dependent Variable:		

Be sure to try to answer before reading on. The independent variable is the *source* of the message (CEO versus attorney versus spokesperson). Remember, when naming a variable, it's good to come up with a word or phrase that captures the way the variable *varies*. Hence, "source" is a good word here. The dependent variable is "perceived spin"—the degree to which the source is seen to be spinning the truth. The dependent variable is going to be the focus of this chapter: How is Aaliyah going to measure "perceived spin"?

Creating a New Measurement Tool: Three Steps

Aaliyah knows from her undergrad class (and you know from Section 3) that it is best to use an **existing instrument** to measure a concept—using a questionnaire that someone has already designed and used is typically better than creating your own. Remembering back to Section 3, try to provide two different reasons why you think it is good to use an *existing* measurement tool rather than creating a new one?

One good reason here is simply minimizing unnecessary work. Don't reinvent the wheel! You wouldn't try to construct a tape measure from scratch: You would just buy a commercially produced one because it's a lot less time-consuming and probably less expensive. A second good reason is that we can be confident that existing tools *work*. The tape measure you pick up at the store will almost certainly measure length more accurately than anything you could build from scratch. Likewise, if a social science measurement tool already exists, then there will be information about it in the research literature—we will know whether it is a high-quality measurement tool from other scholars' reports of using it. The first choice is always to use an existing tool.

However, Aaliyah has scoured Google Scholar (see sidebar) and library databases, and she cannot find an existing measurement tool to assess perceived spin. She is faced with the exciting (but perhaps daunting) task of developing her own new measurement instrument to assess this concept. This chapter will describe some of the steps she will go through and things she will need to pay attention to.

Searching those databases

Google Scholar (https://scholar.google.com/) is a useful tool for hunting down previous research on a topic you are interested in. It indexes a vast number of academic research articles and is searchable in ways similar to regular Google searches. Searching effectively takes a lot of trial and error to develop an "instinct" for what terms to use and how to adjust a search based on what shows up. Don't give up based on what you get on your first attempt. A researcher might search for 5–10 different combinations of words and phrases before hitting on the one that gets him or her what he or she is looking for. Be patient and persistent; remember to look beyond the first page of results!

Figure 7.1 shows an example of a search. In this case, I was looking for a tool to measure the organizational communication climate. Once a promising lead is found, clicking on the title of the article (in blue) or one of the links to the right will take you to a place where you can read the abstract of the article, or perhaps the whole article, via your campus library. Your campus library may also offer communication-specific databases (e.g., Communication and Mass Media Complete) that you can use for your searches. Once you have found a tool that you want to use, read the article carefully and examine the appendix to find the exact wording of items in the measurement tool. If the items are not described in enough detail, look for other articles that have used the same measurement tool, or contact the author of the article: the authors will often be happy to provide more information.

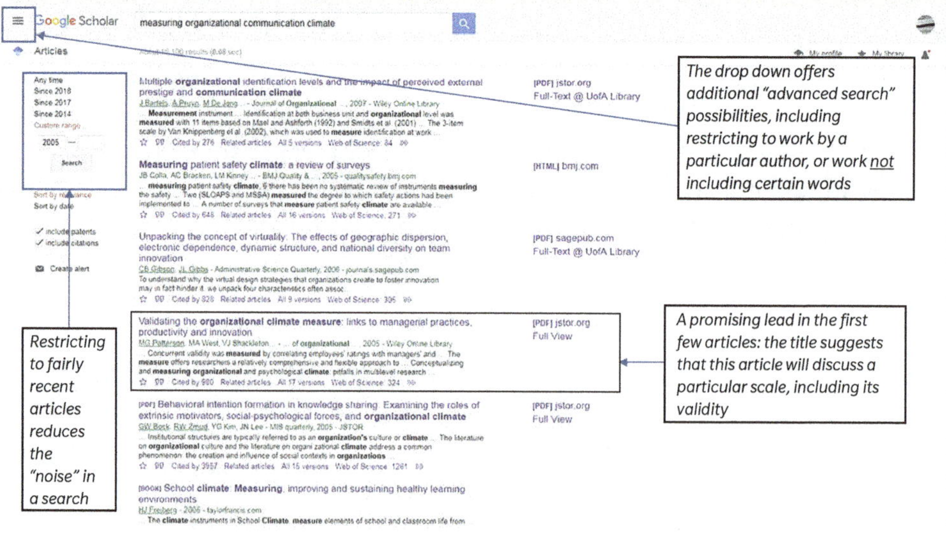

FIGURE 7.1 Searching for articles using Google Scholar

Step 1: Definition

As discussed earlier in the book, a crucial first step in examining any concept is defining it. Aaliyah's dependent variable is perceived spin. She might define this variable in the following manner:

> Perceived spin is a person's *subjective impression* that a message includes information that is *biased, deceptive, or manipulative,* including elements such as omitting relevant information, avoiding direct answers to questions, or attempting to distract the audience from the main issue.

This definition does a few things. First, it makes clear that the variable is concerned with subjective impressions—*perceptions* rather than objective reality. Second, it defines the "content" of the variable—communication that is biased, deceptive, or manipulative. The definition is also clear that it is the *message* that is being evaluated, not the *messenger*. Hence, this concept is distinct from evaluating whether a *person* is seen to be trustworthy. Of course, the messenger might still *influence* perceptions of whether a message includes spin; in fact, that is the focus of Aaliyah's study!

Step 2: Writing a Preliminary Set of Items

Once the concept is defined, the task of building the measurement instrument begins—always with the definition in the back of your mind, of course. Aaliyah decides to use a set of response options called a **Likert scale**. The Likert scale asks people to rate how much they *agree* or *disagree* with a series of statements. It is a useful technique for assessing subjective perceptions of a message, person, or concept. You have probably encountered Likert scales in questionnaires like the following:

> "The store made it easy for me to find what I was looking for."

Strongly Disagree	*Disagree*	*Neither Agree nor Disagree*	*Agree*	*Strongly Agree*

Aaliyah knows the importance of using more than one item in measurement, and so (like most researchers in this situation) she begins by brainstorming a whole bunch of statements that might assess whether a message is perceived to be spin.

When writing potential items, you should always keep the definition of the concept in mind, so here's a reminder of that, with some main points in italics:

> Perceived spin is a person's subjective impression that a message includes *information that is biased, deceptive, or manipulative,* including

elements such as *omitting relevant information, avoiding direct answers to questions,* or *attempting to distract the audience from the main issue.*

Imagine that you have shown someone a message, and you want them to rate the message's *spin* using a Likert scale. What sort of statements might you ask them to agree or disagree with? Try writing *three* items that would work with the Likert response scale and that address Aaliyah's definition of "spin." Note: I'm calling these *items* because they are *not* questions—they should be *statements*: things that someone could agree or disagree with.

Item 1: ______________________________

Item 2: ______________________________

Item 3: ______________________________

The following items are the result of Aaliyah's initial brainstorm. Mark any of these that seem similar to your own.

- *This message omits important information.*
- *Anybody with any sense can see that this message is a lie.*
- *When I listen to this message, I feel really uncertain about what it's saying.*
- *This message is deceptive.*
- *I don't trust this guy.*
- *This message leaves out important information and adds other information that is not true.*
- *This message doesn't answer the actual question.*
- *I would believe a CEO more than an attorney or a company spokesperson.*
- *I don't like this message.*
- *The disingenuous nature of this message is ubiquitous.*
- *If someone were to listen to this message and try to believe what the person is saying, he or she would have a really hard time doing so.*
- *This message tries to distract me from the main issue.*
- *This message tries to manipulate me.*
- *This message is manipulative and deceptive.*
- *The person speaking this message seems untrustworthy.*

I'm sure you can see that some of those questions might be better than others. What criteria should Aaliyah use in deciding which questions are "good" and which she should drop? Table 7.1 outlines the seven key things to *avoid* when writing items like these.

TABLE 7.1 Problems in Writing Questionnaire Items

Problem	Definition/Explanation	Example
Leading questions Loaded language	Items that direct the respondent to a particular answer. Loaded language ("Good parents ...") is sometimes a part of this problem. Use neutral language when wording items and avoid including unnecessary information (e.g., the whole first sentence in the example).	Good parents don't let their young children watch any television. How much television do your kids watch?
Replicating the hypothesis	Items that present the respondent with the research hypothesis and ask for a response. The example is a good question if you are interested in people's *perceptions* of the effects of violent television. But if you are interested in the *effects themselves*, asking people what they *think* the effects are is not a good approach. Just because people *think* that violent TV is harmful doesn't tell you anything about whether it actually *is*!	Do you think that people who watch lots of violent TV will act violently?
Vagueness or incompleteness	Items where the wording makes multiple interpretations possible, thus making responses hard for the researcher to interpret. In the example, some people may think that "media" means television and movies, while others might include time spent on their phones or listening to the radio.	How much media do you consume?
Negative wording	Items that are hard to understand or respond to because of use of negatives ("not" or "un-", for instance). This can be particularly problematic with Likert responses that have "disagree" as an option. "Disagreeing" with a negative becomes a double negative, which means the respondent has to work hard to figure out if he or she is responding correctly.	I dislike ice cream Agree — Disagree

continues on next page

continues from previous page

Problem	Definition/Explanation	Example
Wordy or complex items Use of jargon	Items containing unnecessarily complicated wording or more words than necessary. Write concisely using simple language so the reader will understand easily. "At a ball game, would you be more likely to eat a hot dog or a pretzel?"	In the contextual environment of a professional sporting encounter, would your gastronomic desires lead you toward a hot dog situation or something more like pretzel consumption?
Double-barreled items	Items that ask about two different things at the same time. In the example, whether your professor likes you and whether your professor cares about your future are two separate things. While they might be related, if you want to know about each of them, you should ask them separately.	Does your professor like you and care about your future?
Off topic	Items in a questionnaire should relate directly to the definition of the concept; items unrelated to the definition should be removed.	In a questionnaire measuring *anxiety* in communicating about religion, an item measuring how religious someone is would be off topic. It's about religion, but it's clearly not measuring anxiety.

With the aforementioned ideas in mind, look again at Aaliyah's items and decide if they are good items or bad items, and try to note in the right-hand column why you think that. It might be helpful for you to look at each issue in Table 7.1 for each question.

Item	Good/Bad?	Why?
This message omits important information.		
Anybody with any sense can see that this message is a lie.		
When I listen to this message, I feel really uncertain about what it's saying.		
This message is deceptive.		
I don't trust this guy.		

continues on next page

continues from previous page

Item	Good/Bad?	Why?
This message leaves out important information and adds other information that is not true.		
This message doesn't answer the actual question.		
I would believe a CEO more than an attorney or a company spokesperson.		
I don't like this message.		
The disingenuous nature of this message is ubiquitous.		
If someone were to listen to this message and try to believe what the person is saying they would have a really hard time doing so.		
This message tries to distract me from the main issue.		
This message tries to manipulate me.		
This message is manipulative and deceptive.		
The person speaking this message seems untrustworthy.		

There are some items that are obviously bad and others where you could probably argue the case either way. My thoughts are in Table 7.2.

TABLE 7.2 Analysis of Item Wording

Item	Good/Bad?	Why?
This message omits important information.	Good	—
Anybody with any sense can see that this message is a lie.	Bad	Leading question/loaded wording ("anyone with any sense ...").
When I listen to this message, I feel really uncertain about what it's saying.	Bad	Off topic: Feeling "uncertain" about what a message is saying is probably different from believing that the message is spin or is intentionally deceptive.

continues on next page

continues from previous page

Item	Good/Bad?	Why?
This message is deceptive.	Good	—
I don't trust this guy.	Bad	Off topic: The definition relates to the *message*, not the person sending the message. Also, it is bad for the item to assume that the person sending the message is a "guy"!
This message leaves out important information and adds other information that is not true.	Bad	Double-barreled: Based on the definition of "spin," Aaliyah wants to assess whether the message leaves out important information *and* whether the message includes untrue information, but she shouldn't try to measure both those things with one item!
This message doesn't answer the actual question.	Bad	Negative wording: The negative ("doesn't answer") might make it difficult for people to respond with a "disagree"—this results in a double negative.
I would believe a CEO more than an attorney or a company spokesperson.	Bad	Replicating the hypothesis: This is asking your respondents who they think they believe, but that is not the same as investigating which one they actually believe.
I don't like this message.	Bad	Vague: Someone might dislike a message for reasons other than perceiving it to be "spin." Saying, "Don't like ..." is not specific enough for what Aaliyah is trying to measure.
The disingenuous nature of this message is ubiquitous.	Bad	Wordy/complex: The item contains unnecessarily complex vocabulary.
If someone were to listen to this message and try to believe what the person is saying they would have a really hard time doing so.	Bad	Wordy/complex: Right?
This message tries to distract me from the main issue.	Good	—
This message tries to manipulate me.	Good	—
This message is manipulative and deceptive.	Bad	Double-barreled: Being manipulative and being deceptive are separate things, so this should be two separate questions.
The person speaking this message seems untrustworthy.	Bad	Off topic: Question asks about a person, not the message itself.

Now go back to the three items that you wrote earlier. Go through the criteria in Table 7.1 and see which of your own items you think are good and which you think are bad. If you think they are bad, say why.

Good Item(s)	Bad Item(s)	Reason

From her original brainstorming, Aaliyah is left with four "good" items: This is a great start! These items relate clearly to the original concept's definition: Social scientists refer to this as **face validity**. If just by looking at an item it seems to be a sensible way of measuring the concept, you say that it has face validity. Now would be a good time for her to check that she has covered all the bases in terms of her definition (see Table 7.3):

TABLE 7.3 Checking Items Against a Conceptual Definition

Component of the definition	Item
information that is biased	??
information that is deceptive	*This message is deceptive.*
information that is manipulative	*This message tries to manipulate me.*
omitting relevant information	*This message omits important information.*
avoiding direct answers to questions	??
attempting to distract the audience from the main issue	*This message tries to distract me from the main issue.*

It looks like she has most of the concepts in the definition covered, but she is missing questions relating to the information being biased, and the message is not providing direct answers to questions. The former could be addressed with a simple item like the following:

"This message is biased."

The latter is trickier. An item like, "*This message does not directly answer the important questions,*" could be criticized as creating a double negative—it's difficult to "disagree" with something that is already a negative.

One option with this situation is to word the item positively:

> This message directly answers the important questions.

You'll remember that in Chapter 5, we spent some time discussing the benefits (and some costs) of having a mix of positively and negatively worded items in a scale (i.e., having some **reverse-scored** items). Including one here has the benefit of rounding out the various components of the definition.

Here's a final consideration in creating the scale: If Aaliyah is going to include the positively worded item described earlier (one where agreeing indicates a *lack* of perceived spin), she should probably include a couple more to balance the scale out. People are likely to misread a single positively worded item if it is embedded with five items worded in the opposite direction. It would be good for Aaliyah to include some additional positively worded items. For example,

> *This message is truthful* (positive version of the "deceptive" component).

> *This message contains all the relevant information* (positive version of the "omits relevant information" component).

The process of checking that a measurement instrument covers all of the bases of a concept's definition is called assessing the **content validity** of the measurement tool. If you had a tool to assess fourth-grade math skills, you'd want to make sure it included addition, subtraction, division, and multiplication: That's content validity. Likewise, with any communication concept, you need to make sure that a measurement tool covers the full range of things in the definition.

After this process, Aaliyah has a promising set of eight items. The reverse-scored ("not spin") items are in italics.

> This message is deceptive.
>
> *This message contains all the relevant information.*
>
> This message tries to manipulate me.
>
> This message omits important information.
>
> *This message directly answers the important questions.*
>
> This message tries to distract me from the main issue.
>
> *This message is truthful.*
>
> This message is biased.

These items

- all relate directly to her definition of the concept (face validity),
- collectively appear to cover all the dimensions of the concept (content validity),
- meet the criteria for well-worded items,
- include positively and negatively worded items (not a requirement, but helpful in this instance),
- can comfortably be responded to on the Likert (Strongly Agree — Strongly Disagree) scale, and
- are neither too few or too many.

On that last point, hopefully, you were convinced by the Chapter 5 discussion that single items are not great. You probably also have an intuitive sense that using 100 items to measure "perceived spin" would not be reasonable—people would grow very bored answering the questions. As a researcher, you should aim to use enough items to assess the full range of a concept without exhausting your participants' attention spans and patience! About five to 10 items are normally sufficient to measure most concepts.

The last step here is that Aaliyah needs to format her measure of perceived spin in a way that it is nice for her participants to look at and easy for them to fill out. That includes providing some instructions for her respondents so that they know what they are supposed to do. You can see her final online questionnaire here: https://bit.ly/2IhkNJX. The instructions are important to remember: It may seem obvious to Aaliyah what respondents are supposed to do, but as the researcher, she needs to put herself in the place of a research subject who may need some guidance.

KEY POINT

Response sets. Aaliyah decided to use the Likert scale. There are other types of responses that are possible, depending on exactly what you are measuring. Some examples are in Table 7.4. These would obviously change depending on what you are measuring—with research, it is important to step back and make sure you are being sensible. On "objective frequency," for example, the set of responses here would be good for something most people tend to do with those sorts of frequencies (e.g., watch movies, or eat out). On the other hand, this would be a poor set of options for something that people do more frequently (e.g., check their phones) or less frequently (e.g., attend a wedding). Pretty much everybody checks their phone at least once a day, so you would not have any variation if you used this set of options for that behavior.

TABLE 7.4 Common Response Sets

	Response Set				
Subjective frequency	Very often	Fairly often	Occasionally	Rarely	Never
Objective frequency	Every day	A few times a week	A few times a month	A few times a year	Once a year or less
Satisfaction	Completely satisfied	Mostly satisfied	Neither satisfied nor dissatisfied	Mostly dissatisfied	Completely dissatisfied
Intensity (e.g., for measuring distress)	None	Very mild	Mild	Moderate	Severe
Agreement	Strongly disagree	Disagree	Undecided	Agree	Strongly agree
Comparison	Much more	Somewhat more	About the same	Somewhat less	Much less

Sweat the small stuff

In the process of writing a questionnaire (or constructing one from other people's scales), it is easy to get focused on the technical aspects and forget about the experience of your research subjects. It is critical to make sure your questionnaire *looks* attractive and professional, and that it provides clear instructions for your respondent. The appearance and clarity of your questionnaire tells respondents that you are a professional and that the research you are doing is important. If your questionnaire is sloppily presented or hard to understand, chances are you will get a lot of meaningless data from respondents who think you don't really care about the research—so why should they?!

Once Aaliyah had responses to her questionnaire, she would need to remember to reverse-score the positively worded items so that high numbers would indicate more perceived spin for each of the items (see Chapter 5 if you need a reminder of this reverse-scoring process). Then, for each person who responded to her questionnaire, she could generate a single score representing the extent to which the respondent perceived a message as being "spin." This score would just be the average of all eight items on the scale.

Note that Aaliyah's items require respondents to give one and only one response from a predetermined set of responses—all of the response sets in Table 7.4 do the same. These kinds of questionnaire items are called **closed-ended questions**. Sometimes you might want to get more details and allow your respondents to give you more detail on their feelings (e.g., "Tell us what made you think that the message was deceptive?"). That kind of **open-ended question** allows your respondents to tell you interesting things that you might not have thought of. However, you pay a price in terms of efficiency—it's harder to analyze open-ended responses than closed-ended responses. Later chapters in the book discuss more about how you would go about analyzing free-response answers.

Ethics and question wording

When we talk about wording questions carefully to avoid bias, we are typically talking about researchers *accidentally*, including a question that is poorly worded. However, sometimes "research" includes questions that are deliberately deceptive or leading. The following question was part of a questionnaire sent to me by my local congressional representative—a representative who strongly supported more border security:

continues on next page

continues from previous page

Do you think congresswoman ______ is doing enough to secure our border?

Yes, her efforts are improving border security.

No, she's not doing enough.

Unsure.

Notice that either of the substantive responses supports the representative's agenda. If you check the first box, it means that she's doing a good job. If you check the second box, you are saying that more should be done (which would indicate support of her actual position on the issue). Your only other option is a rather bland "unsure." So, sometimes questions are worded poorly just by accident, but sometimes poor wording is designed to force people into responses that support the question-writer's agenda.

Step 3: Assessing Reliability and Validity of the Tool

Aaliyah has two tasks before she can be confident in using her newly designed questionnaire. She needs to make sure that it measures consistently (**reliability**), and she needs to make sure it measures accurately (**validity**). We'll deal with those in turn. First, though, what you read in the next two sections might sound like a lot of work. Don't lose track of the bigger picture. Aaliyah's firm is looking to make recommendations to Tumblrgram on a major corporate decision. Making those recommendations based on questionable measurement would be a really bad idea!

Measurement Reliability

Any good measurement tool must be consistent. Imagine a tape measure made from elastic. You might measure the same object twice and get two different lengths just because you accidentally stretched the measure a little. You would toss that tape measure in the trash, right? The same is true with social science measurement. Measurements of the same thing at different points in time should show *consistency*. For Aaliyah, this means that the same person assessing the degree to which a particular message is "spin" should give that message roughly the same score at two different points in time. She can test this relatively easily. With a small group of willing volunteers (20 of her coworkers would be fine), she can show them a message (perhaps a video of a White House press conference) and ask them to complete her questionnaire. Then, a couple of days later, she can show the same people the same message and ask them to complete the questionnaire again.

The scores on the spin questionnaire at the two points in time should be related. Or, to be more precise, they should be ***correlated***. The scores at the first point in time are an interval-level measure, and the scores at the second point in time are a second interval-level measure. As you will remember from Chapter 4, we can explore the association between two interval-level measures using correlation (*r*). Aaliyah would expect a strong positive correlation between the two sets of scores in order to claim that her measurement tool is consistent. The correlation won't be perfect (1.0)—people will always vary a little because of chance factors. One person might notice something in the message he or she missed the first time and evaluate the message a little more positively, while another might be in a bad mood on the second occasion and so evaluate it a bit more negatively. The association might look a little like what we see in Figure 7.2. Each dot in the picture represents one person's score at Time 1 (x-axis) and Time 2 (y-axis).

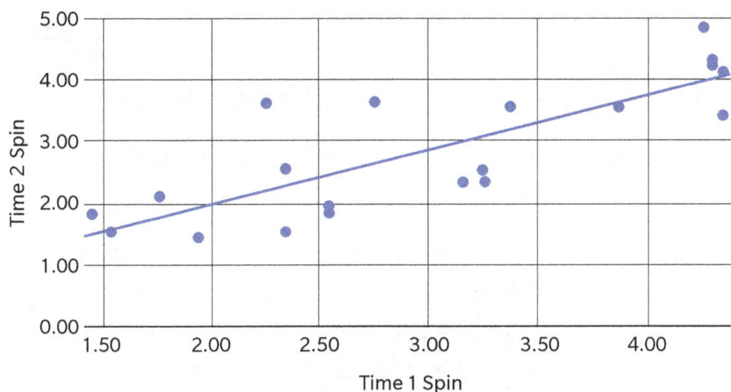

FIGURE 7.2 Association between Time 1 "Spin" and Time 2 "Spin"

As you can see from the chart (and in the Google Sheet of the same data: https://bit.ly/2Glmnhm), Aaliyah's data are doing what she hoped: scores at the two points in time are fairly closely related. The correlation (also calculated in the Google Sheet) is .81. This would be written as "r (18) = .81, $p < .05$"—the 18 is the degrees of freedom ($N - 2$). For this sort of reliability analysis, any correlation greater than .70 indicates strong reliability. So far, so good!

This form of reliability is called (for obvious reasons) **test-retest reliability**. It is important to use this test sensibly. If you are measuring something that *should* fluctuate over time (e.g., "How enjoyable was the last conversation that you had?"), you cannot expect test-retest reliability to be good. People's conversations naturally fluctuate in terms of how enjoyable they are. On the other hand, if you are measuring something that is supposed to be quite stable (e.g., personality, happiness with your marriage), you should reasonably expect good test-retest reliability over even quite long periods of time. The "Going Further" part in this section of the book addresses a different way to assess reliability for measures that are not expected to be stable over time.

What would you do if you went to all this trouble and found that your measure was *not* reliable (the test-retest correlation was only .30, for instance)? Next, write two things that you think you could do to try to improve the reliability of the measure.

Here are some ideas. See if any of them are similar to yours.

- Ask some people to fill out your scale and give you feedback on it—ask them if any items seem confusing.
- Eliminate bad items: The "Going Further" part of this section describes some statistical techniques for identifying bad items, but you can also sometimes just spot them by critically thinking about the wording of your items. Revisiting Figure 7.2 would be a starting point for this examination.
- Add more (good) items: Scales with more items tend to be more reliable, so if you have a really short scale (three items, say), adding a few additional items may improve reliability. This is one reason why using a **multi-item scale** is important—more items mean more reliability.
- Consider whether your items measure multiple *dimensions* of a concept: Sometimes bad reliability can exist because you are actually assessing more than one thing. If Aaliyah had bad reliability for her "perceived spin" measure, she might consider whether "spin" has multiple dimensions. Perhaps the "*deception*" side of spin is different from the "*manipulation*" side of spin, and those two things need to be measured separately.
- Consider whether it is sensible to expect consistency in the measure over time (perhaps it's normal for scores on this construct to vary from day to day).
- Start over: Rethink your strategy and consider if there is a completely different way of assessing the construct (e.g., change your response set, consider an observational measure instead of a self-report measure).

It can be depressing to design a measure and discover that it has poor reliability. But remember your scientific goal is uncovering truth: A measure with poor reliability is unlikely to measure truth, so you need to bite the bullet and rethink your approach.

Measurement Validity

It is a sad truth of measurement that something can be very reliable and also very wrong! If I get on my bathroom scale each morning, and it tells me I weigh 35 pounds every time, then my scale is reliable, but it is also broken! Therefore, when creating a new measure, it is important to assess the **validity** of that measure: Its **truth**. We have already discussed **face validity** and **content validity**, each of which tells you something about the truth of a measure. This section addresses the final area of measurement validity: **criterion-related validity**. The term "criterion related" is used here because this form of validity involves testing your measure against some external standard—a criterion. When tested empirically (using data), does the new measurement tool give us scores that relate sensibly to other measures? The other measures are the criteria.

Aaliyah can do this by looking at associations between her measure of perceived spin and other measures that assess things similar to spin. We already know one such measure—the measure of source credibility from Chapter 3. While (as discussed earlier) the perceived spin of a message and the credibility of the message's source are not identical, we would expect them to be related: More spin should be associated with less credibility. The more you think a message is "spin," the less likely you will perceive its sender to be credible. Another variable that Aaliyah could consider using to assess validity would be people's willingness to actually *do* something. This is often called "behavioral intention." Your perceptions of "spin" in a message from Tumblrgram should be positively associated with your intention to post a negative review or commentary about the company on the Internet.

To test the criterion-related validity of her new spin measure, Aaliyah would recruit a small sample of people to evaluate a message on her spin scale and on both the source credibility measure and a behavioral intention measure.

Behavioral intention is typically measured using a small set of items like the following (Chang, 1998):

I intend to ...

I will try to ...

I will make an effort to ...

Because these items have already been used in other studies and shown to be reliable, Aaliyah can be confident in using them to help test the validity of her spin scale. You can see how these items could be adapted to measure intention to do just about anything. In the case of Aaliyah's validity check, she would phrase them as follows:

I intend to post a negative online review of Tumblrgram.

1	2	3	4	5	6	7
Extremely improbable						*Extremely probable*

I will try to post a negative online review of Tumblrgram.

1	2	3	4	5	6	7
Extremely improbable						*Extremely probable*

I will make an effort to post a negative online review of Tumblrgram.

1	2	3	4	5	6	7
Extremely improbable						*Extremely probable*

As with other scales we have looked at, Aaliyah would average scores of these three items to get a total "behavioral intention to post a negative review" scale.

If her spin scale "works," would she expect positive or negative correlations between the measures? If you are uncertain, drawing a picture of the relationship is a good idea: Plot perceived spin on the X-axis and either source credibility or behavioral intention on the y-axis, and think about whether the association should slope up (positive) or down (negative) from left to right. Remind yourself of *what high numbers mean* on each measure: figuring out the direction of a correlation requires you to be absolutely clear on whether high scores mean more or less behavioral intention, for instance.

After thinking and drawing a picture, complete the following:

There should be a ____________________ correlation between the spin scale and the measure of source credibility.

There should be a _______________ correlation between the spin scale and the measure of behavioral intention to post a negative review.

Aaliyah's predictions for these associations are represented in Figure 7.3. If you thought there should be a negative correlation in the first case, you would be correct. If people perceive a source to be engaging in a lot of "spin," they should typically perceive that source to be low in credibility. If you said the second correlation should be positive, you would also be correct. The more you perceive spin, the more you should be willing to post a negative review. Don't get confused about the fact that these are both bad (negative) things: Often, *negative* things are *positively* correlated with one another. Verbal abuse is bad. Feeling contempt for another person is typically bad. Feeling contempt and verbal abuse are *positively* correlated with one another: The more Person A feels contempt for Person B, the more likely Person A is to abuse Person B verbally.

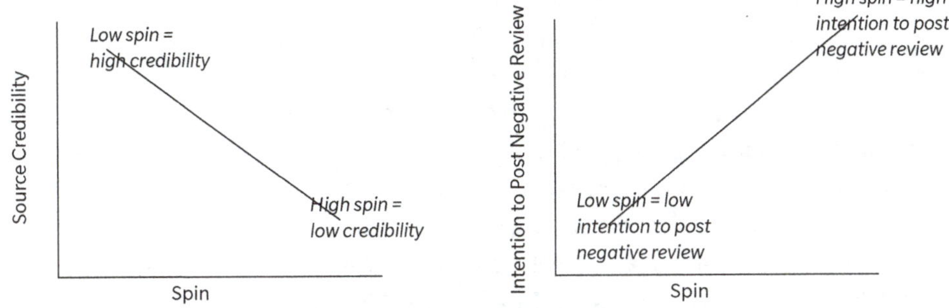

FIGURE 7.3 Predictions for validity tests

In testing validity, it is not just observing a significant effect that matters: The *size* of the effect is also important. Aaliyah would hope to find relatively strong correlations (probably in the realm of .50 or higher) in order to make a case that her spin measure has good criterion-related validity. Table 7.5 illustrates some scenarios that Aaliyah might observe and their implications for the validity of her measure.

TABLE 7.5 Values of Correlation Indicating Different Levels of Validity

	Good Validity	Marginal Validity	Poor Validity	Extremely Poor Validity
Correlation between new "spin" measure and source credibility	−.60	−.15	.05	.30
Correlation between new "spin" measure and intention to post negative review	.55	.20	.10	−.25

If Aaliyah's measure has good validity, she can proceed with using it in her actual research study. If it has marginal validity, she would probably need to look at the individual items and see which ones might be worded badly. She could look at correlations between each *item* and the criterion measure to see if just one or two items are perhaps hurting the overall "spin" scale's validity. If that was the case, she could simply rewrite or delete those items and her scale would be ready to go. If her scale has poor or very poor validity, she might need to go back to the drawing board and create a new measure of "spin." A lot of the steps described for dealing with a measure that has poor reliability would also apply to dealing with a measure that has poor validity.

For now, we'll assume her scale is good to go!

Where do the human subjects come from?

Research is a critical activity in industries such as PR, advertising, and marketing, as well as in universities, of course. Firms in these areas have a number of ways to access people to assist in their research. For "quick and dirty" research (things that need to get done quickly and don't require a nationally representative sample), professionals in these areas might go to a public place like a shopping mall and simply recruit passersby. These are called "intercept" studies. For larger studies, firms in these industries might outsource data gathering to a company that specializes in survey research. Survey research or market research companies like Qualtrics (www.qualtrics.com) can supply large numbers of human respondents from their own "panels" of respondents. Such companies already know quite a lot about their panels, allowing targeting of research to specific groups. Aaliyah, for instance, might decide that she is most interested in responses from people who *use* Tumblrgram. Qualtrics might already have data on which of its panels of volunteers use Tumblrgram, so it could ensure that the responses Aaliyah is receiving come only from those people.

Money changes hands here, of course. Tumblrgram is paying Aaliyah's firm for its services and built into that contract would be the costs of doing the research. If Aaliyah does a mall intercept study, she will be paying the volunteers in the mall out of that budget; she might also need to pay the mall if she is using some of their space for her research. If she uses Qualtrics to help with the research, then Qualtrics gets paid for gathering the data, including Qualtrics paying their panel of respondents.

Writing the Report

There are a lot of moving pieces in what has been discussed so far in this chapter. A good report needs to describe all of the stages in developing the measure. It is helpful to use subheadings and to describe the process chronologically so that a reader can follow what happened in sequence. The Report 7.1 provides the same level of detail that would be required in a scientific report of the process. In Aaliyah's corporate context, a lot of this information might go in an appendix. Corporate reports of research are more likely to include an executive summary that "cuts to the chase" of the main results and provides a set of recommendations for the organization. However, even in such contexts, the specific research procedures will be included somewhere in the report in case someone reading it has questions.

REPORT 7.1 Methods for Developing a Measurement Instrument

Item generation. Development of the perceived spin scale began with writing a pool of 15 items informed by the definition of perceived spin as *a person's subjective impression that a message includes information that is biased, deceptive, or manipulative, including elements such as omitting relevant information, avoiding direct answers to questions, or attempting to distract the audience from the main issue.* Eleven items in the initial pool were eliminated as being insufficiently related to the original definition or for problems with wording (e.g., being double-barreled). The remaining four items were examined for content validity. Two components of the definition were not represented in the items, and so two additional items were developed. One of the newly developed items was positively worded (reflecting a *lack* of spin); as a result, two additional positively worded items were developed to improve the balance of positively and negatively worded items in the scale. The final scale thus had eight items with good face validity and content validity (see Figure 1).

Reliability. Twenty volunteers were shown a video of a spokesperson (extracted from a White House press conference) and responded to the eight perceived spin items on a 1–7 Likert scale. Two days later, they rewatched the video and completed the same items a second time. At both time points, scores for all items were averaged (after reverse scoring the positively worded items). Test-retest reliability for the measure was good, $r(18) = .81, p < .05$.

Criterion-related validity. Twenty volunteer respondents responded to the new measure and responded to a six-item measure of source credibility (from McCroskey & Teven, 1999) and a three-item measure of behavioral intention to post negative reviews of the source organization (adapted from Chang, 1988).

continues on next page

continues from previous page

Indicative of strong criterion-related validity, the perceived spin scale was strongly negatively correlated with the source credibility measure ($r(18) = -.62$, $p < .05$) and positively correlated with the intention to post negative reviews of Tumblrgram ($r(18) = .71$, $p < .05$).

Item
This message is deceptive
This message contains all the relevant information
This message tries to manipulate me
This message omits important information
This message directly answers the important questions
This message tries to distract me from the main issue
This message is truthful
This message is biased

Note. Reverse-scored items are in italics.

FIGURE 1 Perceived spin scale items

The Actual Study

While this chapter has dealt with the measurement issue, it is important to remember that Aaliyah is trying to answer a question about whether different company representatives are seen as higher or lower on perceived spin. With her new (valid and reliable!) measurement instrument, Aaliyah can do her actual research to determine which of Tumblrgram's potential candidates is the best—which one is seen as producing the least spin.

To do this, she would pursue a strategy similar to Andre's in the previous section. She would recruit a group of human subjects, **randomly assign** them to view one of the three Tumblrgram representatives giving a statement about the company, and then ask the research subjects to evaluate the candidates on her new "perceived spin" scale. She knows about good experimental design, so she would make sure that all of the representatives' messages are identical (**experimental control**). She would create the videos herself—with the help of the company reps, of course. Her experimental **manipulation** here would be the difference between the three sources. The next chapter will describe how she would analyze her data.

Other Applications

The procedures described in this chapter apply to many situations in which someone is attempting to develop a new measurement tool. As society changes, we sometimes need to measure new things that nobody has measured before. The extent and manner in which people engage with online social networks, for instance, is something that simply didn't exist 15 years ago, and so we need new measurement tools to assess that.

Similar techniques are also useful when *adapting* existing measures for new applications. Again, in the area of new technology, you might be interested in understanding whether people have feelings of strong connection to YouTube celebrities. While we might not have a measurement tool specific to that, we do have older measurement tools assessing feelings of connection to television characters, for instance. It would be possible to adjust those measures to YouTube, and if you did so, you might want to check that the measures still have reliability and validity for this new context.

These techniques are also useful in creating new measures of variables for which we have existing measures. Yes, I know—we talked about how you *shouldn't* bother creating a new measure when one already exists! That's normally true, but not always. Can you think of two reasons for creating a new measure for something, even though there is already a measure out there?

The two main reasons I have encountered for engaging in this task are as follows:

1. The old measure is too long: Imagine that there is a really good (reliable and valid) measure of communication competence in the literature, for instance, but it requires respondents to fill out 60 questions. For a lot of research studies, that might take too much of the respondents' time. A researcher might use the procedures in this chapter to develop a new "short" version of that 60-item measure. When shortening the measure, you have to demonstrate that the new short version also has reliability and validity.

2. The old measure is outdated: Some concepts simply change over time. If you are interested in prejudice against people based on race, for instance, you have to understand that racism has changed over the years. Very old measures of racial attitudes contained statements that do not make sense today and that many respondents would find entirely offensive. Racial prejudice still exists in our society, but it looks and sounds different from

what it was like 50 or 100 years ago. As society changes, we have developed new ways to ask about this concept. In the 1980s, for example, McConahay, Hardee, & Batts (1981) developed what was called the "Modern Racism Scale" to assess more subtle types of racism. Now, of course, even that "modern" racism scale feels a bit outdated! When new measures of an old concept are developed, they need to be tested for reliability and validity.

Of course, these procedures are limited to things where it is possible (and reasonable) for people to provide self-reports. A self-report measurement is not appropriate as a means for people to report things they cannot know (e.g., their current level of blood oxygen, their future income). There are debates about whether people are able to report things like their motivations accurately—do you know *why* you chose to watch a particular television show over another one? Some people think you do, while others think that your true motivations might be unconscious or inaccessible to you.

Reliability and validity are principles that apply beyond just self-report measures. Perhaps you think that people are not truthful in reporting how much they use their phones. So, you decide to measure phone use via observation (perhaps following people around and counting how many times they look at their phones). You would still need to demonstrate that *that* measure is reliable (e.g., that the measure of phone use on day 1 is correlated with the measure on day 2) and that it is valid (e.g., that the observational measure correlates with scores from an app on the phone that tracks phone activity).

Your Turn

In Chapters 5 and 6, you imagined measuring a variable as the dependent variable in an experiment. Back then you didn't need to worry too much about *how* you measured that dependent variable. Well, now's the time to start worrying! Go back to your responses in Chapters 5 and 6, and write that variable's name here: ____________________. If the variable is something that is impossible to measure using a self-report questionnaire, you might need to think of an alternative for this section. Write a clear, concise *conceptual definition* of that variable, if you have not already done so.

Go through the process like Aaliyah did:

- Decide on a response set (e.g., a Likert scale or similar—see Figure 7.5).
- Brainstorm some ideas for items or questions that might measure your variable.
- Assess those against the criteria for "good" questionnaire items (see Figure 7.2); eliminate or reword items that have problems.

- Check that your remaining items cover all of the aspects of the variable's conceptual definition. If they do not, write additional items so the complete scope of the variable is measured (**content validity**).
- Create the questionnaire using Google Forms or some similar tool.
- Think carefully about how you would test the reliability and validity of your measure—consider some additional variables you might measure that you would expect to be associated with your measure (to assess criterion-related validity).
- Finally, write a report like Aaliyah's describing your new tool: Make sure to reference reliability and validity.

Wrap Up

In this chapter, you have learned how to develop a questionnaire to measure a social science variable and how to identify wording problems with items on a questionnaire. You should also now understand the meaning of reliability and validity, and have some idea of how you might assess reliability and validity for a new measure that you created. These skills will also let you assess someone else's report of a measurement tool: Do they tell you about their reliability and validity, are their items worded well, and do the items cover all the aspects of their variable's conceptual definition?

If you get nothing else from this chapter, remember the following:

1. You should only create a new measuring instrument if you know that a good one doesn't already exist.
2. Reliability indicates the stability of measure over time; validity indicates that it is measuring what you think it's measuring; both are indicators of the quality of the measurement tool.
3. Statistics you have already learned (e.g., correlation) are used to examine reliability and validity, as well as being used to test hypotheses.

Key Chapter Concepts

Closed-ended questions: Questions with a limited and predetermined set of response options from which respondents much pick. Responses involving picking a single number (e.g., on a 1–10 scale) or category (e.g., the religious group you identify with the most) are closed-ended questions. See also **Open-ended questions**.

Content validity: The extent to which a measurement scale assesses the full breadth of a concept. If you were measuring *communication competence*, a scale that only assessed your public speaking skills would have weak content validity. A scale that assessed your communication abilities in public settings (e.g., giving a speech, asking a question in a group setting) and private settings (e.g., having a conversation with a stranger) would have stronger content validity.

Criterion-related validity: The extent to which a measure is associated with other measures that it "should" be related to (the criterion measures). A measure of communication competence should be related to your success in persuading other people, or ratings of your public speaking performance, or your ability to maintain successful interpersonal relationships. If it is unrelated to any of those things, it's probably not a valid measure of communication competence.

Double-barreled items: Items in a questionnaire that ask two things at once. "How much do you like your home and family?" is double-barreled: You might love your family but dislike your home (or vice versa). Double-barreled items should be avoided.

Existing instrument: A measurement tool that has been used in published research. Typically, using an existing instrument (assuming it has good **reliability** and **validity**) is better than making up your own instrument—don't reinvent the wheel.

Face validity: The impression that a scale measures what it is supposed to measure based on a close examination of the items.

Leading questions: Items on a questionnaire that "push" the respondent toward responding in a particular way. These should be avoided.

Likert scales: A format for a questionnaire. Respondents are given a statement (or series of statements) on some topic and asked how much they agree with each statement, often on a 1–5 or 1–7 scale ranging from "strongly disagree" to "strongly agree."

Measurement reliability: The consistency or stability of a measurement tool. Reliability is often measured by assessing whether scores on a measure are stable over time (**test-retest reliability**). Together with **measurement validity**, measurement reliability is an indicator of the quality of a measurement tool.

Measurement validity: The degree to which a measurement tool *accurately* measures the underlying concept. A questionnaire to measure public speaking confidence is valid if it genuinely assesses how much (or little) confidence someone has when he or she is going to give a speech. Together with **measurement reliability**, measurement validity is an indicator of the quality of a measurement tool. **Face validity, content validity**, and **criterion-related validity** are all types of measurement validity.

Multi-item scale: A questionnaire that measures a concept with more than one question or item; typically, the responses to all of the items are averaged (after **reverse-scoring**) to result in a single score.

Negative wording: Questions containing a "not" or similar. Can be useful in generating items for **reverse-scoring** but should be used carefully to avoid respondent confusion over double negatives.

Open-ended questions: Questions without fixed response choices. If you can speak or write freely in response to a question, it is an open-ended question. If you have to pick from a predetermined set of choices, it is a **closed-ended question.** Most measurement tools use closed-ended questions, but open-ended questions are useful if you are seeking feedback on a questionnaire, for instance.

Reliability: See **Measurement reliability.**

Reverse-scoring: The process of changing numerical responses to questions that are asked in the opposite direction to what is being measured. See Chapter 5 for a detailed discussion.

Test-retest reliability: The correlation between scores on a measurement tool at two points in time (T1 and T2). Measurement tools with strong T1–T2 correlations have good test-retest reliability. See also **Measurement reliability.**

Validity: See **Measurement validity.**

Credit

CHAPTER 8

Reporting the Research: One-Way Analysis of Variance

Aaliyah has developed a scale to measure perceived spin and used it to measure perceptions of spin for three potential representatives of Tumblrgram. As discussed in the previous chapter, she has already done some analysis to assess the reliability and validity of the measure. You were already familiar with the correlation analysis she used there, for instance. This chapter is going to focus on her actual research question:

> RQ: Which source (CEO, company attorney, company spokesperson) is seen as engaging in the most spin?

Let's imagine that Aaliyah has now collected data from 150 people. The people were recruited with the assistance of Qualtrics, who ensured that all of the respondents were regular Tumblrgram users. Remember from the previous chapter that Aaliyah uses good **experimental design** in collecting these data (see Chapter 5 for a reminder of what is required for something to count as an experiment).

- The respondents were **randomly assigned** to one of three conditions: 50 people watched the CEO present a message, 50 watched the Tumblrgram attorney present the message, and 50 watched the spokesperson. Remember, random assignment ensures that the three groups of people are equivalent to one another at the start of the study.
- She would make sure that the wording of all of the messages is identical (**experimental control**). This ensures that any differences in perceptions are due to the person giving the message, not the content of the message.

After watching the video, respondents reported their feelings about the message using Aaliyah's spin scale.

After averaging the people's answers on the eight items from the scale, Aaliyah's data will look like what is shown in this section's Google Sheet (experiment data tab: https://bit.ly/2Glmnhm). The spreadsheet is arranged in three columns; each represents the average score for 50 different people in three experimental conditions (evaluating the message from the CEO, the attorney, or the spokesperson, respectively). If you scroll to the bottom of the 50 scores, you can see the means and standard deviations for each group, along with a chart.

Equal numbers in groups

For this book, we are going to focus on the simplest situations where there are equal numbers of people in groups. It is possible to do experiments and analyze results with unequal numbers (e.g., if Aaliyah had 40 people in the CEO group, but 50 in the other two groups). The analysis gets a bit more complicated, however, and is not possible in Google Sheets. The software described in the "Going Further" section (JASP) can do this sort of analysis, so if you want to try, read that section.

Thinking back to what you already know, what are the independent and dependent variables here, and what are their levels of measurement?

	Name	Level of Measurement
Independent Variable		
Dependent Variable		

Hopefully, you indicated that the independent variable is message *source* (CEO/attorney/spokesperson) and that it is a categorical measure. Different experimental conditions typically make a categorical variable—they represent variation in some quality or state, not variation in a quantity. And, hopefully, you indicated that the dependent variable is *perceived spin*, and that is an interval-level measure; it is made up of numerical scores.

In Chapter 6, we compared two groups of people (categorical independent variable) on an interval-level dependent variable using an independent samples *t*-test. That test doesn't work for the current situation, however, because it can only compare *two* groups of people, and in the current example, we need to compare *three* groups. Remember, don't confuse the number of *variables* with the number of levels or categories within the variables—here we have one independent variable (*message source*) with three levels (*CEO, attorney, spokesperson*). Using the updated statistical decision flowchart in Figure 8.1, which statistical test do you think you should use in the current scenario?

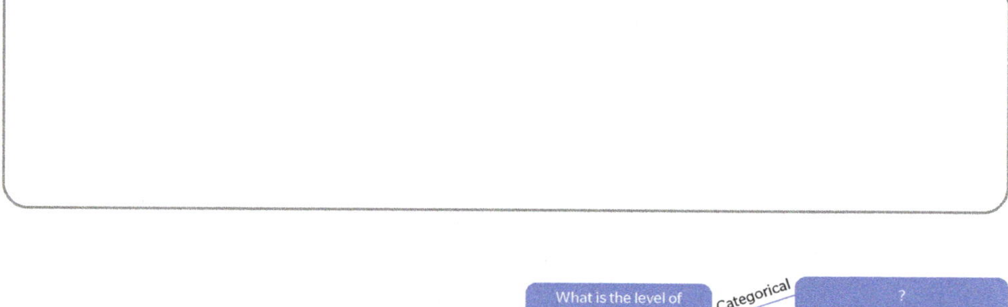

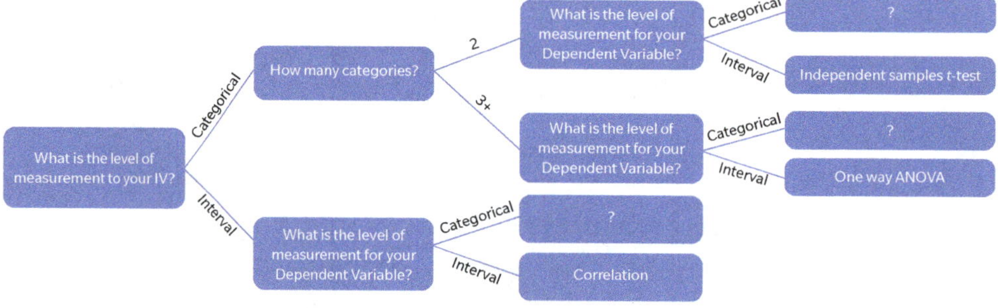

FIGURE 8.1 Statistical choice decision tree

If you wanted, you could run an independent samples *t*-test comparing the CEO and the attorney, and another independent samples *t*-test comparing the CEO and the spokesperson, and yet another independent samples *t*-test comparing the spokesperson and the attorney. However, that's not particularly efficient, and it also causes some statistical problems (that we don't need to get into here). The correct answer is the **one-way ANOVA**—ANOVA stands for **analysis of variance**. "One-way" means that you have only one independent variable.

The one-way ANOVA will compare the means for multiple groups (we have three here, but it can do more than three). It provides an answer to the question, "Are these means all the same?" The means being all the same is, of course, the null hypothesis.

Running the Analysis: One-Way ANOVA

You can run the one-way ANOVA in Google Sheets using the XLMiner ToolPak (see Chapter 6 for a reminder on how to install this if you haven't already). Once you have it installed, in the Google Sheet, go to "Add-Ons—XL Miner Analysis ToolPak—Start."

To run the analysis, select "ANOVA: Single Factor" and enter the range for your data in the "Input Range" area. It is a good idea to have headings for your data columns, and if you do then check the "Labels in the First Row" box. You can leave the "alpha" at "0.05" and then enter a blank area of your Google Sheet for the "Output Range." As always, make sure the output isn't going to write over your data! Figure 8.2 illustrates the commands Aaliyah used to get the output shown in this chapter's Google Sheet ANOVA tab.

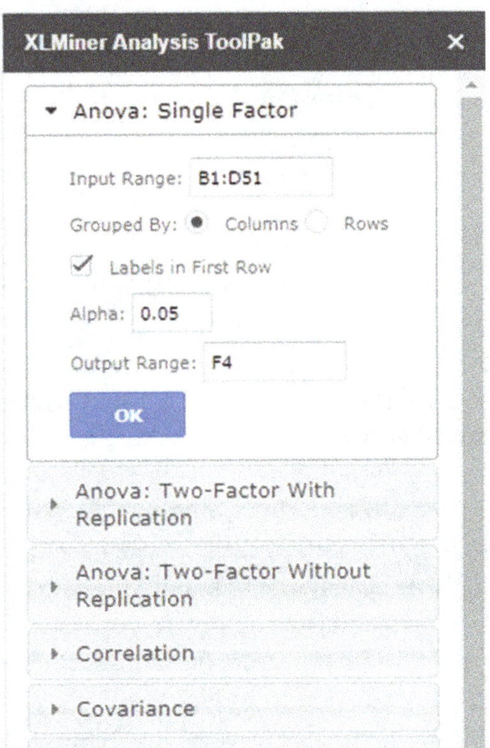

FIGURE 8.2 XLMiner analysis one-way ANOVA

The output is also displayed in Figure 8.3. If you run the analysis for these data, you should get identical output; the only thing Aaliyah has changed in Figure 8.3 is rounding some of the numbers to make things look consistent and easier to read. You can also see this in the ANOVA tab of the Google Sheet (https://bit.ly/2Glmnhm).

Anova: Single Factor

SUMMARY

Groups	Count	Sum	Average	Variance
CEO	50	152.92	3.06	1.04
Attorney	50	142.92	2.86	0.73
Spokesperson	50	174.79	3.50	1.02

ANOVA

Source of Variation	SS	df	MS	F	P-value	F crit
Between Groups	10.63	2	5.31	5.73	0.0040	3.06
Within Groups	136.36	147	0.93			
Total	146.99	149				

FIGURE 8.3 One-way ANOVA output

The important elements in the output are highlighted. First, Aaliyah will look at the means (averages) for the three groups (highlighted in yellow). Remember that "spin" is bad, so *low* scores here are better. She can see right away that the spokesperson condition had the highest perceived spin scores, with the other two conditions falling somewhat lower. In other words, it seems like if you want to avoid perceptions of spin, you should avoid using a spokesperson and instead use someone who has a different role in the company.

As you know from earlier chapters in the book, just seeing a difference between means isn't quite enough. Aaliyah needs to know whether these differences might just be due to chance—can she reject the null hypothesis? Can she be confident that these groups are *actually* different from one another? That is what the ANOVA is for, and the lower part of the output in Figure 8.3 shows the most important information; again, it is highlighted. The most important information is in pink: this is the *p*-value. Aaliyah knows that any *p*-value less than 0.05 indicates that the null hypothesis is unlikely to be true. Can she reject the null hypothesis in this situation?

This *p*-value (0.0040) is definitely less than 0.05, so she can reject the null hypothesis. The determination of the null hypothesis being true is done based on the *F*-statistic (highlighted in blue) and the degrees of freedom (highlighted in green).

The *F*-statistic is a lot like the *t*-statistic in that it compares **variance between groups** and **variance within groups.** You might remember Figure 6.5 in Chapter 6, which illustrated how the *t*-test involves a ratio of between group and within group variation. The same applies to the one-way ANOVA, but the one-way ANOVA does it with more than two groups. Figure 8.4 illustrates this idea with three groups. As in Chapter 6, you would probably be most confident that the differences between the groups are "real" in scenario D of the figure (big differences between groups, small differences within groups). Likewise, area A is where you would be least confident (small differences between groups, big differences within groups). The *F*-statistic in Figure 8.3 represents this ratio—when differences *between* group means are bigger, and variation *within* groups is smaller, the *F*-statistic will be bigger. A bigger *F*-statistic tells us that the null hypothesis is *less* likely to be true.

When reporting the *F*-statistic, Aaliyah will need to report *both* of the degrees of freedom numbers highlighted green in Figure 8.3. The first represents the number of groups Aaliyah is examining (minus 1). Aaliyah is examining three groups, so the first degrees of freedom number is 2, because 3 − 1 = 2. If she was examining four groups, this number would be 3, because 4 − 1 = 3. The second degrees of freedom number indicates the number of people in the study minus the number of groups: 150 − 3 = 147. Therefore, Aaliyah's one-way ANOVA statistic has (2, 147) degrees of freedom. To report this *F*-statistic, Aaliyah would write,

$$F(2, 147) = 5.73, p < .05.$$

This statistic tells Aaliyah that the means of these three groups are not the same. Put differently, Aaliyah can now conclude that it *matters* who Tumblrgram puts in front of the public; the company's potential representatives are not interchangeable or equal. There's more we need to do, but this is our starting point.

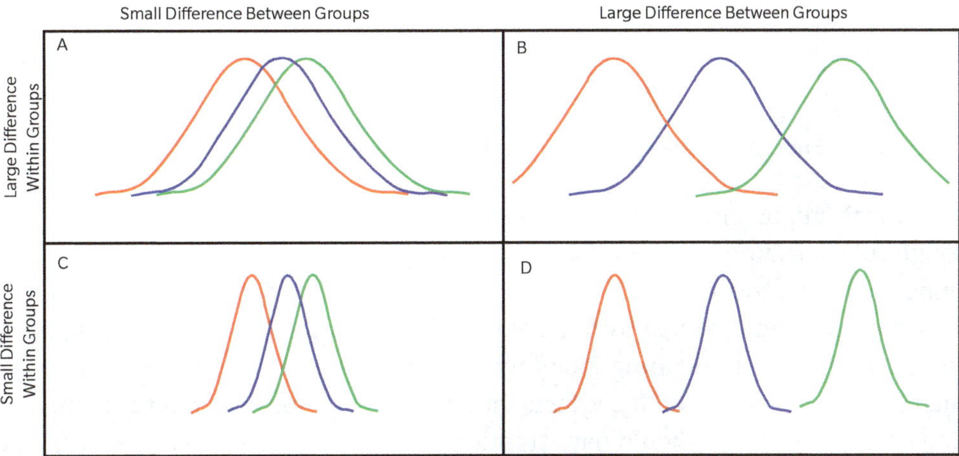

FIGURE 8.4 Between and within group differences in one-way ANOVA

Effect Size

It's exciting for Aaliyah to find a significant effect, but as we discussed in Chapters 4 and 6, just finding a significant effect isn't everything. Aaliyah is also interested in how *big* the effect is. If the effect is tiny, her advice to Tumblrgram should be a bit more muted; if it's a huge effect, then she will need to tell them that the choice of spokesperson is critical.

In one-way ANOVA, effect size is calculated by dividing two numbers from the SS column in Figure 8.3: The $SS_{\text{Between Groups}}$ (10.63) and the SS_{Total} (146.99) from the first column of numbers. The result is called **eta-squared** and is written η^2.

$$\eta^2 = 10.63 / 146.99 = 0.07$$

The write-up of the results presented earlier can now be extended to include this eta-squared:

$$F(2, 147) = 5.73, p < .05, \eta^2 = 0.07.$$

This number can be converted to a percentage by multiplying it by 100. An $\eta^2 = .07$ is equivalent to 7%. But what does it mean? Using this number, Aaliyah can say that "7% of the variation in perceived spin is explained by the source." Or, more generally, 7% of the variation in her dependent variable is explained by her independent variable. It can be useful to think about this like a pie chart. Imagine the entire pie represents all of the variation in people's "perceived spin" scores—every difference between one person's score and another person's score. The eta-squared (η^2) statistic tells us that 7% of all that variation is due to the source of the message. The other 93% is because of other factors (see Figure 8.5).

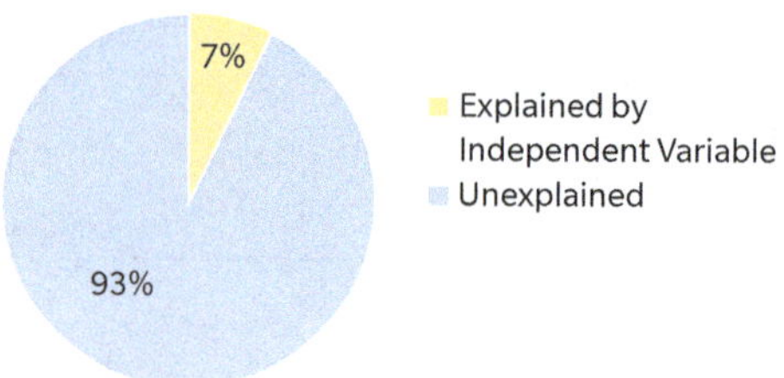

FIGURE 8.5 Effect size represented as a pie chart

Aaliyah might think that 7% is not very much, but it's not a small effect. A rough rule of thumb for effect sizes with eta-squared is provided in Table 8.1. It's important with social science effect sizes to remember that human behavior is very complex and is driven by hundreds of factors, some of which are unique to individual people. Explaining 7% of what's going on with a single experimental manipulation is not trivial. It suggests that the choice of spokesperson does matter and that Tumblrgram should pay attention.

TABLE 8.1 **Rules of Thumb for Effect Size With Eta-Squared**

η^2	Effect
< .01	Very small, perhaps trivial
.01	Small
.09	Medium
.25+	Large

Visualizing the Effect

Aaliyah will want to graph the effect to get a sense of what it looks like visually, and this is easy to do in Google Sheets. At the bottom of the ANOVA tab for this section's Google Sheet (https://bit.ly/2Glmnhm), you can see that Aaliyah has calculated the means along with the labels for each group. You can create the chart by (a) selecting the three means and the labels, (b) clicking "Insert—Chart," and then (c) selecting "Line Chart." This should create something similar to Figure 8.6. By now, you should be able to edit the chart: Adjust its properties so that it looks how you want it to (click the three dots in the top right of the chart and experiment!).

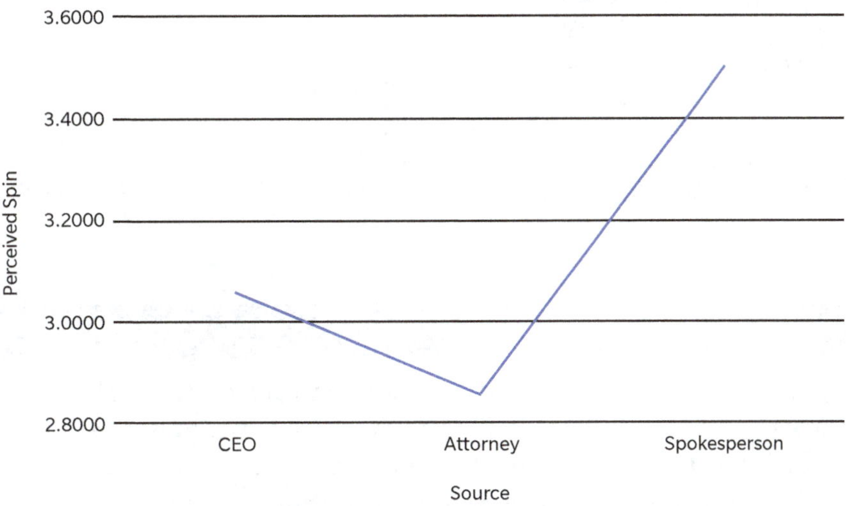

FIGURE 8.6 Plot of means for one-way ANOVA

Figure 8.7 displays the means from Aaliyah's study, showing clearly that the spokesperson was perceived as engaged in the most "spin." And the differences look very large from this image. Visually, the difference between the spokesperson and the attorney seems substantial. However, Aaliyah needs to be aware of her responsibility (as a scientist) to report accurately and fairly what she found. The difference between the attorney and the spokesperson is actually just a difference of .64 on a 1–5 scale, which is not trivial, but not as big as it looks in Figure 8.7. As a contrast, consider Aaliyah's second try at generating a graph (Figure 8.8). This chart displays the same effect as Figure 8.7, but with the full 1–5 range on the y-axis. You can see that the effect "looks" a little less impressive here. Scientists are always tempted to make things that they have found seem important. It is important to be aware of the **ethical** responsibility to represent what you find objectively so that readers aren't tricked into thinking that it's somehow bigger or more important than it actually is. Thinking carefully about how to represent effects visually is a big part of this.

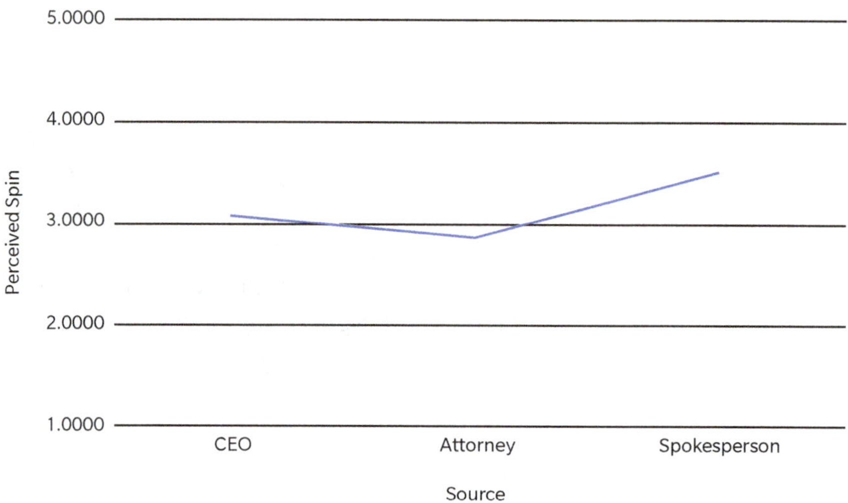

FIGURE 8.7 Improved plot of means for one-way ANOVA incorporating the full range of dependent variable

Writing the Report

Writing the results of an ANOVA is similar to writing up a *t*-test, but you need to report on three groups instead of just two. As with the *t*-test, it is important to report the test statistic (F) and its significance level (p), as well as the effect size (η^2). Including a chart displaying the means can also be helpful to allow the reader to visualize your effects.

REPORT 8.1 Results for One-Way ANOVA

The three sources' messages differed significantly in terms of their perceived spin, $F(2, 147) = 5.73$, $p < .05$, $\eta^2 = .07$. The attorney was seen as displaying the lowest level of perceived spin ($M = 2.86$, $SD = 0.85$), followed by the CEO ($M = 3.06$, $SD = 1.02$) and the spokesperson ($M = 3.50$, $SD = 1.01$). The means are displayed in Figure 1.

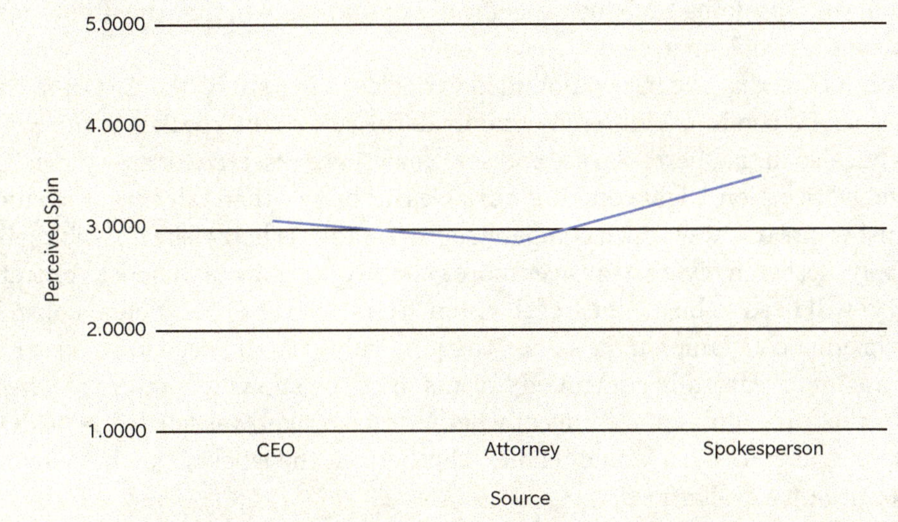

FIGURE 1 Means of perceived spin for three different company representatives

Confounded Variables in Theoretical and Practical Research

Aaliyah has done a good experiment for the particular purposes she has—figuring out which spokesperson this particular company should use. However, her experiment would not be very useful for *another* company trying to figure out which spokesperson they should use. Why?

A key problem in Aaliyah's study is that she is dealing with specific individuals who are the actual people doing the jobs (CEO, spokesperson, attorney) for Tumblrgram. That means that the group of people in the "CEO" condition might have seen a white woman in her mid-40s with a low-pitched voice who is above average in terms of attractiveness. Meanwhile, the people in the "spokesperson" condition might have seen a black man with a midwestern accent wearing a bright pink tie. While Aaliyah could control the *content* of the message the spokespeople were delivering, she couldn't control all of the differences between the specific people: Indeed, she was doing the study specifically to find out whether the differences between the people mattered.

This means that she has confounded variables in her study: the CEO and the spokesperson conditions differed not only in the role of the speaker in the company but also in that person's race and sex. Sometimes research for a very specific individual situation might confound variables in the way that Aaliyah's study did. She just wants to know which company representative is best—she doesn't really care *why*. Research trying to answer more general questions (and hence generate theory) will need to be more careful with matters such as experimental control. To help other companies in the same situation, Aaliyah would need to do research that was more carefully controlled; for instance, by showing viewers *identical* videos that only differed in terms of whether the speaker was labeled as "CEO" or "spokesperson." That would tell her whether just the label of "spokesperson" causes negative evaluations.

Other Applications

Social science research often involves comparisons of more than two groups. If you want to compare religious groups, racial groups, members of different fraternities/sororities, or students from different academic majors, you will need to compare more than just two groups. As illustrated in the current chapter, if you want to run an experiment with more than two conditions, you likewise will be comparing more than two groups.

Imagine, for instance, a situation in which you wanted to see whether people learn more from television, radio, or Internet news. You would probably do an experiment where you exposed people to one of those three news sources for a specific period of time and then measured their knowledge of the content. What would your independent variable and dependent variable be?

Independent variable: Name of variable: ____________________

Levels of variable: ____________________

Dependent variable: ____________________

For the independent variable, a good label would be something like "medium type," and its levels would be television, radio, and Internet. Your research question concerns whether medium type influences people's learning or knowledge, so a term like learning or knowledge would be good for the dependent variable. To do your analysis, you would need to use a one-way ANOVA to understand if knowledge differed across media.

ANOVA is a very powerful statistical technique. The one-way ANOVA described in this chapter can be extended to any number of groups. You can compare four, five, or 25 groups using this technique. Be aware, however, that you need a reasonable number of people in *each* group (about 30 minimum). So, if you want to compare 25 groups, you'll need data from 750 people!

ANOVA extends beyond situations with just one independent variable. The current chapter described the one-way ANOVA (one independent variable); Chapter 12 describes how ANOVA can be used with more than one IV.

ANOVA can also be used when the same people are in *all* of the experimental conditions or groups—similar to the **paired t-test** described in Chapter 6. Imagine a situation, for instance, in which the same people consumed three different news stories—one on the radio, one on television, and one on the Internet—and you measured their learning from each story. The independent and dependent variables would be the same as described earlier. But because it's the same people in each condition rather than different people, you cannot do the analysis using a one-way ANOVA. This "within subjects" or **repeated measures ANOVA,** uses different math from the one-way ANOVA and isn't possible in Google Sheets. It can be done using the JASP software described in the "Going Further" section.

In other words, ANOVA is not a single statistical test, but rather a large family of related tests that can be used for different types of data. If someone tells you that they analyzed their data "using ANOVA," you should ask, "What kind of ANOVA?!"

Your Turn

In Chapter 7, you developed a multi-item measurement scale—this will be your *dependent variable* for the current example. Remind yourself of what that variable is:

Dependent variable =

Now, think of a categorical variable with *three categories* that might influence scores on that variable. You might think of an experimental manipulation with three different levels that might affect your multi-item measure. For this, you could just build on the manipulation you had previously developed in Chapter 5—simply think of a third option to go along with the two you already have. Or you could think of a demographic variable that might be associated with your multi-item measure. For example, for ethnicity, you could choose three ethnic categories, or for religion, you could pick three religious groups that you think might differ on your dependent variable. This will be your independent variable for this example; write its name and list the three categories/conditions.

Independent variable = Label: ________________________________

Categories: ________________________________

You can create this study using Google Forms, or some other tool, or make up data in a Google Sheet (organize it exactly like Aaliyah's). Either way, using the skills you've learned in this chapter, analyze your data using a one-way ANOVA and write a summary like Aaliyah's for your results. Be sure to include an explanation of exactly what the data *mean*.

Wrap Up

In this chapter, you have learned how to analyze data to compare means across three (or more) groups. You have learned to calculate a one-way ANOVA in Google Sheets and interpret the output. You know how to calculate a measure of effect size for the one-way ANOVA and how to represent its effects visually. You have also learned the importance of being ethical in that presentation of data. Finally, you know how to write the results of a one-way ANOVA analysis.

If you get nothing else from this chapter, remember the following:

1. You can compare the means of three or more groups of people using a one-way ANOVA.
2. The size of the ANOVA's F-statistic is determined by how much the group means differ and how much variation there is *within* each of the groups. Bigger differences between groups and smaller variation within groups leads to a big F and more likelihood of statistical significance.
3. Visual representations of data should strive to represent what was found accurately rather than seeking to exaggerate the size of the effects.

Key Chapter Concepts

Analysis of variance (ANOVA): A family of statistical tools used for comparing means (averages) between groups of people.

Confounded variables: In an experiment, a confound occurs when an experimenter (typically inadvertently) manipulates two variables simultaneously. If you run an experiment in which one group of people see a "violent" television show (which happens to be a cartoon), while another group sees a non-violent show (which happens to be live action), then you have confounded level of violence (high vs. low) with video format (cartoon vs. live action). This is a problem because any effects you observe *might* be because of the violence, or might be because of the video format. Avoid confounded variables!

Eta-squared (η^2): A measure of effect size for ANOVA, typically calculated by dividing the sum of squares (SS) for the particular effect under consideration by the SS_{total}. In the one-way ANOVA, this means dividing $SS_{between\ groups}$ by SS_{total}. Eta-squared ranges from 0 to 1, and larger eta-squareds indicate a bigger effect. The number represents how much variance in the dependent variable is being explained by the independent variable (e.g., an eta-squared of .25 indicates that 25% of the variance has been explained).

Ethical responsibility in visual representations: Scientists have an obligation to represent the truth and not use clever graphical manipulations to exaggerate or overemphasize effects. One simple way to do this is to include the full range of the dependent variable on the y-axis or at least to alert your reader when you are not doing so.

F-statistic: The statistic used by **analysis of variance** to test hypotheses. The **F**-statistic gets bigger when **variation between groups** is large and **variation within groups** is small (see Figure 8.4).

One-way ANOVA: A type of **analysis of variance** that examines the effects of a single categorical independent variable on an interval-level dependent variable.

Standard deviation (*SD*): A measure of **variation within groups** of people, the square root of the **variance.**

Variance: A measure of variation within a group of people; can be obtained by squaring the **standard deviation.**

Variation between groups: The extent to which the mean of one group of people differs from the mean of another group of people. The ANOVA tests whether such differences are statistically significant by using the **F-statistic.**

Variation within groups: It is rare that a group of people will all score the same on any measure. Within any group of people, the within group variation is the extent to which they differ from one another. Sometimes most people score fairly similar to one another (small variation within groups), and sometimes they differ wildly (large variation within groups). Variation within groups is measured with statistics such as the **standard deviation** or **variance** (see Chapter 2).

Section Wrap

Section Summary

This section of the book has described how to develop a new measurement tool and how to assess that tool for reliability and validity. Reliability and validity are the two key criteria by which we judge whether a particular measurement instrument is of high quality. Reliability can be assessed by examining consistency over time; validity is assessed by considering face validity, content validity, and criterion-related validity—all indicators of whether a measurement tool is measuring what it was *intended* to measure. In Chapter 8, the new measurement tool was used as the dependent variable in an experiment featuring three groups. The chapter introduced the one-way ANOVA as the appropriate statistical tool for comparing means across more than two groups.

Going Further

There are two subsections in this "Going Further" section. One provides an additional method for assessing the reliability of a multi-item measure. The other addresses a useful "follow-up" that can be done with the one-way ANOVA analysis described in this chapter. For both sections, you will need to use the JASP software—see the "Going Further" part of Section 2 for details on downloading and installing that software.

Advanced reliability. As mentioned in the chapter, there are ways to assess measurement reliability other than test-retest reliability. One commonly used technique assesses whether all the items in a multi-item scale are related to one another. This technique is useful if you are not able to gather data at two points in time or if you are measuring something that you don't expect to be consistent over time (e.g., how much you enjoyed the last conversation you had).

The goal of a multi-item measure (e.g., Aaliyah's eight-item spin scale) is that each item contributes something of its own, but that all the items are measuring some underlying concept. In Aaliyah's case, she wants all eight of her items to be measuring something about "perceived spin." If all the items are meant to be measuring the same thing, they should all be associated with each other to some extent. This is sometimes called "internal consistency"—the degree to which a set of items in a measure are consistent with one another. A statistic called **Cronbach's alpha** assesses this form of reliability. The maximum score for Cronbach's alpha is 1, and a good measurement instrument typically has a Cronbach's alpha of at least 0.70.

Imagine that Aaliyah did a pilot test of her measure with 20 people: A copy of what those data might look like is available in a JASP file at the following link: http://bit.ly/2zca6sn (you will need to download the file and open it in JASP). You can see that there are scores from 20 people for eight questions (Aaliyah's eight items). To test Cronbach's alpha, click on "Descriptives—Reliability Analysis," and drag all eight questions from the left box into the right box (see Figure 8.8). You should see results on the right of the screen telling you that the Cronbach's alpha is .562. That value is not above .70, indicating that her scale does *not* have good reliability.

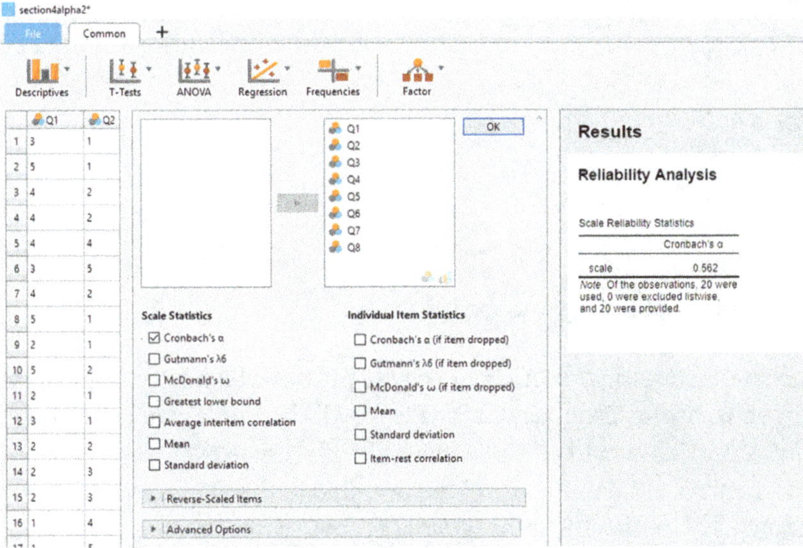

FIGURE 8.8 Calculating Cronbach's alpha with JASP

One good way to find out *why* the alpha is low is to click the "Cronbach's α (if Item Dropped)" checkbox (see Figure 8.9).

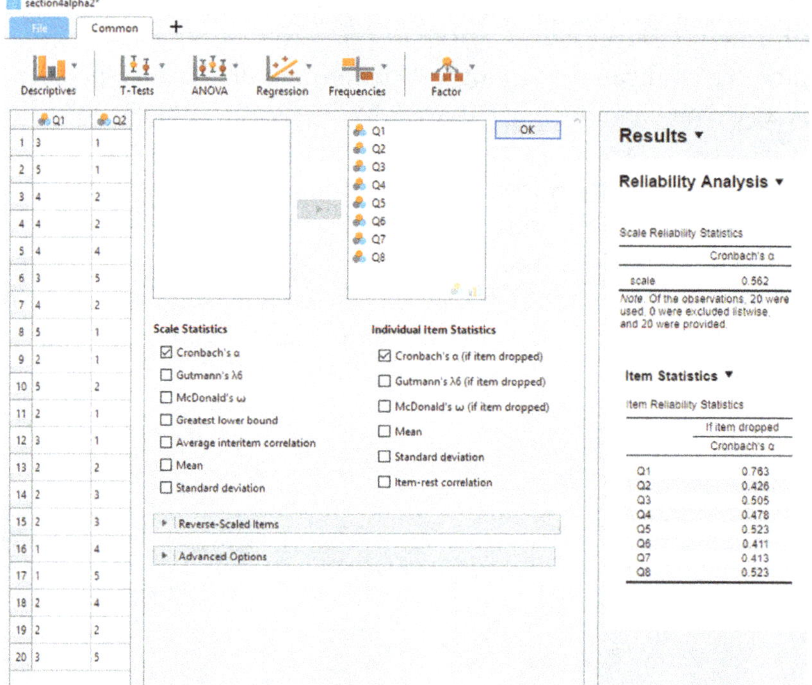

FIGURE 8.9 Using alpha (if item dropped) in JASP

In the "item statistics" section of the output (on the bottom right), this now tells Aaliyah what the Cronbach's alpha is for all the items *except one*. It does this *repeatedly*, reporting what the alpha would be if Q1 was excluded, then if Q2 was excluded, then Q3, etc. For instance, the first line in the "Item Statistics" area tells Aaliyah that the Cronbach's alpha *without Q1* is .763. That score is above .70, thus indicating good reliability. Aaliyah now knows that if she uses just Questions 2–8, she will have good reliability. Question 1 is "bad." Perhaps some subjects misread Q1, or it doesn't quite measure the same thing as the other seven items, or maybe it's worded poorly so the respondents were confused. If Aaliyah had results like this, she could just proceed using *only* Q2–Q8. Alternatively, if Q1 was important for content validity, she could work on rewriting Q1 and gathering more pilot data to check the reliability of the scale with the new and improved Q1.

If you want to check that you understand, go back and run the reliability analysis again, but *just using* Q2–Q8—the Cronbach's alpha is indeed .763 (see Figure 8.10). So, Cronbach's alpha provides an additional tool for demonstrating that a scale is reliable and for figuring out which items might be causing problems if the scale is not reliable.

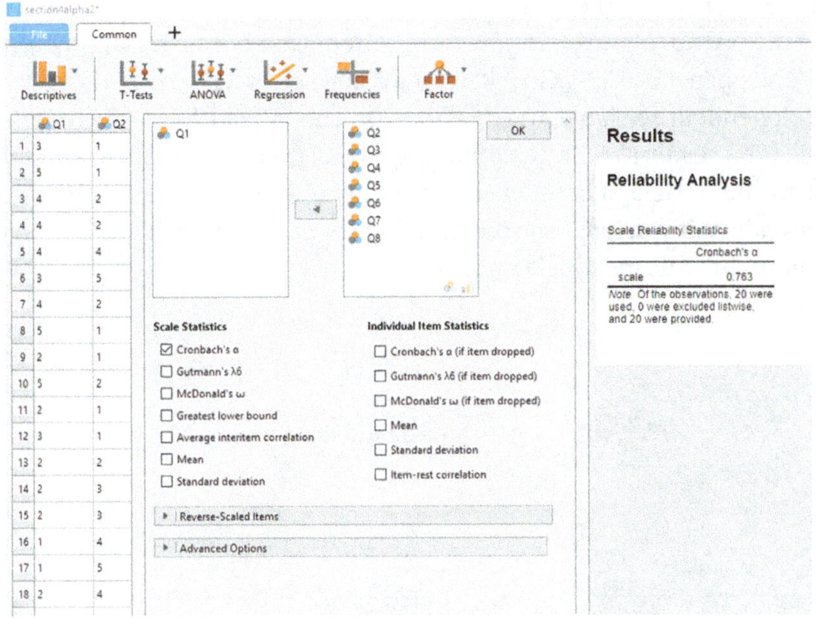

FIGURE 8.10 Cronbach's alpha of improved scale

What would Aaliyah's Cronbach's alpha be if she used all the items except item 4 (i.e., she constructed a scale from Q1, Q2, Q3, Q5, Q6, Q7, and Q8)? Would that scale have good reliability?

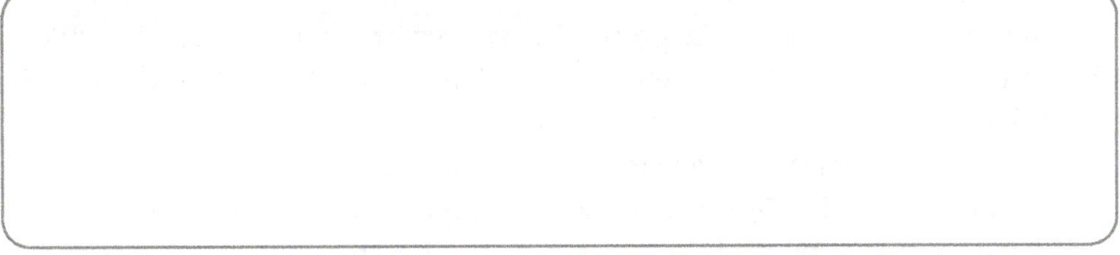

The alpha in this case would be .478—a lot lower than .70! That version of her scale would not be a good option.

Following-up on a significant one-way ANOVA. One area of the chapter that might have bothered you is some vagueness in what the one-way ANOVA tells us. Because her analysis was significant, Aaliyah knew that the three groups were not the same. But she didn't really know precisely *which* group(s) were different from which other groups. She can find out this additional detail using what are called *post hoc* tests. "Post hoc" just means "after the fact"—these are tests you do after having found a significant ANOVA to provide you with more detail on the results.

The JASP version of the data from Aaliyah's study is available at the following link (http://bit.ly/2KHfbh9). If you want to replicate her process, download the data file and open it in JASP. Go to "ANOVA" and select "ANOVA." Indicate "Spin" as your dependent variable and "Source" as the "Fixed Factor" (independent variable). The result should look like Figure 8.11; the numbers are exactly the same as in the Google Sheet. One bonus of using JASP for this analysis is that it will easily adjust if you have unequal numbers of people in each group, something that is more difficult in Google Sheets.

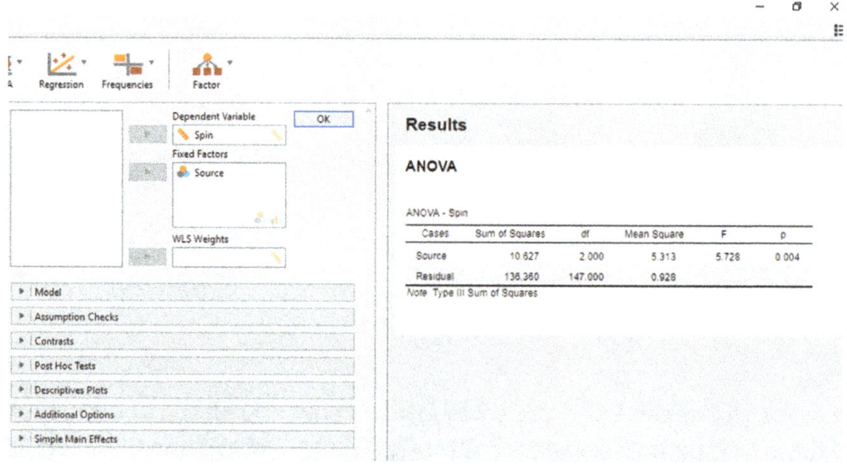

FIGURE 8.11 One-way ANOVA in JASP

To figure out which *specific* group differences are significant, go to "Post Hoc Tests" and move "Source" into the right-hand box. "Tukey" should already be checked—Tukey tests are the most common form of post hoc test. The new output tells you exactly which groups are different from other groups (see Figure 8.12 for the output). In Figure 8.13, each row represents a comparison between two of the three groups, and the column on the far right provides the *p*-value, indicating whether that comparison is significant. The first row represents the CEO-attorney comparison, and you can see from the "p_{tukey}" column that this is *not* significant: the *p*-value is *not* less than .05. The next row compares the CEO and the spokesperson, and this row is also not significant (although it's close!). The final row represents the comparison of the attorney and the spokesperson, and this comparison *is* significant (0.003 < .05). So, the one-way ANOVA told Aaliyah that these three groups were not all the same. The post hoc tests tell her that the only statistically meaningful difference is the one between the attorney and the spokesperson.

Post Hoc Tests

Post Hoc Comparisons - Source

		Mean Difference	SE	t	P_{tukey}
CEO	Attorney	0.200	0.193	1.038	0.554
	Spokesperson	−0.437	0.193	−2.271	0.063
Attorney	Spokesperson	−0.637	0.193	−3.309	0.003

FIGURE 8.12 Post hoc tests in JASP

With this additional information, Aaliyah's write-up would look more like the following:

REPORT 8.2 Results for One-Way ANOVA With Post Hoc Tests

Evaluations of the three targets in terms of their perceived spin were significantly different, $F(2, 147) = 5.73, p < .05, \eta^2 = .07$. Post hoc Tukey tests indicated that the spokesperson ($M = 3.50, SD = 1.01$) was seen as displaying significantly higher spin than the attorney ($M = 2.86, SD = 0.85$). Perceptions of the CEO's spin ($M = 3.06, SD = 1.02$) were in between the other two and not significantly different from either. The means are displayed in Figure 1.

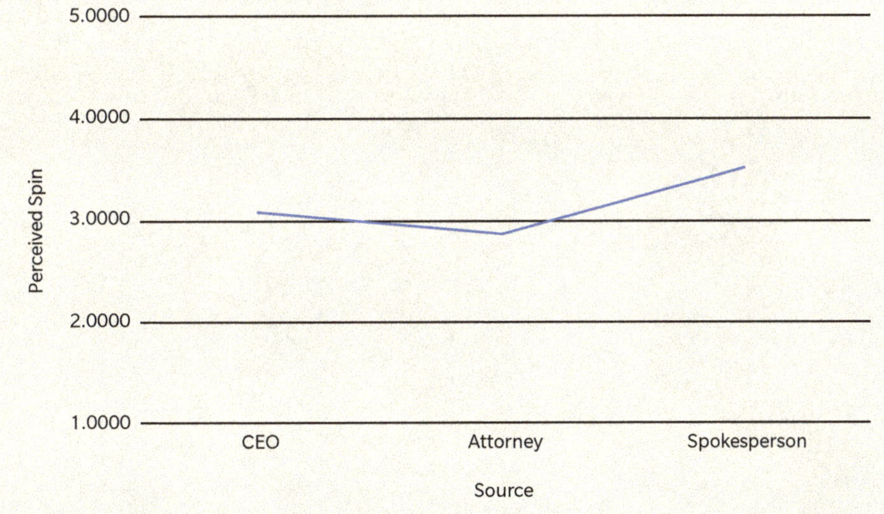

FIGURE 1 Means of perceived spin for three different company representatives

Credits

Fig. 8.8: Copyright © by The JASP Team.

Fig. 8.9: Copyright © by The JASP Team.

Fig. 8.10: Copyright © by The JASP Team.

Fig. 8.11: Copyright © by The JASP Team.

Fig. 8.12: Copyright © by Random.org.

SECTION 5

Advanced Sampling From a Population: Do Facebook Ads About Physical Exercise Reach Middle-Schoolers?

By the end of this section, you will be able to:

- Design a strategy for gathering data using a multistage cluster sample
- Evaluate the ethical implications of gathering data from samples of people designated as vulnerable
- Understand the implications of representative (versus non-representative) samples for external validity
- Clearly distinguish between random assignment and random sampling
- Calculate a chi-square test of contingency using Google Sheets and write a report of the results of that analysis
- Distinguish between Type 1 and Type 2 errors in statistical hypothesis testing

CHAPTER 9

Doing the Research: Sampling

You were briefly introduced to Francisco at the start of the book. Francisco is a communication major doing an internship with the local government health agency from his city—Bakersville. The city has been doing a health promotion campaign trying to get middle schoolers to exercise more. As part of evaluating the effectiveness of this program, they have asked Francisco to assess whether (and which) middle schoolers in Bakersville have actually *seen* the messages that have been distributed on social media.

Developing the Research Question/Hypothesis

Francisco has a fairly simple first research question.

> RQ1: How many middle schoolers in Bakersville have seen the "Get Active" campaign messages?

This is a *descriptive* research question—there is no hypothesis here, just a need to "describe" a situation. Francisco has also been tasked with answering an additional question, however. The city is concerned that physical activity is seen as a "boy" thing. They are particularly interested in making sure that their messages reach boys and girls equally. Hence, he has an additional research question:

> RQ2: Do boys or girls see the "Get Active" campaign messages more?

Because this RQ contains two variables, it is also possible to express it as a (nondirectional) hypothesis. Try to write the hypothesis here:

The hypothesis will be nondirectional because Francisco doesn't have any reason to predict that one sex will see the message more than the other. If he knew, for instance, that middle school boys used social media a lot more than girls, then he would have a reason to predict that boys were more likely to see the messages and hence write the following directional hypothesis:

> H: Boys are more likely to see "Get Active" campaign messages than girls.

And if he knew that girls pay more attention to advertising messages than boys, then he might make the opposite directional hypothesis:

> H: Girls are more likely to see "Get Active" campaign messages than boys.

However, Francisco doesn't actually know either of those things, so his best bet here is a *non*directional hypothesis, which could be written similarly to any of the following:

> H: There are sex differences in exposure to "Get Active" campaign messages.

> H: There will be differences between boys and girls in their exposure to "Get Active" campaign messages.

> H: Girls and boys will differ in whether they have seen "Get Active" campaign messages.

If you wrote something like one of those three options, then you understand how a nondirectional hypothesis should be structured.

Who to Study? The Importance of a Representative Sample

As in Cassandra's example in the early chapters of this book, Francisco really needs a representative sample for his research. The city wants to know how many middle schoolers in the entire city have seen the messages, not just the number in a particular school. But they don't have the resources to actually ask every middle schooler about his or her exposure. This is where representative (**random**) sampling is useful: Francisco can gather data from a sample that will allow him to make inferences about the entire **population**.

In Cassandra's example, you will remember that she persuaded the registrar of the college to allow her to randomly sample from their list of all enrolled students. If Cassandra's college had 23,000 students enrolled, for instance, Cassandra

Random Integer Generator

This form allows you to generate random integers. The randomness comes from atmospheric noise, which for many purposes is better than the pseudo-random number algorithms typically used in computer programs.

Part 1: The Integers

Generate [50] random integers (maximum 10,000).

Each integer should have a value between [1] and [23000] (both inclusive; limits ±1,000,000,000).

Format in [5] column(s).

Part 2: Go!

Be patient! It may take a little while to generate your numbers ...

[Get Numbers] [Reset Form] [Switch to Advanced Mode]

Random Integer Generator

Here are your random numbers:

8661	19382	10980	4250	15665
12570	16845	15982	4949	16763
12558	21600	7842	18174	8863
8665	14480	17413	11065	7950
7057	16316	17515	2509	3431
1137	18410	8874	14898	14183
5334	4098	15173	20800	21443
1208	225	20871	703	22035
10096	19454	18859	7563	6545
1158	8454	10099	10124	17321

Timestamp: 2018-04-17 16:39:06 UTC

[Again!] [Go Back]

Note: The numbers are generated left to right, i.e.,

FIGURE 9.1 Using www.random.org to generate truly random numbers

could just number them from 1 to 23,000. Using a random number generator (e.g., https://www.random.org/integers/), she could then request a list of 50 numbers between 1 and 23,000—see Figure 9.1. This kind of sample is called a **simple random sample**. You have a list of all the members of the population, and you randomly select from that list.

A "random" reminder. Remember that "random" is very different from "haphazard." When scientists do something random, that means they are trying very hard to do something without any bias. Computer scientists work very hard to get computers to generate truly random numbers. And social scientists work hard to make sure that when they draw a random sample, everyone in the population has an equal chance of being in that sample. Picking the first 50 people you run into, or the passengers on a particular subway car isn't random—it's arbitrary or haphazard.

A New Type of Representative Sample: The Multistage Cluster Sample

In Francisco's case, there is no list of all of the middle school students in the city. Just because Francisco doesn't have such a list doesn't mean that he can't get a random sample. He is going to need to think creatively, however. He is encountering a somewhat common scenario for researchers: He doesn't have a list of the things he wants to sample, but he does have a list of the places where those things "exist." Where do middle schoolers exist? In middle schools! So even though no *list* of the students exists, Francisco does know where to find the students. He could get a list of all the public middle schools directly from the local school district's website. Lists of private schools are available through national government databases (e.g., the National Center for Education Statistics: https://nces.ed.gov/surveys/pss/privateschoolsearch/), state departments of education, or even using tools like Google Maps. Let's imagine that Bakersville is a pretty large city, and Francisco ends up with a list of 200 middle schools.

Once Francisco has this list, he could try contacting *all* of the schools, but that would take more time and use more resources than he has available. Instead, he randomly samples *schools* from the list. A random sample of schools taken from a list of *all* schools (the *population* of schools) will *represent* all the schools. Random sampling doesn't just work for people! You can randomly sample pretty much anything: a sample of countries from a list of all countries, a sample of newspapers from a list of all newspapers, or a sample of days in the year from the list of all the days in the year. There are populations of countries, newspapers, and days in the year, just like there are populations of people. Just make sure you are following the rules for random sampling: every item has to have an equal chance of being selected.

Francisco randomly samples 25 schools from the list of 200. As Cassandra did, he could just number the schools from 1 to 200, and use www.random.org to give him 25 numbers randomly selected from the numbers 1 to 200. Those 25 numbers would be the schools that he would target for his research. See Figure 9.1 for an illustration of using random.org.

Once Francisco has that random sample of schools, he can then contact each school and request their cooperation with his research. For now, we'll assume they all agree and are willing to give Francisco a list of their students. Francisco now has the problem that the 25 schools contain thousands of students, and he doesn't need thousands of students to do his research. The simplest way to reduce the complexity of this task is for him to randomly sample again—this time from the students *within* each school. If he selects just 20 students from each school, he will have 500 student respondents, which is plenty for his needs. As with the previous random sample, within each school, he would take his list of all the students, number them, and use a random number generator to select the 20 students he will use in his research.

The final sample of students that Francisco just obtained is called a **multistage cluster sample**. This sort of sample is characterized by (1) sampling larger units (e.g., schools) in which objects (e.g., students) are collected and *then* (2) randomly sampling the objects (students) from within the selected larger units (i.e., only the schools that were selected in Step 1). Francisco's process is illustrated in Figure 9.2.

The multistage cluster sample has two main advantages over a simple random sample:

1. As is clear from Francisco's example, you can use the multistage cluster sample for situations when a simple random sample isn't an option because you don't have a list of the population.

2. The multistage sample can reduce the time and effort required to gather data. If Francisco *did* have a list of all the students in the city and used a simple random sample, he might have to visit 200 schools to collect his data, perhaps only meeting with one or two students at each school. Using the multistage cluster sample, he only has to visit 25 schools.

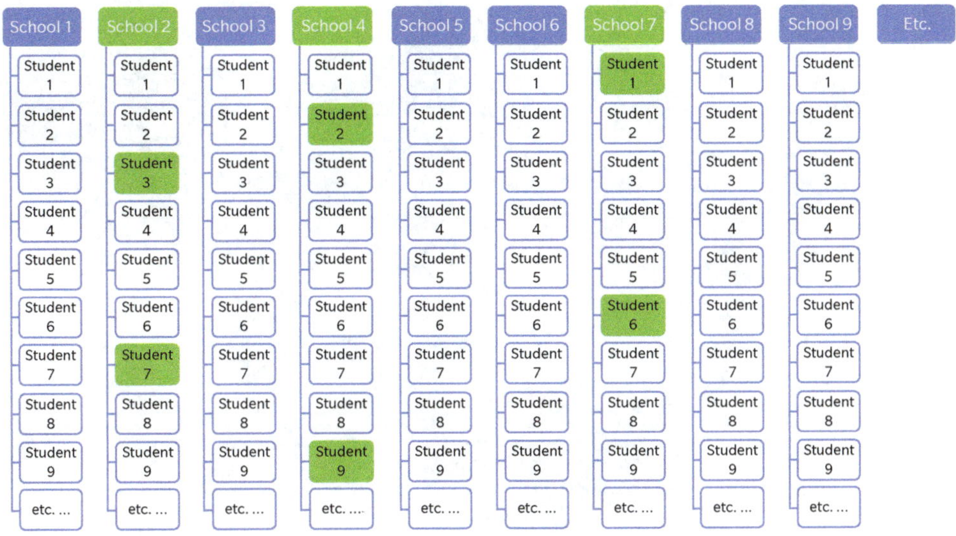

FIGURE 9.2 Illustration of multistage cluster sample. Note. Green indicates selected items. Only some schools are randomly selected from a list of all the schools. Once the school is selected, students are randomly selected from within just those schools. Blue indicates schools that were not selected, so no students from within those schools are selected. Likewise, the not-green students were not selected.

As you might guess, there's a price to pay for this "trick" of sampling schools and then students within schools. Remember from Chapter 1 the idea of **sampling error.** When you draw a random sample from a population, it represents that population, but not perfectly. The difference between the true characteristics of the entire population and the characteristics of the sample is called sampling error. Sampling error is introduced whenever random sampling happens. In Francisco's multistage cluster sample, there is sampling error in sampling schools from the population of schools: the sample of schools doesn't perfectly represent the entire population of schools. Then there is *additional* sampling error in randomly sampling the students from within those schools: in any given school, the sample of students doesn't perfectly represent all of the students in that school. Hence sampling error in a multistage cluster sample tends to be larger than with a simple random sample. Figure 9.3 illustrates this.

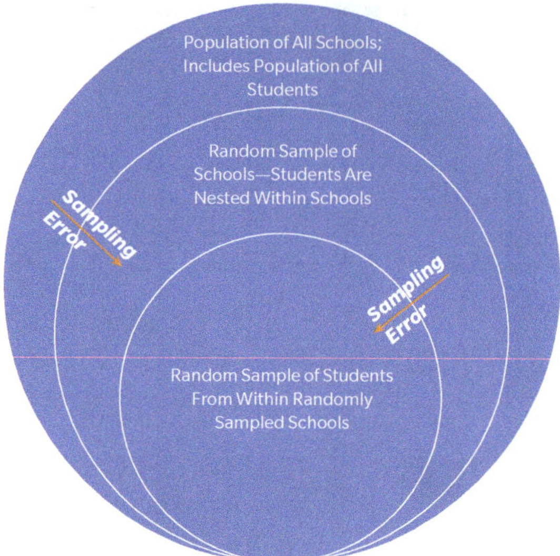

FIGURE 9.3 Sampling error in a multistage cluster sample

The "cure" for sampling error is to have a larger sample: Larger samples have less sampling error, and hence a larger sample can "make up for" the additional sampling error in a multistage cluster sample. Francisco has a sample of 500 students, which is a pretty good number for his purposes.

Can you think of another situation in which you might use a multistage cluster sample?

The "Other Applications" section of this chapter will provide additional examples—see if something similar to what you thought of is there.

Not all research needs a representative sample

There are plenty of situations in which a representative sample is not essential for a research study. Sometimes a **convenience sample** is fine. A convenience sample, as the name suggests, is just a group of people that is easily accessible to the researcher, even if it doesn't represent any population in particular. If you are interested in whether being exposed to scary movies increases the number of nightmares people have, you probably don't need a representative sample. You take a group of people, randomly assign half of them to watch some scary movies, and half of them to watch some nonscary movies, and then measure how many nightmares they have. You could do this with college students, retired U.S. Navy veterans, Olympic athletes, or elementary school kids (although their parents might have something to say about that!). You are just interested in whether the effect *occurs*, not whether you can make some claim about nightmares in the entire population. Random samples take time and money to gather, so it's important to ask yourself if you really need one before investing that effort. The "Going Further" part of this section provides more detail about different types of samples for those who are interested.

Doing Research in the Field: Practical Considerations

For most of this chapter, we have been assuming that Francisco's sampling process will go smoothly. However, in the real world, there are lots of problems he might run into in getting his final sample. Write three problems you think he might encounter: What are three ways in which he might end up with a *less-than-perfect* sample?

Sampling often depends on people cooperating, and people don't always cooperate! Francisco will be calling up the principals of the middle schools and asking them if he can do the study. Some of the principals might say "no." Francisco will also be asking parents if they agree (consent) to have their kids be in the research study. The parents might say "no." Their children will also be asked whether they agree (assent) to be in the study. The kids might say no. Some children might be absent from school on the day that Francisco is collecting data. Some of these issues might result in **sampling bias**. Remember that sampling bias is when the sample differs in a systematic way from the population (instead of in an arbitrary or random way, which is **sampling error**). For instance, children from low-income families are more likely to be absent from school than kids from higher income families (Balfanz & Byrnes, 2012). Francisco's sample is, therefore, likely to be *systematically* different from the population in terms of family income: He will have more kids from higher income families in his sample than exist in the population.

There also might be children who are missed altogether by Francisco's process. Homeschooled children are probably the most obvious group (their schools aren't on any formal list that he is likely to access). He would also miss kids who have dropped out of school for some reason—homeless children and children whose parents have "lost control" or just don't care. So, while his process will generate a very nice sample in theory, in practice, things are often a lot "messier"!

Francisco can minimize some of these problems with simple professional behavior. He should be professional in approaching the schools and parents, and be able to articulate the importance of the research. People are more likely to agree to be in research if they think it "matters" and if the person heading up the research behaves appropriately. Problems in getting people to participate are not disasters for Francisco's research. What he must do, however, is let his readers (the health agency for which he's doing the work) know about them. When reporting on sampling procedures, one ethical responsibility that researchers have is to accurately report on all of the "mess." In the "Writing the Report" section, you will see an example of how deviations from perfect sampling are reported to the reader—this involves reporting specific numbers. Francisco needs to report the exact percentage of schools that agreed to participate relative to the number that were originally asked and likewise for the parents (these numbers are called **response rates**). The reader can then make an informed decision on how much these problems might influence Francisco's ability to generalize from his sample to the broader population.

The ability to generalize gained by using a representative sample is part of **external validity**. External validity is the *degree to which your research can be applied to people, places, or circumstances outside the research setting*. The more your sample represents or generalizes to a broader population, the better your external validity. If the sample represents a bigger population, then your research findings with that sample can be applied to the bigger population. There are a number of other factors in research that can improve external validity, including the following:

- Designing research materials that reflect real life: If you create a video for your research study, it should "look like" a real video that people might encounter in their real lives. The more realistic the video is, the more likely people's responses will reflect their real-life reactions to similar videos.
- Designing research procedures that reflect real life: If people are watching a video in your study, it is better if they watch the video in a similar setting to how they normally watch videos. Maybe on their own laptop in a comfortable chair or sitting on a couch watching a TV rather than sitting in a classroom watching a projection onto a screen.
- Using **unobtrusive measurement**: While a lot of the measures we discuss in this book involve self-reports, measures that the research subject is unaware of will enhance external validity. If somebody doesn't even know that he or she is being measured, then that person's behavior will be natural, which means external validity will be good. In Francisco's study, it would help his external validity if he could surreptitiously monitor the research subjects' social media use without them knowing. There are, of course, other problems with doing that: unobtrusive measures can get into areas of violating people's privacy!

Research Ethics: Informed Consent and Assent, Vulnerable Populations

In most cases, human beings must **consent** to participating in research (see sidebar later for exceptions). You cannot do research on people without asking their consent first, and their consent should be informed: The idea of **informed consent** means that potential research subjects understand what they are getting into before they agree to do the study. There are four key components to informed consent. Research subjects must be told the following:

1. The activities the research will involve and how much time they will take: Some studies might just involve filling out a short questionnaire, while others might involve reporting to a lab every day for two weeks, having blood drawn, and watching scary videos. Potential research participants need to be told the details before they commit to a study.
2. Any risks associated with participating: In a simple questionnaire study, the risks might be minimal, but in a more extensive study, the risks might involve physical pain (e.g., from a blood draw or a stamina test) or psychological concerns (e.g., being scared by a scary video or being asked about traumatic events from a person's life). Research subjects should know about these risks before they decide to participate.
3. Any benefits associated with participating: Benefits are rare in social science research, but some studies might provide information about improving personal relationships or communication skills. These are also relevant to the decision to participate, and the subjects should be made aware of them.
4. The compensation provided for participating: For instance, if someone is being paid money, or receiving extra credit in a class for participating, that should be communicated clearly.

Benefits and compensation are easy to confuse. Benefits are positive consequences from the research itself. For instance, participating in a study of a new form of marital therapy might potentially improve your marriage. Compensation is a positive consequence that is *not* a part of the research, including incentives the researcher offers to get someone to agree to participate (typically a payment, extra credit in a class, or maybe free pizza!).

Francisco has an additional challenge in getting informed consent. Because his research subjects are legal minors, he needs to get their *parents'* consent. Children fall into a category of people who are called "vulnerable populations" for research purposes—*people whose ability to provide informed consent is regarded as being limited*. Can you think of three other groups of people who might be treated in this manner?

See the following "Key Point!" section to see if you were on target.

Research ethics: Vulnerable populations. Populations can be vulnerable either because they have personal characteristics that impair their decision making or because they are in a situation in which their autonomy is restricted in some way. Children are the classic example of the former case—as a society, we have determined that people below 18 lack fully adult decision-making ability and hence can't make important decisions without some assistance. Another group of people in this category would be people with cognitive impairments that restrict their decision making. Pregnant women also fall into this category: While being pregnant doesn't impair decision-making ability, research ethics also demand attention to the fetus, and so there are particular protections for pregnant women in research that might have consequences for the fetus. People who are currently using substances known to impair decision making (e.g., heroin addicts) would also fall into this category.

The classic example of people in situations with limited autonomy is prisoners. While most prisoners have normal decision-making skills, they are all in a situation in which their ability to make decisions is constrained by their environment. Without careful use of informed consent, prisoners might feel pressured to participate in research by their captors.

As you can see, sometimes the definition of who is vulnerable might vary depending on the situation. Research in many organizations needs to attend to vulnerability concerns if there is a chance that workers feel forced to participate in research by their bosses, for instance. People with certain illnesses might be considered vulnerable if they feel coerced to participate with (perhaps false) the promise of a potential cure. Researchers need to be aware of the need to provide informed consent carefully to people in these situations and to arrange the research environment to minimize coercion. For instance, if you are asking people in an organization to complete a questionnaire for research, their participation should occur in an environment where their boss can't monitor them and where the boss is not aware of whether someone declines to participate.

Once Francisco has selected his sample, he will need the school's assistance in sending a letter home to the parents explaining the research, and he will have to wait for the parents to respond. Assuming the parents agree (this is called **parental permission**), he will also need to explain the study carefully to the students themselves and get them to agree to participate (this is called child or minor **assent**).

Francisco's letter to the parents is in Figure 9.4—this is typical of such letters. Can you identify the benefit the participants will experience and the compensation they will be provided?

Benefit: ____________________

Compensation: ____________________

Remember that a benefit is a positive outcome from the study itself, either for the participant or for the community. So the benefit in this study is the potential for better community health; the participants themselves are unlikely to experience any personal benefit. The compensation is what the subject receives in exchange for doing the study—a reward or payment that is independent of the content of the study itself. In this study, the compensation is the snack.

INTRODUCTION
Your child has been invited to join a research study jointly organized by Bakersville Department of Health and Bakersville University to look at their social media use and exposure to health messages on social media. Please take whatever time you need to discuss the study with your family and friends, or anyone else you wish to. The decision to let you child join, or not to join, is up to you.

In this research study, we are investigating whether certain health messages placed on social media are reaching their intended audience. Our research is intended to improve the health of young people in Bakersville.

WHAT IS INVOLVED IN THE STUDY?
Your child will be asked to tell us how much they have used social media, whether they have seen specific messages on social media, and to provide us with some basic demographic information. We think this will take him/her 10–15 minutes. Your child will be answering questions on a questionnaire.

The investigators may stop the study or take your child out of the study at any time they judge it is in your child's best interest. They may also remove your child from the study for various other reasons. They can do this without your consent. Your child can stop participating at any time. If your child stops he/she will not lose any benefits.

RISKS
This study involves few risks: there is a chance your child may feel slightly uncomfortable in answering some questions.

BENEFITS TO TAKING PART IN THE STUDY?
We do not expect that your child will personally experience benefits from participating in this study. Others may benefit in the future from the information we find in this study if we can better target health information to young people.

CONFIDENTIALITY
Your child's name will not be used when data from this study are published. Your child's name will be separated from their data as soon as data collection is complete, and there will be no way to reconnect the information. Your child's data are anonymous.

INCENTIVES
Each child who participates will receive a choice of a healthy snack to thank them for participating.

YOUR CHILD'S RIGHTS AS A RESEARCH PARTICIPANT?
Participation in this study is voluntary. Your child has the right not to participate at all or to leave the study at any time. Deciding not to participate or choosing to leave the study will not result in any penalty or loss of benefits to which your child is entitled, and it will not harm his/her relationship with the school or teachers at the school. If your child decides to leave the study, s/he simply should stop completing the questionnaire.

CONTACTS FOR QUESTIONS OR PROBLEMS?
Call Francisco Obregon at 417-555-1212 or email him (francisco@email123.com) if you have questions about the study, any problems, if your child experiences any unexpected physical or psychological discomforts, any injuries, or think that something unusual or unexpected is happening.

Permission for a Child to Participate in Research
As parent or legal guardian. I authorize ______________________________ (child's name) to become a participant in the research study described in this form.

______________________________ ______________
Parent or Legal Guardian's Signature Date

FIGURE 9.4 Example consent letter for parents in a study involving children

Exceptions to informed consent

While informed consent is the norm for research, it is not always required for communication researchers. Exceptions to the informed consent requirement typically fall into three big categories: cases of minimal risk, cases where consent is not possible, and research not involving human subjects. These can sometimes overlap.

- **Minimal risk.** If there is virtually no conceivable harm that could come to the research subjects as a result of your research, informed consent requirements are often waived. Simple questionnaires about noncontroversial topics being completed by nonvulnerable populations are a good example here. There may still be a requirement that you provide respondents with some basic information related to consent (e.g., how long the research will take and what they will get in return), but you will not need to gather signatures, for instance.
- **Cases where obtaining consent is impossible or impractical.** If as a researcher you go to a soccer stadium to observe crowd behavior and do not intervene in the situation at all, you do not need to seek the consent of all the fans. This extends to the Internet, where you can observe and analyze public behavior (e.g., Yelp! reviews) without asking permission. However, not everyone "on the Internet" is necessarily public enough to count here. If, for instance, you gain access to a discussion board that is intended only for people with a specific disease, publishing analysis of the contents of that site would not necessarily be OK without getting consent from the participants. People on such a site might have a reasonable expectation that their comments are only intended for a particular audience.
- **Archival research, or research with no human subjects.** Perhaps it is obvious, but you do not need to seek consent if there are no people involved in your research (e.g., you are studying magazine articles or annual reports from organizations). Even studies of archives that relate to individual people may be exempt from consent requirements if, for instance, the people are dead or the records are anonymous.

Note: These are *not* typically exceptions to getting Institutional Review Board (IRB) approval to do your research. If you are going to that soccer stadium to observe the fans, it would be a good idea to describe the research to your IRB so that the members can give you permission *not* to get consent from the fans. Ultimately, the IRB decides whether your research needs to obtain informed consent.

There is one case where the IRB does not need to be involved at all: Class projects! So long as the data collection you do in a class is *only* for the purpose of the class, then you do not need to seek consent, and you don't need to run it by the IRB. Your instructor is in charge of making sure that you are not engaged in activities that could cause anyone harm.

The Research

The focus of this chapter has been on Francisco's sampling process and the ethical issues in dealing with vulnerable populations. But let's not lose track of his actual research! Once he has collected his sample and obtained parental consent and child assent, he has to actually ask these students some questions. It is likely that he will do the research in the school to make it convenient for the children, so the data collection will need to be quick. He also needs to be aware of the ages of the children when asking the questions: some middle schoolers can be quite advanced, but he also needs to be prepared for kids who may have limited levels of literacy. Hence, he should consider offering an "interview" option as well as a standard questionnaire (see the following "Key Point!" section).

Interviews versus questionnaires. For any research in which respondents are being asked questions, the researcher should think about whether it is better to do an interview or use a written questionnaire.

Can you think of one advantage for the researcher of using an interview and one advantage of using a written questionnaire?

Advantages of interviews. For a lot of work with young people (and other populations with low levels of literacy), it can be helpful to do the research using interviews (asking the questions orally) rather than with a written questionnaire. Almost everyone can respond to questions asked orally, but many people struggle with written materials. Interviews also offer the advantage of both parties being able to seek clarification. An interviewee can ask for a question to be explained and clarified, and an interviewer can ask for more detail in a response, for instance. Interviews also help with maintaining the respondent's attention. In a written questionnaire, the respondent might "zone out" and stop paying attention. This is very rarely the case in a spoken interview.

Advantages of questionnaires. The primary advantage of questionnaires is efficiency. You can typically only interview one person at a time, and interviews have to be scheduled, resulting in a lot of downtime between interviews and sometimes even travel to get from one interview to the next. On the other hand, an almost unlimited number of people can fill out a questionnaire simultaneously. Questionnaires are also quicker for respondents; you can read and respond to a lot more questions in written form than spoken form—reading and circling answers is just a quicker process than speaking the questions and answers. If you remember that "time is money," then you will understand that this means questionnaires are typically a lot less expensive than interviews. Questionnaires also offer advantages for anonymity—if you are asking about sensitive topics or things people might be hesitant to answer (e.g., drug use, sexual fantasies), you may get more accurate data in an anonymous questionnaire than a face-to-face conversation. Questionnaires also have the advantage of minimizing investigator influence or bias. In an interview, there is always the chance that the person asking the questions does so in a manner that influences the responses—perhaps via subtle nonverbal signals that the interviewer isn't even aware of. That sort of influence is much less likely with a written questionnaire.

TABLE 9.1 Pros and Cons of Interviews and Questionnaires

Dimension of Evaluation	Interviews	Questionnaires	Winner
Time/money	Take more time/ cost more	Take less time/ cost less	Questionnaires
Confidentiality (including perceived confidentiality)	Less confidential	More confidential	Questionnaires
Investigator influence/bias	More chance of influence	Less chance of influence	Questionnaires
Detail in data/opportunities for interaction with research subjects	High	Low	Interviews
Options for low literacy subjects, including children	Good	Bad	Interviews

These relative advantages (and hence also disadvantages) are summarized in Table 9.1. What should be clear is that the decision about whether to use an interview or questionnaire will depend on *who* you are studying, *what* you are studying, and what *resources* you have available. Later chapters will discuss uses of interviews in qualitative research.

For the purposes of our needs here, we are going to focus on just one simple question from Francisco's study, even though he probably would ask more questions. The following is the question we will focus on:

> We have been putting messages on Facebook and Instagram to encourage people your age to get more exercise. Which of the following messages do you remember seeing on Facebook or Instagram in the past week? Pick only the one message you are most confident you have seen.

- ☐ Be strong!
- ☐ Have a blast!
- ☐ Move your body!
- ☐ Get active!
- ☐ Be a moving star!
- ☐ Go for it!
- ☐ Dance yourself fit!
- ☐ I don't remember seeing any of these messages

The correct answer here is "Get Active!" Francisco will score everyone who checks *only* that box as having seen the message; everyone who checks other boxes will be scored as not having seen the message.

Writing the Report

This report describes the sampling process, including noting when the sampling was unsuccessful (e.g., when schools declined to participate).

REPORT 9.1 Methods for Multistage Cluster Sample

Sample. We obtained a random multistage cluster sample of middle school students from a large midwestern city. Twenty-five middle schools in the city were randomly sampled from a list of all accredited middle schools; the list was obtained from the state department of education. Each selected school's principal was contacted and asked if the school was willing to participate. When schools indicated they were unwilling, additional schools were randomly selected from the list to replace the declining schools. A total of 30 schools were asked and 25 agreements obtained (a school response rate of 83%).

Each school provided a list of all enrolled students, and a random sample of 22 students was taken from each list (for a total of 550 students contacted). Our target was 20 students per school, but additional students were contacted to allow for attrition. Some students' parents declined the request to have their children participate, or the students were no-shows to the research. This resulted in a final sample of 500 students from a total of 550 students who were contacted (a response rate of 91%).

The final sample was 50% female, 50% male, and ethnically diverse (46% white, 22% black/African American, 17 % Hispanic, 12% Asian American, 6% Native American, 12% other; numbers do not sum to 100% because respondents could select more than one category).

Measures. Respondents were asked to identify a fitness-related message they had seen on social media in the past week. They were given a list of eight options—the target program message ("Get active!") along with seven distractors. Individuals who selected "Get active!" were scored as having seen the program message, and everyone else was scored as not having seen it. Demographic information (including respondent sex) was also collected.

Other Applications

As mentioned in the text, multistage cluster samples can be useful for many situations where the things you want to research are nested in some larger units. If you want to study a national sample of police officers, there probably is no list of those people. But you could find a list of all U.S. police departments, randomly select departments from that list, and then randomly sample police officers from within those sampled departments. There is no list of everyone employed by a major- or minor-league sports franchise. But there are lists of the teams in those leagues: You can sample teams and then sample employees from within the sampled teams. Lots of "organizational" contexts are hence good situations for multistage cluster sampling. It is also useful in media research. If you want to study magazine advertising, for instance, you could generate a random sample of magazines (from a publisher's list of all widely read magazines) and then sample issues from *just* those magazines you selected. Similarly, you could randomly sample network television shows and then sample episodes from just the selected shows.

Your Turn

Take a moment to remind yourself of your ongoing project. Look back at the previous chapters' "Your Turn" sections to refamiliarize yourself with what you have been doing so far. For our current purposes, imagine that you wanted to collect data from one of the following populations:

a) representatives in state legislatures,

b) members of religious communities (e.g., churches, synagogues, mosques), or

c) married couples attending marriage counseling with a licensed therapist.

Pick whichever one of those options might be the most relevant for the study you are interested in pursuing. Following the model laid out by Francisco, write a description of the steps you would go through to obtain a multistage cluster sample from one of those three populations. Try to be as detailed as possible. Think about what specific lists you would be sampling from, where you would get those lists, and how you would draw the sample. Write the report.

Wrap Up

In this chapter, you have learned how to draw a multistage cluster sample to obtain a representative sample from a population. You have learned some of the practical problems in doing research, especially in community settings (e.g., people or organizations who do not want to participate in your research). You have learned the importance of being thorough in reporting problems you encountered in your data collection so that readers are fully informed about what you did. You have also learned some of the ethical challenges associated with doing research involving vulnerable populations, such as children or prisoners.

If you get nothing else from this chapter, remember the following:

1. There are different ways to obtain a random sample—if there is no list from which to draw a **simple random sample**, you can be creative by using something like a **multistage cluster sample.**

2. The **external validity** of a study is increased by using representative samples, procedures and materials that are similar to what people encounter in their real lives, and (if possible) unobtrusive measures.

3. There is increased ethical scrutiny of research that involves **vulnerable populations** (e.g., children, prisoners, people with cognitive impairments, pregnant women).

Key Chapter Concepts

Convenience sample: A type of **nonrepresentative sample**. A convenience sample is any group of people (or other objects) that is easily accessible to the researcher. For college professors, college students are often the convenience sample of choice.

External validity: The extent to which a research study's findings can be generalized to other people, places, situations, etc. A study done in a natural setting with a representative sample using unobtrusive measurement would have high external validity.

Institutional Review Board (IRB): An oversight committee charged with checking that research follows appropriate ethical procedures. Researchers planning a research project need to have it approved by an IRB before proceeding with the work.

Nonrepresentative sample: A sample not randomly selected from a population. For example, a **convenience sample.** Research done with nonrepresentative samples has less **external validity** than work done with **representative samples**, but many scientific questions can still be answered with nonrepresentative samples.

Multistage cluster sampling: A form of **representative sampling** in which larger units are randomly sampled, and then smaller units from within the larger units are sampled to provide the final sample. To obtain a multistage cluster sample of zoo animals, you might first randomly sample zoos and then randomly sample animals from within the sampled zoos.

Population: The entire universe of items from which a sample is drawn. The population of books in a library would be defined by every book on the shelf or perhaps every book listed in the electronic catalog.

Random: In science, random means doing something in a *completely* unsystematic and unbiased manner. Being random does not mean being haphazard, but rather it means being *completely* unpredictable. With **random sampling**, there is no way to predict who will be selected for a sample. With **random assignment**, there is no way to predict whether someone will be assigned to group A or group B. Flipping a fair coin is truly, scientifically random. Asking a friend to choose "heads or tails" is not truly scientifically random (people pick "heads" more than they pick "tails").

Random sampling: See **Representative sampling.**

Representative sampling: Sampling in which the goal is to obtain a sample (of people or other objects) that represents some larger population. Often used interchangeably with **random sampling**.

Response rate: The percentage of people (or other units, e.g., schools) that actually generate usable data for a study, relative to the total number that were sampled. If you ask 70 professors to answer your questionnaire and only 35 provide responses, your response rate is 50%.

Sampling error: The natural difference between a sample and the population. A **representative sample** will probably not have exactly the same mean as the population from which it was drawn. This difference is sampling error. The more a sample differs from the population, the greater the sampling error. Larger samples have less sampling error (they are more accurate) than smaller samples. **Multistage cluster samples** have more sampling error than **simple random samples.**

Simple random sampling: A form of representative sampling in which the sample is drawn at **random** from a list of all the people (or other objects) in the population.

Unobtrusive measurement: Measurement performed when the person is unaware that he or she is being measured. A researcher who measures exercise use by checking your entrance and exit times on the gym's computer system is using unobtrusive measurement. A researcher who asks you how often you exercise is not. Unobtrusive measurement has high external validity because it doesn't rely on someone's memory or self-presentation (which might be biased).

Vulnerable populations: Populations that receive additional protection from university **IRBs**—children, prisoners, and people with cognitive impairments, among others. Any group of people whose decision-making ability is seen to be impaired or restricted is treated as a vulnerable population.

Credit

Fig. 9.1: Copyright © by Random.org.

■ CHAPTER 10

Reporting the Research: Comparing Frequencies Using Chi-Square

Remember that Francisco was dealing with the following nondirectional hypothesis:

> H: Girls and boys will differ in whether they have seen "Get Active!" campaign messages.

What would Francisco's *null* hypothesis say?

If the research hypothesis says that girls and boys will differ, then the null hypothesis should say something about girls and boys *not* differing. Wording like "*girls and boys will not differ in whether they have seen 'Get Active!' campaign messages*" or "*there will be no sex differences in whether people have been exposed to 'Get Active!' messages*" would work just fine.

In the following boxes, fill out the name of Francisco's independent and dependent variables, what their levels of measurement are (categorical, ordinal, or interval), and how many levels exist for each. Remember, the levels of a variable reflect what different options/scores someone might have on each variable (e.g., for a measure of political party registration, the options might be Republican, Democrat, or Independent, and thus that variable would have *three* levels).

	Name	Level of Measurement	# of Levels
Independent Variable			
Dependent Variable			

Understanding Francisco's Data

Hopefully, you identified the two variables as sex (girl/boy) and exposure to message (yes/no). As discussed earlier in the book, sometimes "sex" can be more complex than just the two categories of male and female (e.g., transgender, non-binary). For the purposes of illustrating the analysis here, we are just dealing with the two most common categories (male and female). This is, of course, a categorical variable—male and female are categories. The dependent variable is exposure to the message. In Francisco's study, this was measured as a simple yes-no variable, which makes it also a categorical variable. As with sex, there are different ways this could have been measured—e.g., if it had been measured as a total number of exposures, it would have been an interval-level variable. Your table should have looked something like this:

	Name	Level of Measurement	# of Levels
Independent Variable	Sex	Categorical	2
Dependent Variable	Exposure to message	Categorical	2

Remember that Francisco gathered data from 500 school children, and for our purposes, we're going to imagine that he recruited exactly 250 boys and 250 girls. The Google Sheet for this chapter shows you what Francisco's data would look like—and indeed what any data set involving two categorical variables would look like: See the "data" tab at https://bit.ly/2HPvaba.

Each variable has its own column, and each row represents a single person. There are 500 rows of data: Row 1 gives the variable names, so the data go down to row 501. When you first look at the spreadsheet, you will just see a lot of 1's—these are just the boys (boy is coded 1) who didn't see the message (*not* seeing the message is coded 1). If you scroll down, you will start to see different combinations of scores, as summarized in Table 10.1.

TABLE 10.1 Four Possible Combinations of Two Two-Level Categorical Variables

Sex (1 = boy, 2 = girl)	Message Exposure (1 = didn't see it; 2 = did see it)	What combinations of scores represent
1	1	Boys who didn't see the message
1	2	Boys who did see the message
2	1	Girls who didn't see the message
2	2	Girls who did see the message

This data set provides a nice example of why statistical summaries are useful: It is very difficult to scroll down all 500 lines and quickly see what's going on with the data. Alternative ways of looking at the data make the task a lot less taxing and informative, and Francisco will implement some of those techniques in this chapter.

Which Statistical Test to Use?

If Francisco was looking at our earlier statistical decision tree to find out which statistical test to use, he would be frustrated, because it doesn't have an option for a situation with two categorical variables. Never fear—the decision tree is continuing to grow! The latest expanded version is in Figure 10.1.

Which statistical test should Francisco use?

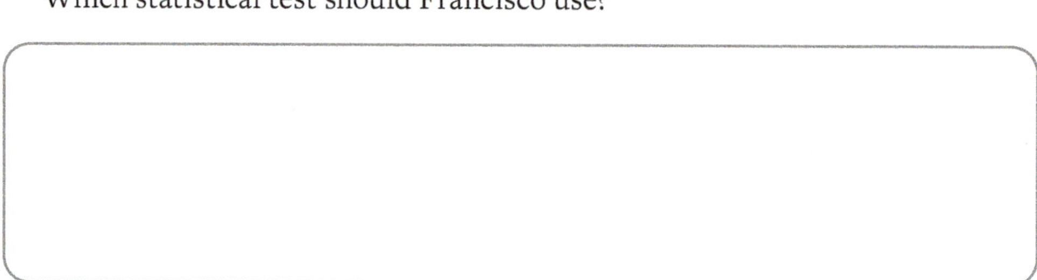

Francisco should start at the left side: His independent variable is categorical and has two categories (levels). The dependent variable is also categorical, and so he will be using the **chi-square test of contingency.** You can see from the decision tree that he would also use the same test if his variables had more than two levels (categories); however, this chapter will only be dealing with the simplest situation: two variables, each with two categories.

The chi-square test follows a fairly logical process of comparing the frequencies *observed* in each cell, relative to the frequencies that would be *expected* in each cell *if the null hypothesis was true* (**observed values** and **expected values**). More details on the calculation process and logic of the test are provided in the "Going Further" section. The observed frequencies are Francisco's data (https://bit.ly/2HPvaba). The Google Sheet's chi-square tab includes a tool for converting the 500 lines of data into a simple 2 × 2 table of frequencies (also displayed in Table 10.2). As is now easy to see, there are 187 boys who didn't see the message (187 rows with scores of "1" in both columns), 153 girls who didn't see the message, 63 boys who did see the message, and 97 girls who did see the message.

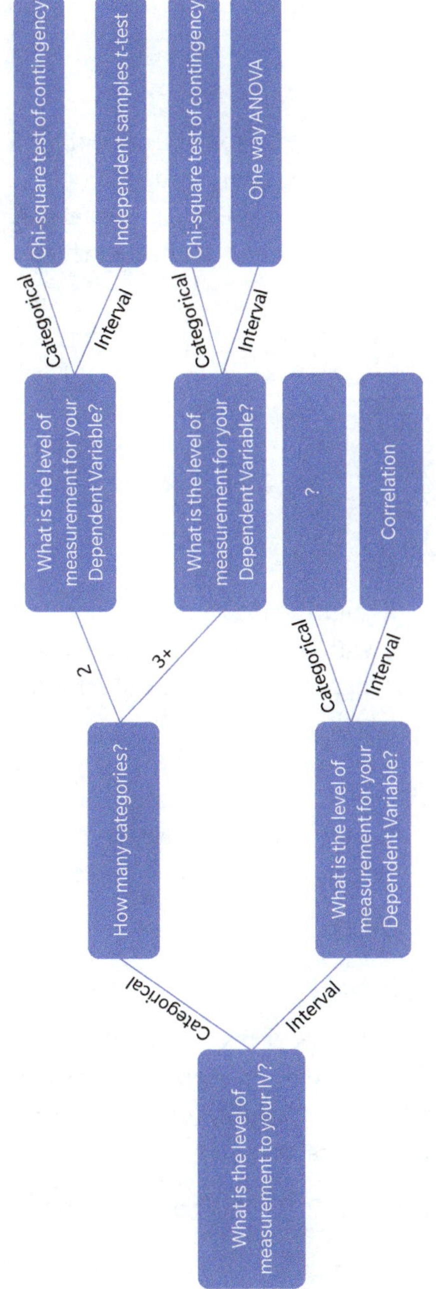

FIGURE 10.1 Statistical decision tree

TABLE 10.2 Observed Frequencies

	Didn't See Message	Did See Message
Boys	187	63
Girls	153	97

Based on this table of frequencies (sometimes called a contingency table), Google Sheets can calculate the chi-square statistic (shown immediately below the table in the Google Sheet). Francisco is most concerned with seeing whether there are any sex differences, and so he looks first at the *p*-value. Is this test statistically significant?

If you thought the test was significant, you'd be correct. The reported *p*-value in the Google Sheet is 0.0011, which is definitely smaller than 0.05, and so $p < .05$, which means that the test is significant. A significant effect in this case means that Francisco can reject the null hypothesis—remember that his null hypothesis was that girls and boys would be equally likely to see the message. The table shows us that 97 out of 250 girls saw the message, but only 63 out of 250 boys saw the message. So girls are significantly more likely to see the message than boys are. The next section describes more about the details of interpreting and writing this effect.

Effect Size and Write-Up

Francisco is almost prepared to report his chi-square statistic. As with previous statistics, he needs to report his degrees of freedom. Degrees of freedom in chi-square are based on the following formula (where rows and columns mean the number of categories for each variable).

$$(\text{\# of rows} - 1) \times (\text{\# of columns} - 1)$$

What are Francisco's degrees of freedom?

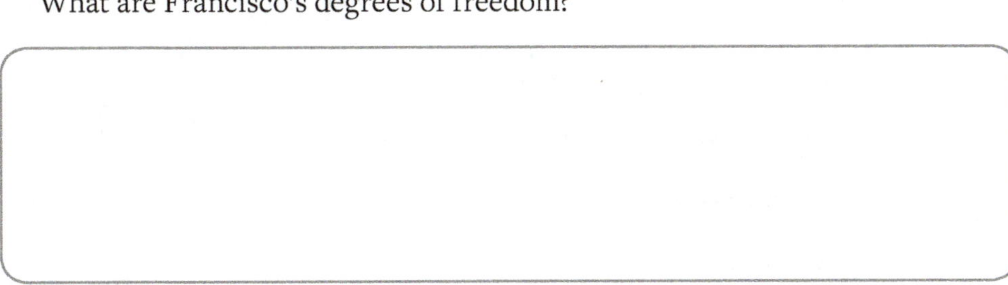

Francisco has two rows in Table 10.2 (boys and girls) and two columns (didn't see and did see). The degrees of freedom are

$$(2 - 1) \times (2 - 1) = 1 \times 1 = 1.$$

In the other statistical tests, we've learned that degrees of freedom are closely related to sample size. That is not the case for chi-square, so when reporting chi-square, Francisco will also need to report his sample size ($N = 500$).

The chi-square statistic is like the *t*-statistic in that you cannot figure out how big the effect is just from looking at the size of the chi-square. To understand the chi-square statistic fully, Francisco will also need an additional statistic called Cramer's *V*. Cramer's *V* is a lot like a correlation coefficient: It can range from 0 to 1, and the bigger it is, the bigger the effect. Rules of thumb for interpreting *V* as an effect size are in Table 10.4. The *V* statistic for Francisco's data is computed automatically in the Google Sheet's chi-square tab (https://bit.ly/2HPvaba).

TABLE 10.3 Interpreting Cramer's *V* as a Measure of Effect Size

Cramer's *V*	Effect
< .10	Very small, perhaps trivial
.10	Small
.30	Medium
.50+	Large

Francisco's write-up will look like this:

> A greater proportion of girls (97/250: 38.8%) than boys (63/250: 25.2%) had seen the "Get Active!" message, χ^2 (1, $N = 500$) = 10.63, $p < .05$, Cramer's $V = .15$.

Details on where all the "bits" of this write-up come from are in Figure 10.2.

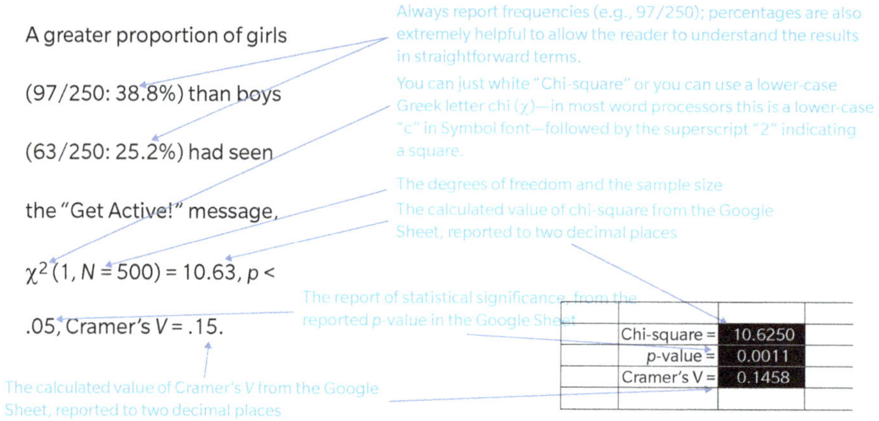

A greater proportion of girls (97/250: 38.8%) than boys (63/250: 25.2%) had seen the "Get Active!" message, $\chi^2(1, N = 500) = 10.63, p <$ .05, Cramer's $V = .15$.

Always report frequencies (e.g., 97/250); percentages are also extremely helpful to allow the reader to understand the results in straightforward terms.

You can just white "Chi-square" or you can use a lower-case Greek letter chi (χ)—in most word processors this is a lower-case "c" in Symbol font—followed by the superscript "2" indicating a square.

The degrees of freedom and the sample size

The calculated value of chi-square from the Google Sheet, reported to two decimal places

The report of statistical significance, from the reported *p*-value in the Google Sheet

The calculated value of Cramer's *V* from the Google Sheet, reported to two decimal places

Chi-square =	10.6250
p-value =	0.0011
Cramer's V =	0.1458

FIGURE 10.2 Translating the Google Sheet into your write-up

A Little More on *p* < .05

Let's do a brief thought experiment. Remember that Francisco found that girls saw messages on social media more than boys, $p < .05$. The p being *less than* .05 means that there's less than a 5% chance of the null hypothesis being true: Francisco can comfortably reject the idea that the boys and girls are the same. Now, imagine that Francisco's study gets some publicity and other health communication researchers around the country start doing research to see if girls see more health messages on social media than boys do. And imagine that in all of those follow-up studies, the researchers find that there's *no* difference between boys and girls—in statistical terms, $p > .05$. Remember, saying that p is greater than .05 means that there's a fairly large (greater than 5%) chance that the null hypothesis is true, so the researchers are not at all comfortable rejecting it. They want to say that boys and girls don't differ. Something weird is happening; it looks like Francisco's findings were perhaps wrong.

Francisco has been wondering about that .05 in $p < .05$ (remember, this is called the alpha level). The statement "$p < .05$" means the null hypothesis is quite unlikely to be true in the larger population. Does this mean that it's *impossible* that the null hypothesis is true?

Yes No

No! If there is a less than a 5% chance that something might be true, that doesn't mean there's a zero chance that it's true. Remember that when we're talking about the null hypothesis, we're talking about what we *think* is the case in the entire population. But Francisco is working only with a *sample* from that population, so there is always some uncertainty in drawing an inference about the population from the sample.

For all the statistical tests that say $p < .05$ and reject the null hypothesis, *some* of them are incorrect: The null hypothesis is actually true. In Francisco's case, he concluded that girls in the population saw the message more than boys ($p < .05$). There is a small chance (less than 5%) that in fact girls and boys (in the population) saw the message an equal amount, in which case, Francisco's conclusion is in error. Given what the other researchers around the country have found, it is looking like Francisco's conclusion was incorrect. Francisco didn't make a mistake, and there's no immediate way for him to tell that there's a problem, but his conclusion about the null hypothesis was in error. This type of error is called a **Type 1 error**: Francisco has *rejected the null hypothesis, even though it is actually true.*

While Francisco can't know right away that his research may have involved a Type 1 error, he learns about it from the subsequent research. As more studies roll in showing no differences between boys and girls, perhaps even Francisco himself decides to do another study on the topic and finds out that there is no sex difference in his second study. This reveals the power and importance of scientific **replication**. Replication is the process of redoing a study to check the findings. Through replicating their own and others' work, scientists find cases where the original findings don't seem to replicate; those situations often uncover that an original study might have included a Type 1 error.

You might also find out about a Type 1 error if the research led to some sort of program or intervention in society. Imagine that a researcher did a high-quality scientific study showing that banning baseball caps from schools eliminated bullying. What might schools do in response to that sort of study?

You probably figured out that some schools might decide to ban baseball caps. Now, what if those schools then observed that just as much bullying was going on as before the cap ban. So, the cap ban had no effect on bullying? What would the schools say about the original study?

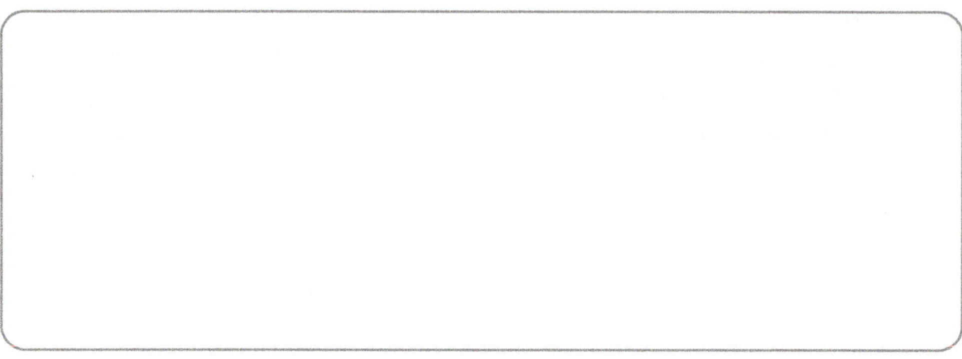

They'd probably just say that it was wrong. But, as noted earlier, it was a well-done scientific research study—it wasn't wrong in the sense of being inaccurate or biased. It was just wrong in the sense that the researcher got unlucky and the data involved a Type 1 error. We only find that out when future research can't replicate the results or when interventions based on a study just don't work.

KEY POINT

Type 1 errors (*falsely rejecting the null hypothesis*) are inevitable when using standard statistical hypothesis testing procedures. We typically find out about them when subsequent studies fail to replicate an effect or when an intervention based on a research study fails.

You can, of course, reduce your chances of a Type 1 error by changing the alpha level. If you set alpha at .01, then everything described earlier will have a reduced likelihood of occurring: If the null hypothesis was true, you would only incorrectly reject it 1% of the time. However, there is a price to pay for this, as elaborated next.

If you're thinking that the term "Type 1 error" suggests that there might be a Type 2 error, you'd be correct. A **Type 2 error** occurs when a researcher *does not* reject the null hypothesis (the researcher says that $p > .05$), but in the population, the null hypothesis is actually false.

Imagine that Francisco had concluded based on his data that there is *no* difference between boys and girls in their exposure to social media messages but subsequently large numbers of researchers found that, in fact, there *is*. That situation would suggest that Francisco committed a Type 2 error—again, replication can help to uncover this type of error.

Type 2 errors are more likely with studies involving small samples and studies examining small effect sizes. Having a large sample size in a social science study is a bit like having a really powerful telescope for an astronomer. You can see more detail, and you are more likely to find effects (if they exist) with a large sample size; this means that you are less likely to make a Type 2 error. This point reflects the important concept of **statistical power**: Statistics have more power if they are better able to reject a null hypothesis correctly. Large samples provide more statistical power.

Sample size doesn't change your chances of making a Type 1 error. Type 2 errors are more likely to occur if you set your alpha level lower—this is the "price to pay" mentioned earlier. If you set alpha at .01, you are *less* likely to make a Type 1 error, but *more* likely to make a Type 2 error.

Type 1 and Type 2 errors. Type 1 errors involve falsely rejecting a null hypothesis—saying that there is an effect (a difference, a correlation) when in fact there isn't. Type 2 errors involve falsely saying a null hypothesis is true—saying there is ***no*** difference or correlation when in fact there *is*. Type 1 errors occur naturally, and there is no way to completely avoid them. Type 2 errors are more common when sample sizes are low and when research examines small effect sizes. The differences between the two types of errors are summarized in Table 10.4.

TABLE 10.4 **Summary of Type 1 and Type 2 Errors**

	In reality, the null hypothesis is true (there really is NO effect in the population as a whole).	**In reality, the null hypothesis is false (there really IS an effect in the population as a whole).**
The statistical test says to reject null ($p < .05$)	***Type 1 error***—Null is rejected even though it is true.	***Correct decision***—The null hypothesis is rejected when it is false.
Statistical test says not to reject null ($p > .05$)	***Correct decision***—The null hypothesis is not rejected, and it is actually true.	***Type 2 error***—The null hypothesis is not rejected, even though it is false.

Look at the scenarios in the response box that follows and decide whether a Type 1 error or a Type 2 error has happened. In some cases, no error has occurred. The answers appear afterward in Table 10.5. When looking at these, remember that, of course, a researcher doesn't know the "in reality" part: We're briefly imagining that we are omniscient! If you already know definitively whether something is true, you don't need to do research!

Situation	Type of Error (Type 1, Type 2, or No Error)
In reality, doing crosswords doesn't affect people's spelling. Your study finds no difference in spelling ability when people do (vs. don't do) crosswords.	
You do a study and find a statistical difference in IQ between a group of men and a group of women. In reality, men and women don't differ in terms of intelligence.	
In reality, there's no such thing as a psychic. You do a study and determine that a group of self-described psychics have "special powers" compared to regular people.	
Your study says that watching *Sesame Street* doesn't help kids learn to read. In reality, it does.	
In reality, playing violent video games makes people more aggressive. In your study, you statistically find that 30 minutes of *Halo* results in people behaving more aggressively.	

TABLE 10.5 Answers to Response Box Above

Situation	Type of Error (Type 1, Type 2, or No Error)
In reality, doing crosswords doesn't affect people's spelling. Your study finds no difference in spelling ability when people do (vs. don't do) crosswords.	There is no error here. Crosswords have no effect in reality (null hypothesis true), and the study concludes that there's no effect ($p > .05$).
You do a study and find a statistical difference in IQ between a group of men and a group of women. In reality, men and women don't differ in terms of intelligence.	This is a Type 1 error. In reality, there is no effect, but the study says that there is ($p < .05$). Subsequent studies finding no difference will probably emerge, and this research finding will be revealed as an error.
In reality, there's no such thing as a psychic. You do a study and determine that a group of self-described psychics have "special powers" compared to regular people.	This is also a Type 1 error. There is no difference between psychics and regular people in terms of their "powers" (the null hypothesis is true), but the research says there is a difference. Again, replication should uncover the error.

continues on next page

continues from previous page

Situation	Type of Error (Type 1, Type 2, or No Error)
Your study says that watching *Sesame Street* doesn't help kids learn to read. In reality, it does.	This is a Type 2 error. Your study is saying that the show has no effect ($p > .05$); you're saying that the null hypothesis is true. But, in fact, the null hypothesis is false, and the show really does have effects. Possibly, you did the study with a rather small sample size.
In reality, playing violent video games makes people more aggressive. In your study, you statistically find that 30 minutes of *Halo* results in people behaving more aggressively.	There is no error here. Your study shows what we know to be true for the population. You are rejecting the null hypothesis, and the null hypothesis is indeed false.

Visualizing Categorical Data

Along with reporting the statistics, providing a visual to illustrate the findings can be very helpful. A stacked column chart (see Figure 10.3) is one simple and informative technique for representing categorical data. As you can see, the height of each column represents all of the respondents of one sex, and the shading within the bar represents the proportion that did (or did not) see the message. It is immediately clear from the visual not only that more girls saw the message but also *how many more*. This provides a clear visual of the size of the difference between the two groups. You can create a stacked column chart in Google Sheets by highlighting the table of frequencies (including the row and column labels) and selecting "Insert-Chart-Stacked Column Chart." See the "Visualizing" tab in this section's Google Sheet (https://bit.ly/2HPvaba) for details.

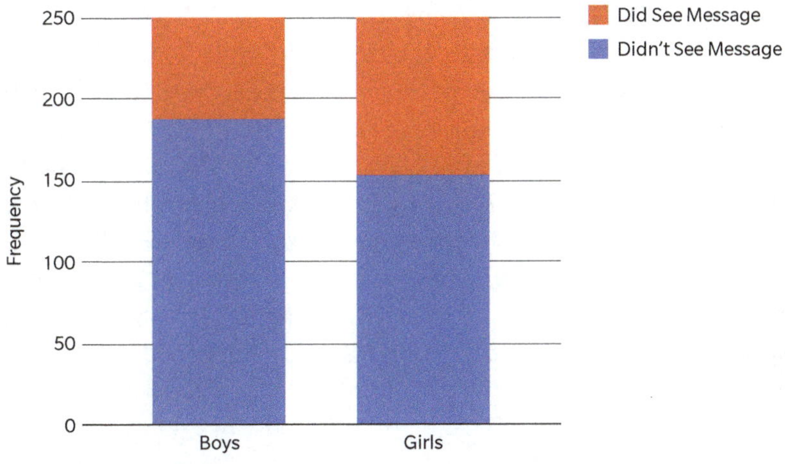

FIGURE 10.3 A stacked column chart

Confidence Intervals

You will remember that earlier in the book we looked at **confidence intervals**—ways of estimating a range within which the true population value of a statistic probably lies. The same thing is possible with the categorical data we are dealing with in this chapter. Two pieces of information will help you understand the process Francisco is going to use here.

1. Calculating confidence intervals for frequencies relies on using proportions. A proportion is just like a percentage but expressed out of "1" instead of out of "100." A proportion of .46 is identical to 46%.

2. The confidence interval is calculated around a single frequency. So, while Francisco had certain numbers of girls (and boys) who *saw* the message and certain numbers of girls (and boys) who *didn't* see the message, the confidence interval just focuses on one of those numbers. Francisco is more interested in the number of participants who saw the message, so we're going to focus on that.

Before reading on, think briefly about the girls in Francisco's study. In total, 38.8% of them had seen the "Get Active!" message. If you had to guess the likely range within which the population value lies, what would you guess? Think about a range of percentages *around* 38.8%.

In the Google Sheet's "Confidence Interval" tab (https://bit.ly/2HPvaba), Francisco can see that 97 girls saw the message (pink cell), out of a total of 250. This is equal to 38.8% of the girls, or a proportion of .388 (97/250). That proportion is calculated in the red highlighted cell. To the right of the red highlighted cell is the 95% confidence interval: (.3276, .4484). In percentage terms, this means that Francisco is 95% sure (his confidence level) that between 32.76% and 44.84% (confidence interval) of girls in the entire population would have seen the message. Notice that this is a range spread *around* the actual sample number of 38.8%. How close was your estimate to this range? This confidence interval is illustrated in Figure 10.4.

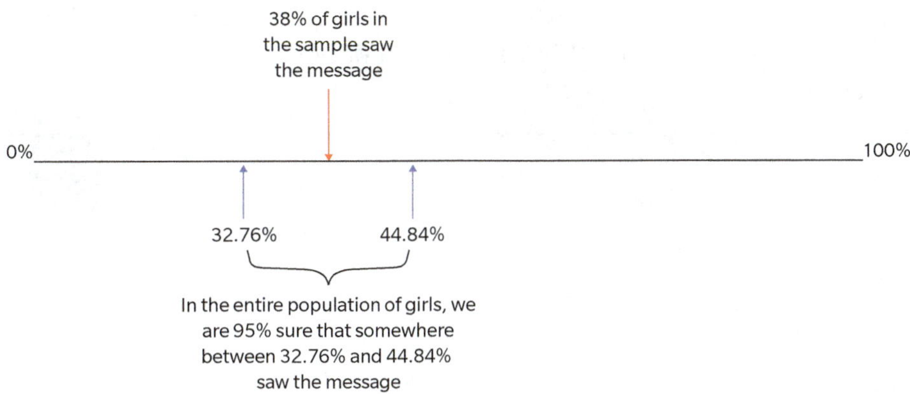

FIGURE 10.4 Confidence interval for number of girls in the population exposed to the message

Can you identify the confidence interval for boys?

The same calculation for boys indicates that between 19.82% and 30.58% of boys saw the message; and, again, because this is a 95% confidence interval, Francisco can say that he is 95% sure that the true population number is somewhere in that range.

Confidence intervals are useful with categorical data because they give you a very clear idea of how much potential "wiggle room" there is in a particular number. Imagine you are gauging customer satisfaction with a customer service chatline. Perhaps you find that 62% of customers say they are satisfied. Your interpretation of that number might change dramatically in the following two scenarios:

a) The 95% confidence interval falls between 60% and 64%.

b) The 95% confidence interval falls between 32% and 92%.

In scenario (a), you know that the true population number really is pretty close to 62%, and you can decide whether that's a good enough level of satisfaction for your business. In the second scenario, the confidence interval is telling you that you actually have almost no idea what the actual population value is—knowing that it could be anywhere between 32% and 92% is only a little better than knowing it could be between 0% and 100% (which, of course, you know without bothering to gather any data!). Given what you have learned about **sampling error** and what makes samples more accurate, what do you think might explain the difference between scenario (a) and (b)? What might make one of these confidence intervals bigger or smaller?

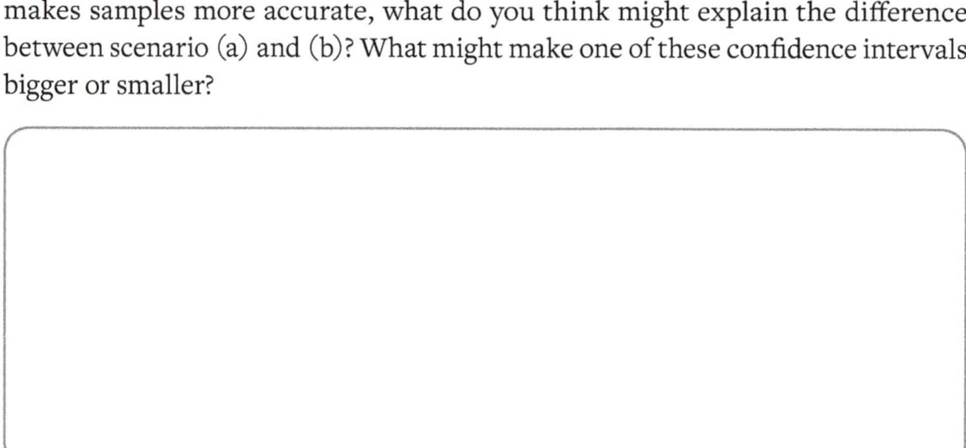

If you responded with something concerning the size of the sample or the number of people in the research study, you would be correct. Larger samples have less sampling error, which means that they are more accurate. More accurate samples allow you to be more confident in estimating the true population value, which makes confidence intervals narrower. Scenario (a) would have had a much larger sample than Scenario (b).

Writing the Report

Francisco's report (Report 10.1) is now just a question of combining the pieces we have already covered. People often omit the confidence intervals in this sort of report, although they are quite important for the reasons outlined earlier. The local health agency for which Francisco is working is interested in message exposure in the entire population, not just in one sample. The confidence interval provides more information about that.

REPORT 10.1 Results of Chi-Square Analysis

A greater proportion of girls (97/250: 38.8%) than boys (63/250: 25.2%) had seen the "Get Active!" message, χ^2 (1, N = 500) = 10.63, $p < .05$, Cramer's V = .15. The 95% confidence intervals indicate that the true population value of exposure for girls is between 32.76% and 44.84%, while for boys, it is between 19.82% and 30.58%. The results are graphically represented in Figure 1.

continues on next page

continues from previous page

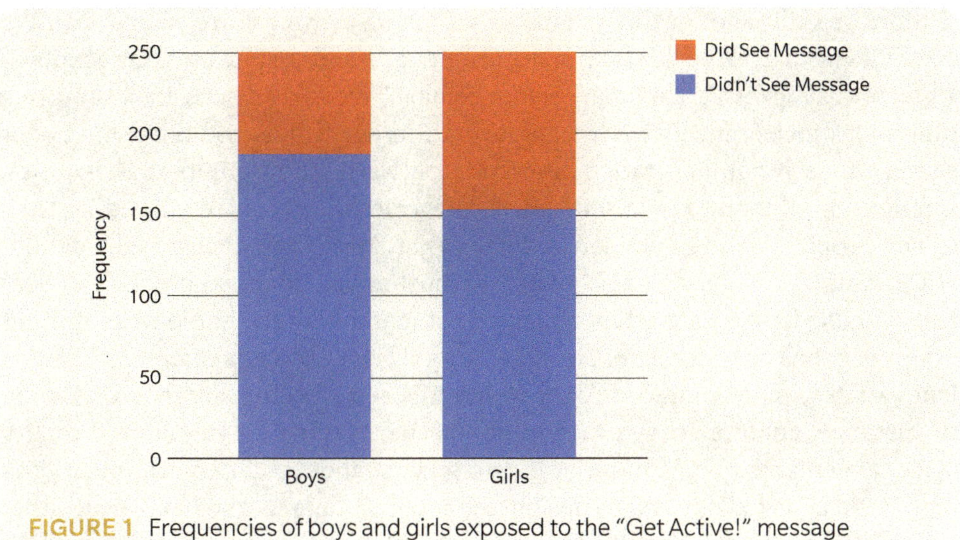

FIGURE 1 Frequencies of boys and girls exposed to the "Get Active!" message

Other Applications

The confidence intervals discussed in this chapter are things you encounter in the news on a fairly regular basis. They are the core of a lot of political polling. For instance, a 2018 poll by the Gallup organization that received widespread news coverage indicated that 37% of U.S. voters believed that President Trump deserved to be reelected (https://bit.ly/2KaEWG7). Based on a sample of about 1,300 registered U.S. voters, this poll had a "margin of error" of "plus or minus 3%." That 3% represents the 95% confidence interval. It says that the true value in the population is somewhere between 3% *below* 37% (i.e., 34%) and 3% above 37% (i.e., 40%). In other words, it is saying that in the population, somewhere between 34% and 40% of voters believed that Trump deserved reelection at that point in time. This is illustrated in Figure 10.5.

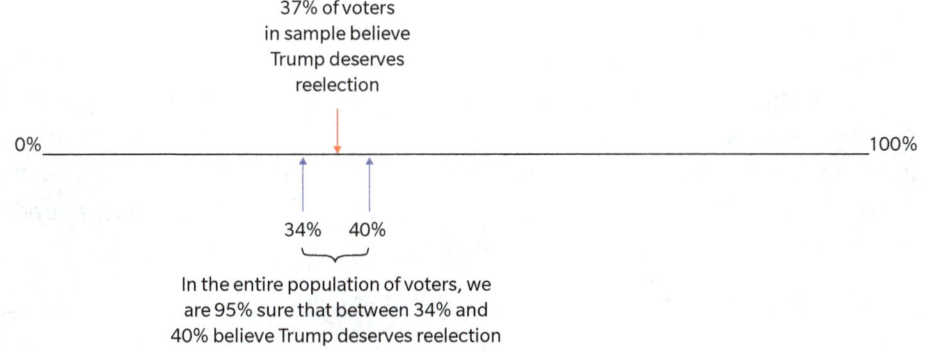

FIGURE 10.5 Voters believing Trump deserves reelection

More broadly, a lot of the variables that interest us most are categorical. We are endlessly fascinated by sex and sex differences, and despite growing acknowledgment that sex isn't just "male versus female," most lay discussions about sex differences focus on those two categories. Similar things could be said about examinations of communication differences between ethnic groups, nationalities, or religions. All tend to be discussed as categories ("Are Italians friendlier than French people?"), and so chi-square analyses are needed to analyze such data.

Categorical variables are also central to most experiments, where the independent variable is represented by some sort of manipulation that leaves different groups of people in different experimental conditions. Add in a categorical dependent variable, and you need the sort of analysis described in this chapter. Think, for instance, about a study examining whether playing an augmented reality (AR) game makes people more or less observant about their environment. You might send people out to walk a designated route on campus and have them either play Pokémon GO (AR condition) or just walk the route without doing anything else. Somewhere on the route, you place a colorful soccer ball in a clearly visible location, and on their return, you ask the participants whether they saw any sporting equipment. Those who correctly remember the soccer ball are scored as being "observant." Example data for this experiment are shown in the "Additional Example" tab of the Google Sheet (https://bit.ly/2HPvaba). You can see that the structure reflects Francisco's study almost exactly, even though the study itself is completely unrelated.

Your Turn

You already have one categorical variable with two levels as part of your ongoing project—the independent variable from Chapter 6's "Your Turn" section. Go back to that section and remind yourself of that variable (it may help to also look at the "Your Turn" section in Chapter 5). What is the variable?

Independent variable: ______________________________

For the current section, think about a *categorical* variable with two levels that you might use as a dependent variable. This might be a simple measure of whether someone engages in a behavior or not, gives a "yes" versus a "no" response to a question, or chooses X or Y. Think about the example from earlier where we measured whether someone noticed a soccer ball or didn't notice it. Think of a variable with this sort of structure that you think is influenced by your independent variable. Give that variable a name here.

Dependent variable: ______________________________

To check that this is set up correctly, make sure that you can organize your independent and dependent variable into a 2 × 2 grid as shown next:

		Dependent variable	
		Category 1	Category 2
Independent variable	Category 1		
	Category 2		

Reproduce this table, entering your variable names and category labels in the following grid:

Using this as your template, either gather data from classmates or make up data, do the chi-square analysis using Google Sheets, and write up your analysis like Francisco did.

Wrap Up

In this chapter, you have learned how to calculate a chi-square statistic in Google Sheets by applying the statistic to understanding the relationship between two categorical variables. You have learned how to calculate the appropriate measure of **effect size** for this analysis and how to represent it graphically. You have also learned how to calculate confidence intervals for frequencies and how to write up this analysis. In addition, you have learned the difference between Type 1 and Type 2 errors in the statistical hypothesis testing process.

If you get nothing else from this chapter, remember the following:

1. The chi-square test is used to analyze categorical data.
2. Cramer's *V* is the appropriate measure of effect size for a chi-square.
3. Type 1 errors occur when research incorrectly rejects the null hypothesis (says that there *is* an effect but, in reality, there is not). Type 2 errors occur when research incorrectly *accepts* the null hypothesis (incorrectly says there is no effect when in reality there is).

Key Chapter Concepts

Chi-square (χ^2) analysis: The most basic method for analyzing associations between categorical variables. The chi-square statistic gets bigger as differences between **observed values** and **expected values** get larger.

Expected values: The frequencies you would see in any particular "cell" in a research design *if the null hypothesis were true*. Imagine studying a potential association between subscribing to Netflix and subscribing to cable. If there is no association between those two variables, then you would *expect* to see that the proportion of Netflix subscribers among cable subscribers is roughly the same as the number of Netflix subscribers among those who don't have cable TV. More details on expected values are provided in the "Going Further" section. See also **observed values, chi-square statistic.**

Observed values: The frequencies in any particular "cell" in a research design. Imagine studying a potential association between subscribing to Netflix (yes/no) and subscribing to cable TV (yes/no). If your data included 52 people who subscribe to Netflix but don't subscribe to cable, then 52 is the observed value in that cell. See also **Expected values, Chi-square statistic.**

Statistical power: The chance of correctly rejecting a null hypothesis, statistical power is essentially the opposite of **Type 2 error.** The more statistical power you have, the less likely you are to commit a Type 2 error. The simplest way to increase statistical power is to increase sample size—have large numbers of people in your study. See also **Type 2 error.**

Type 1 error: Incorrectly rejecting the null hypothesis. A researcher's data indicate an association between reading romance novels and having a good sex life. In the population as a whole, however, there's *no* association between those two things. This researcher has committed a Type 1 error. See also **Type 2 error.**

Type 2 error: Incorrectly accepting the null hypothesis. A researcher's data indicate *no* association between reading romance novels and having a good sex life. In the population as a whole, however, there *is* an association between those two things. This researcher has committed a Type 2 error. See also **Statistical power** and **Type 1 error.**

Section Wrap

Section Summary

This section has discussed a form of representative sampling—multistage cluster sampling—which is useful when a list of the entire population isn't available. It describes the process of randomly sampling units in which members of the population are contained and then sampling the population members from within those units. The section also describes special protections for certain populations (including children) when doing research with them and more broadly the importance of seeking participants' permission for their involvement in research. The second chapter in the section describes the chi-square (χ^2) statistic as a commonly used way of testing hypotheses with categorical data. It also describes Type 1 and Type 2 errors as issues in the statistical hypothesis testing process.

Going Further

There are two subsections in this "Going Further" section. The first provides a little more detail on how the "expected" frequencies in the chi-square statistic are calculated. The second provides more detail on some other methods of sampling, including nonrepresentative sampling.

Expected frequencies in the chi-square calculation. The expected frequencies are the frequencies we would expect to see if the null hypothesis were true. That doesn't necessarily mean that there will be equal "expected" frequencies in each cell. It means that the expected frequencies will reflect the column and row *totals*.

Francisco had equal numbers of boys and girls in his study (250 of each, see the row totals in Table 10.6).

TABLE 10.6 Observed Frequencies

	Didn't See Message	Did See Message	TOTAL
Boys	187	63	250
Girls	153	97	250
TOTAL:	340	160	**500**

So, the expected frequencies should have an equal number of boys and girls within each column. However, more people *didn't* see the message (340) than *did* see it (160)—see the column totals in Table 10.6 or the Google Sheet's "chi-square" tab (https://bit.ly/2HPvaba). So, the expected frequencies under the null hypothesis should reflect more people *not* seeing the message than seeing it in the same ratio as in the overall data.

The expected frequencies should, therefore, reflect equal numbers of boys and girls, and more people *not* seeing the message versus seeing it. Table 10.7 shows what these expected frequencies should look like.

TABLE 10.7 Expected Frequencies

	Didn't See Message	Did See Message	TOTAL
Boys	170	80	250
Girls	170	80	250
TOTAL:	340	160	**500**

You can see that the pattern of the row and column totals in Table 10.6 is reflected in the cell values in Table 10.7—higher expected values for "didn't see the message" than "did see the message" and equal numbers of boys and girls. Thus these reflect the pattern you would expect if the row and column totals stayed the same, but there was no difference between boys and girls in their likelihood of seeing the message.

Calculating the expected frequencies in Table 10.7 is pretty straightforward if you want to do it by hand. The formula is just

(Row Total * Column Total) / Grand Total.

So, for the top left cell, the calculation is

(250 * 340) / 500 = 170.

How would you calculate the expected value for girls who did see the message?

For girls who did see the message, your calculation should have been (250 * 160) / 500 = 80.

The chi-square calculation then involves comparing the observed versus expected values. The bigger the differences between the observed data and the null hypothesis ("expected") data, the bigger the chi-square statistic and the more likely it is that Francisco will reject the null hypothesis. Each difference between an observed and expected value reflects some way in which boys or girls are more or less likely to have seen the message than would be expected just based on how much people in general saw the message.

Sampling. So far, the book has talked about **simple random sampling** (drawing people at random from a list of the entire population) and **multistage cluster sampling** (drawing larger units at random from a population of units and then drawing people at random from within those larger units). These are types of representative (or random) sampling. There is one additional form of representative sampling that it is good to be familiar with. **Stratified sampling** is used when researchers are particularly concerned about representing subsections of a population accurately relative to their presence in the population. For instance, if you wanted a random sample of communication undergraduates from a particular college, you might want to consider the fact that these undergrads tend to skew female. At my university right now, our undergraduate population is about 68% female. If I used a simple random sample from that population, it would probably be close to 68% female, but not exactly that number (because of sampling error). I could, however, intentionally create a sample that was *exactly* 68% female. I would do this by separating my list of all the communication undergraduates into two lists: one of all the women and one of all the men. If I were drawing a sample of 100 students, I'd then draw exactly 68 names (at random, of course) from the list of women and 32 names from the list of men.

Stratified sampling is useful because it reduces sampling error for the overall sample. With stratified sampling, one source of error (in our example, error associated with the sample not perfectly representing the population in terms of sex) is completely removed. The sample is "perfect" in terms of its gender composition. This is the benefit of this form of sampling. Can you think of one potential cost, or limitation, or problem with stratified sampling?

Stratified sampling is a strong form of sampling and doesn't have many limitations—so if you had trouble thinking of an answer, that's OK! The main reason why people *don't* always use stratified sampling is simply a logistical one. It's not often the case that you have access to a list of the entire population that includes a relevant stratifying "factor." In the earlier example, I would need to find a list of all communication majors at my school that *included* whether they were male or female. Maybe I could do that somewhere in the student records system, or maybe not. With larger populations, it becomes increasingly difficult: Getting a list of all registered voters that included their sex would start to become very complicated.

Sex, of course, is not the only variable that you can use to stratify populations. Can you think of two others?

Pretty much any categorical variable might be used to stratify a sample: I have seen samples stratified by race, religion, sexuality, political affiliation, and even things like whether people attended college or not. Most of the time, the extra effort required to stratify means it is only done when the research topic and the stratifying variable are connected (e.g., stratifying by political affiliation in a study of politics, stratifying by sex or sexuality in a study of sexual attitudes).

You now know a little about three forms of representative or random sampling: simple random sampling, multistage cluster sampling, and stratified sampling (Table 10.8).

TABLE 10.8 Types of Representative and Nonrepresentative Sample

	Description	Advantages	Disadvantages
Representative (Random) Samples	All representative samples involve objects (typically people) being drawn at random from a population.	Ability to generalize to a population	Time-consuming, expensive, logistically challenging

continues on next page

continues from previous page

	Description	Advantages	Disadvantages
Simple Random Sample	Objects in the sample are randomly chosen from a list of the entire population.	The simplest (easiest, cheapest) form of representative sampling	Requires a list of the entire population
Multistage Cluster Sample	Objects in the sample are randomly chosen from higher level units (schools, organizations, etc.), which are themselves randomly chosen from a population of all such higher level units.	Useful when a list of the entire population isn't available	Complicated multistage process. Subject to higher levels of sampling error
Stratified Sample	The population is divided (stratified) according to some categorical distinction (e.g., sex, race). Objects are randomly chosen from within those categories to achieve a sample that perfectly represents the population composition on that dimension.	Low levels of sampling error	Requires a list of everyone in the population, along with information about all those people on the stratifying variable (e.g., knowing their sex)
Nonrepresentative (Nonrandom) Samples	Nonrepresentative samples involve objects (typically people) being drawn in some manner other than truly random.	Easy, cheap, quick	Cannot generalize to a population—subject to ***sampling bias***
Convenience Sample	Any sample of objects that is available to the researcher to use (e.g., a class of students, passersby at a particular location).	Very easy to obtain	Cannot generalize to population, convenience samples may be unusual (e.g., a group of college students is, pretty much by definition, more educated than the population as a whole)

continues on next page

continues from previous page

	Description	Advantages	Disadvantages
Quota Sample	The nonrepresentative version of a stratified sample: a convenience sample with a pre-determined demographic makeup; a *non-random* sample of 67% female and 33% male undergraduates from a communication major would be a quota sample.	Easy to obtain, may represent the population on at least one dimension (e.g., having the same breakdown by sex)	Requires some knowledge of the population to match sample characteristics to population characteristics. Still doesn't permit generalization to population
Purposive Sample	A sample where the goal is to study a very specific group of people with unique knowledge or experience. If your research question asks about security officers in school environments, you will need to intentionally target those people in your sampling.	Necessary when the target group has unique knowledge, or the research question asks specifically about that type of person	Limits results to members of that group. Doesn't permit generalization to the population. Easy to end up with a certain subtype of person—e.g., those who are more willing to disclose their membership in the group of interest).
Snowball Sample	A sample obtained by contacting a small number of people belonging to a specific population and asking them to refer you to other people also in that population (e.g., asking U.S. military veterans to connect you to other veterans).	Good way to find groups of people who might otherwise be hard to reach, efficient (uses research subjects to also help with recruitment)	May result in samples that are very similar to one another. For example, if a veteran refers you to another veteran, the second veteran may be similar to the first given that they are friends. Doesn't permit generalization to the population

As has been noted a couple of times already, not all research needs a random sample, and many research studies are done without random samples. If you want to study whether taking away people's phones causes them to experience psychological distress, then there is very little reason to go to the trouble of drawing a random sample from the population to do the study. Any sample of people who use phones would be sufficient for you to demonstrate that the effect exists, which is your primary goal. There are different types of nonrandom samples, which are summarized in Table 10.8, along with the representative samples already discussed.

Using the information provided earlier, try to identify what sort of sample is being recruited in the scenarios in Table 10.9 (the answers are in Table 10.10).

TABLE 10.9 Identifying Types of Sample

Example	Type of Sample
1. I sample a group of 5-year-old kids at my local park (after asking their parents, of course).	
2. I stand in the mall and pick the first 50 men and 50 women who pass by.	
3. The Bakersville University student population is 78% undergraduate and 22% graduate students. I randomly sample exactly 78% undergrads and 22% grads from the student population.	
4. I randomly sample bars from all the bars in the downtown area and then randomly sample people from within each of the sampled bars.	
5. I visit a local support group for opioid addicts and ask them to participate in my research. In addition, I ask them to help me recruit their friends who are also addicts.	
6. I randomly sample television shows from a list of all major network and cable channels and then randomly sample individual episodes of those shows from their entire seasons.	

TABLE 10.10

Answers
1. This is a convenience sample: I am just using my local park (convenient), and I am not using any form of random sampling.
2. This is also a nonrandom sample: The fact that I'm specifically attempting to get equal numbers of men and women suggests this is a quota sample. I am trying to match the population on one dimension.
3. This is a random sample of some sort: That I am attempting to make my sample perfectly match the population on one specific characteristic (undergrad versus grad) indicates that this is a stratified sample.

continues on next page

continues from previous page

4. This is another random sample: The sequential process of randomly sampling bars and then randomly sampling from within bars tells you that this is a multistage cluster sample.

5. This is a classic snowball sample: There is no attempt at random sampling, and I'm getting my respondents to help me recruit other people who share their specific characteristics.

6. This is another multistage cluster sample: This one illustrates that it's not always people who we are sampling. In this case, we want a representative sample of television episodes, and we can achieve that by sampling shows and then sampling episodes from within the selected shows' seasons.

SECTION 6

Factorial Design: Are Older or Younger People More Judgmental About a Politician Appearing on BuzzFeed?

By the end of this section, you will be able to:

- ✔ Identify a factorial design
- ✔ Distinguish between main effects and interaction effects
- ✔ Be able to determine whether a particular set of results might include an interaction effect and be able to graph the means from a factorial design
- ✔ Be able to write hypotheses reflecting main effects and interaction effects
- ✔ Be able to perform and write up a factorial ANOVA analysis

CHAPTER 11

Doing the Research: Factorial Design

Remember Andre from Section 3? He's back! In Section 3, we learned that Andre was interested in whether a political candidate was perceived as less credible if the candidate appeared on BuzzFeed. He ran an experiment, manipulating whether a video of the candidate was identified as coming from BuzzFeed and then measured perceptions of the candidate's credibility. Surprisingly, he found that a candidate appearing on BuzzFeed was actually seen as *more* credible than a candidate appearing on a video that wasn't identified as being from BuzzFeed.

As you can imagine, his campaign office was pretty interested in this effect. Is it really true that they can create positive perceptions of their candidate just by having her appear on an online news platform? They have asked Andre to investigate more. In thinking about the effect, Andre starts to wonder whether age might play a role. Younger people are accustomed to getting their news from a variety of online platforms rather than just traditional news outlets, and young people might, therefore, view a platform like BuzzFeed as a credible source. They might even view a candidate appearing on BuzzFeed as being more "in touch" with their generation. On the other hand, older people might not have heard of BuzzFeed or might discount its credibility relative to "real" journalism.

Let's reframe Andre's idea in terms of variables. First, remember the original issue he was interested in: whether exposure to a BuzzFeed video (relative to a control) changes perceptions of candidate credibility. What were the original independent and dependent variables for this question?

Independent variable: ______________________________

Dependent variable: ______________________________

If you are following (or remembering!) correctly, then you should have identified that exposure to the BuzzFeed video (versus control) was the independent variable, and the credibility of the candidate was the dependent variable.

Andre's new idea introduces *another* variable—the age of the respondent. He is saying that the association between exposure to the BuzzFeed video and candidate credibility *changes* depending on the respondent's age. When the respondent is young, the effect of BuzzFeed on credibility is positive, but when the respondent is old, the effect of BuzzFeed on credibility may be negative or perhaps neutral. These kinds of "it depends" issues are examined using what is called a **factorial design**.

Factorial Design

Andre's new variable—age—can be considered another independent variable in his experiment. Nothing in the experiment could *influence* the respondents' ages, so age cannot be a dependent variable. This research study now has *two independent variables:*

1. Exposure to the BuzzFeed video
2. Age

And the research also, of course, has a dependent variable (credibility). This is what defines a factorial design: A factorial design occurs when a research study involves more than one categorical independent variable influencing a dependent variable.

Continuous versus categorical variables revisited

To keep things simple, Andre is treating age as a categorical variable with just two categories (younger and older). Of course, age is actually an interval-level variable, and most researchers would want to keep it that way. However, converting an interval-level variable to a categorical variable (high/low, young/old, above/below average) can be helpful in some situations. In Andre's case, as will become clearer here, having just two categories for age will make interpreting his effects a lot easier.

Figure 11.1 shows this in its simplest form: Each of the independent variables is thought to affect the dependent variable.

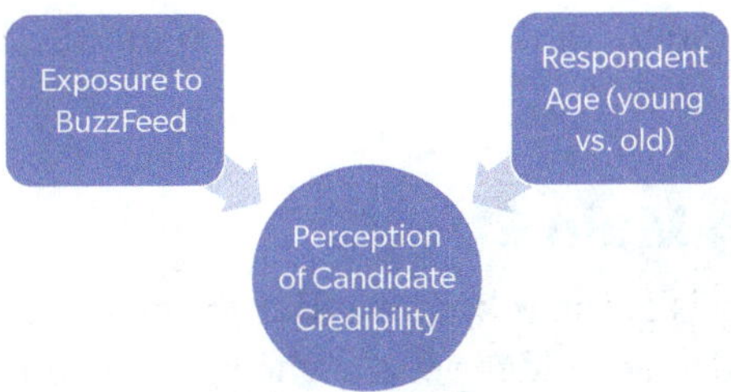

FIGURE 11.1 Andre's independent and dependent variables

However, Figure 11.1 doesn't reflect Andre's idea. The two arrows in this illustration might reflect questions like the following:

- **Question 1:** Do people who see a BuzzFeed video evaluate a candidate as more (or less) credible than people who see a control video?
- **Question 2:** Do young people evaluate a candidate as more (or less) credible than older people?

These are interesting questions, but they are not what Andre was interested in. He was interested in whether the answer to Question 1 *depends on* the other independent variable (age). So, there is actually a third question here:

- **Question 3:** Does the effect of being exposed to a BuzzFeed video on perceptions of candidate credibility *depend on* respondent age?

This is illustrated in Figure 11.2 by the "Exposure to BuzzFeed × Respondent age" box.

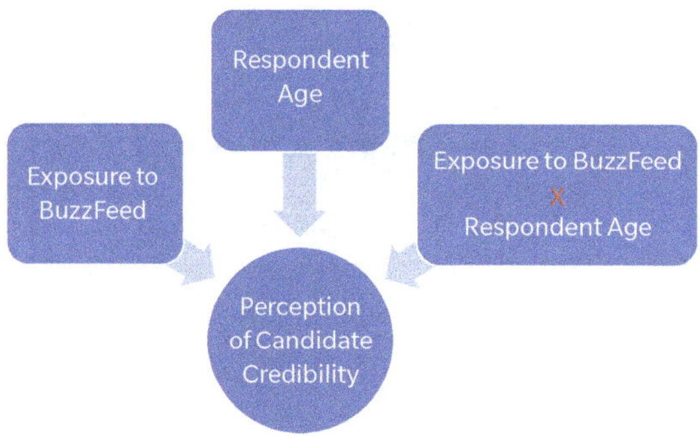

FIGURE 11.2 Andre's independent and dependent variables incorporating the interaction effect

The first two questions represent what we will call **main effects** questions. The third question reflects what we will call an **interaction effect**. In a factorial design like the one here, we will be considering two main effects and one interaction effect. It is easiest to understand main effects and interaction effects by looking at some examples.

Understanding Main Effects

Andre's research study is going to involve four groups of people: younger people who view the BuzzFeed video, older people who view the BuzzFeed video, younger people who view the control video, and older people who view the control video. You can see these groups organized in Figure 11.3.

	Control	BuzzFeed
Younger	Younger people who view the control video	Younger people who view the BuzzFeed video
Older	Older people who view the control video	Older people who view the BuzzFeed video

FIGURE 11.3 Groups of people in a factorial design

If you can imagine doing the study, you would end up with scores (averages) for each of these groups in terms of their perceptions of the candidate's credibility. Consider part A of Figure 11.4. The young people in the control condition rated the candidate (on average) a **4** on credibility, as did the older people in the control condition. The younger people in the BuzzFeed condition rated the candidate a **6** on credibility, and the older people did as well. In this example, it is clear that the candidate in the BuzzFeed video is rated higher on credibility than the candidate in the control video. Andre would call this a ***main effect*** **for the video variable.** It's an effect because there is a difference between those two groups. On the other hand, there is no difference between young people and old people in either condition (young and old both score 4 in the control condition and both score 6 in the BuzzFeed condition), so there's ***no*** **main effect for age.**

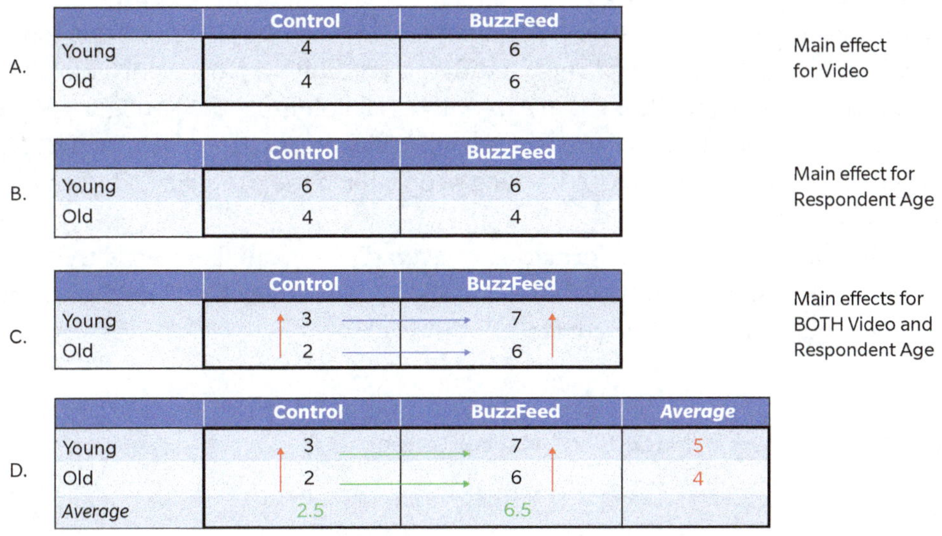

A. Main effect for Video

	Control	BuzzFeed
Young	4	6
Old	4	6

B. Main effect for Respondent Age

	Control	BuzzFeed
Young	6	6
Old	4	4

C. Main effects for BOTH Video and Respondent Age

	Control	BuzzFeed
Young	3	7
Old	2	6

D.

	Control	BuzzFeed	*Average*
Young	3	7	5
Old	2	6	4
Average	2.5	6.5	

FIGURE 11.4 Examples of main effects: numbers in cells are average scores

Statistical significance

To introduce main effects and interaction effects, in this section, we'll be looking at numbers and assuming that differences are meaningful. As discussed already in this book, sometimes two numbers can be different but not *statistically significantly* different. For any effects in a factorial design, you need to test for significance to see if a main effect or interaction effect is actually statistically significant. That's going to wait for the next chapter: For now, just assume that any differences are "real."

In Figure 11.4(B), something different is going on. Here the younger people rate the candidate a 6 (on average) in both the BuzzFeed and control conditions (with no difference between those conditions), while the older people (in both conditions) rate the candidate a 4. So, younger people like the candidate more, and the video has no effect. Andre would call this **a main effect for age but no main effect for video condition.**

In Figure 11.4(C), things start getting a little more complicated, but by taking things slowly, Andre can see what's going on. First, he looks across the rows: In both rows, the BuzzFeed video score is 4 points higher than the control video score (the green arrows). This tells him that there is a main effect for viewing the BuzzFeed video. No matter what age you are, viewing the BuzzFeed video increases your perceptions of the candidate's credibility. Now Andre looks up and down the columns (the red arrows). In both columns, the younger people score one point higher than the older people, indicating a main effect for age. No matter which video they watched, young people liked the candidate a little more than older people.

Andre can see this same information by averaging the numbers along the rows and down the columns (see part D of Figure 11.4). He averages both columns, and sees an average of 2.5 for the control condition:

$$(3 + 2) / 2 = 2.5$$

but an average of 6.5 for the BuzzFeed condition:

$$(7 + 6) / 2 = 6.5.$$

The BuzzFeed condition people (on average) like the candidate more than the control condition people. By examining the row averages, he can see similarly that younger people like the candidate more than older people. So here Andre sees *both* main effects at the same time: With these data, he could say that there is **a main effect for video condition *and* a main effect for age.**

Look at the patterns in Figure 11.5. Try to identify whether they represent main effects for video, age, or both.

A.

	Control	BuzzFeed
Young	4	4
Old	5	5

Main effect for Video? Y N
Main effect for Age? Y N

B.

	Control	BuzzFeed
Young	2	4
Old	4	6

Main effect for Video? Y N
Main effect for Age? Y N

C.

	Control	BuzzFeed
Young	3	6
Old	3	6

Main effect for Video? Y N
Main effect for Age? Y N

D.

	Control	BuzzFeed
Young	3	3
Old	3	3

Main effect for Video? Y N
Main effect for Age? Y N

FIGURE 11.5 Which main effects are present?

The next section will explain the answers to Figure 11.5 using graphs to help.

Graphing in Factorial Design

Rather than staring at tables of numbers, it can often be easier to look at a chart. It's pretty straightforward to convert these tables of means into charts that illustrate the effects (see "Key Point" for the relevant steps). The "Chapter 11 Charts: 1" tab of this section's Google Sheet (https://bit.ly/2xzn6rd) has charts of all the numbers in Figure 11.5. In Part A, the red dashed line (representing older participants) is higher overall than the blue line (younger participants). Older people rate the politician's credibility higher than younger people on average—a main effect for age. The lines are horizontal—they don't slope up or down—so the x-axis variable (video) has no effect. There is no main effect for video condition. Part A answer: video-no, age-yes.

Part B shows the same general trend for age—red line higher than blue—indicating a main effect for age. The lines also slope upward, indicating that the politician was evaluated as more credible in the BuzzFeed video than the control video. You would be correct if you said "yes" to both main effects in part B of Figure 11.5. Part B answer: video-yes, age-yes.

The graph for C shows the upward slope (main effect for video), but the lines for the two age groups are directly on top of each other, so there is no main effect for age. Part C answer: video-yes, age-no.

Finally, part D shows flat lines that are completely on top of one another, so there is nothing going on here—no main effects. Part D answer: video-no, age-no.

To the right of the charts in the Google Sheet, the tables of means are repeated along with the row and column averages. You should be able to connect the interpretation of the graphs with the interpretation of these averages. For instance, in part A, there is no difference in the two column means (both are 4.5), which again tells you that there is no video main effect. But there is a difference in the row means (4 versus 5), indicating a main effect for age.

Creating factorial design charts in Google Sheets. In Google Sheets, enter your numbers into a new sheet so that it looks like the examples in the chapter sheet: https://bit.ly/2xzn6rd. Highlight the numbers (and the row/column labels) and use the menus: "Insert—Chart" and select "Line Chart". Depending on what you want the display to look like, you can click the box to "Switch Rows and Columns"; this determines whether young–old or BuzzFeed–control are listed on the x-axis. Then you need to "customize" to make the chart look how you want. You can adjust the vertical axis to reflect the true range of the scale (min = 1, max = 7) and add a label for that axis (vertical axis title: "credibility"), for instance. It can be useful to change the colors and end markers for the lines on the chart as well. In some charts (e.g., examples C and D), it is possible for the two lines to end up "on top of" each other, which can be confusing unless it is visually clear that both lines are in the same place. Using one dashed and one solid line can help in those situations. You can do this via "Customize—Series—Apply to" and then selecting one line at a time.

It should be clear by now that a given set of results may include no effects at all, either main effect on its own or both main effects. In the next chapter, we will get into more detail about how to actually test these effects statistically.

One thing you may have noticed in these examples is that the lines in the charts are always parallel and in some cases even directly on top of each other. It is not always the case that the charts are so pretty, which brings us to the second type of effect mentioned earlier: interaction effects.

Understanding Interaction Effects

Let's begin our discussion of interaction effects by looking at the numbers in Figure 11.6. If he follows the rules from before, Andre should conclude that there are no main effects here (and he would be correct). On average, the young and old people scored the same (4) and the BuzzFeed and control video people scored the same (also 4). If he just looked at main effects, Andre would conclude that there is nothing going on. But the numbers within the table are not all the same, and if you try to interpret them, it's clear that something IS going on. What's going on is an **interaction effect.**

A	Control	BuzzFeed
Young	3	5
Old	5	3

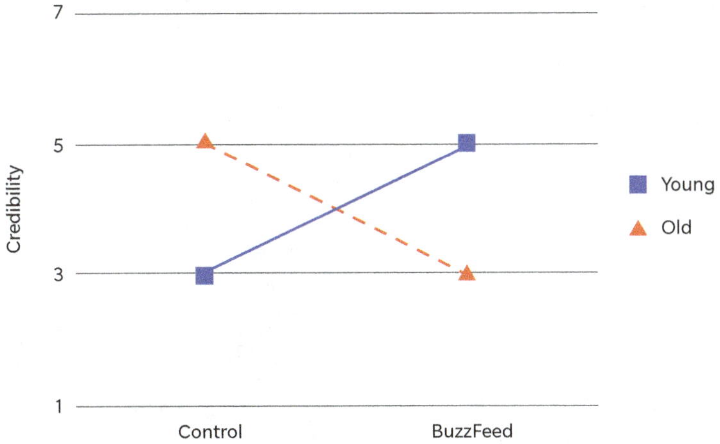

FIGURE 11.6 Means and chart demonstrating interaction effect, Part A

Remind yourself again of the basic question that Andre was trying to answer: Does appearing on BuzzFeed help or hurt a candidate's credibility? If the data looked like Figure 11.6, then the answer would be "it depends!" What it depends on is the *other* independent variable: age. When the respondents were young, it looks like appearing on BuzzFeed *helps* the candidate's credibility (the upward sloping blue line). However, when the respondents were older, appearing on BuzzFeed *hurt* the candidate's credibility (downward sloping red line). This is the essence of an interaction effect: Whatever effects occur for one of the independent variables *differ* depending on the other independent variable. When describing an interaction effect, it can be very helpful to describe it by looking at the table one row at a time. For example,

> **[First row of table] For younger people ...** the BuzzFeed video *increases* perceptions of credibility compared to the control, but

> **[Second row of table] for older people ...** the BuzzFeed video *decreases* perceptions of credibility compared to the control.

You can also see these numbers and charts in the "Chapter 11 Charts 2" tab of the Google Sheet (https://bit.ly/2xzn6rd).

Now, look at Figure 11.7 (and part B of the Google Sheet tab). Here you see a different kind of pattern but, again, one that indicates an interaction ("it depends") effect.

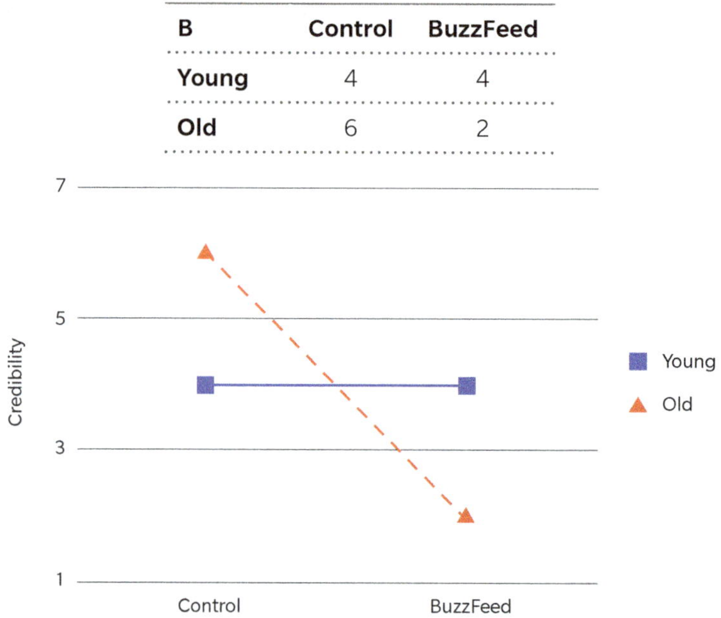

B	Control	BuzzFeed
Young	4	4
Old	6	2

FIGURE 11.7 Means and chart demonstrating interaction effect, Part B

Try describing this effect:

For younger people ... ____

____, but

For older people ... ____

____.

From looking at the numbers on the chart, you should be able to see that the video has no effect for young people; they score a 4 on average no matter which video they watched. On the other hand, older people saw the candidate as very credible in the control video condition, but not at all credible in the BuzzFeed condition. Andre might describe this effect by saying,

> For younger people, the video source has no effect, but for older people, the BuzzFeed video results in lower levels of perceived credibility compared to the control video.

Try doing the same for the remaining two charts in the Google sheet (C and D). In some cases, you might notice that the direction of the effect is the same (e.g., the BuzzFeed video improves credibility perceptions), but the *size* of the effect is different. In those cases, you can note that explicitly by saying that there is a *larger* effect for one group but a *smaller* effect for the other group.

Part C:

For younger people ... ______________________________

______________________________, but

For older people ... ______________________________

______________________________.

Part D:

For younger people ... ______________________________

______________________________, but

For older people ... ______________________________

______________________________.

For chart C, Andre would say that for younger people, the BuzzFeed video increased perceptions of credibility substantially, but for older people, the BuzzFeed video increased perceptions of credibility just a little. For chart D, Andre would say that for younger people, the BuzzFeed video increased perceptions of credibility, but for older people, the BuzzFeed video decreased perceptions of credibility.

Three important things to remember about interaction effects should be clear from these examples:

First, when you graph an interaction effect, you end up with lines that are *not* parallel. In fact, this is one way to spot whether you may be looking at an interaction effect in your data: If the lines are parallel, you do NOT have an interaction effect.

Second, it is possible to have **any combination of main effects** along with the interaction effect. Consider the four examples we just looked at and see the row and column means (the red and green numbers on the right-hand side in the Google Sheet: https://bit.ly/2xzn6rd). All the examples featured interaction effects. Example A featured *no* main effects—young and old people had the same overall mean, and the control and BuzzFeed conditions had the same means as well. Example B included a main effect for video type in addition to the interaction effect (on average, people liked the control video more; there were no age differences, so no main effect for age). Example C featured *both* main effects and the interaction. Example D featured a main effect for age, but not a main effect for video type. We can say that the two main effects and the interaction effect are **independent effects**—any combination of those effects (or lack of effects) is possible.

Third, note that the *main effects* are often somewhat deceptive if you interpret them without also considering the interaction effect. Example B provides a good example of this. The main effect says that, on average, credibility perceptions were higher in the control video condition than the BuzzFeed condition (see the green-column means to the right in the Google Sheet). However, that effect is entirely due to what was going on among the *older* participants; among young people, the video had absolutely no effect. So, you should always be cautious when interpreting main effects if an interaction effect is also present.

Spotting interaction effects

As described earlier, a common way to spot whether you have a possible interaction effect is to look at the lines in the chart. If they are parallel, you don't have an interaction effect. There are other ways to spot these effects, however, if you don't always want to draw the chart. One easy technique is just to look at the differences between the numbers within the cells. Consider Figure 11.8.

	Control		BuzzFeed
Young	4	Difference of +1 →	5
Old	6	Difference of −3 →	3

FIGURE 11.8 Identifying interaction effects from means

The red arrow shows that the BuzzFeed condition results in a score one point higher than the control condition (average of 5 in the BuzzFeed condition, four in the control condition) for the young respondents. On the other hand, the

continues on next page

continues from previous page

BuzzFeed condition results in a score 3 points *lower* for the older respondents (illustrated by the green arrow). If the difference in the top row is *different* from the difference in the bottom row, then that indicates a possible interaction effect. The differences don't have to be in different directions: If the score increases by 2 in the top row and increases by 4 in the bottom, that also suggests an interaction. Similarly, if the score increases by 2 in the top row (+2) and decreases by 2 in the bottom row (−2) that would suggest an interaction. The only scenario *not* indicating an interaction is exactly the same difference in each row (e.g., +2 in the top row and +2 in the bottom). The next chapter will discuss how to determine whether differences are large enough to call them statistically significant.

Writing Hypotheses in Factorial Design

Andre's study involves two independent variables, each of which has a potential main effect, as well as the interaction between those two independent variables. He, therefore, can generate three separate hypotheses. The main effect hypotheses will be relatively straightforward: They are just like hypotheses you've seen before. Notice, though, that each refers to just one of the independent variables: He doesn't talk about age in the video-type hypothesis, and he doesn't talk about video type in the age hypothesis:

> H1: A political candidate who appears on BuzzFeed will be perceived as less credible than a candidate who does not appear on BuzzFeed.

> H2: Older people evaluate political candidates as less credible than younger people do.

Of course, Andre's predictions might be the opposite (e.g., that younger people evaluate the candidate as less credible); these are just examples.

Interaction effect hypotheses are more complicated to write because they involve more variables. One useful trick is to refer to the main effect hypotheses in writing the interaction to provide some "shorthand." An example of an interaction effect hypothesis for Andre's study is the following:

> H3: The effect described in H1 will be stronger for older respondents and weaker for younger respondents.

This hypothesis says that BuzzFeed has a negative effect on perceptions of credibility but that that effect is *especially strong* for older people. Another way to write an interaction hypothesis is to break it down into sections. First, make the general prediction that there will be an interaction effect; next, describe the nature of the effect for one group (or one condition) and then for the other group (or other condition). The following provides an example of this; it makes a slightly different prediction from the previous hypothesis.

> H3: Video type (BuzzFeed versus control) will interact with respondent age in predicting perceptions of candidate credibility. When respondents are younger, they will perceive the candidate to be more credible in the BuzzFeed condition as compared to the control; when respondents are older, they will perceive the candidate to be less credible in the BuzzFeed condition as compared to the control.

As you can see, this hypothesis is longer, but it does clearly lay out the prediction without having to refer back to previous hypotheses. There's no one correct way to write these types of hypotheses, just put in the time to make sure that what you are predicting is clear to your reader.

Writing the Report

This chapter shows that sometimes an existing research study gets repeated with a new tweak or addition. In Andre's case, the tweak was very simple: Just by measuring and analyzing the respondent's age, he was able to start answering questions about an interaction effect in the data. The report (Report 11.1) for his methods is, therefore, very similar to the one in Chapter 5. There is an added sentence noting that he measured age and split it into two categories; it's important if you are making this sort of change in your data that it be clearly described. You can't just say that you have a younger and older group without saying what defines someone as being in one group or the other. Apart from that, everything here should be fairly familiar.

continues from previous page

REPORT 11.1 Methods for Experimental Study With Factorial Design

Participants. A convenience sample of 200 people was recruited at a suburban midwestern shopping mall. Shoppers were approached, shown a form featuring information about the study, and asked if they would participate in exchange for $10. Volunteers were 55% female, 38% male, and 7% nonbinary/third gender, and diverse in terms of age (M = 42.32 years, SD = 8.27, Range = 18–73). For the purposes of this study, age was split into two categories: younger (under 30 years old: N = 100) and older (30 and over: N = 100). The sample was also diverse in terms of race and ethnicity (42% white, 25% Latino/a/x, 33% black/African American, 15% Asian American; numbers do not total to 100% because respondents could select more than one option).

Procedures. Participants who agreed to participate were escorted to a private area to complete the study. They sat in front of a computer and were asked to watch a video of a middle-aged female political candidate being interviewed about state and national political issues. Participants were instructed to "try to get an impression of the candidate" while watching the video. The participants were randomly assigned to see either a version of the video featuring the logo of a social media website (BuzzFeed) or a version with no logo (control). All other aspects of the video were identical. After watching the video, respondents completed a computer-based questionnaire assessing perceptions of the candidate's trustworthiness (described next). The entire procedure took approximately 15 minutes, after which respondents were debriefed and paid $10.

Measures. We measured perceptions of the candidate's trustworthiness using McCroskey and Teven's (1999) trustworthiness scale (one component of their ethos/credibility measure). Six semantic differential items tapped perceptions of the candidate as dishonest, trustworthy, dishonorable, immoral, ethical, and genuine using a 1–7 scale. After recoding reverse-scored items, scores were averaged to yield the measure of perceived trustworthiness (M = 4.53, SD = 1.35).

Other Applications

Examining main effects and interaction effects requires having multiple categorical independent variables. Andre's research involved two independent variables. One of those was a manipulated experimental variable (video type) and one was nonexperimental (age). To examine main effects and interaction effects, it doesn't matter whether your independent variables come from an experiment or not.

Some people use the term "factorial design" strictly to refer to experiments, but I am using it more broadly here to refer to any study in which main effects and interaction effects are being examined.

It would be possible to examine main effects and interaction effects using data that were entirely nonexperimental. Andre, for instance, might take advantage of a situation in which his candidate had appeared in a BuzzFeed video and on some other platform (e.g., a television news show). Using a survey, he could find people who had seen one or the other of those appearances (but not both) and ask them how credible they found the candidate. He could also measure the respondents' ages. This would allow him to do exactly the same analysis of main effects and interactions as described in this chapter but with nonexperimental data.

Similarly, it is possible to design a study in which *both* independent variables are manipulated. Andre could have manipulated the content of the video in other ways—for instance, whether the politician was talking about substance (policy issues, legislation) or providing more personal information (e.g., family background). When combined, those two variables would result in the factorial design illustrated in Figure 11.9.

	Control	BuzzFeed
Talking about policy issues	People watch a non-BuzzFeed video in which the candidate talks about policy	People watch a BuzzFeed video in which the candidate talks about policy
Talking about personal issues	People watch a non-BuzzFeed video in which the candidate talks about personal issues	People watch a BuzzFeed video in which the candidate talks about personal issues

FIGURE 11.9 Example of factorial design using experimental variables

And, of course, examination of main effects and interaction effects is not restricted to the issues Andre was examining. Perhaps you are interested in what prepares students to have the communication skills they need for a job interview. You might predict that their skills would be influenced by having taken a communication class during college (versus not having taken one) and whether they have previous work experience. Figure 11.10 illustrates this as a problem in which main effects and interaction effects could be investigated. Perhaps, for instance, taking a communication class is effective for people who have work experience (and can apply the skills learned in the class) but ineffective for those without prior experience (who aren't able to apply the class material to the real world). The means in Figure 11.10 show that sort of pattern: an interaction effect.

	Have Prior Work Experience	Do Not Have Prior Work Experience
Taken a COMM class in college	6	3
Not taken a COMM class in college	3	3

FIGURE 11.10 Interaction between prior work experience and communication training predicting interviewing skills

Finally, let's talk about theory. As mentioned earlier in the chapter, interaction effects tell you about "it depends" questions. They tell you that an effect works one way in one situation or for one group of people, but differently in another situation or for another group of people. These effects are very helpful in developing *theories* for how the world works. Most things in our universe don't have the same effect for everyone all the time. Watching too much violent media can make people act more aggressively, but not all the people all the time. A full understanding of the effects of violent media, therefore, requires looking at interaction effects. A good advertising campaign for a campus gym will cause people to work out more. But not all the people all the time. A full understanding of advertising campaigns requires looking at interaction effects. Seeing which other independent variables interact with exposure to the advertising message helps us understand why the message works for some people some of the time, but not for others. The more we understand when, where, why, and for whom, particular effects occur, the better we understand those effects and, hence, the better our theories are.

This chapter has described the simplest type of factorial design: one involving just two independent variables, each with just two categories. Factorial designs can get much more complicated, with more than two independent variables and independent variables with more than two categories. Those designs would be the subject for a more advanced book than this one, but the same general principles apply, as you've learned in this chapter.

Another Example

Main effects and interaction effects can be complicated to understand, and another example might be helpful. If you are still not entirely certain about factorial design, this section presents a completely different example to provide some additional practice.

Imagine you are running a study examining what motivates students to talk to their professors. You come up with two ideas for variables that might cause a student to go to office hours. You think students are more likely to do it (a) when they've received a bad grade and (b) when the class is in their major. You run an experiment where students imagine being in a class and either (a) receiving a bad grade versus an OK grade, that is (b) in a class that is in their major versus not in their major. After imagining this scenario, the students rate how likely they are to visit their professor during office hours from 1 to 7:

1	2	3	4	5	6	7
Definitely WOULD *NOT* go see my professor						Definitely WOULD go see my professor

This is a factorial design, and you can see it illustrated in the Google Sheet (https://bit.ly/2xzn6rd, tab "Extra Example"). You have two independent variables and, of course, a dependent variable. List them below (the order of the two independent variables doesn't matter):

Independent variable 1: ______________________________

Independent variable 2: ______________________________

Dependent variable: ______________________________

Hopefully, you came up with something like the following:

Independent variable 1: Grade (OK vs. bad)

Independent variable 2: Class (In major vs. not in major)

Dependent variable: Likelihood of visiting professor

As you look at the Google Sheet, remember that the numbers represent *averages*. For instance, if you had 25 people imagine that they got an OK grade in a nonmajor class, the "3" in the top-left box in the Google Sheet is the average for those 25 people. On average, they leaned a little toward *not* going to see their professor.

Before reading on, look at the first example (A) in the Google Sheet and decide whether there is a main effect for either variable and if there is an interaction effect. Feel free to use the chart and the row/column means on the right-hand side of the chart.

Main effect for grade? Y N

Main effect for class? Y N

Interaction effect? Y N

For any effects that you think exist, try to write a sentence describing them. Leave it blank if you think there is no effect:

Main effect for grade? ____

____

Main effect for class? ____

____

Interaction effect? ____

____

Looking at the chart, you can see that the lines are parallel, indicating that there is not an interaction effect. You can also spot this lack of interaction effect by comparing the differences across the rows. In both rows, the difference between the two numbers is the same: zero (i.e., the difference between 3 and 3 in the top row, and 6 vs. 6 in the bottom row).

In terms of main effects, you can see that the red line (people who received a bad grade) is higher than the blue line (people with an OK grade), which indicates a main effect for the grade variable. People who got bad grades are more likely to visit the professor than people who got OK grades. The lines are flat rather than sloped, indicating no effect for whether the class was in the person's major or not. You can also spot the main effects by looking at the row and column averages off to the right. The column averages for people in the major and not in the major are the same (green numbers: both 4.5) indicating no difference on this variable. The row averages (red numbers) are not the same 6 vs. 3: Again, this shows that people with a bad grade were more likely (6) to say they'd visit the professor than people with an OK grade (3).

Try doing the same for the remaining three examples in the Google Sheet (https://bit.ly/2xzn6rd: "Ch. 11 Extra Example" tab). For B, the chart and row and column means are provided. For C and D, they are not, but it will definitely help you to draw the chart and calculate the row and column means.

Example B

Main effect for grade? Y N

Main effect for class? Y N

Interaction effect? Y N

For any effects that you think exist, try to write a sentence describing them:

____

____

____

Example C

Main effect for grade? Y N

Main effect for class? Y N

Interaction effect? Y N

For any effects that you think exist, try to write a sentence describing them:

____

____

____

Example D

Main effect for grade? Y N

Main effect for class? Y N

Interaction effect? Y N

For any effects that you think exist, try to write a sentence describing them:

____

____

____

Answers are provided in the "Ch 11, Extra 2" tab of the Google Sheet.

Your Turn

In the "Your Turn" sections of previous chapters you have been developing an experimental study. By now, you should have a fairly clear vision for your experimental **manipulation**'s influence on a dependent variable. Remind yourself of that design right now:

My independent variable is: ____________________________

My dependent variable is: ____________________________

Now, think about an "it depends" question to expand your study. Does your effect work differently for one group of people compared to another? Or does the effect work differently in one situation compared to another? Brainstorm some ideas for a *second independent variable* that might interact with your main independent variable to create some interesting effects. The only requirement (to make your life easy!) is that the variable be a *categorical* variable with just *two categories*. So, you'll need to be comparing two different demographic groups, for instance, or an experimental variable with just two conditions (high/low, experimental/control, radio/television, indoors/outdoors, etc.).

Do the following:

- Come up with a name for this new variable, and write a brief conceptual definition of it.

- Write three to four sentences describing how you would either manipulate (if it's an experimental variable) or measure (if it's not experimental) that variable (i.e., your operational definition). Again, remember that this operational definition should result in just two groups of people.
- Write three hypotheses: **main effect** hypotheses for your two independent variables and an **interaction effect** hypothesis for the interaction between them. Feel free to copy the general structure from the hypotheses Andre developed.
- Draw a table of "hypothetical" means and a graph of those means, like the Google Sheet and Figure 11.6. What do you expect to find?
- If you are planning to collect actual data (e.g., in your class), expand your Google Form (or whatever you are using to collect data) to accommodate this additional variable.

Wrap Up

In this chapter, you have learned what defines a factorial design: It is a research design with multiple categorical variables. You have learned how to distinguish the effects of each independent variable on the dependent variable as distinct "main effects." You have also begun to understand that the effect of one independent variable can *change* depending on the other independent variable: an effect called an interaction effect.

If you get nothing else from this chapter, remember the following:

1. A main effect is an effect for *one* independent variable; an interaction effect is a joint effect of both independent variables.
2. Main effects and interaction effects are independent of one another: It is possible to have any one of them without the other or to have any combination of them (including none of them in a really boring study!).
3. A good description of an interaction effect typically emerges from moving slowly and row by row in a table of means. Describe the effect in the first row and then move down and describe the effect in the second row. An example of this was provided earlier and is repeated here:

   For younger people ... the BuzzFeed video *increases* perceptions of credibility compared to the control, but

   for older people ... the BuzzFeed video *decreases* perceptions of credibility compared to the control.

Key Chapter Concepts

Factorial design: A situation in which you have multiple categorical independent variables and are able to examine **main effects** and **interaction effects**.

Interaction effects: In a **factorial design**, when the effect of one independent variable varies depending on the level of the other independent variable. Potential interaction effects are identifiable in graphs of means by the presence of *non*-parallel lines. Descriptions of interaction effects often involve statements of how the effect of one independent variable *depends on* the levels of the other independent variable.

Main effects: In a **factorial design**, when there is a difference in the levels of one independent variable averaging across the levels of the other independent variable. You should be cautious in interpreting main effects when you also have interaction effects: Interaction effects indicate that the pattern of a main effect changes under certain circumstances or for certain people.

Manipulation: When a researcher controls the values of a variable rather than letting them vary naturally.

■ CHAPTER 12

Reporting the Research: Factorial ANOVA

Andre has his data! You will remember from the previous chapter that he manipulated whether people saw a politician appearing either in a BuzzFeed video or a control video (i.e., one without a BuzzFeed logo). He also measured respondents' ages and split them into two groups: under 30 and 30+. He measured their perceptions of the politician in terms of her credibility. He now needs to analyze the data to find out whether his hypotheses are supported. He had three hypotheses:

> H1: A political candidate who appears on BuzzFeed will be perceived as less credible than a candidate who does not appear on BuzzFeed.
>
> H2: Older people evaluate political candidates as less credible than younger people do.
>
> H3: The effect described in H1 will be stronger for older respondents and weaker for younger respondents.

Which Test? The Decision Tree Updated

To test these hypotheses, he will need a form of analysis that can incorporate multiple independent variables. The decision tree continues to grow (Figure 12.1).

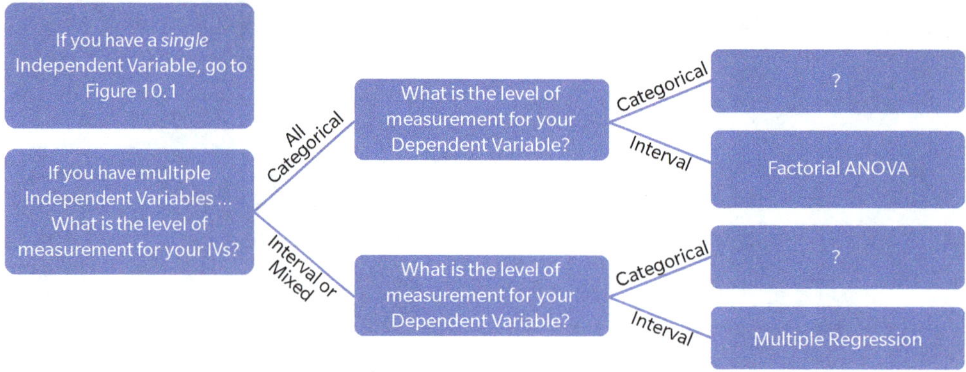

FIGURE 12.1 The updated statistical decision tree

Figure 12.1 shows the decision tree for situations with multiple independent variables—the tests we've already looked at involving just one independent variable have been excluded to simplify the image (go back to Figure 10.1 to see those). Once you have identified that you have multiple independent variables, you need to decide whether they are all categorical-level variables or if at least some of them are interval-level variables. All of Andre's independent variables are categorical. Then you need to decide if your *dependent* variable is categorical or interval—the measure of politician credibility is interval level. This means that Andre will be using the factorial ANOVA (factorial analysis of variance) to do his analysis. We've already encountered ANOVA in Chapter 8—there we were using it to analyze just one independent variable with more than two categories. Now we are using a different version of ANOVA for a situation with *multiple* independent variables. Let's look at how we run and interpret this analysis.

The Data

To do a factorial ANOVA within Google Sheets, you'll need to have the data organized in a rather specific form. Looking at Andre's data will help you understand: Go to the Google Sheet for this section (https://bit.ly/2xzn6rd) and click on the "Ch.12 Data" tab at the bottom of the page. You'll see two columns of numbers—each number represents one person's score on the credibility variable. The left column contains scores from the older (30+ years old) respondents. The right column contains numbers from the under 30. The data are then organized vertically by experimental condition. The first 50 rows are for people in the control condition, and the second 50 rows (you'll need to scroll down!) are for people in the BuzzFeed condition. So, in the Google Sheet, you'll see

- red numbers for the 50 older people in the control condition,
- blue numbers for the 50 younger people in the control condition,
- scroll down to see green numbers for the 50 older people in the BuzzFeed condition, and
- scroll down to see pink numbers for the 50 younger people in the BuzzFeed condition.

The labels for the age groups are at the top of each column, and the labels for the experimental conditions are off to the left on the first line of each condition: Control is on the first line of the control condition, and BuzzFeed is written to the left for the first line of the BuzzFeed condition.

When you organize your own data, it's *critical* to lay it out exactly as shown in this example or the analysis won't be able to interpret what you are giving it. If you have something other than 50 people in each condition, you would add or remove rows, but the basic structure should stay the same. To keep things simple, we are only going to be dealing with situations where you have the same number of people in all conditions. This is called a "balanced design." ANOVA can also be used to analyze designs with different numbers of people in conditions but that adds complications that we don't need to deal with in this book.

The Analysis

To do the factorial ANOVA analysis, Andre needs the XLMiner Analysis ToolPak up and running (see Chapter 6 for instructions on installing). Go to "Add-Ons—XLMiner Analysis ToolPak—Start" to get it running. Andre's data and analysis are shown in the Google Sheet (https://bit.ly/2xzn6rd: tab "Ch. 12 Analysis"). In XLMiner, the factorial ANOVA that Andre needs to use is called "ANOVA: Two Factor With Replication." The commands Andre entered in the XLMiner to get his results are shown in Figure 12.2.

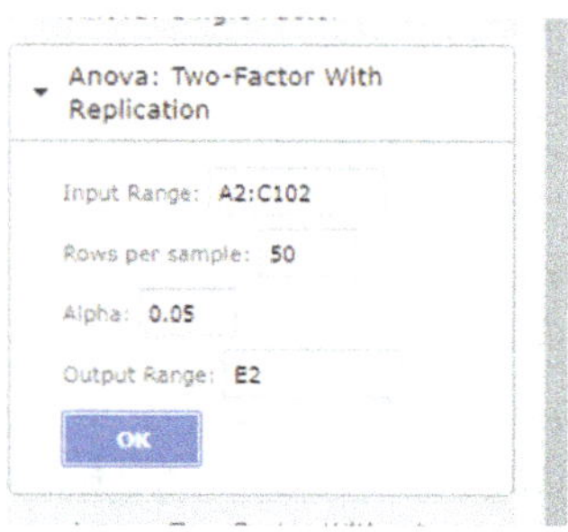

FIGURE 12.2 Factorial ANOVA commands in XLMiner

He had to enter the input range for all the data, including the *labels* for the age groups and experimental conditions. In his data, this is cell A2 to cell C102 (input range: A2:C102). He had 50 people in *each* age + video condition (rows per sample: 50). We always use the default alpha of 0.05 (see Chapter 6). The output range can be anywhere, but you need to make sure that the output doesn't overwrite your data—E2 is safe here (output range: E2).

Figure 12.3 shows Andre's results alongside the XLMiner commands and his data. There is a lot to go through here, but we'll go slowly. In the figures from here on out (and the Google Sheets tab "Ch.12 Brief"), I have added a few labels and reduced the number of decimal places to make the output a little easier to look at. I highly recommend that you do this when you start looking at your own output: Sometimes Google Sheets gives you a lot of decimal places, which can be daunting to look at. Things are easier to process if you are only looking at the decimal places you need. In most cases, two decimals are plenty. You can reduce decimal places by selecting whatever cells you want reduced and going to "Format—Number—0.00."

Anova: Two-Factor With Replication

SUMMARY

Control	Older	Younger	Total
Count	50	50	100
Sum	213	206	419
Average	4.26	4.12	4.19
Variance	1.298367347	1.291428571	1.286767677

Buzzfeed	Older	Younger	Total
Count	50	50	100
Sum	227	260	487
Average	4.54	5.2	4.87
Variance	2.049387755	2.081632653	2.154646465

Total	Older	Younger
Count	100	100
Sum	440	466
Average	4.4	4.66
Variance	1.676767677	1.964040404

ANOVA

Source of Variatio	*SS*	*df*	*MS*	*F*	*P-value*	*F crit*
Sample	23.12	1	23.12	13.76023321	0.000270407084	3.88934082
Columns	3.38	1	3.38	2.011660391	0.1576824323	3.88934082
Interaction	8	1	8	4.761326369	0.03029537887	3.88934082
Within	329.32	196	1.680204082			
Total	363.82	199				

Anova: Single Factor
Anova: Two-Factor With Replication
Input Range: A2:C102
Rows per sample: 50
Alpha: 0.05
Output Range: C13
OK
Anova: Two-Factor Without Replication
Correlation
Covariance
Descriptive Statistics
Exponential Smoothing
F-Test Two-Sample for Variances
Fourier Analysis
Histogram
Linear Regression
Logistic Regression
Moving Average
Random Number Generation

FIGURE 12.3 Factorial ANOVA output from Google Sheet

Figure 12.4 starts to unpack the top part of the output. This is the area that tells you the averages for all the groups, which will ultimately be the most important information in understanding any effects Andre observes. The two main columns in the table report information for the older and younger people, and the first two blocks of information report on the control and BuzzFeed conditions, respectively. You can see from the boxes Andre has inserted that the mean for older people in the control condition, for instance, is a 4.26. This can be inserted into the table we use to understand effects in factorial designs. Likewise, the other three means can be moved into that table. From this, Andre can immediately start to get a sense of the pattern of effects. For instance, it is already clear that the BuzzFeed video seems to be getting higher scores than the control video.

	Control	BuzzFeed
Younger	4.12	5.20
Older	4.26	4.54

SUMMARY

Control	*Older*	*Younger*	*Total*
Count	50	50	100
Sum	213	206	419
Average	4.26	4.12	4.19
Variance	1.30	1.29	1.29

BuzzFeed	*Older*	*Younger*	*Total*
Count	50	50	100
Sum	227	260	487
Average	4.54	5.20	4.87
Variance	2.05	2.08	2.15

Total	*Older*	*Younger*
Count	100	100
Sum	440	446
Average	4.40	4.66
Variance	1.68	1.96

Means for older and younger people in the control condition

Means for older and younger people in the BuzzFeed condition

FIGURE 12.4 Deriving cell means from factorial ANOVA output

Figure 12.5 shows how to get the row and column means from the same part of the output. The far-right column gives information about scores in the two video conditions (averaging across people in the different age groups). And the lower area of the table gives the averages for older and younger people. These can be included in the previous table as shown in Figure 12.5. Because we have equal numbers of people in each **cell** (50), we can also just average across rows or down columns to get these same numbers—for example, (4.12 + 5.20) / 2 = 4.66. You can see from Figure 12.5 that younger people see the candidate as more credible (4.66) than older people (4.40), and the BuzzFeed condition results in higher evaluations of credibility (4.87) than the control condition (4.87). We don't yet know whether those differences are large enough to be statistically significant.

	Control	BuzzFeed	
Younger	4.12	5.20	4.66
Older	4.26	4.54	4.40
	4.19	4.87	

SUMMARY			
Control	*Older*	*Younger*	*Total*
Count	50	50	100
Sum	213	206	419
Average	4.26	4.12	4.19
Variance	1.30	1.29	1.29
BuzzFeed	*Older*	*Younger*	*Total*
Count	50	50	100
Sum	227	260	487
Average	4.54	5.20	4.87
Variance	2.05	2.08	2.15
Total	*Older*	*Younger*	
Count	100	100	
Sum	440	466	
Average	4.40	4.66	
Variance	1.68	1.96	

Means for the Control and BuzzFeed conditions (including people from both age groups)

Means for older and younger people (across both video conditions)

FIGURE 12.5 Deriving row and column means from factorial ANOVA output

Figure 12.6 breaks down the bottom part of the table, which is where the actual factorial ANOVA is reported: This part of the output is often called the **F-table** because it is where the *F*-statistics are reported. Because we are testing three hypotheses, there are three rows in the table related to those hypotheses. The first row relates to the video main effect (H1), the second to the age main effect (H2), and the third to the **interaction effect.**

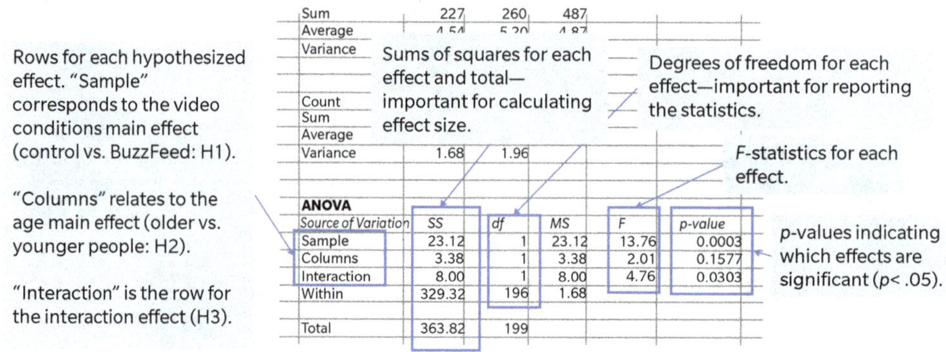

ANOVA					
Source of Variation	*SS*	*df*	*MS*	*F*	*p-value*
Sample	23.12	1	23.12	13.76	0.0003
Columns	3.38	1	3.38	2.01	0.1577
Interaction	8.00	1	8.00	4.76	0.0303
Within	329.32	196	1.68		
Total	363.82	199			

FIGURE 12.6 Elements of factorial ANOVA statistical output: The *F*-table

A good place to start looking at Figure 12.6 is at the far right, where you can find the *p*-values for each of the key effects. Remember, *p*-values tell you the probability of the null hypothesis being true; A *p*-value below 0.05 means that an effect is statistically significant. Think back to the previous chapter just briefly here. In Chapter 11, we were happy just interpreting any differences between means as if they were important or significant. Now that we are learning the proper analysis, we need to remind ourselves that sometimes differences between means are not significant: Two numbers might be different, but the difference is not big enough for us to have confidence that it is "real." It is the tests of statistical significance in the factorial ANOVA that tell us which differences we can have confidence in.

The *p*-value in the first row is 0.0003: That number is clearly less than 0.05 ($p < .05$), and so Andre can conclude that this effect is statistically significant. There is a significant difference between the BuzzFeed and the control conditions. It's important, of course, now to look at the means to understand what this main effect is telling us. From Figure 12.5, what would you conclude about this main effect: In which condition do people see the politician as more credible?

Andre looks at the column means (in green) in Figure 12.5 and sees that the BuzzFeed group ($M = 4.87$) scored higher than the control group ($M = 4.19$). He knows that difference is significant, and so he can conclude that there is a main effect for video type such that people in the BuzzFeed condition viewed the politician as more credible than people in the control video condition.

The *p*-value in the second row is 0.1577: That number is larger than 0.05, and so Andre concludes that this effect is *not* statistically significant ($p > .05$). There is no significant difference between the older and younger people in the study—no main effect for age. So, even though the means for older and younger people are slightly different (see the row means in red in Figure 12.5), they are *not different enough* for us to discuss that difference as being real. Older and younger people do not differ statistically in their perceptions of the candidate's credibility.

Finally, the *p*-value in the third row is 0.0303: That number is less than 0.05, and so Andre concludes that the interaction effect *is* statistically significant. He needs to look at the means and a chart to understand this. In the Google Sheet (https://bit.ly/2xzn6rd), the tab "Ch. 12 Chart" shows the chart (Chapter 11 described how to create these charts); see also Figure 12.7. Remember the idea from Chapter 11 of going one row at a time in the table (or indeed one line at a time in the chart)? How would you describe this chart? Focus on describing what's going on for the younger people first (the blue line/blue numbers) and then the older people (the red line/red numbers.

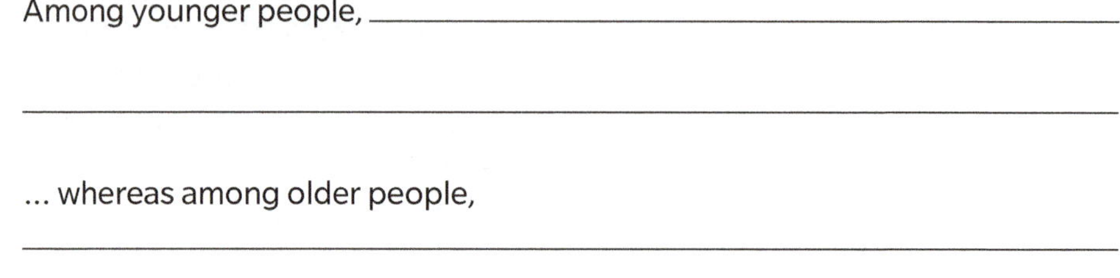

Among younger people, ____

____

... whereas among older people,

____

____.

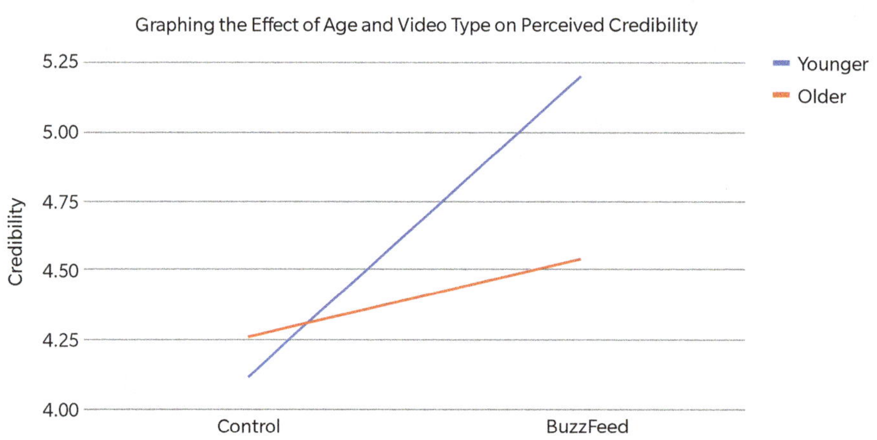

FIGURE 12.7 Graphing the significant interaction effect

Andre writes the following:

> Among younger people, credibility ratings were much higher in the BuzzFeed condition than the control condition, whereas among older people, the difference between the two video conditions, although in the same direction, was much smaller.

He could also have written the following:

> Among younger people, credibility ratings were much higher in the BuzzFeed condition than the control condition, whereas among older people, credibility ratings were only slightly higher in the BuzzFeed condition than the control condition.

Or if you want to get creative ...

> For all participants, credibility ratings were higher in the BuzzFeed condition than the control condition, but this difference was bigger among the younger than the older participants.

All the descriptions capture the nature of the differences observed across the four means, and all would be a good way of describing the chart.

Effect Size

We know from earlier chapters that statistical significance isn't all Andre should care about. Statistical significance doesn't tell us how *big* an effect is, it just tells us that the effect is real. With one-way ANOVA (remember Chapter 8), we used **eta-squared (η^2)** as a measure of effect size. Factorial ANOVA uses the same statistic. But because we have three different hypotheses, we also have *three different* eta-squareds. The eta-squared for any individual effect in ANOVA is calculated from the sums of squares, as illustrated in Figure 12.8.

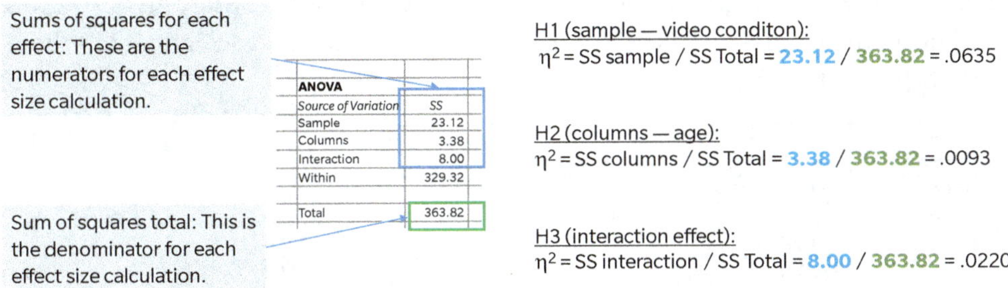

FIGURE 12.8 Calculating a measure of effect size in factorial ANOVA

Degrees of freedom in factorial ANOVA

You might remember from Chapter 8 that *F*-statistics always have two numbers for degrees of freedom—one representing the number of groups and one representing the number of people in the study. With the factorial ANOVA, these degrees of freedom are reported for each effect (the two main effects and the interaction effect). In our case, the degrees of freedom for the different effects are all the same, but that is not always the case. Figure 12.9 gives you some idea of where Andre gets the degrees of freedom to report for his analysis. As you can see, for the video type (sample) main effect, he first uses the degrees of freedom from the "sample" row (which represents the video main effect: red text), and then the degrees of freedom from the "within" row (blue text). This "within" row represents the total number of people in the study minus the number of groups (Andre had four groups total: young-BuzzFeed, young-control, old-BuzzFeed, old-control: 200 – 4 = 196). For the other effects, he follows the same procedure, using the degrees of freedom for the effect's row (always 1 in this case) and the degrees of freedom from the "within" row. The degrees of freedom for all Andre's effects will be (1, 196).

Writing the Report

As you can probably already tell, writing the results of a factorial ANOVA is going to be a little more complicated than the previous reports, because you are reporting *three* tests rather than just one (two main effects and one interaction effect). Andre just needs to remember to stay organized and report one effect at a time (you'll notice in his write-up [Report 12.1] that each hypothesis gets its own paragraph). Andre will need to report the test statistic (F) and its significance level (p), as well as the effect size (η^2) for each effect. As with previous reports, he will also need to report the degrees of freedom for each statistic (see sidebar). Because Andre has a significant interaction effect, including a chart displaying the means is very important to help his readers understand the general pattern of effects. Figure 12.9 might be helpful to you in understanding where all of Andre's numbers come from—all of the numbers are color coded so you can match them from the output to the write-up.

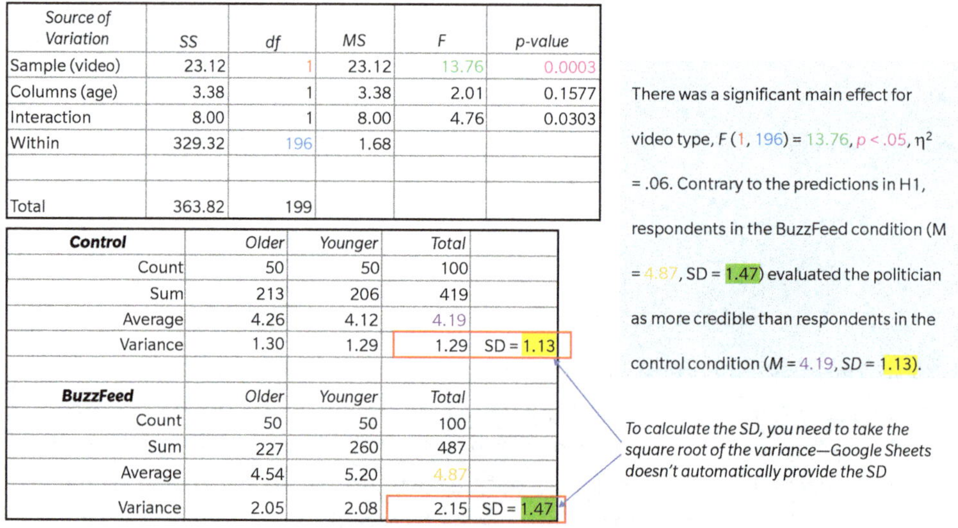

Source of Variation	*SS*	*df*	*MS*	*F*	*p-value*
Sample (video)	23.12	1	23.12	13.76	0.0003
Columns (age)	3.38	1	3.38	2.01	0.1577
Interaction	8.00	1	8.00	4.76	0.0303
Within	329.32	196	1.68		
Total	363.82	199			

Control	*Older*	*Younger*	*Total*	
Count	50	50	100	
Sum	213	206	419	
Average	4.26	4.12	4.19	
Variance	1.30	1.29	1.29	SD = 1.13
BuzzFeed	*Older*	*Younger*	*Total*	
Count	50	50	100	
Sum	227	260	487	
Average	4.54	5.20	4.87	
Variance	2.05	2.08	2.15	SD = 1.47

FIGURE 12.9 Deriving write-up of factorial ANOVA from output

REPORT 12.1 Results for Factorial ANOVA

There was a significant main effect for video type, $F(1, 196) = 13.76$, $p < .05$, $\eta^2 = .06$. Contrary to the predictions in H1, respondents in the BuzzFeed condition ($M = 4.87$, $SD = 1.47$) evaluated the politician as *more* credible than respondents in the control condition ($M = 4.19$, $SD = 1.14$).

There was no support for H2: There was no significant main effect for subject age, $F(1, 196) = 2.01$, $p > .05$.

There was a significant interaction effect, $F(1, 196) = 4.76$, $p < .05$, $\eta^2 = .02$. Among younger people, credibility ratings were much higher in the BuzzFeed condition ($M = 5.20$, $SD = 1.44$) than the control condition ($M = 4.12$, $SD = 1.14$), whereas among older people, credibility ratings were only slightly higher in the BuzzFeed condition ($M = 4.54$, $SD = 1.43$) than the control condition ($M = 4.26$, $SD = 1.14$). This pattern is displayed in Figure 1. The pattern does not reflect the predictions in H3: Specifically, H3 predicted stronger effects (and in the opposite direction) for older respondents, but the data indicate stronger effects among younger people.

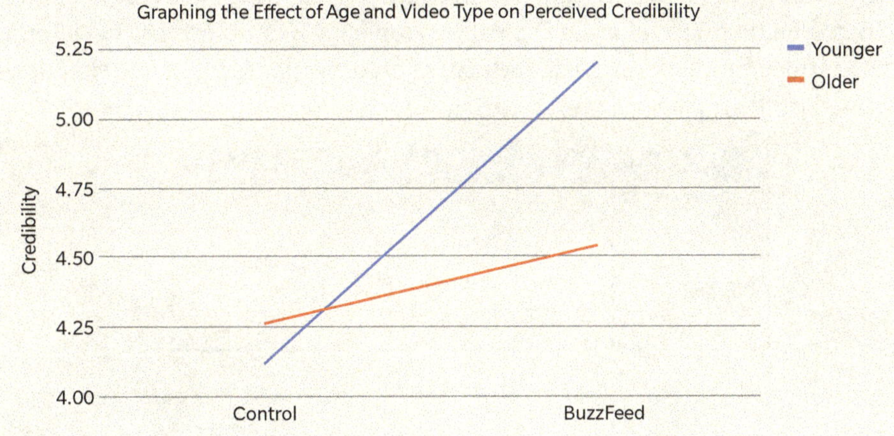

FIGURE 1 Means of perceived credibility for two age groups across the two video conditions

NOTES: Andre could also report the means and the eta-squared for H2 if he wanted. Often, people don't report the effect size for nonsignificant effects because there is no effect statistically speaking, and so the size of the "effect" isn't very important! But it's not wrong to do so. As has occurred in previous chapters, Andre's hypotheses were not supported. While there were significant effects, those effects were not in the direction predicted. Sometimes, this can seem like a disaster for a scientific study—imagine testing a new drug and finding that it actually makes people's health *worse* rather than better! But unexpected findings can be quite interesting, showing you that the world works differently than you thought and therefore giving you new understanding.

KEY POINT

Don't *assume* that a significant effect indicates support for your hypothesis: It might mean exactly the opposite!

Other Applications

As described in the "Other Applications" section of the previous chapter, factorial designs are very broadly useful across the theoretical and applied social sciences. In this section, I'll discuss two statistical extensions of what you've already learned.

Remember that in Andre's example, there were 200 people spread across four groups, with 50 people in each group. Of course, that means that each individual person was only in *one* "cell" of the design. That doesn't have to be the case. In research designs called "repeated measures" or "within subjects" designs, the same person can appear in more than one cell of the design. For example, imagine that Andre was interested in how *long lasting* the effects of the BuzzFeed video are. Do they last until election day?! He might assign people to a BuzzFeed or control condition and then measure how credible they thought the political candidate was. But then he might contact the same people *again* a month or two later and ask them once more about the candidate's credibility. You can see this design illustrated in the top section of Figure 12.10.

	Control	BuzzFeed
Time 1 (T1)	50 people (Group A), average score on credibility	50 people (Group B), average score on credibility
Two Months Later (T2)	The same 50 people (Group A), average score on credibility	The same 50 people (Group B), average score on credibility

Example Results A	Control	BuzzFeed
Time 1 (T1)	3	6
Two Months Later (T2)	3	6

Example Results B	Control	BuzzFeed
Time 1 (T1)	3	6
Two Months Later (T2)	3	6

FIGURE 12.10 Factorial design featuring a repeated measures variable (time)

As you can see, Figure 12.10 resembles the factorial design we have been looking at throughout this chapter. There are two independent variables (video type: BuzzFeed/control and time: T1/T2). That results in four cells in the design. The only difference is that the *same* people are measured in two cells of the design (T1 and T2). Look at the first example set of results (A) in the bottom portion of the figure. What main effects and interaction effects might be significant here?

Hopefully, you identified that *just* the main effect for video is significant. The BuzzFeed video is better, and that effect is consistent across time (BuzzFeed is better at T1, and it's *equally* better at T2).

How about the example results B? Which effects are significant?

Hopefully, here you identified that *all three* effects might be significant—both main effects and the interaction. On average, by calculating the row and column means, T1 scores are higher than T2 scores, and the BuzzFeed condition is better than the control. However, both of those effects become unimportant relative to the interaction effect. The interaction effect tells you that the BuzzFeed condition "worked" at T1—BuzzFeed scores are higher than the control scores there. However, this effect completely disappears at T2. If Andre found this pattern of effects, what sort of advice might he give his campaign team?

This would be useful information for Andre's team. One fairly clear message would be that if they want to "use" the BuzzFeed effect (have their candidate benefit by appearing on BuzzFeed), they would need to schedule the appearance fairly close to the election. It looks like the BuzzFeed benefit wears off over time.

There are advantages to designs where people are measured more than once. You can see that it lets you track trends over time. It also increases the **efficiency** of your research. Notice that with this design, you are "reusing" the respondents, and so you can examine a design with four cells, with 50 people in each cell, even though you only have 100 people total. This can make doing research less expensive and make your statistics more powerful.

However, you must be aware that the analysis for designs where the same people pop up in more than one place is different from the analysis for designs where people only appear once. A separate type of ANOVA called "**within subjects**" or "repeated measures" factorial ANOVA is required, and right now, Google Sheets doesn't do that sort of analysis. If this is reminding you of how there are different *t*-tests for "independent samples" and "paired" situations, then you are correct; this is exactly the same issue.

For your own research, if you plan on using Google Sheets for analysis, you should focus on designs where you only measure people a single time.

Your Turn

In Chapter 11, you designed an extension of your study for the class so that it involved a factorial design. Remind yourself of your idea here.

My first independent variable: ____________________

My second independent variable: ____________________

My dependent variable: ____________________

At this point, double-check that (a) both independent variables are categorical and have only two categories, (b) you are not planning on measuring people on the dependent variable more than once, and (c) that the dependent variable is interval level. You should be able to organize your design to look like the following:

		Second independent variable name:	
		Category 1 label	Category 2 label
First independent variable name	Category 1 label		
	Category 2 label		

If you are collecting real data, or just making data up, now is the time to do it. Once you have your numbers, organize them in the same way as the Google Sheet for this chapter, and run your factorial ANOVA. Write the results just like Andre did. Including a chart like Andre's will be helpful, and it is essential if you find an interaction effect.

Wrap Up

In this chapter, you have learned how to analyze a design involving multiple categorical independent variables using the factorial ANOVA. You now know how to interpret two main effects and an interaction effect within the analysis, and how to calculate an effect size for each of those effects. You know how to create a graph of the means and how to write the results.

If you get nothing else from this chapter, remember the following:

1. Factorial ANOVA is the statistical test for situations where you have multiple categorical independent variables and an interval-level dependent variable.
2. A main effect is an effect for *one* independent variable; an interaction effect is a joint effect of both independent variables.
3. A significant interaction effect should make you cautious in your interpretation of any main effects.

Key Chapter Concepts

Cell: A cell in a factorial design is a unique combination of levels of the independent variables. For example, in a study of the effects of medium (television or radio) and volume (loud versus quiet) on understanding of news, "loud television" would be one cell in the design.

Degrees of freedom (*df*): As with the one-way ANOVA, *F*-statistics in factorial ANOVA have two numbers for degrees of freedom. The first gives you some idea of how many categories the independent variables have; for instance, with a main effect, the first number tells you the number of categories for that variable minus one. The second number gives you an approximation of the sample size: it is the sample size minus the total number of cells in the design.

Eta-squared (η^2): A measure of effect size for ANOVA, typically calculated by dividing the sum of squares (SS) for the effect under consideration by the SS_{total}. In the one-way ANOVA, this means dividing $SS_{between\ groups}$ by SS_{total}. In factorial ANOVA it would be, for instance, the SS for the interaction divided by the SS_{total}. Eta-squared ranges from 0 to 1, and larger eta-squareds indicate a bigger effect. The number represents how much variance in the dependent variable is being explained by the independent variable (e.g., an eta-squared of .25 for the interaction effect would indicate that 25% of the variance in the dependent variable is explained by the interaction between the two independent variables).

F-table: The portion of the statistical output from a factorial ANOVA that reports the *F*-statistics, *p*-values, and related information.

Interaction effect: A significant interaction effect tells you that the effect of one independent variable on the dependent variable changes (significantly) depending on the value of the other independent variable.

Interpreting and graphing cell means: Interaction effects can take many forms; properly interpreting them requires thinking about the pattern of means. Often, graphing the means in the form illustrated in the chapter can help with interpretation.

Within subjects variables: Independent variables for which participants in the study participate in more than one condition or "cell" of the design (e.g., being measured at more than one point in time or receiving more than one experimental treatment).

Section Wrap

Section Summary

This section has introduced the idea of having more than one independent variable in a research design. It uses the simplest form of factorial design—two categorical independent variables, each with two levels (or categories). Within this design, the section has distinguished between main effects and interaction effects. The first chapter described conceptually how main effects and interaction effects differ, while the second chapter described specifically how to analyze a factorial design using factorial ANOVA in Google Sheets.

Going Further

We're again going to look at the same analysis in JASP and observe a few additional pieces of information available there. The JASP data file is downloadable here: http://bit.ly/2NPQI7N.

The first thing to notice about the JASP data set is that it is organized in a different way than the Google Sheets data. Each variable in the analysis gets its own column, including the dependent variable: All the credibility scores are in a *single* column. The "video" column simply reflects whether people are in the control or the BuzzFeed condition. The "age" column just reflects whether people are younger or older. This might take a little while to get used to, but it is more intuitive for thinking about independent and dependent variables. Each variable (whether independent or dependent) gets its own column.

Once you understand the data organization, you can move to analysis. Go to "ANOVA—ANOVA," and put "credibility" as the dependent variable and both "video" and "age" as fixed factors (the independent variables). Under "descriptive plots," move "video" into the "horizontal axis" area and "age" into the "separate lines" area. You should get output exactly like that in Figure 12.11.

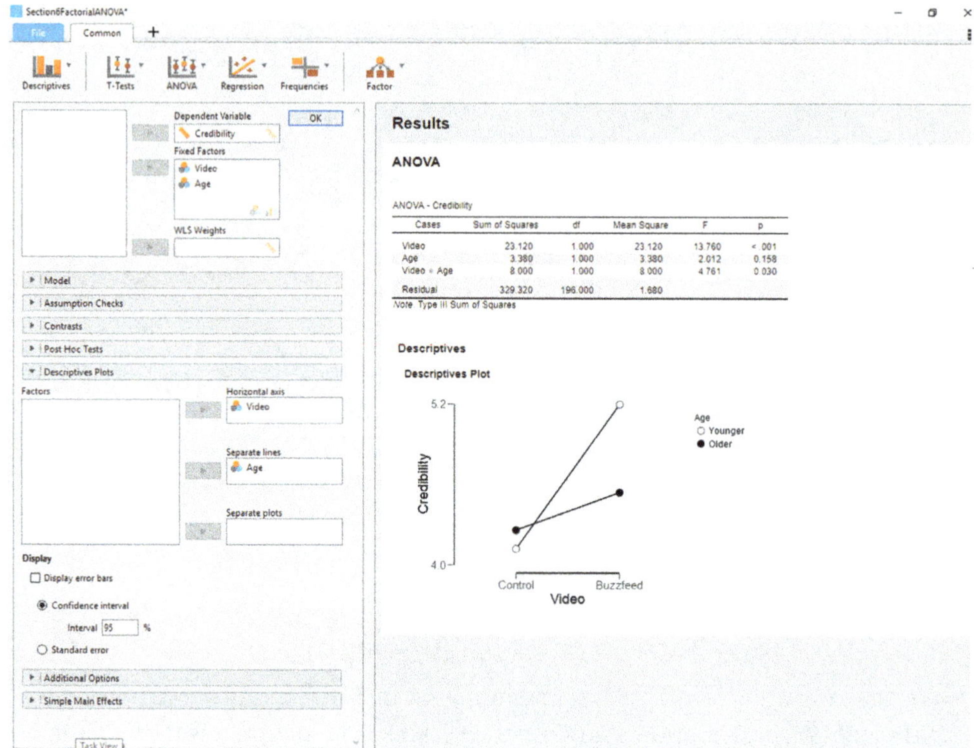

FIGURE 12.11 Factorial ANOVA output from JASP

All these results are the same as the Google Sheets analysis, and the chart is the same except for cosmetic differences. Notice that in its current form, the graph truncates the y-axis and makes the effect look larger than it is; if you were presenting this chart, you should adjust the y-axis to reflect the actual scale of the variable. Under "Additional Options" you can request that the output also include "Estimates of Effect Size," which will give you the eta-squared numbers we calculated earlier (saving you some calculation!) and descriptive statistics (means and standard deviations) for each group.

The new information that you can get from JASP comes in the "simple main effects" section of the analysis. If you go to that section and enter "video" as the simple effect factor and "age" as the moderator factor 1, you get the additional output in Figure 12.12 (which also illustrates how to request this analysis).

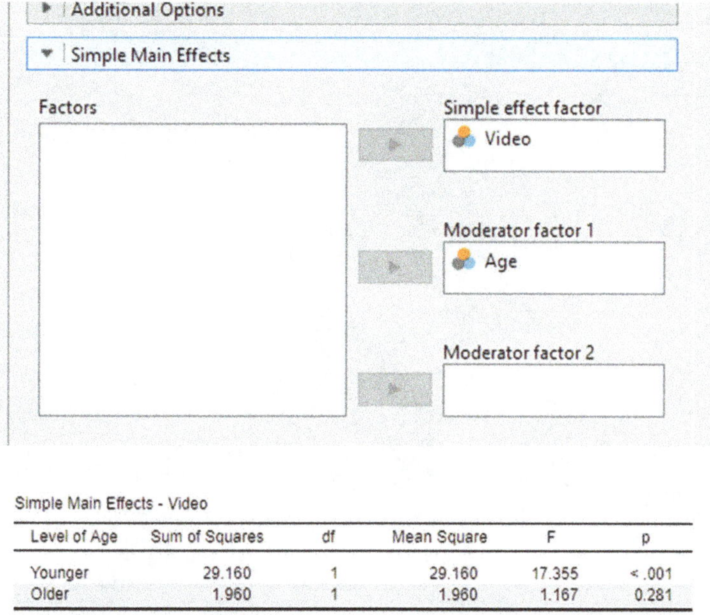

Simple Main Effects - Video

Level of Age	Sum of Squares	df	Mean Square	F	p
Younger	29.160	1	29.160	17.355	< .001
Older	1.960	1	1.960	1.167	0.281

FIGURE 12.12 Requesting simple main effects in JASP

These simple main effects test differences between means *within* the factorial design. So the row for "younger" in Figure 12.12 is telling Andre whether the BuzzFeed and control conditions are significantly different *just among younger people*. The row marked "older" is doing the same but *just among older people*. Looking at the *p*-values on the far right, you should be able to see that the effect among younger people is statistically significant: Young people who watched the BuzzFeed video saw the candidate as *significantly* more credible than young people who watched the control video. On the other hand, the effect among older people is not significant: There is no statistical difference between older people who saw the BuzzFeed video and older people who saw the control video. Just by looking at the chart, we knew that the effect among younger people was bigger (the line for younger people is steeper, indicating a bigger difference between means). But it is only with this test of simple main effects that we can confirm that that difference is significant. Likewise, while we could see that the effect among older people was smaller, we didn't know if the effect was significant or not: Perhaps the effect is still "real," even though it's smaller. The test of simple main effects tells us that the effect, statistically speaking, is not different from zero. These simple main effects tests are another helpful way to break down the detailed meaning of an interaction effect.

Credits

Fig. 12.2: Copyright © by Frontline Systems, Inc.

Fig. 12.3: Copyright © by Frontline Systems, Inc.

SECTION 7

Content Analysis of the Web: Did the Fitness Campaign Work?

By the end of this section, you will be able to:

- ✔ Write definitions and code naturally occurring communication using content analysis
- ✔ Describe the process of checking intercoder reliability
- ✔ Describe key stages in training content analysis coders
- ✔ Distinguish between simple and multiple regression
- ✔ Describe why it is sometimes important to statistically control variables
- ✔ Write the results of a regression analysis

CHAPTER 13

Doing the Research: Content Analysis

You might remember Francisco from Section 5. Francisco studied 500 middle school students from Bakersville, assessing whether they had seen a "Get Active!" social media fitness campaign designed by the local government health agency. He found that about 40% of girls had seen the message, but only about a quarter of boys. The agency has now asked him to assess whether the students who did see the message engaged in more exercise and specifically whether seeing the message multiple times helped increase its effect. The health agency will use this information to decide how much of its budget to invest in sponsored social media postings. If repeated exposures increase the effectiveness of the message, then they will want to invest enough in the program to give a good chance of students being exposed multiple times.

The research question that Francisco begins with is as follows:

> RQ: Is repeated exposure to the "Get Active!" campaign on social media associated with higher levels of physical exercise?

Following the techniques learned already in this book, you could probably imagine Francisco giving the students a questionnaire asking them how often they have seen the message and how often they exercise. That would be one option for doing this research. Francisco has another idea, however, that capitalizes on these students' heavy use of social media. He is going to analyze their social media accounts to examine both how often they have seen the relevant message and how much they have been exercising. This technique has one major advantage over the questionnaire: It avoids responses that are **socially desirable**. Socially desirable responses are ones that a research subject might give you not because they are true, but because the subject thinks it's what you want to hear or because it's a socially acceptable answer.

How will Francisco go about this? He is going to use a technique called **content analysis**. As the name suggests, content analysis is a systematic examination of the content of a set of messages. The content being examined might be "surface"-level features, such as how many words there are in a newspaper article: This is sometimes called **manifest content**. It might also be content that is subtler or hidden, such as underlying themes or biases in television shows: This is called

latent content. In Francisco's case, the messages are the children's social media posts during the period the "Get Active!" campaign was running, and the content he is interested in is anything indicating exposure to the campaign, and anything indicating that the kids are engaged in physical activity.

A key term for content analysis is **coding**. Coding is the process of taking a message and scoring it or putting it into a category so as to be able to compare it to other messages. Consider a half-hour TV show. You could code the TV show based on how many male (versus female) characters it contained. This would involve watching the show and counting of all the people on screen how many are male and how many are female. Once you had done this, you could say you had "coded the show for character sex." Coding is just the process of translating the natural content of a message into numerical scores representing specific variables. If you coded a newspaper for number of political stories, you would simply go through the newspaper and count how many stories were political (as well as probably how many were not about politics). Coding is done by **coders**. Coders are people who use a set of **coding definitions** and rules determined by the researcher to generate the data (e.g., they are the people who watch the television show and decide for each character whether the person is male or female).

Why not an experiment?

As discussed earlier in the book, experiments are typically considered the best way to demonstrate a causal relationship. And given that Francisco is interested in whether the "Get Active!" campaign *caused* kids to engage in more exercise, you might wonder why he isn't using an experiment. In the case of a social media campaign like the one Francisco is investigating, randomly assigning some children to receive the message and others to not receive it is logistically very complicated. The campaign is buying placements for its message on the social media site, and that process probably won't allow for individual-level assignment. In cases like this where the researcher is trying to investigate the efficacy of an intervention in the real world, a true experiment may not be possible, and so creative alternatives like Francisco's plan become necessary.

Gathering the Data

You will recall in the previous chapter about Francisco's project that we spent some time discussing how to get consent to do research with children. The same processes would apply in terms of getting access to the children's social media accounts. Francisco would need to get permission from both the parents *and* the children in order to view their accounts. For the purposes of this chapter, we will assume he has engaged in this process and gained consent from 100 students (and parents) to look at their social media accounts.

It turns out that this population of middle schoolers almost exclusively uses the social networking app "Instabook," and so Francisco's analysis will focus on that app. Instabook features posts that can include photos and/or text, similar to a number of other popular social networks. Posts are typically very short and can be a mix of things by the account owner (the child in this case) and advertising and promotional messages. Francisco, of course, is particularly interested in the "Get Active!" message that appeared among each child's Instabook posts.

Francisco is working with a sample of 100 middle schoolers and examining all of their social media posts over a period of four weeks. How many posts total do you think Francisco might be dealing with? Guess a number.

Once he has gathered all of the students' posts, he discovers that each child posts an average of about eight times a day. That means that he has collected about 22,000 posts. Yes—you read that number correctly! Four weeks is 28 days, multiplied by 8 posts a day (224 posts per student) multiplied by 100 students gives us 22,400 posts.

Francisco has a number of tasks ahead of him. He needs to develop a plan to sample the messages he will code, to code the messages, and then actually do the coding. Then, of course, he will need to analyze the data—something we'll discuss in Chapter 14.

Sampling Messages

Previous chapters have discussed how to draw a sample of people from a population. In those cases, random (representative) samples are used to get a sample of people who represent the population—a sample from which claims can be made about the entire population of people. Nonrandom samples are used when generalizing to a population isn't the main goal of the research. **Sampling**, however, is not just for people! Biologists sample individual animals from populations of animals. Airline safety researchers sample individual airplanes from fleets (populations) of aircraft. And communication researchers sample messages from **populations of messages**.

As will become clearer when we describe the coding process, Francisco can't possibly analyze all 22,400 of the posts he has gathered, and so he will need to **sample** from the population of posts (messages) in order to have a manageable data set to analyze. He knows that if he randomly samples posts, he will be able to generalize from his sample to the entire population of 22,400 messages without having to analyze every single message.

Francisco wants to make sure that every student is represented in his sample, and so he samples 20 messages from each student over the course of the 4-week period of the study. To make sure that his sample represents the complete time frame, he also breaks this down by week, sampling five posts per student per week. As you can see from Figure 13.1, this results in a sample of 2,000 posts. This is still a lot, but more manageable than 22,000!

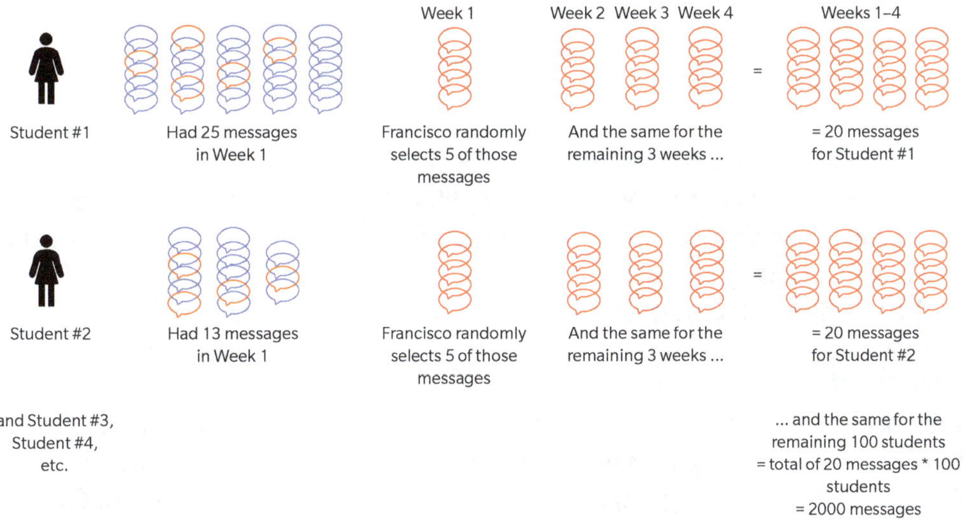

FIGURE 13.1 Illustration of sampling messages over weeks for multiple students

The first tab in the Google Sheet for this section illustrates what these text data would look like (see the "Posts" tab at http://bit.ly/2MHGfOO).

Unitizing

In Francisco's study, it is fairly clear what an individual "unit" is: It's a post. Because of how social media is formatted, an individual "post" is easy to identify. In other contexts, it can be harder. If you were coding the sex of characters in a television show, for instance, you might struggle to define what a "character" is. Is it anybody who appears on screen (good luck with a shot of a crowd in a football stadium!), or anybody who speaks (what if a group of people all speak at the same time?), or only major characters in the show (and how do you define major?). Hence, before you can code a message, it is often necessary to define what the units are that you are coding. This process is called unitizing and can sometimes be just as complicated as the subsequent coding process. In a small group discussion, for instance, coding when one person stops talking and another starts can be very complex. Human interaction doesn't always have nice clear exchanges of speaking turns: people interrupt, talk simultaneously, have side conversations, and offer supportive back channels ("mm-hmm"). If you were doing research in a situation like this, you would need clear definitions of what counts as a speaking "turn."

Developing a Coding System

Francisco needs to derive two important bits of information from the analysis: the extent to which students were exposed to the "Get Active!" message and the extent to which they engaged in physical activity. We will deal with these in turn, as they require different levels of complexity in their analysis.

Get Active!

Presence of the "Get Active!" campaign in a student's feed is a relatively easy thing to code. Each campaign message contains specific text—specifically the "Get Active!" tagline. Assuming that very few other posts on Instabook will feature this phrase (!), it is quite easy to identify the number of campaign posts in any student's feed. Indeed, this task is so easy, it is perfectly suited for a computer. Computers are adept at reading text and identifying specific phrases; they can do so accurately and incredibly efficiently. While it might take a human many hours to read through all of the Instabook posts to find the ones from the "Get Active!" campaign, a computer can do so in a matter of a few seconds. This sort of task can be done directly in Google Sheets (and similar spreadsheet software, such as Excel). The second tab in the Google Sheet for this chapter ("Text Analysis" tab at http://bit.ly/2MHGfOO) shows this process in action with a small sample of text and explains how to accomplish this sort of coding. This is very easy for the computer to code because Francisco is looking for one very precise phrase: He is looking for **manifest** content.

Computer-aided text analysis

As is clear from the "Get Active!" coding, computers are good at searching for specific words and phrases. Computers can also uncover more **latent** content in text. The program LIWC (http://liwc.wpengine.com/) codes language for *sets* of words that indicate broader underlying psychological concepts. For instance, the program codes language relating to *causation* by coding the frequency of words like "because" and "effect," and codes *power* by counting words like "bully" or "superior." The overall presence of such words indicates that the writer/speaker was psychologically concerned with those concepts. Even more complex and subtle coding is possible by machine learning and artificial intelligence techniques that are still in their infancy. The next decade is likely to see massive steps forward in researchers' ability to feed text into computers and get a startling array of analysis back concerning very subtle and deep aspects of the language. Visuals, and especially video, are considerably more difficult for computers to code, but progress is being made in this area too.

Engaging in Physical Activity

Identifying the extent to which the children engaged in physical activity from their Instabook posts is more challenging than the coding in the previous section. Here Francisco may be looking for more *latent* content in the posts. All of the posts about exercising won't say exactly the same thing; some may just imply that exercise is occurring, and some posts about exercising won't reflect precisely what Francisco is interested in (i.e., posts reflecting that the person doing the posting has actually exercised or is planning to).

This last point reveals (again) the importance of a good **conceptual definition**. Francisco needs to define what he's going to be looking for in the posts in order to be able to measure them properly. He writes the following conceptual definition:

> An exercise post describes voluntary physical activity engaged in by the poster, a plan to engage in physical activity, or a desire to engage in said activity. The physical activity being described must extend beyond that required for everyday activities. The physical activity being described must be logistically feasible.

Notice how the definition establishes boundaries for what kinds of posts are going to count and which are not. Descriptions of unrealistic physical activity ("I'm going to climb Mt. Everest this afternoon") don't count and neither do descriptions of activity that is just a part of daily life (e.g., "I missed the bus this morning and had to walk to school"). For posts to count, they must describe *voluntary* activity (again, the walking to school post doesn't count, nor would a post about a physical education class at school). Descriptions of a desire to engage in activity do count, but they would need to meet the other criteria too: the activity being desired would need to be voluntary and the like. Other people might write a slightly different definition of what a physical activity post consists of, but Francisco's seems sufficient for now.

Francisco needs to convert this conceptual definition into an **operational definition**. Operational definitions in content analysis are different from those in, for instance, survey research. For a questionnaire study, the operational definition of a variable might be the set of questions you are going to ask, their response options, and instructions for calculating the score. In a content analysis, the operational definition is the list of instructions for the **coders**.

Based on all of the preceding discussion, Francisco ends up with the coding system in Figure 13.2. Notice that this system involves two elements: a set of definitions and instructions, and a reporting tool (the "coding sheet"). Often, the reporting tool is electronic so that as the coders do their work, the data are recorded automatically; you can see an electronic version of the coding sheet at this link: http://bit.ly/2NBBndP.

Coding instructions

Consider each post individually. Write the child ID and post# on the coding sheet.
You may consider the time and date of posting when making judgments about whether a post counts as a physical activity post.

Code as a "Physical activity" post if the post indicates:

a) an intent by the poster to engage in physical activity ("Let's go play baseball!")
b) a desire of the poster to engage in physical activity ("I wish I had someone to play tennis with")
c) indication of past physical activity by the poster ("so tired from my long run this afternoon")

Do not code as "Physical activity" if

a) No physical activity is described
b) The physical activity described is unrealistic ("Might as well try to swim across the Atlantic ...")
c) The physical activity described is non-voluntary. For instance, physical activity as part of daily activity ("My dad made me help him build a wall this afternoon; exhausted!")
d) Physical activity *not* by the poster (e.g., "You guys played great out there today!").

Coding sheet (see electronic version here: http://bit.ly/2NBBndP)

Child ID: ________
Post #: ________
Physical Activity (circle one): Yes No

FIGURE 13.2 Francisco's coding scheme: Coding instructions and coding sheet

Training Coders, Intercoder Reliability, and Coding

While Francisco might be tempted to just look through the posts himself and decide which ones are exercise posts, that isn't the ideal method. What might be wrong with Francisco making these decisions on his own?

You probably thought that Francisco might be biased in some way, and that would be the primary concern. Perhaps he wants the "Get Active!" campaign to work and so would be more likely to classify a post as an exercise post if he notices that the child has seen more of the "Get Active!" messages. You might also have been concerned that just having one person make all these judgments will lead to problems. Francisco might get tired or bored looking at a whole bunch of posts and deciding if they are going to count as exercise posts. Both of these would be reasonable concerns. He needs coders who are **independent**: this means is that they are not directly involved in other parts of the research project (and hence can be unbiased) and that they are unaware of the specific hypotheses being examined. This reduces the possibility of bias.

Once the coding system is set up, Francisco will need to find some coders to implement it. Depending on the situation, coders can sometimes be undergraduate students looking for independent study credit, employees who help with research as part of their jobs, or temporary workers. We'll assume that Francisco has recruited Sam and Jo to help him with his coding; they are student workers at the health department.

Once Francisco has his coders, he needs to **train** them to use his coding scheme. While he has carefully written the instructions, the coders will need some practice and help to get used to the process. He'll need to train coders until they are good enough to do the actual coding. This raises the question of what "good enough" means when it comes to coding in content analysis. The key way to judge whether coding has been performed effectively is **intercoder reliability.** Intercoder reliability is a measure of how much different coders agree with one another when they code objects (while not consulting with one another). If different coders operating independently can agree on whether a particular post is an exercise post (or isn't), then that's a good indication that Francisco's coding scheme is good. If they cannot agree with one another, then his scheme probably isn't good. Intercoder reliability is measured using a statistic called Krippendorff's alpha. Krippendorff's alpha has a maximum value of 1. Typically, values above .70 are treated as acceptable. Francisco will be hoping he can get his coders to a level of reliability greater than .70. In the "Going Further" part, you can learn how to calculate intercoder reliability.

Francisco will need to engage in at least three main steps for effective coder training. For some of this training, he will use actual posts, but not posts from the final data set. Remember that Francisco collected a lot of data but is only going to use 20 posts per subject for the actual coding. All those other posts can be used to help train the coders. We'll call all these leftover posts the "training posts."

a) Explain the coding system to the coders: Before coders can attempt to code, they will need an explanation of the procedures and some education about what the definitions in Francisco's coding scheme mean. This might also involve looking at some of the "training posts" just mentioned and discussing as a group how they might be coded.

b) Have the coders practice with a set of training posts (again, a reminder that these are *not* part of the final data set; they also shouldn't use posts that they discussed in the previous step). Francisco might pick a small set of posts (perhaps 50 total) and have the coders practice with those. For this part of the coding, they will need to do their work *independently*. Earlier, we said that it's important for the coders to be independent of Francisco and unaware of the goals of the project, so they are not biased. Now we are learning of an additional reason for that independence: They need to be independent of each other. Once they are actually doing coding, they can't consult with each other about their decisions, because the coders influencing one another could also be a source of bias.

c) If the practice coding reliability is bad (Krippendorff's alpha below .70), then Francisco will need to do additional work to improve the coders' reliability. Can you think of two things that Francisco might do to improve his coders' reliability?

If you do content analysis, you shouldn't despair if the coders are unreliable on the first trial. It's very common for it to take a while for coders to get proficient with a coding system. The more complex the scheme, the more training and practice will be needed. If Francisco's coders don't have excellent reliability, then things Francisco can do include the following:

Look at the specific training posts on which they disagree. Imagine, for instance, that the coders disagreed about whether the following counted as an exercise post:

"Are you ready for some football?"

One of the coders saw this as expressing a desire to play football, while the other (familiar with the tagline for ESPN's *Monday Night Football*) interpreted it as indicating that the person was going to *watch* some football on TV. Based on this discussion, Francisco would clarify in his coding system how coders should interpret similar content. What do you think he might do?

One possible thing for coders to consider would be the timing of the post (something that could easily be kept as part of the coding): If the post happened at 8:30 pm Eastern on a Monday night, then coders could use that information to weigh the relative possibility of it actually reflecting physical activity!

Or imagine the coders disagreeing on a post like the following:

"Gotta run!"

Perhaps one coder interpreted it as indicating a desire to go jogging, while the other thought it reflected someone closing a conversation ("Nice talking to you, gotta run!"). What could Francisco do to adjust his coding scheme for this disagreement?

In this case, Francisco would probably need to discuss the nature of Instabook—is it a platform where people have the type of online conversations where "gotta run" might serve the function of closing a conversation? If not—if people mostly post updates but don't interact with one another—then it would be best to understand this statement as an exercise post. In the coding scheme, Francisco might add a description of how Instabook works so that information could be used in interpreting posts. Depending on how the data were organized, Francisco could also allow coders to use the context (e.g., by considering the posts before and after this post to see if those posts provide any clues as to the poster's intent). This sort of fix would be implemented by adding a sentence to the coding scheme saying something like, "For ambiguous posts, you may consider the post immediately preceding and following in order to understand context. Do not go beyond the immediately preceding and following posts." Why do you think Francisco might limit the "context" to the immediately preceding and following posts?

I can imagine two reasons he might do this. First, if coders start looking through someone's entire posting history, they might be biased by completely separate posts. For example, if they see that the person is on the football team, they'd assume that a post was a physical activity post, whereas the same post might not be coded as physical activity if they see that the person is on the chess team. If you want people to code individual posts, then looking at the immediate context might be helpful, but you want to avoid introducing bias that might be caused by finding out too much extraneous information about the poster. Second, Francisco might simply be trying to keep the coding process efficient: If his coders go looking through hundreds of other posts just to try to interpret *one*, they might never finish their work! Scientific accuracy is always the top priority, of course, but researchers must also be realistic about designing tasks they can actually finish.

As you can see, discussion of disagreements and clarifying the coding system can be very useful tools for improving reliability. If the coders ran into similar issues subsequently, they'd have a better idea of how to deal with them. All of this has to happen *before* the "real" coding begins. Once you start coding the actual sample, you can't change the coding scheme or procedures, so the training process is critical to make sure everything is right before you start gathering the real data.

Of course, sometimes it is possible that a particular *coder* is really the problem. If a researcher has three coders, it is possible to see if two of the coders have good reliability with one another, but the third coder is frequently disagreeing. This might reveal a different perspective of the third coder (e.g., perhaps he or she is from a different cultural or age group that views the messages differently), or maybe the person is simply not being careful enough in his or her coding and needs to be assigned to a different task. Francisco only has two coders, but if he notices that one of the coders is repeatedly coding materials in ways that don't make sense or that don't follow basic instructions, he should consider hiring a replacement!

The examples of disagreements also reflect why it is difficult to achieve perfect reliability between coders. Human communication is often ambiguous, and messages can have multiple meanings that depend on context and on the particular person. When doing content analysis, you are sometimes trying to make judgments about the meaning of messages without having all of the context available. All social science measurement has some "error" in it: we can't measure human social behavior with the accuracy that we can measure the temperature of a liquid or the speed of an Olympic sprinter.

Exhaustive and mutually exclusive category systems

Francisco's category system is fairly straightforward: A post is coded either as reflecting physical activity or not. However, this system illustrates two characteristics of how variables must be organized in content analysis coding: The categories to be coded must be exhaustive and mutually exclusive.

Exhaustive: For a coding system to be exhaustive, every item being coded must fit in a category. When Francisco's coders are working, they do not have the option of looking at a post and "passing" if they don't know where to put it. Every single post has to be coded into one of the available categories. A coding system that doesn't have a home for every option is a bad system. Imagine a coding scheme for web pages where they are coded according to whether they are sites for (a) businesses, (b) nonprofits, or (c) government entities. This would work fine until you run into a personal website or a website for a small community group, which isn't officially a nonprofit. For the coding system to work, it would need to either have additional categories for those situations or (sometimes a good option) an "other" category to capture all of the cases that didn't fit into the main three categories.

continues on next page

continues from previous page

Mutually exclusive: If a category system is mutually exclusive, then something can only belong in one category: there is no possibility for it to be coded into multiple categories. Imagine trying to code those websites into categories like (a) business, (b) nonprofit, (c) government, and (d) religious. These are not mutually exclusive categories because some religious sites might also be nonprofits, and others might be businesses (e.g., a religious book store).

Clearly, for Francisco, he doesn't have any concerns on this front: His categories are clearly exhaustive (if it is not an exercise post, it goes in the "not" category) and mutually exclusive (something can't be both an exercise post and not an exercise post). But as you saw earlier, other situations are not as clear-cut. If you design your own category system, make sure to think carefully about whether there might be things that don't fit in any category or that fit in more than one category.

Validity of Coding

Coding is measurement—the process of taking a set of messages and categorizing or scoring them is the content analysis equivalent of a person completing a questionnaire. As noted earlier, reliability is a big deal in content analysis, and assessing intercoder reliability is essential to demonstrating the quality of the measurement. Validity is often given less attention, but it is also important. You might remember from Chapter 7 that we looked at three types of validity:

Face validity: The general impression that a tool measures what it is supposed to measure based on a close examination of the tool.

Content validity: The extent to which a measurement scale assesses the full breadth of a concept. If you were measuring *communication competence*, a scale that only assessed your public speaking skills would have weak content validity. A scale that assessed your communication abilities in public settings (e.g., giving a speech, asking a question in a group setting) and private settings (e.g., having a conversation with a stranger) would have stronger content validity.

Criterion-related validity: The extent to which a measure is associated with other measures that it "should" be related to (the criterion measures). A measure of communication competence should be related to your success in persuading other people, or ratings of your public speaking performance, or your ability to maintain successful interpersonal relationships. If it is unrelated to any of those things, it's probably not a valid measure of communication competence.

Francisco can apply these aspects of validity assessment to content analysis.

Face validity: This one is easy. The goal in face validity is simply to look at whether, on the face of it, the measurement is reasonable. This process will occur throughout the coding training and particularly as Francisco examines the "errors" his coders make. When he sees something being coded incorrectly, or coders disagreeing on how to code something, he will get insight into the face validity of his coding scheme. Note: This also gives some indication of the connection between reliability and validity; often, a lack of reliability is symptomatic of a validity problem.

Content validity: Once Francisco has conceptually defined what exercise counts as, checking the content validity of his coding system is as simple as double-checking that all of the possible aspects of an exercise post appear in his coding system.

Criterion-related validity: This is often the most challenging form of validity for a content analysis. To check the criterion-related validity of a content analysis coding system, you need data from some other source to confirm the accuracy of your coding. If you are coding the sex of television characters, for instance, what else could you look at to see if the characters are really of the sex that you coded them as?

Perhaps you could look up the actors' sex in a database. While occasionally actors might play someone of a different sex, most of the time, they'll play someone of their own sex. Or you could look at information about a show to see how the characters were being referenced (e.g., use of "he" or "she" in describing a character). If you found repeated indications that your coders had coded someone as one sex while the actor was a different sex or other information about the show referred to the character as a different sex, that would indicate a validity problem.

How about for Francisco? What could he do to check the validity of his coding for the students' levels of exercise by examining its association with some other measure?

Francisco has the advantage that he is coding something for real people—people he can ask questions about in real life. He could ask students to self-report on their exercise or ask their parents or teachers how physically active the students are. If he found a low correlation between the Instabook coding and independent reports of physical activity, that might suggest that the Instabook measure was not valid. However, it might also indicate that the students' self-reports or their parents' or teachers' reports were not valid—in fact, remember that he used the Instabook coding precisely because he wasn't sure that students would accurately report their own physical activity levels! A really great alternate way to assess validity here might be having some of the students wear an activity monitor (e.g., a Fitbit watch) to see if their true activity levels reflected the scores from coding Instabook. Can you think of any disadvantages of using the Fitbit method?

I think there are two main disadvantages of this method. First, it would be rather expensive. Unless Francisco can convince Fitbit to give him the watches (might be worth a try!), he will need to buy quite a few of them, and the local health department might not have that sort of budget. Second, it's possible that the watches themselves might change the students' levels of physical activity. That's kind of the point of the watches. So, Francisco might be actually changing the students' activity simply by observing them—the opposite of what he was seeking by using **unobtrusive measurement**. As you've seen elsewhere in the book, this is another illustration where there isn't a perfect solution to the problem, but there are a number of options with various pros and cons. Part of learning to think like a researcher is identifying the pros and cons of the different options available and then making the best choice dependent on your specific research goals and resources.

Observer effects

Francisco's concern that giving students' Fitbit watches might change their activity levels is a good example of what is sometimes called an observer effect. Observer effects happen when the mere act of observing something changes the thing being observed. The term Hawthorne effect is sometimes used to describe this effect because of one of the earliest demonstrations of it. In research done at a factory called Hawthorne Works, researchers are said to have discovered that almost any intervention they did with the workers ended up increasing productivity. That result suggests that merely being observed increased productivity, no matter what the actual intervention involved. There is some controversy about the scientific details of the original Hawthorne study, but the idea that sometimes observation can change what is observed is fairly well accepted. If you place a camera in someone's bedroom, it's fairly intuitive that some of their bedroom behavior might change! As social scientists, it's important for us to be aware that even our research studies are social activities, and people's social behavior changes depending on the context they are in; when people are in an experiment or filling out a survey, they may not behave the same way they do when they are not in those situations.

Writing the Report

Describing a content analysis is similar to describing any other method. It is important for Francisco to tell his readers about the steps in his process so that they can judge the quality of his work and, at least in theory, replicate his analysis (Report 13.1). This means providing details on the conceptual and operational definitions, information on intercoder reliability, and all the other steps described earlier. Often, these descriptions can get quite complicated; giving an overview of the process at the start can be useful.

REPORT 13.1 Methods for Content Analysis

Overview. We obtained a random sample of Instabook posts from middle school students. The presence of "Get Active!" messages and references to physical activity in the posts was assessed using computer-aided text analysis.

continues on next page

continues from previous page

Sample. Students (*N* = 100) were recruited from a middle school in a large midwestern city. The sample was 50% female, 50% male, and ethnically diverse (46% white, 22% black/African American, 17 % Hispanic, 12% Asian American, 6% Native American, 12% other; numbers do not sum to 100% because respondents could select more than one category).

The students and their parents consented to grant the researchers access to their Instabook accounts; Instabook is the most widely used social network among this age group of students (Social Media Now, 2019). From all of the posts on an individual's Instabook account, we randomly sampled five posts per week over a 4-week period for a total of 20 posts per student and hence 2,000 posts total. Posts included posts by the student him/herself as well as third-party posts to the student's account by advertisers (including the "Get Active!" campaign).

Coding. "Get Active!" messages were counted using computer-assisted text analysis in Google Sheets. The number of instances of the phrase "Get Active!" was counted; it was assumed that all such instances were sponsored posts by the "Get Active!" campaign. The number (out of 20 posts) was recorded as the student's score (*M* = 3.34, *SD* = 2.00).

The presence of physical activity by the students (as reported in Instabook posts) was coded using traditional content analysis techniques. I developed a preliminary operational definition for what would indicate physical activity in an Instabook post. Through meetings and practice coding sessions with two independent coders (both trained undergraduate research assistants), the operational definitions were refined to the final coding system shown in Figure 1. Each student post in the sample was then coded by both assistants (Krippendorff's alpha = .82). Students received a final score for the total number of physical exercise posts in their sample; this score could range from 0 to 20 (*M* = 5.58, *SD* = 2.35).

Code as an "Engaging in physical activity" if the post indicates:

a) An intent by the poster to engage in physical activity ("Let's go play baseball!")
b) A desire of the poster to engage in physical activity ("I wish I had someone to play tennis with")
c) Indication of past physical activity by the poster ("so tired from my long run this afternoon")

Do not code as a physical activity post if:

a) No physical activity is described
b) The physical activity described is unrealistic ("Might as well try to swim across the Atlantic ...")
c) The physical activity described is non-voluntary. For instance, physical activity as part of daily activity ("My dad made me help him build a wall this afternoon; exhausted!")
d) Physical activity *not* by the poster (e.g., "You guys played great out there today!")

FIGURE 1 Coding "engaging in physical activity" instructions

Other Applications

Content analysis is widely used in the discipline of communication. As an academic field that is focused on messages, understanding the content of messages is obviously very important, and content analysis provides a systematic quantitative method of uncovering that content. Content analysis is useful when the goal is a pure understanding of content. These can be purely descriptive studies:

- How many news stories report on candidate A versus candidate B?
- What percentage of TV shows feature a major character of a minority ethnicity?

Such studies can also examine associations between content variables:

- Do TV shows featuring nudity (e.g., *Game of Thrones*) include more verbal references to sex than shows not featuring nudity?
- Do major newspapers describe Democratic politicians using more positive words than Republican politicians?

The first example looks at the association between visual representations and verbal representations; both are aspects of content. The second looks at whether the content suggests a political bias by looking at associations between *who* is being described and *how* they are being described.

Content analysis can also be used as part of examinations of questions that go beyond content. For example, examining whether news coverage is associated with public preferences for political candidates would involve two sources of data:

1. Examination of the nature of news coverage about different candidates using content analysis, and
2. People's preferences for candidates (probably assessed using a survey, or political polling data, or perhaps even voting outcomes).

Similarly, imagine a study examining whether the temperature in a room influences the frequency with which people use heat-related metaphors in their speech (e.g., "He's super-hot!" "You need to cool down a little" "Now we're cooking!"). The researcher might use an experiment in which he or she can control the temperature in a room and record people having conversations when it's either warm or cool in the space. To measure the dependent variable, the researcher might well use content analysis to code for how often heat metaphors appear in the conversations. In this sort of example, the content analysis is a critical part of the process, but the entire study is more than simply a content analysis. Hence, while we often refer to a study as being "an experiment" or "a content analysis," it's important to remember that some studies involve components of multiple distinct methods.

Typically, content analysis involves coding considerably more variables than in Francisco's example. For instance, Mastro and Figueroa-Caballero (2018) examined over 1,000 television characters to understand how people of different body types were portrayed. They coded the characters' body types (obviously) but also their attractiveness and how intelligent they were portrayed, as well as their sex, race, and likeability. Each of those factors was a different variable that had to be defined, coders had to be trained, and then the coders had to code reliably. Among other findings, these researchers showed that women were more likely to be portrayed as underweight than men; overweight characters were portrayed as less intelligent than non-overweight characters; underweight characters were the most likable.

As discussed earlier in the chapter, content analysis is not always the best research method for examining causal associations between variables, and there are many other questions for which content analysis is not the best solution (as is true with all methods—see the "Key Point" section). Nonetheless, it can be a very useful technique for systematically examining the content of messages; for researchers in a discipline that focuses on messages, this is obviously pretty important!

KEY POINT

As we move toward the end of the parts of the book devoted to quantitative methods, it is worth summarizing when and why to use specific types of quantitative technique. As you can see in Figure 13.3, there are some fairly simple rules to help guide decisions about which method to use. When examining causal questions (does X cause Y?), it is best to use an experiment, so long as the key independent variable can be manipulated. If manipulation is not possible, then most of the time, a survey is the next best option. When describing a population or looking for associations between variables in a population, the key guiding issue is understanding the characteristics of the population. If you are describing a population of humans or trying to understand associations between variables in a population of humans, then a survey is your best bet. If the population is *messages*, then a content analysis is the best technique. As noted earlier, combinations of these techniques are also possible. For instance, you might run an experiment but use content analysis to score the dependent variable. Perhaps most importantly, remember that the method you use should be driven by the questions you are trying to answer. Occasionally, a student will show up in my office and say, "I really want to do a content analysis!" I always tell the student that doing a research study because he or she likes a method is rarely a good idea: Decide what ***question*** you are trying to answer and then decide on the most appropriate method to answer that question.

Hypothesis/Research Question specifies causal relationship
- IV can ethically and logistically be manipulated → Experiment
- IV cannot ethically or logistically be manipulated → Survey

H/RQ asks about population characteristics
- Population is humans → Survey
- Population is messages → Content analysis

H/RQ asks about correlations (associations between variables)
- Variables relate to humans → Survey
- Variables relate to messages → Content analysis

FIGURE 13.3 Selecting a method for communication research

Your Turn

For this "Your Turn" section, I'm going to give you a bit more of a specific task than in the previous sections, because the specific project you have been developing might not be suitable for a content analysis. Instead, imagine that you are interested in the amount of detail provided on university health services websites concerning sexually transmitted diseases (STDs). As part of this study, you decide to do a content analysis of that sort of information for a large number of universities. It might help here to briefly look at a couple of universities to see what kind of information they provide (or don't provide) to help generate ideas for how you might measure this. Do the following:

- Decide how you would sample the information you were interested in. Which universities will you examine, and how will they be selected, and which web pages from their health services sites will you focus on?
- Write a brief **conceptual definition** of your main variable (level of detail in STD information). Your definition should be clear on what you mean by STD information (general background or specifically health-related prevention/treatment information?) and what you mean by detail (e.g., amount of information, or explicitness, or specificity in guidance and services described).
- Develop a coding scheme for assessing the level of detail using a content analysis. If you were to have coders look at the websites for a number of university health services sites, what instructions would you need to give them to allow them to "score" those sites in terms of the level of detail provided. Would they just count words, or look for specific types of information, or

assess the diversity of services offered? Remember, this is your operational definition, so it should be consistent with your conceptual definition.

Write your plan using an organization similar to Francisco's (see "Writing the Report"). Make sure that you have developed detailed enough information that you could actually have independent coders do this work for you ... after some training, of course!

Wrap Up

In this chapter, you have learned how to systematically measure the content of messages using content analysis. The chapter has explained that it is possible to sample messages in similar ways to how you sample people: by drawing random samples so that your sample represents the population of all the messages. You should now understand that coding messages requires careful definitions of variables and instructions for coders in how to apply those definitions. You should also now have some understanding of how we examine the reliability and validity of measurement in a content analysis.

If you get nothing else from this chapter, remember the following:

1. Random samples of messages represent populations of messages, much as random samples of people represent populations of people.
2. Careful training is essential for coders to be able to code messages reliably, and during training, sometimes the instructions for coders are adjusted to make the coding more systematic.
3. Intercoder reliability is an index of how much independent coders agree about the application of a coding system; reliability above .70 is acceptable.

Key Chapter Concepts

Coders: The people who do the coding. Typically, we want these people to be **independent**, and we want more than one coder so we can calculate **intercoder reliability**.

Coding definitions: In order to code variables, it is important to have clear conceptual and operational definitions of those variables. See **Conceptual definition.**

Conceptual definition: In content analysis, as with other methods, the conceptual definition of a variable is the verbal description of what the variable represents. See **Coding definition**.

Content analysis: The systematic analysis of messages to reveal patterns in their content.

Independent coders: Independent **coders** are coders who (a) are largely unaware of the specific goals or hypotheses of the research project (and, hence, obviously are not the actual researchers) and (b) do not consult with one another or attempt to influence one another while doing the coding.

Intercoder reliability: The level of agreement between at least two independent coders on a particular coded variable. Intercoder reliability is best assessed using a statistical measure such as Krippendorff's alpha; typically values of alpha above .70 are viewed as acceptable. Low reliability between coders should be investigated during coder training, and further training or adjustment of the coding system should be attempted to improve reliability. If a variable cannot be coded reliably after repeated attempts, it should probably be dropped from the content analysis.

Latent content: The content of a message that is below the surface—not immediately obvious. Coding a movie as expressing optimistic or pessimistic themes would involve coding latent content. It requires deep understanding of the narrative of the movie and probably a weighing of different elements in the story to reach an overall conclusion about the movie's pessimism or optimism.

Manifest content: The content of a message that is on the surface—easy and obvious to see. Coding whether a movie is animated or live action is coding manifest content (although there are movies that involve elements of both, which would require careful operational definitions).

Observer effects: Effects that occur simply because researchers are observing a situation.

Operational definition: In content analysis, the operational definition of the variable is the set of instructions for how to code the message. This would involve clear definitions, procedures for coding (including how to record codes), and instructions for dealing with ambiguous or unclear cases.

Populations of messages: Just like people, messages exist in populations. All issues of *Sports Illustrated*, or every Disney animated movie, or the entire congressional record all count as populations of messages. Often, content analysis can't examine an entire population of messages, so it is necessary to **sample** from that population to achieve a manageable set of messages to code.

Sampling: As in dealing with populations of people, sometimes a **population of messages** is too large for a researcher to examine every one of them. Random (representative) sampling from a population of messages results in a smaller sample of messages that represents the population. For instance, if you are interested in portrayals of women in *Time* magazine but don't have the resources to code every single issue of *Time*, you might randomly sample one issue of the magazine from every year since its inception (in 1923), thus yielding somewhere close to 100 issues to code rather than over 5,000!

Socially desirable: When research subjects tell you something because it's the most socially acceptable response or because it makes them look good, they are engaging in socially desirable responding. Using **unobtrusive measurement** (rather than self-report questionnaires) is a way to avoid getting socially desirable responses from respondents.

Training: It is essential to train coders carefully so they can code a sample of messages with acceptable levels of intercoder reliability. Training typically involves the presentation of the coding scheme by the researcher, some practice coding of messages not in the actual sample, and discussion of disagreements between coders in the practice coding. It may also involve some revision of the coding scheme.

Unitizing: For some type of messages, it isn't absolutely clear where one message ends and another begins. For instance, in a conversation, you might not be certain what counts as a single speaking "turn." If someone tries but fails to interrupt, does that count as a turn? If someone says "mm-hmm" just to indicate that he or she is listening, is that a turn? Unitizing is the process of taking a stream of messages and identifying what the discrete units to be coded are.

Unobtrusive measurement: Measuring something in a way that the things being measured are not aware that they are being measured. Observing someone's behavior in a public space, analyzing the president's tweets, or studying organizations by looking at their press releases and online presence would all be unobtrusive measurement. While the behaviors being produced by the person (or president or organization) are public, the targets of your research have no idea that you are examining that information for specific reasons.

CHAPTER 14

Reporting the Research: Multiple Regression

Francisco now has the data to examine his question from the previous chapter. The data are displayed in the "Final Data" tab of this section's Google Sheet (http://bit.ly/2MHGfOO). You should now be used to this sort of data structure. Each row represents one child's scores, and each column represents a variable. Francisco has four variables, so this data set is a bit larger than previous ones we've seen, but the basic structure is the same. The four columns in the data represent

1. frequency of exposure to the "Get Active!" Message,
2. sex (**1** here represents boys and **2** represents girls),
3. overall use of social media, and
4. frequency of exercising.

Why does he have four variables when he's really only interested in the association between being exposed to the "Get Active!" messages and whether the kids exercise? The other two variables (sex and overall social media use) are variables he thinks might be important to also consider here. He thinks that kids' sex might influence their activity levels—maybe boys are socialized to do more sports, and so it will be important to factor that into his analysis. Similarly, he wants to factor in overall levels of social media use. Any child who uses a lot of social media will also see more "Get Active!" messages—people reading his report might want him to consider that when he writes his report. One important lesson in this chapter will be how Francisco can "factor in" variables other than the ones he is directly interested in.

Which Statistical Test to Use? Introducing Simple Regression

This chapter introduces a new statistical test called regression. It is first worth returning to the very first statistical test we learned about in this book: correlation. Imagine that Francisco just wanted to see whether exposure to the "Get Active!" campaign was associated with exercise. If you remember back to the first decision tree we saw (reproduced here as Figure 14.1), you would use correlation to examine that question.

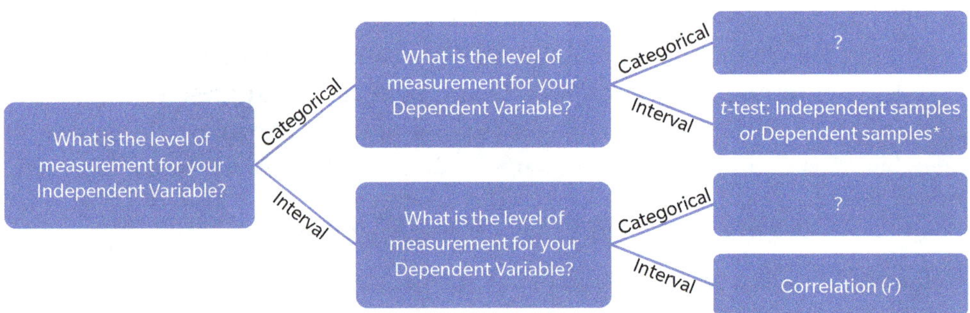

*Independent samples tests are used when samples are unrelated to one another. Dependent samples tests are used when samples are related or when measures are taken on the same group of people at more than one point in time.

FIGURE 14.1 Statistical decision tree

Both the independent and dependent variable are interval-level variables. Do you remember how to calculate a correlation? Make a copy of Francisco's data and calculate a correlation. What do you find?

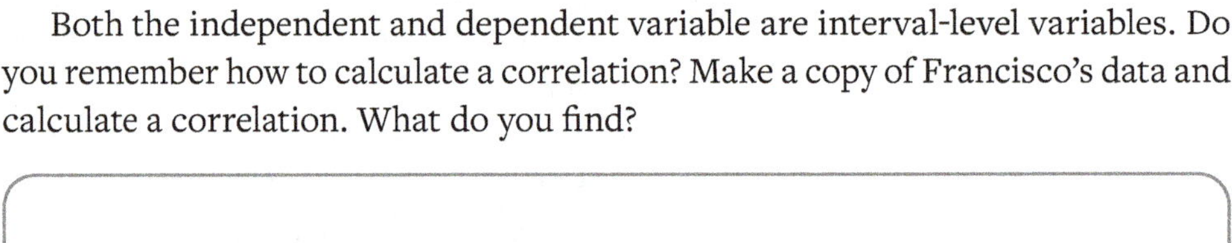

The results are in the "Correlation" tab of the Google Sheet (http://bit.ly/2MHGfOO). You should have said that the two variables are positively correlated, $r = .28$. If you didn't find that correlation, go back and double-check the steps you went through.

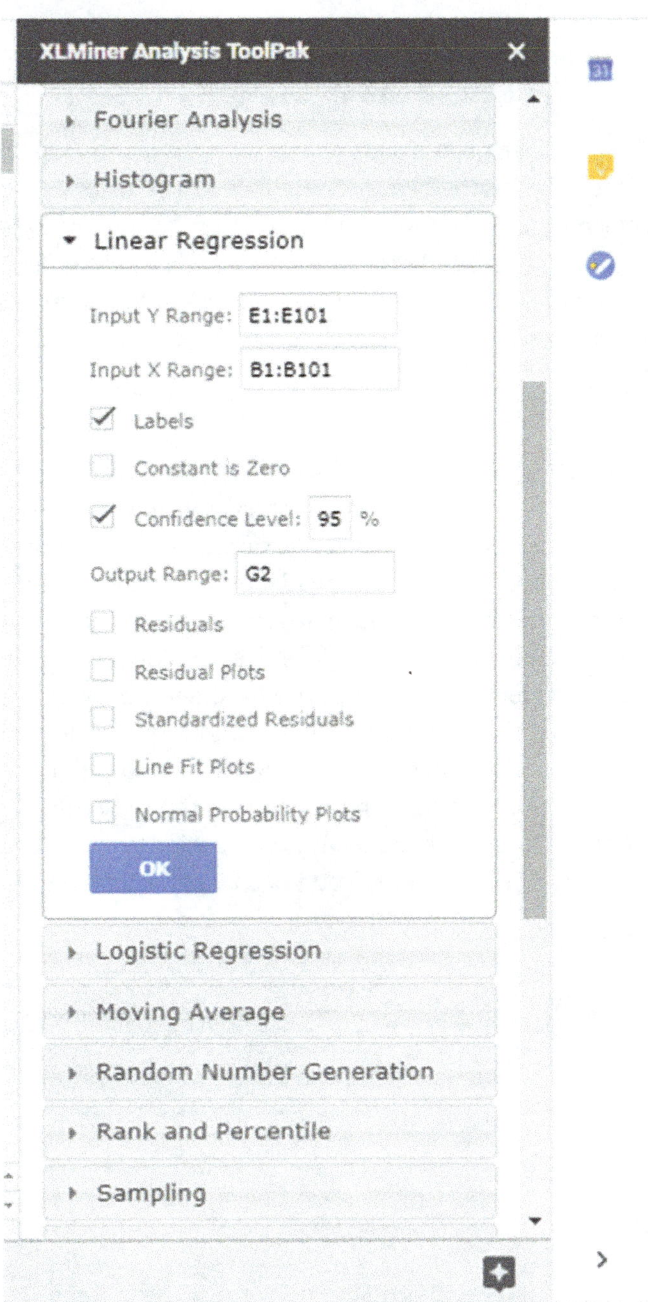

FIGURE 14.2 Simple regression command in Google Sheets

Independent variables are predictors; dependent variables are outcomes

Sometimes the language people use to describe variables changes with different statistical tests. That is the case with regression. Instead of talking about "**independent variables**" and "dependent variables" researchers will often talk about "predictors" or "**predictor variables**" and "outcomes" or "**outcome variables.**" Sometimes the term "**criterion variable**" is used for the outcome or dependent variable. I won't be using that term here, but you might see it elsewhere.

The statistical technique called **regression** is very closely connected to correlation; it also tests for associations between interval-level variables. Let's see what Francisco finds when he uses regression to examine the question we just looked at. The simple regression tab of the spreadsheet shows this same analysis but performed using regression (the "linear regression" command in the XLMiner Analysis ToolPak). **Simple regression** means a regression analysis with one independent and one dependent variable. Figure 14.2 shows how you would define the analysis, and Figure 14.3 shows the output with annotations to help you understand it (you can also see the output in the simple regression table on the Google Sheet: http://bit.ly/2MHGfOO). As with other analyses, I've tidied it by reducing the number of decimal places: This makes it much easier to read. There is a lot of information, but just a few key pieces you need to pay attention to.

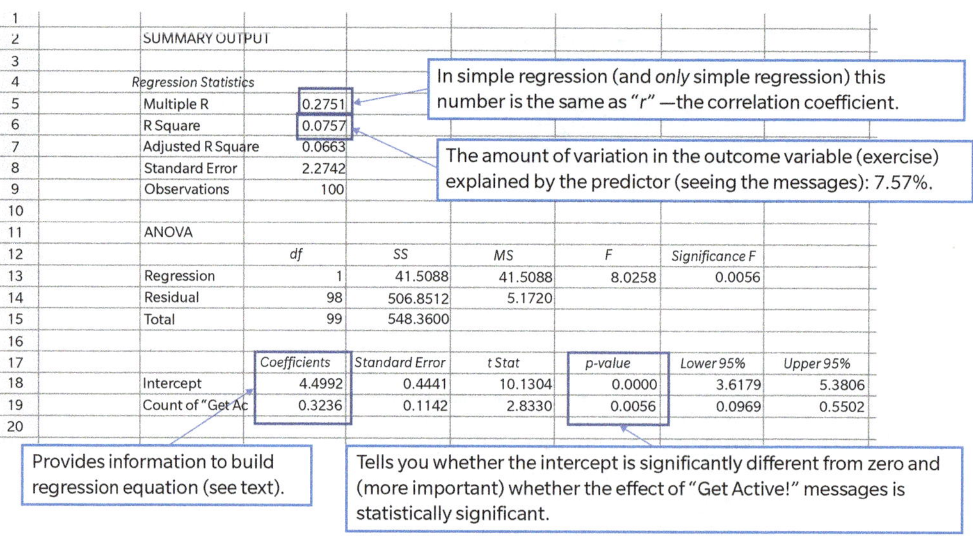

1							
2	SUMMARY OUTPUT						
3							
4	*Regression Statistics*						
5	Multiple R	0.2751					
6	R Square	0.0757					
7	Adjusted R Square	0.0663					
8	Standard Error	2.2742					
9	Observations	100					
10							
11	ANOVA						
12		*df*	*SS*	*MS*	*F*	*Significance F*	
13	Regression	1	41.5088	41.5088	8.0258	0.0056	
14	Residual	98	506.8512	5.1720			
15	Total	99	548.3600				
16							
17		*Coefficients*	*Standard Error*	*t Stat*	*p-value*	*Lower 95%*	*Upper 95%*
18	Intercept	4.4992	0.4441	10.1304	0.0000	3.6179	5.3806
19	Count of "Get Ac	0.3236	0.1142	2.8330	0.0056	0.0969	0.5502
20							

FIGURE 14.3 Annotated simple regression output from Google Sheets

Simple regression has a couple of advantages over correlation. First (and this is just a quirk with Google Sheets), you can get the *p*-value directly from the regression analysis. You might remember that in Chapter 4, we calculated a confidence interval for *r* in order to find out whether it was statistically significant. You don't need to do that with regression. If you look at the *p*-value in the Google Sheet analysis, you can see that it is .0056. What would you conclude about the effect here? Is it statistically significant?

You should have concluded that the effect is statistically significant. Combined with the fact that regression coefficient is positive, this means that as people's exposure to the campaign increases, so too does their level of physical exercise, and that association is not just due to chance.

Second (and more substantively), regression provides Francisco with the information he needs to *predict* people's scores on the dependent variable from their scores on the independent variable. You probably remember from middle school math class that a straight line is defined by an equation:

$$y = ax + b.$$

In the equation, "y" is the score on the y-axis (the vertical axis), and "x" is the score on the x-axis (the horizontal axis). The "a" is the slope of the line (how steeply does it go up (or down) for each unit change in x?), and "b" is the intercept. Where does the line cross the y-axis?

So, a line with the equation **y = 3x + 2** would cross the y-axis at the value of 2 and would be fairly steep and positive (it increases 3 points on y for every increase of 1 on x) (see Figure 14.4).

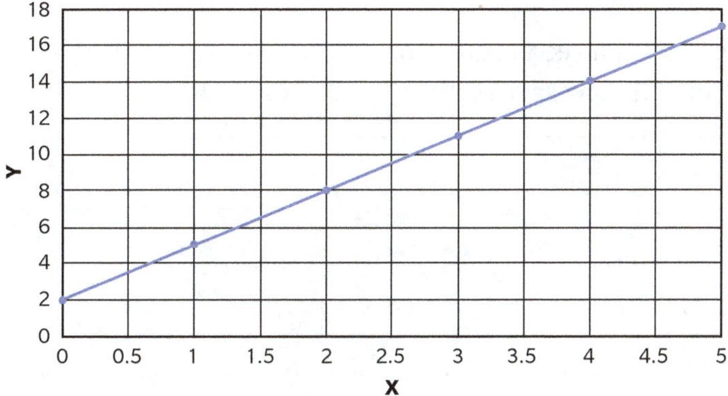

FIGURE 14.4 Straight line corresponding to formula y = 3x + 2

A line with the equation $\mathbf{y = -0.5x + 5}$ would cross the y-axis at the value of 5 and would be less steep and *negative* (it ***de***creases half a point on y for every increase of 1 on x). Try drawing a chart representing this equation: $\mathbf{y = -0.5x + 5}$.

Now, instead of thinking about "x" and "y" as simply axes on a chart, think of them as variables: exposure to "Get Active!" messages (x) and exercise behavior (y). Now the charts become meaningful and knowing the formula for the line is important. The formula lets us answer questions like, "How much does someone exercise if the person sees the "Get Active!" message four times?" Or, "How much *more* would someone exercise if the person saw the message one additional time?"

Let's answer those questions, imagining for now that the equation followed the line:

$$y = 3x + 2,$$

as illustrated in Figure 14.4. In variable form, this would be

Frequency of exercise = 3 (exposure to "Get Active!" messages) + 2.

How often does someone exercise if the person sees see the "Get Active!" message four times?

To solve the equation, you would just insert the number "4" in the slot for "exposure to Get Active!" messages and do the math.

$$\text{Frequency of exercise} = (3 * 4) + 2$$

$$= 12 + 2$$

$$= 14$$

Now think about our second question: "How much *more* would someone exercise if the person saw the message one additional time?" What is your answer here?

You could answer this question by just recalculating the line for the next highest value. For example, since we already know the predicted exercise value for someone who saw the message four times, we could now calculate for someone who saw the message five times.

$$\text{Frequency of exercise} = (3 * 5) + 2$$
$$= 15 + 2$$
$$= 17$$

So, by increasing message exposure by 1, we increase exercise by 3 (from 14 to 17), and given that it's a straight line, this will be the case no matter what the starting value. An easier way to solve this is just to realize that the change in y for one change in x is the *slope* of the line (the "a" in **y** = **ax** + **b**).

There's another interesting question that we can answer here: "How much would someone exercise if the person didn't see any messages at all?" What is your answer here?

You could answer this question by recalculating the line for a message value of zero.

$$\text{Frequency of exercise} = (3 * 0) + 2$$
$$= 0 + 2$$
$$= 2$$

People who never saw a "Get Active!" message would be expected to score a 2 on the exercise variable. An easier way to solve this is to realize that if x = 0, then the answer is just the *intercept* of the line (the "b" in **y** = **ax** + **b**).

This is a level of detail that we can't provide just from a correlation analysis and so is another advantage of regression.

To understand how to do this in practice with real data, check out the "coefficients" in the "Simple Regression" Google Sheet tab and Figure 14.3. You can see that there is a coefficient for the intercept and a coefficient for the "Get Active!"

variable (see the bottom-left corner of the output in Figure 14.3). These are, respectively, the intercept and slope values, and so you can create the actual regression equation as follows:

Frequency of exercise =
0.3236 (exposure to "Get Active!" messages) + 4.4992.

All of the calculations you did above, you could now repeat with this "real" equation. The only difference is that real numbers tend to be a bit messier. You can see right away that if someone never saw a message, the person would be expected to have an exercise score of 4.4992 (the intercept). And that for each message a person sees, his or her exercise score should increase by 0.3236 (the slope). What exercise score would you predict for someone who saw eight "Get Active!" messages?

To figure this out, you would just insert the number 8 into the formula for exposure to "Get Active!" messages and do the math.

$$\text{Frequency of exercise} = (0.3236 * 8) + 4.4992$$
$$= 2.5888 + 4.4992$$
$$= 7.088$$

Regression is a very powerful technique for predicting how someone will score on a particular variable given the person's score on another variable.

Distinguishing Simple Regression From Multiple Regression

Simple regression is great if you want to look at the association between one predictor variable and one outcome. Francisco, however, doesn't have just one independent variable. He has three variables that he thinks might be associated with activity levels:

- Overall social media use
- Sex
- Exposure to "Get Active!" messages

Regression can be extended to look at all of these variables simultaneously. This allows Francisco to see if *each* variable has a statistical effect, *controlling for* the other variables. What does "controlling for" mean? To understand this, it's useful to think about Francisco's finding that "Get Active!" campaign messages are associated with kids' level of exercise. Can Francisco conclude that the messages ***cause*** the exercise?

Yes No

Of course, the answer here is no. Correlation doesn't mean causality. Can you think of one explanation for why being exposed to "Get Active!" messages might be correlated with actually being more active, even though the messages don't *cause* the exercise behavior?

There are a lot of possible answers to this question. Here's one. Remember Aaliyah from earlier in the book? She tells Francisco that what *he* thinks is an effect of the "Get Active!" campaign is *really* an effect of *overall social media use.* She says that kids who use social media a lot also exercise a lot so that they can look good in their selfies! If that is the case, then the association between being exposed to the "Get Active!" campaign messages and exercise would just be a side effect of the overall effect of social media use. Kids who use social media a lot both (1) see a lot of the "Get Active!" messages and (2) exercise a lot. Figure 14.5 illustrates this, which is sometimes called a "third variable" effect. Two variables are related to one another, but their association occurs because each of them is related to a third variable (in this case, overall social media use).

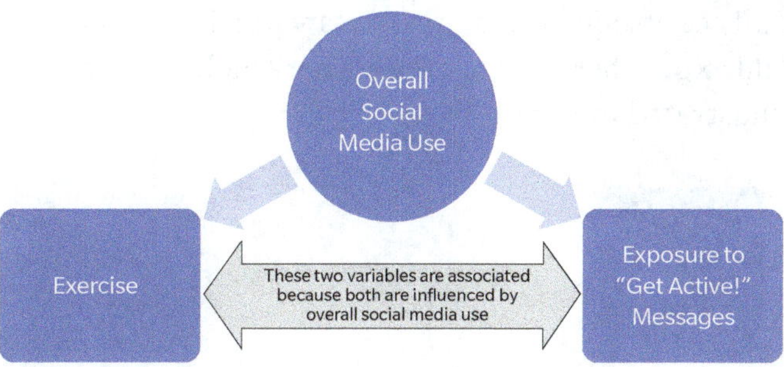

FIGURE 14.5 Illustration of third variable effect

Third variables can lead researchers to erroneous conclusions. If "Get Active!" exposure and exercising are associated purely because each of them is associated with overall social media use (Figure 14.5), then a careless researcher might look at them and conclude that one caused the other ("Get Active!" exposure helped encourage kids to exercise), even though that clearly wouldn't be true.

One way for Francisco to solve this potential problem is to **statistically control** overall social media use while looking at the association between "Get Active!" exposure and exercise behavior. What does "statistically control" mean? Here are a couple of answers to that question. See if one of them helps you understand what it means to statistically control for a variable.

a) One way to think of this is to imagine that you could (statistically) make everyone in the population have the same value for a particular variable. So, if Francisco does his analysis *controlling for* overall social media use, then he is making it as if everyone in the data set has exactly the same overall social media use value. Once everyone is (statistically) scoring the same on overall social media use, any association between exercise and exposure to "Get Active!" messages can't be because of social media use.

b) Another way to think of this is to consider scores on your key variable as being *relative to* the variable you are controlling for. For Francisco, this would mean that scores on "Get Active!" exposure are adjusted. Instead of just being how often someone is exposed to the campaign messages, the scores instead become how much more (or less) someone is exposed to the campaign message, *relative to* how much you'd expect the person to be exposed based on his or her overall social media use. There might be one person in the data (Jim) who uses more social media than average but somehow saw a below average number of the "Get Active!" messages. So, Jim would score very *low* on the statistically controlled measure of "Get Active!" exposure. He saw *way* fewer "Get Active!" messages than he should have. On the other hand, Maria uses a lot of social media and saw a large number of the messages. She would score about "average" on the statistically controlled measure: She saw roughly the number of messages you would expect her to see based on her (high) level of social media use. This is illustrated in Figure 14.6.

FIGURE 14.6 Illustration of association between "Get Active!" exposure and exercise, controlling for overall social media use

Regression (specifically multiple regression—details coming in the next section) allows the researcher to include statistical **control variables**, which can increase your confidence that there is a "real" association between two variables by excluding any potential effects of a third (or fourth, or fifth!) variable.

Regression has two big advantages over correlation (and one silly one in Google Sheets):

a) Important: You can use information from a regression to make specific predictions about someone's scores on a dependent variable given the person's score on an independent variable.

b) Important: A regression analysis can incorporate more than one predictor variable; this is called **multiple regression**. Multiple regression allows you to **statistically control** for variables in the analysis.

c) Silly: In Google Sheets, you can get the *p*-value for an association directly from a regression analysis; In correlation, you have to take some extra steps to figure out if a correlation is statistically significant. Most statistical software will also tell you the significance for a correlation, so this is just a Google Sheets idiosyncrasy.

Multiple Regression: Francisco's Analysis

Remember, again, Francisco's analysis: He has three independent (predictor) variables:

- Overall social media use
- Sex
- Exposure to "Get Active!" messages

He wants to use all three of those to predict activity levels so as to provide a rigorous test of whether the "Get Active!" messages might have worked among this group of kids. Figure 14.7 illustrates this analysis.

To find this out, Francisco will perform a multiple regression analysis with three predictors (overall social media use, sex, and exposure to "Get Active!" messages). The commands for running the analysis are in Figure 14.8. You can see that the commands are almost identical to those for simple regression, except that the input X range now includes three columns (columns B–D, all predictor variables) instead of one. The output is in Figure 14.9 (again, simplified by reducing the number of decimal places; you can also see the analysis in the "Multiple Regression" tab in the Google Sheet: http://bit.ly/2MHGfOO). Figure 14.9 provides information on how to interpret the results.

Sex
Overall Social Media Use
Exposure to "Get Active!" Messages
Exercise

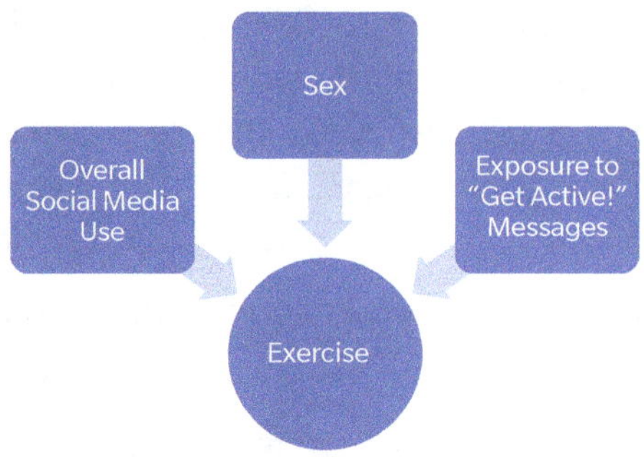

FIGURE 14.7 Illustration of Francisco's analysis model

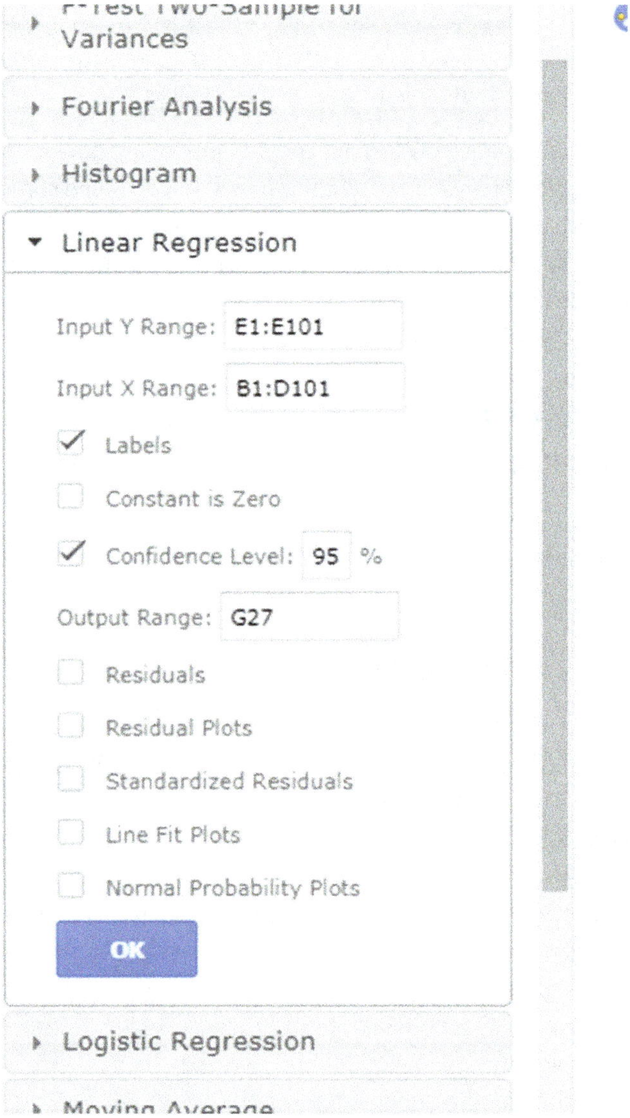

Variances
Fourier Analysis
Histogram
Linear Regression
Input Y Range: E1:E101
Input X Range: B1:D101
Labels
Constant is Zero
Confidence Level: 95 %
Output Range: G27
Residuals
Residual Plots
Standardized Residuals
Line Fit Plots
Normal Probability Plots
OK
Logistic Regression

FIGURE 14.8 XLDataMiner format for multiple regression

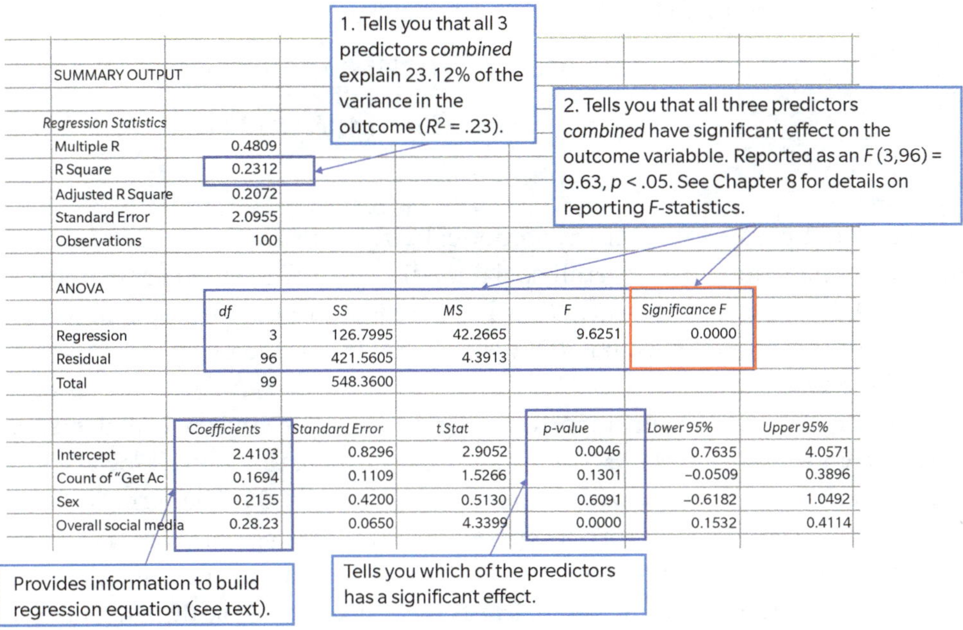

SUMMARY OUTPUT

Regression Statistics	
Multiple R	0.4809
R Square	0.2312
Adjusted R Square	0.2072
Standard Error	2.0955
Observations	100

ANOVA

	df	*SS*	*MS*	*F*	*Significance F*
Regression	3	126.7995	42.2665	9.6251	0.0000
Residual	96	421.5605	4.3913		
Total	99	548.3600			

	Coefficients	*Standard Error*	*t Stat*	*p-value*	*Lower 95%*	*Upper 95%*
Intercept	2.4103	0.8296	2.9052	0.0046	0.7635	4.0571
Count of "Get Ac	0.1694	0.1109	1.5266	0.1301	−0.0509	0.3896
Sex	0.2155	0.4200	0.5130	0.6091	−0.6182	1.0492
Overall social media	0.28.23	0.0650	4.3399	0.0000	0.1532	0.4114

FIGURE 14.9 Annotated multiple regression output

The output contains some important information. First, Francisco can see from the ***R square*** (***R^2***) that about 23% of the variation in exercise is explained by the three variables in the equation (all of them combined). Second, the analysis tells him that the three predictors as a set explain statistically *significant* variance—the 23% **variance explained** number is significantly different from zero. Francisco's measurements help us understand quite a bit about how much people exercise, and they explain something "real" about exercise—something more than just chance. Third, the information provided in the multiple regression analysis allows Francisco to build an equation for predicting exercise from the three predictors. Remember that the top number in the "coefficients" column is the value of the intercept, and the other three now represent "slope" scores for each of the respective variables. So, the regression equation now is

Exercise = 0.1694 ("Get Active!" exposure) + 0.2155 (sex) +
0.2823 (Overall social media exposure) + 2.4103.

Imagine a respondent who saw three "Get Active!" messages, who was a girl (sex = 2), and who had an overall social media score of 5. What would you predict her exercise score to be?

There are a lot of numbers to plug in here, but the math isn't complicated.

$$\begin{aligned}\text{Exercise} &= 0.1694\,(3) + 0.2155\,(2) + 0.2823\,(5) + 2.4103 \\ &= 0.5082 + 0.431 + 1.4115 + 2.4103 \\ &= 4.761\end{aligned}$$

We would predict that the hypothetical girl who saw three "Get Active!" messages and who had an overall social media score of 5 would score approximately 4.8 on the exercise variable. These are just predictions, of course: She might score higher or lower, but 4.761 is our best "informed guess" for what she should score.

The "slopes" are typically reported using the letter "*B*" and are called **unstandardized regression coefficients.** For instance, the slope for the "overall social media use" variable would be reported as follows: $B = 0.28$, $p < .05$. The term "unstandardized" means that you can't compare these numbers against one another: A smaller *B* can be significant and a larger *B* nonsignificant in the same data set. This is because the size of the coefficient is influenced by the scale being used to measure the variable (a 1–100 scale will result in very different coefficients than a 1–10 scale). You know that you can't compare two temperatures if one is measured in Celsius and the other in Fahrenheit; comparing two unstandardized regression coefficients is a similar scenario. There are also "**standardized regression coefficients**," typically reported as **β (beta)**, but you can't calculate those directly in Google Sheets. Standardized coefficients are similar to the correlation coefficient, and they *can* be compared directly to one another—a bigger beta means a bigger effect. The "Going Further" section in this part of the book shows you how to calculate standardized regression coefficients using JASP.

The most critical information, of course, is the significance of each coefficient—that tells Francisco whether the variable is doing anything significant in explaining the outcome. He can see from the results (or Figure 14.9) that the "overall social media use" variable is the only one that is statistically significant. Sex didn't explain significant variation ($p = .61$) and neither did exposure to the "Get Active!" messages ($p = .13$). So, even though there was a significant correlation between exposure to the messages and exercise, once the regression analysis controlled for overall social media use, the effect disappeared.

Remember that Aaliyah had told Francisco that people who use social media a lot also exercise heavily so they can look good in their selfies? Right now, Aaliyah's saying "I told you so!" to Francisco. Unfortunately, Francisco will need to go to the Health Department and tell them that, at least on this one measure, exposure to the "Get Active!" messages does not appear to influence exercise behavior.

Research doesn't always give you the results you expect, or the results you want. That's why we do research! If we always found what we expected, we wouldn't need to actually gather data. This is also why it's dangerous to just "assume" that something is true; it's always possible that the data will surprise you!

Path Diagrams

While not always necessary, sometimes it can be helpful to represent the results of a regression visually in a diagram like Figure 14.10. As you can see, this represents the regression coefficients on pathways between predictor and outcome variables, and indicates which of the pathways is significant. This kind of model is called a **path model**, and you can probably imagine that as multiple regressions get more complicated, this sort of visual can be quite useful in providing an "at a glance" idea of the results. It is also possible to change the style of the lines to emphasize which results are nonsignificant (see the more heavily weighted line in Figure 14.10).

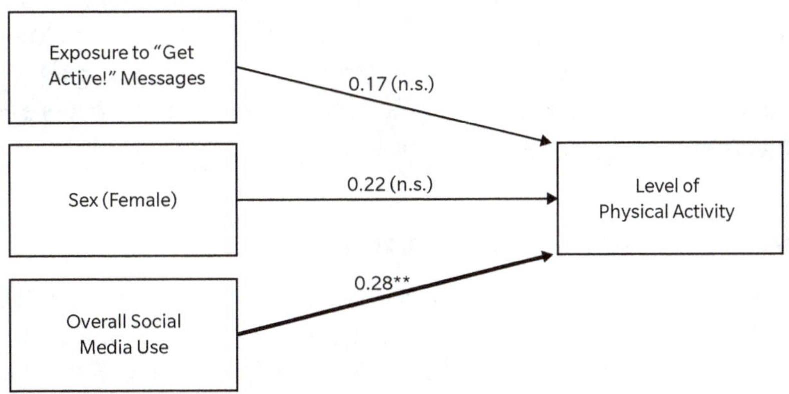

Notes:
Numbers on paths are unstandardized regression coefficients.
Non-significant paths are marked with "n.s."
** $p < .01$

FIGURE 14.10 Path diagram for predictors of physical activity

Distinguishing Multiple Regression From Factorial ANOVA

You now know two statistical techniques that look at the effects of multiple independent variables on a single dependent variable: multiple regression and factorial ANOVA. You will remember from Chapter 12 that factorial ANOVA is used when you have multiple categorical independent variables and an interval-level dependent variable. You now know from the current chapter that multiple regression is used when you have multiple interval level predictors (independent variables) and an interval level outcome (dependent variable). You can also see from Francisco's analysis that categorical predictors with only two levels (sex in Francisco's case) can also be included in a multiple regression. These are called **dichotomous variables**. In general, it's easier to look at interactions between independent variables in ANOVA than in multiple regression. And it's *much* easier to look at independent variables with more than two levels in ANOVA. You can*not* use categorical variables with more than two levels (e.g., something like religion) in regression without some additional mathematical gymnastics that go beyond the scope of this book. Meanwhile, it is more complicated to try to work with interval level predictors in ANOVA. So, both of these techniques are useful for slightly different types of data. And if you pursue your studies, you'll discover that they are actually more closely related than their division in this book implies.

Writing the Report

When writing up the results of a regression (Report 14.1), make sure to tell your reader all of the variables that were included in the analysis; even if a variable is included just as a statistical control, it's important for the reader to know it was included. It is also useful to specify whether what you're reporting are standardized or unstandardized regression coefficients. If the results were more complex, a path diagram like Figure 14.10 could also be included.

REPORT 14.1 Results for Multiple Regression

Multiple regression was used to test the RQ: Is repeated exposure to the "Get Active!" campaign on social media associated with higher levels of physical exercise? In addition to the primary variable of interest (exposure to "Get Active!" messages), two control variables were included as predictors: sex and overall social media use. The outcome variable was the measure of exercise derived from our content analysis.

The overall regression equation was significant, $F(3,96) = 9.63$, $p < .05$. All three predictors combined explained 23.12% of the variance in the outcome variable. Examination of the unstandardized regression coefficients revealed that exercise was significantly predicted by overall social media use, $B = 0.28$, $p < .05$. Sex was not a significant predictor, $B = 0.22$, $p > .05$. Contrary to our expectations, exposure to "Get Active!" messages was also not a significant predictor, $B = 0.17$, $p > .05$. The data indicate that repeated exposure to the "Get Active!" campaign did not increase exercise use among this group of students when their overall level of social media use is controlled.

To keep things simple, this chapter has included positive regression coefficients. However, just like a correlation coefficient, a regression coefficient can also be negative. If in Francisco's subject population people who used social media more were *less* likely to exercise, then the beta coefficient for social media use would be negative. Negative coefficients can be significant, and when they are significant, they are just as important as positive coefficients. Obviously, it is very important to pay attention to whether a coefficient is negative or positive—a negative coefficient is telling you precisely the opposite of what a positive coefficient is telling you.

Other Applications

Multiple regression analysis is one of the most widely used techniques across the social and physical sciences. In survey research, especially, being able to control for some variables while examining the effects of other variables is critical to correctly interpreting results. Here are some examples:

- Does the length of a group discussion influence the quality of a decision the group makes, controlling for the level of information provided to the group?
- Does quality of communication in a marriage influence the length of the marriage, controlling for the age at which the couple was first married?
- Does watching violent television influence aggressive behavior, controlling for sex?
- Does engaging in political discussion predict voting, controlling for geographical distance from a polling location?
- Does looking at other people's selfies influence self-esteem, controlling for overall focus on body image?

On your own, or in a small group, you might want to think about or discuss why each of the aforementioned control variables might be important.

Your Turn

Visit the "Your Turn" tab in the Google Sheet for this section (http://bit.ly/2MHGfOO). The data here represent scores from a study examining whether class attendance in a public speaking class influences scores on an end-of-semester speech. The researcher decided it was important to statistically control for scores on communication apprehension at the start of the semester. Why do you think she did that?

People who are really high on communication apprehension might skip class a lot (perhaps because they are scared to do a speech) and might do worse on the end-of-semester assignment (because they're scared). This is a great example of a situation where a control variable is important. For this "Your Turn" assignment, run the regression analysis predicting the end-of-semester score from both communication apprehension and class attendance scores. Write up the results using the earlier model as a guide. Be very careful to pay attention to whether the coefficients are positive or negative. Does class attendance help people's performance? Does communication apprehension *hurt* people's performance? Write the results in a separate document. If you have time during class or outside class time, it will be useful to compare your peers' write-up with your own to see if you reached the same conclusions.

Wrap Up

In this chapter, you have learned how to perform a regression analysis in Google Sheets and write up the results. Regression analysis allows you to predict scores on an outcome variable from scores on a predictor variable and to test whether predictors are statistically significant in their association with the outcome. By drawing a path diagram, multiple regression allows for a clear visual representation of complex associations between variables. Regression is a very widely used statistical tool across all the sciences.

If you get nothing else from this chapter, remember the following:

1. Simple regression analysis has one predictor (independent) variable and one outcome (dependent) variable.
2. Multiple regression analysis is useful for statistically controlling variables: If you control for a variable when doing an analysis, you effectively rule out that variable as a plausible alternative explanation for anything you find.
3. Regression yields unstandardized coefficients (which let you predict dependent variable scores using a regression equation) and standardized

coefficients (betas, which can be compared across predictors, allowing you to understand which predictors are the strongest).

Key Chapter Concepts

Beta coefficients: These are *standardized* regression coefficients (beta). Beta tells you the strength of the association between any individual predictor variable and the outcome variable. In a simple regression, beta is the same as the correlation coefficient (*r*). One beta coefficient can be compared against another one: a bigger beta means bigger effect. Google Sheets does not report betas. See also **Unstandardized regression coefficients**.

Causality: The idea that changes in one variable are the reason for changes in another variable. Regression and correlation measure associations between variables, but an association doesn't mean that one variable *causes* another. Methods like experiments are how causality is demonstrated. **Multiple regression** can help in the search for causal relationships by incorporating **control variables**.

Control variables: A control variable is included in a **multiple regression** analysis typically to control for potential alternative explanations and hence increase the strength of an argument that the **predictor variables** cause changes in the **outcome variable**.

Criterion variable: In regression analysis, researchers sometimes use this term to mean the same thing as **dependent variable** or **outcome variable**. This chapter uses the term "outcome variable." It's the variable you are trying to predict.

Dichotomous variables: Categorical variables with only two categories (e.g., living vs. dead, U.S. citizen vs. non-U.S. citizen, full-time student vs. part-time student). Standard regression analysis can incorporate predictor variables that are dichotomous, but you should not include other categorical variables as predictors (e.g., ones with three or more categories).

Independent variable: A variable that is seen as predicting, causing, or influencing a dependent variable. In regression, the term **predictor variable** is often used instead of the term **independent variable,** but they essentially mean the same thing.

Multiple regression: Regression analysis with more than one **predictor variable.**

Outcome variable: In regression analysis, researchers use this term to mean the same thing as **dependent variable**. Sometimes the term "criterion variable" is also used to mean the same thing.

Path models: Visual models representing the predictor and criterion variables in a multiple regression, typically including the regression coefficients for the paths between the variables.

Predictor variable: In regression, this term is typically used to mean the same thing as **independent variable**—a variable that is predicting the outcome variable.

Simple regression: A regression analysis with only one **predictor variable.**

Standardized regression coefficients (β): See **Beta.**

R^2: A common measure of variance explained by a regression analysis. The statistic ranges from 0 to 1, and a score of zero indicates 0% of the variance is explained, while a score of 1 indicates that 100% of the variance is explained.

R square: See **R^2**

Regression analysis: A set of statistical techniques for predicting scores on an **outcome variable** from one or more **predictor variables.** In the regression analysis covered in this book, the predictor variables must be either interval-level variables or **dichotomous variables.**

Unstandardized regression coefficients (*B*): Regression coefficients that are reported in the units of the original variables. These coefficients allow computation of the regression equation (to predict scores on the outcome from scores of the predictor variables). However, these coefficients cannot be compared against one another: A bigger unstandardized regression coefficient does *not* mean a bigger effect. See also **Beta coefficients.**

Variance explained: A measure of effect size for a regression analysis. The variance explained in the outcome variable by the predictor variable(s) tells us how accurate our predictions will be. If 100% of the variance is explained, then if we know someone's scores on the predictor variables, we will be able to predict their scores on the outcome variable perfectly. If 0% of the variance is explained, then our predictor variable(s) are literally useless: They don't help us predict at all. Variance explained is typically measured with **R^2.**

Section Wrap

Section Summary

This section has introduced you to content analysis and regression analysis. Content analysis is a way of systematically analyzing the content of messages by having independent coders score the content according to your instructions (coding). Careful training of coders and checking that coders reach the same conclusion about a message when working independently (intercoder reliability) is important for ensuring the quality of conclusions in a content analysis. Regression analysis is highly related to correlation analysis but allows you to examine the influence of multiple predictor (independent) variables on a dependent variable (multiple regression). Among other things, this means you can statistically control variables. Of course, you don't just use regression analysis for analyzing data from content analysis: The type of method (e.g., content analysis, experiment, survey) and the type of analysis (regression, ANOVA, *t*-test, etc.) are separate decisions, and any form of analysis might be used for data coming from any sort of method.

Going Further

This "Going Further" section includes two subsections. First, I show you how to calculate intercoder reliability using a convenient Internet resource. Second, I show you how to calculate a multiple regression in JASP. This technique allows you to see standardized regression coefficients.

Calculating Intercoder Reliability

It is essential to be able to calculate intercoder reliability if you are doing a content analysis. It is relatively simple to do so using the tools available at http://bit.ly/2LcEbua.

I will briefly describe how to calculate reliability on a small set of data. In the "Going Further" tab of this section's Google Sheet (http://bit.ly/2MHGfOO), you will see a set of data with 15 rows and three columns. Notice that none of the rows or columns have any labels; this is a requirement for using the calculation software; obviously, in a real project, you would need to keep careful notes somewhere on the meaning of the data given that you can't include labels for in the sheet itself!

This data set represents the work of three coders (the three columns) coding 15 objects (the 15 rows). For instance, imagine that you had hired Joe, Julia, and Pedro to code 15 TV shows. The numbers represent the codes—for instance, perhaps you asked them to count how often any characters on the shows mention alcohol consumption. So the first row here would represent a situation in which all three coders (Joe, Julia, and Pedro) watched a particular show, and they all counted just one reference to alcohol consumption. Just from skimming the data, you should be able to see that in most cases, the three coders agree on their scores. However, they are not perfect. In row 4, there's a television show in which Joe and Julia counted two references to alcohol, but Pedro counted three. To calculate the Krippendorff's alpha reliability coefficient, do the following steps:

1. In the Google Sheet, click on "File—Download As" and select "Comma-Separated Values (.csv, Current Sheet)." Make a note of where this file saves to.
2. Go to http://bit.ly/2LcEbua.
3. Scroll down to the brown box (see Figure 14.11).
4. Check the box for "Interval"; this tells the system that the coders were dealing with a numerical "scale" type variable, not a categorical variable.
5. Click on "Choose File" and navigate to the .CSV file you saved in step (a).
6. Click on "Calculate Reliability."

If you have used ReCal OIR before, you may submit your data file for calculation via the form below. If you are a first-time user, please read the documentation first. (*Note: failure to format data files properly may produce incorrect results!*) You should also read ReCal's very short license agreement before use.

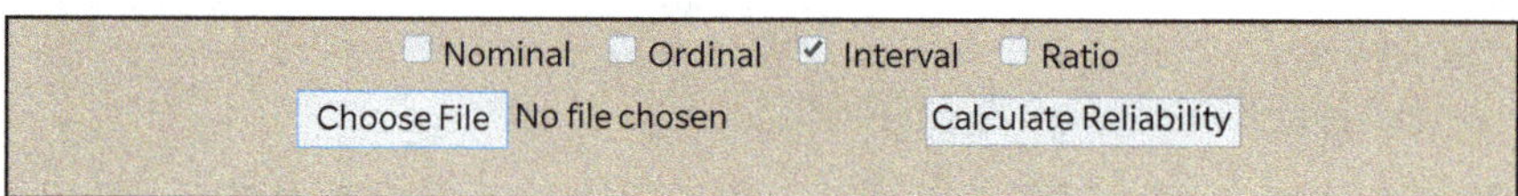

Documentation

ReCal OIR operates under the following requirements and assumptions:

- Data should be nominal, ordinal, interval, or ratio

FIGURE 14.11 Using an online tool to calculate intercoder reliability

If you follow these steps, you should see a result telling you that Krippendorff's alpha is .931. If you recall from the chapter, this is very good reliability (anything above .70 is acceptable). You would be satisfied that your coders are able to independently code and agree with one another most of the time. You would follow the same procedures if the coders were coding categorical variables (e.g., coding the race of television characters), but when you visited the website, you would select "Nominal" instead of "Interval."

Multiple Regression in JASP

To calculate the multiple regression analysis using JASP, you can download and open the JASP file located here: http://bit.ly/2UvnQoV. These are the data from the Google Sheet now in JASP format. To compute the multiple regression in JASP, click on "Regression—Linear Regression" to get to the dialog box. As you can see in Figure 14.12, you would then enter "references to physical exercise" as the "dependent variable" and the three predictors in the "Covariate" box (in JASP terminology, "covariate" is the same as "predictor"). Click "OK." The results that appear should be the same as you calculated in the Google Sheet. For example, if you look at the "unstandardized" column in the JASP output, you'll see the same numbers you got in the "coefficients" column in the Google Sheet: the unstandardized regression coefficients (B). The most immediate advantage of JASP for this analysis is that it tells you the *standardized* regression coefficients (beta—β). These are in the "standardized" column in the JASP output, and they help you understand the relative size of the effects. For example, you can see that the beta for overall social media use is .410—almost three times bigger than the effect for the "Get Active!" exposure. So, even if "Get Active!" exposure had been significant, it would still have been the case that overall social media exposure had substantially larger effects. You cannot draw this sort of conclusion from the unstandardized coefficients because each coefficient is measured in different units.

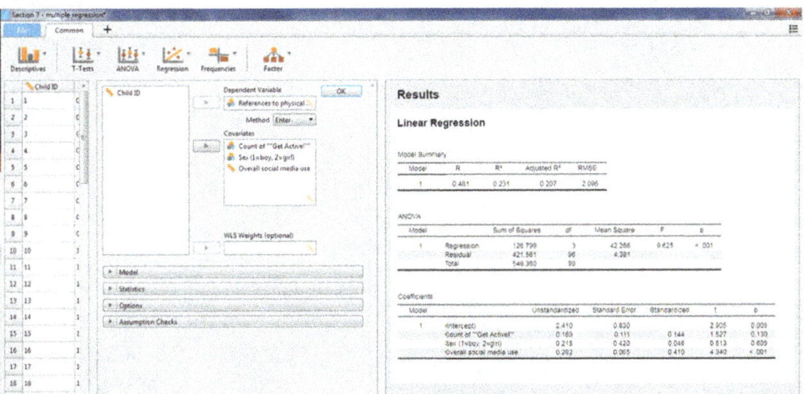

FIGURE 14.12 Multiple regression commands and output in JASP

Credits

Fig. 14.2: Copyright © by Google.
Fig. 14.8: Copyright © by Google.
Fig. 14.11: Copyright © by ReCal.
Fig. 14.12: Copyright © by The JASP Team.

SECTION 8

Qualitative Research: Exploring the Communicative Power of Music

By the end of this section, you will be able to:

- ✔ Articulate the key differences between qualitative and quantitative research
- ✔ Describe important considerations in creating an interview protocol
- ✔ Discuss when interviews or focus groups are more appropriate to a research question
- ✔ Discuss key considerations in recording and transcribing language data
- ✔ Describe key elements that build rapport and trust in qualitative research
- ✔ Distinguish between open coding and axial coding of qualitative data
- ✔ Perform and write up a simple thematic analysis of text

CHAPTER 15

Doing the Research: Interviews and Focus Groups

Remember Aaliyah from Section 4? She has moved on from the PR firm and is now working in a music company's market research department. Her company is discussing how to market music to young adults as they struggle with the new reality where people stream music rather than buying it. They have given Aaliyah the task of finding out more about young people's peak experiences of music listening: When does music listening result in particularly intense experiences? The company is interested in how to use those situations and moments to enhance the profile of their artists among listeners (and hence sell concert tickets, merchandise, etc.). As a former communication major, Aaliyah is interested in exploring the social dimensions of those peak moments. Do they happen in social settings, and are other people involved in the experiences? Among other things, she is interested in times when music results in people feeling a sense of unity with all humanity—a rather specific form of intense musical experience. She develops the following research question: What are the individual and social aspects of peak musical experiences?

Notice that this question is a bit broader than some of the questions we've addressed previously. It doesn't contain clear independent or dependent variables, and it suggests an exploration of lots of different types of phenomena. It is an ideal question for a **qualitative** approach. Qualitative research often asks "how?" or "what types?" kinds of questions, while quantitative research typically investigates "does it?" type questions (e.g., does X lead to Y?). Qualitative researchers rarely ask "yes/no" type questions or questions with a single specific "correct" answer. They also rarely ask questions about causality. They typically work with research questions rather than hypotheses.

Look at the examples in Figure 15.1 and decide whether each is most likely to be addressed using a qualitative or quantitative research method.

	Qualitative	Quantitative
1. Does X cause Y?		
2. What are the different types of communication that occur in a particular context?		
3. Is there an association between a certain type of communication and a particular outcome?		
4. If you expose people to a specific stimulus (e.g., a video), does it change their subsequent communication?		
5. What are the various ways in which people get comfortable in a new social context?		
6. How does a particular social organization "work"? What are the rules by which people operate?		
7. How many times do people do a particular behavior in a day?		

FIGURE 15.1 Qualitative or quantitative?

Probably, a *quantitative* researcher would be most drawn to questions 1, 3, 4, and 7. These are all questions that ask about whether one thing causes another or that require a single answer (either a yes/no or a single number). On the other hand, questions 2, 5, and 6 are questions for which the answers are more detailed and complex. There's no single answer to these questions, and the researcher will need to present a variety of "types" or strategies or examples of rules in order to address the issue. These are perfect types of questions for qualitative data and analysis.

Aaliyah decides to use **interviews** to ask young people about their peak musical experiences. Interviews will allow her to gather information about the wide variety in such experiences in the young people's "own words," thus allowing her to understand a wide range of experiences. Interviews will also give her the opportunity to ask follow-up questions, so as to probe the details of individual lived experiences.

Sampling

Who will Aaliyah be studying? As in a quantitative research study, Aaliyah should first decide what her population consists of. What counts as "young people?" Based on a popular theory of "emerging adulthood," she elects to examine 18- to 25-year-olds. People in this age group consume a lot of music, and the record company believes it's a group that is developing *lifetime* tastes in music. It is a valuable demographic. In qualitative research, **sampling** to obtain a group that is *representative* of the population is less common than in quantitative research. Rather, the goal is often to obtain a sample that is diverse and large enough to uncover the full range of people's experiences. The goal may also be to sample specific people with particular special knowledge or investment in the topic. Aaliyah wants to make sure she gets the broadest set of descriptions that she can to answer her question fully. She is not going to be counting or attempting to generalize to a population, so the mathematical representativeness of her sample is not a concern.

With this age group, and given Aaliyah's research goals, can you think of two places you might go in order to find the sample?

You probably immediately thought of a college campus. Young adults dominate campuses, and so colleges would be a great place to start. If focusing on college campuses, Aaliyah should retain her interest in getting a diverse sample: Only going to an elite private school would yield a restricted sample. Mixing public and private schools and including community colleges (especially ones in a variety of neighborhoods) would get her a more diverse group. However, college students don't represent the full range of 18- to 25-year-olds, so Aaliyah would also want to consider other options. You might have thought of doing interviews *at* musical events, which would be a reasonable strategy. Again, though, you wouldn't want to focus only on such situations (and especially not on just *one* such event), because some people might have intense musical experiences but never attend concerts. You'll remember that Andre in Chapter 11 used a mall intercept design to recruit subjects. That sort of approach would also work. A lot of the recruitment issues (where to find subjects, whether to pay them, etc.) are similar across qualitative and quantitative research. Aaliyah recruits her participants using flyers at a local university and a community college in a low-income neighborhood. She also recruits participants using targeted advertising on a social media site popular among the 18–25 age group; social media ads can be directed specifically to people who fit the required characteristics, which is very helpful for recruiting.

Purposive sampling in qualitative research

You might recall from Table 10.8 a brief discussion of purposive sampling. This is sampling where the researcher intentionally selects a certain type of person for his or her sample. In qualitative research, purposive sampling is a common way to gain specific perspective on the topic of interest. In Aaliyah's case, she might seek out people with particularly in-depth knowledge or understanding of the youth music scene (e.g., popular local DJs or musicians, radio station managers, concert promoters). She might also use snowball sampling techniques (see Table 10.8, again), by asking some of her respondents to refer her to friends of theirs who are particularly involved in music.

Qualitative research often uses smaller samples than quantitative research. It can be relatively easy to gather quantitative questionnaire data from 500 people; questionnaires can often be completed by a large group simultaneously or online without the need for supervision. But it would be immensely time-consuming to interview 500 people because each interview happens one at a time. Also, after a while, those people probably wouldn't be telling Aaliyah anything new: It would be a waste of her time and their time. This illustrates a key rule for sampling with qualitative research: **saturation**. Saturation occurs when additional data collection does not yield any new information.

How will Aaliyah know whether she is reaching a point of data saturation? Qualitative researchers keep **memos** throughout their data collection process. By reflecting on the data collection process in these memos, the researcher begins data analysis while still doing data collection. And this initial analysis will help Aaliyah become aware of when responses from her interviewees become redundant. Rather than determining a sample size ahead of time, Aaliyah should decide on the *minimum* number of interviews required to get a diverse sample—perhaps 20. Then, during the interview process, Aaliyah will make time after each interview to write memos on the interview process (e.g., noting particularly interesting ideas, themes shared with previous interviews, new themes or ideas). Thus she will constantly be monitoring for how much new information is emerging. This can happen even if Aaliyah doesn't do all of the interviews herself. If she is working in a team, then the team will be meeting regularly and discussing their memos, as well as sharing their memos in some sort of online team workspace. Through this process, Aaliyah will become aware of when responses from interviewees become redundant. Memos are sometimes subdivided into process memos (reflecting on the interview process, e.g., whether the order of questioning should be changed) and analytic memos (reflecting on the content of responses—the preliminary stages of data analysis).

Types of interviews

Interviews are used for many research purposes, and so many types of research interviews exist. Here are three of the most common.

Structured interview survey: This is the oral equivalent of a questionnaire, as already discussed in Chapter 9. In these interviews, the research subject is presented with a set of very specific questions, often with restricted answer choices (multiple choice, yes/no, etc.). There is limited scope for follow-up questions or elaborations. This form of interview is useful if you want the equivalent of questionnaire responses but are concerned that the research respondents either won't pay sufficient attention to your questions or are unable to respond to a questionnaire (e.g., with research on young children). As with most closed-ended questionnaires, the data from this sort of interview would typically be analyzed quantitatively.

Structured qualitative interview: This is an interview where you are interested in the open-ended responses of the interviewees and want to give them opportunities to describe their experiences in their own words. However, you still have a specific set of questions that you want to ask, and you are planning on asking them in a fairly specific order. There is the option to ask follow-up questions, but the follow-ups will be focused on specific research goals (e.g., seeking clarification, asking for additional examples).

Unstructured qualitative interview: In these interviews, the researcher has a general goal in mind (e.g., to understand what is going on in a particular social context) but only a very limited guiding structure for the interview. An interviewer interested in understanding more about life in prison might want to talk to corrections officers about their experiences. However, if the researcher doesn't know much about prisons, she might ask very general questions (e.g., "tell me about your daily work routine") and then listen carefully and build a conversation from those responses. That is, the researcher assumes that the interviews will *lead her* to the important questions rather than going into the research assuming that she knows what the important questions are.

Aaliyah's research most closely resembles the middle category—a structured qualitative interview. Some researchers also use the term **"semi-structured interview"** to mean an interview containing some quite structured sections and some sections that are expected to be more free-flowing. Whether structured or unstructured, qualitative interviews are typically analyzed using qualitative analysis techniques.

Developing Interview Questions and an Interview Protocol

Obviously, the questions Aaliyah asks during an interview are critically important in determining the quality of responses that she gets. Remember Aaliyah's original question: What are the individual and social aspects of peak musical experiences? And remember that she was particularly interested in young people's experiences of music providing a sense of unity with all of humanity. Before proceeding, write three questions that you think Aaliyah should ask her interviewees:

Preliminary interview questions:

1. ______________________________
2. ______________________________
3. ______________________________

Aaliyah's question-writing process will probably begin with her narrowing down some of the important areas in which she wants to ask questions: That is, she may need to define the *scope* of her study a bit more before she can decide what she is going to ask people. She brainstorms the following broad areas of questioning:

- The importance of music
- The role of music in the interviewee's social lives
- Different types of intense musical experiences the interviewee has experienced
    - When and where and with whom those events occurred
    - What music was associated with those events

These broad parameters help Aaliyah develop a preliminary set of questions much like the following:

What music do you listen to most often?

[*Depending on the detail in their responses*]

Any other types?

When do you typically listen to ______?

Overall, how important would you say music is in your life. Tell me about the importance of music in your life?

[*Depending on the detail in their responses, these follow-up prompts*]

If you could no longer listen to music, how would that make you feel?

Are there times when music is particularly important for you?

Can you describe for me a time when you had a particularly intense reaction to a piece of music or a musical event?

[*Depending on the detail in their responses*]

Who was with you when that happened?

What music were you listening to?

Where were you?

Tell me more about how you felt.

What made you feel that way? Was it just the music or other things in the moment?

What about the music made you feel that way?

Sometimes when people are listening to music or watching a musical performance, they have experiences such as the following: *feeling one with all humanity, feeling a bond with people of all cultures, feeling like the music overcomes barriers between people.* Try to think of a time when you felt this way because of music. Please describe the experience.

[*Depending on the detail in their responses*]

What music were you listening to?

Who were you with?

How did it make you feel?

Why do you think you still remember this experience?

Having established the questions that she wants to ask, Aaliyah should also consider the order in which to ask them. Notice that in the earlier examples, the order takes the interviewee from fairly general questions about music listening into more specific (and more personal) questions about intense emotional experiences. Moving from the general to the specific is sometimes called a "funnel" approach to the interview. The inverted funnel (as you might expect) takes the reverse approach, moving from a specific question to more general ones.

Can you think of one interview situation where you might want to use the funnel and one where you might use the inverted funnel?

The funnel (general to specific) is useful when: ______________________________

____

The inverted funnel (specific to general) is useful when: ______________________

____

The funnel strategy can be useful when (as with Aaliyah's approach) the questions become progressively more personal or perhaps more difficult to answer. It is good to make the interviewee comfortable with simple and not-too-personal questions before delving deeper. A funnel can also be useful when the researcher doesn't quite know what she is looking for—remember the prison example from earlier. If you're uncertain about what is important in a setting, beginning with very general questions will help reveal what is important for the people who live in that setting and help you transition into more specific questions based on your own growing understanding.

The inverted funnel can be useful when the researcher is interested in how specific events or experiences play out in someone's life. For example, if a researcher was interested in understanding the importance of someone's first live concert experience, he might begin with quite "narrow" questions about that experience (when it happened, who was there) to orient the interviewee to the situation. Later in the interview, he'd move to broader questions (what the event meant to the interviewee and meaningful memories) that would get at deeper emotional consequences. In this sense, the inverted funnel can often be a good way to establish common ground between interviewer and interviewee, and provide a point of reference for the rest of the interview. After the initial question, the remainder of the time and questions can refer back to "*Weather Report* at the Dominion Theater in 1981," for example, as a common reference point.

In developing her plan for the interview, Aaliyah needs to consider any additional information or instructions she wants to share with the interviewee. Her interviewees will need to provide **informed consent** to be in the study. So, Aaliyah will need to tell them about the confidentiality of their responses, any compensation, costs, or benefits they might receive, and the like (see Chapter 9). The complete package of her materials is called the **interview protocol**: an introductory script, questions, potential prompts, and any closing "thank you" or other **debriefing.** Key parts of Aaliyah's interview protocol are in Figure 15.2.

Welcome

Welcome, and thank you for participating in this interview. I appreciate you being here to share your thoughts. Before we start. I'm going to have you read and sign a consent form for our research study. Please let me know if you have any questions. *[Provide consent form. Note: this is also a step that could be accomplished online ahead of the meeting.]*

I would like to record this conversation so I can remember everything you said later. Is that OK? *[Get verbal consent before turning on recorder]*

Ground Rules / Introduction

We are here to discuss your experiences listening to music. Remember: there aren't any right or wrong answers. I will treat everything you say confidentially, and any published reports of our discussion here won't include your name or any information that could identify you. We'll be here for about 45 minutes. Do you have any questions? *[Answer any questions.]* Are you ready to begin? OK, my first question is ... *[Proceed with questions and probes below]*

Main Question	*Potential Follow-Up Probes*
Tell me about the importance of music in your life	If you could no longer listen to music, how would that make you feel? Are there times when music seems particularly important?
What music do you listen to most often?	Any other types? When do you typically listen to_______?
Can you remember a time when you had a particularly intense reaction to a piece of music or a musical event?	Who was with you when that happened? What music were you listening to? Tell me more about how you felt. What made you feel that way—was it just the music, or other things in the moment? What about the music made you feel that way?
Sometimes when people are listening to music or watching a musical performance, they have experiences such as the following: • **"Feeling one with all humanity"** • **"Feeling a bond with people of all cultures"** • **"Feeling like the music overcomes barriers between people"** **Please try to think of a time when you felt this way because of music. Please describe the experience.**	What music were you listening to? Who were you with? How did it make you feel? Why do you think you still remember this experience?
Is there anything else you would like to say about this topic: anything we haven't covered but that you think might be important?	

Closing / Thanks

Thank you again for participating in our study. Do you have any other questions about the study before we finish? *[Respond to questions.]* OK. I'm going to turn off the recorder now. Thank you again for participating. *[Distribute compensation money or record participation for extra credit, if applicable. Immediately after respondent leaves, record any additional field notes concerning the interview.]*

FIGURE 15.2 Aaliyah's interview protocol

Building Trust Through Rapport and Professionalism

One factor determining the quality of responses in interview research is **rapport**. Aaliyah needs to build rapport with her respondents; they need to feel comfortable talking to her and enjoy the experience. She wants them to talk openly to her and disclose information about important moments in their lives. They are only likely to do so if they *trust* her. What can Aaliyah do to enhance trust and rapport in the interview? List at least three things.

Rapport builders:

1. ______________________________

2. ______________________________

3. ______________________________

Rapport for an interviewer stems from at least three important factors (and I'm guessing you already thought of some of them!).

1. **Professionalism.** Interviewees are more likely to trust an interviewer who behaves in a professional manner and who appears to be "legitimate." On a surface level, this means that Aaliyah should dress professionally, correspond in a professional manner with the interviewees before the interview (e.g., use a university e-mail address, double-check all correspondence for errors), show up on time for appointments, and address the interviewee appropriately—typically with a title and last name: "Ms. X" rather than "Susie" or "Dude!" On a higher level, it means making sure that all appropriate protocols are followed. Interviews are still human subjects research, and so Aaliyah will need to follow all of the steps in getting her research approved and providing informed consent for the research subjects. Interviewees need to be convinced that their responses will be treated with respect and confidentiality.

2. **Appropriate environment.** *Where* you hold an interview can be as important as who you are interviewing or the questions you ask. In a noisy or unpleasant environment, your recorder might not pick up what the interviewee is saying, and in a public place, the interviewee might be unwilling to talk about the things that you want to ask about. If you are doing research about work, the workplace might be the *worst* place to do the research—a person might (rightly) be hesitant to share everything he or she feels about the boss when she is in the room next door! Aaliyah should ensure that her interviews happen in a location that is comfortable for the interviewees and where she can effectively record their responses.

3. **Interpersonal connection.** This is the holy grail of interviewing. If Aaliyah is doing her job, she will quickly develop a positive relationship with her

> interviewees; they will *enjoy* talking to her. There are simple things that enhance this connection. Following the basic rules for politeness, smiling, articulating speech, and demonstrating attention when the interviewee is talking (by nodding or making eye contact, for instance) will go a long way. An additional important skill in interviewing is maintaining a nonjudgmental mind-set. If Aaliyah is a music lover, it might be difficult for her to hear someone say, "I just don't care about music very much," or "I only listen to Kenny G." But in order to keep the interview moving and maintain the respondent's trust, she will need to avoid frowning or looking disturbed by such comments. The sequence in which Aaliyah asks questions can also help build this connection. In this study, for instance (and as noted earlier), asking about deep emotional responses probably shouldn't be the first thing that she asks about. Some preliminary questions about music in general will help build the connection and allow for more comfortable discussion of the deeper emotional stuff later on. That is, the earlier parts of the interview help build rapport and trust for the later sections.

Building rapport in other qualitative research settings might involve additional skills. For instance, if a researcher is doing *long-term* **observations** of behavior in an organization, rapport might be built by offering some exchange to the organization (e.g., free consulting work, a summary of the research conclusions). A researcher in a foreign-language setting will build rapport by learning and speaking the other language. A researcher in a school will build rapport by offering to meet with parents, teachers, and administrators.

Ultimately, remember that rapport isn't an end in itself. Rapport is the road to trust. While you can develop rapport fairly quickly (by positive interpersonal behaviors), trust develops over time, both within an interview (with assurances of confidentiality and demonstrations of empathy) and in the long term (e.g., by showing repeated professional behavior, following through on commitments, meeting appointments, and the like). Useful and illuminating qualitative data emerge from situations where there is mutual trust between researcher and research participant.

Training interviewers

A lot of the time, qualitative researchers will do their own interviews. In cases where they use research assistants to help them, those research assistants will need extensive training. No matter what kind of interview, training on issues of professionalism and maintaining a pleasant demeanor will be important.

continues on next page

continues from previous page

For structured interview surveys, the interviewers will need training on asking the questions in the *same way* to all respondents (consistency). Subtle differences in how questions are asked can yield different responses, thus contaminating the data. With semi-structured and unstructured qualitative interviewing, the interviewer will need training in areas such as listening carefully, knowing when and how to ask follow-up questions, behaving in a nonjudgmental manner, and keeping the interview moving from one question to the next. Doing an interview is not the same as having a chat. It's a skill that requires training and practice.

Balancing Flexibility and Consistency in Managing an Interview

Aaliyah's research involves a structured (or semi-structured) qualitative interview (see "Types of Interview" sidebar). She wants to understand a broad range of experiences that people have had and gain insight into those experiences. Hence, as we already discussed in how she formulated her questions, she wants to ask a fixed set of questions in a certain sequence, but also wants to remain flexible in terms of asking follow-up questions. She needs to retain control of the interview and move through her interview protocol as well. What problems might she encounter if she allowed the interview to go in any direction the respondent wanted to talk about? Think of at least two.

Problems with a completely unstructured interview:

1. ______________________________

2. ______________________________

Aaliyah's primary concerns with letting the interview go in any direction would be that she wouldn't get the information she actually wants. If a respondent spends a lot of time talking about how his ex-girlfriend really loved music and how much he misses her ... that might be interesting for research on emotional breakups, but it's not helpful for a study of intense musical experiences! A skill that interviewers develop over time is how to sensitively redirect the exchange back to the topic. You can pivot an interview back to the main topic by (a) acknowledging the interviewee's feelings or experiences and then (b) using those feelings or experiences to return to the interview protocol. Aaliyah might deal with the ex-girlfriend situation by saying, "Wow, it sounds like you had a tough time during that breakup. I'm sorry to hear that. Can you think of any other times when you had an intense reaction to music?" A (related) problem with allowing the interview to be completely unstructured is time. After 30 minutes discussing the interviewee's breakup, Aaliyah might get back onto the topic she was interested in, but she'd have wasted 30 minutes. Doing that repeatedly would result in a lot of irrelevant data, and a tremendous waste of resources.

Focus Groups: Costs and Benefits of a "Group Interview"

Instead of one-on-one interviews, Aaliyah could use **focus groups** for her study. A focus group is a small group discussion on a topic led by a moderator (the focus group equivalent of the interviewer). The moderator asks questions and keeps the discussion flowing, sometimes intervening to "call on" particular people (e.g., those who haven't said much) or to redirect the discussion. A moderator is less the center of attention than the interviewer in an interview: Often the moderator wants to remain somewhat invisible, allowing the group members to get on a roll discussing the topic among themselves. Focus groups typically last for 60–90 minutes and involve fewer than 10 participants. Focus group moderators sometimes find it helpful to have an assistant who takes detailed notes—writing down aspects of nonverbal behavior and other subtle group dynamics that occur during the meeting. Those notes can assist with subsequent transcription and analysis.

Field notes and memos

A qualitative researcher keeps a number of different kinds of notes in the course of a project. A researcher observing a social situation will take **field notes**, recording the details of specific activities he or she sees going on, as well as reflections on what is observed (the very earliest stages of analysis). Field notes are discussed a little more in the next chapter. A researcher doing interviews or focus groups will also record memos during the process of data collection and analysis. These memos will include reflections on the research process (How are the interviews going? How might the process be improved?), reflections on specific issues in that interview (Did the person seem comfortable? Are there unique circumstances surrounding this interview that the researcher will need to remember later on?), and preliminary analysis (Did the interview reflect a specific theme that is important to the research question? Are some commonalities across multiple interviews starting to emerge?). Taking these memos soon after the interview helps with recall. Memos can be kept in a physical notebook, in an online resource shared by a research team, or in qualitative analysis software (described in the next chapter). Using qualitative analysis software, a researcher might immediately upload the audio file of an interview to the software and attach memos related to the interview to that audio file.

Can you think of any advantages of a focus group over a one-on-one interview for Aaliyah? Try to think of two.

1. ______________________________

2. ______________________________

If you thought of something concerning people "feeding off" one another's answers, then you captured a key advantage. In a small group, one person's responses will often trigger an idea, thought, or experience in another person—quite possibly something that person would not have come up with in a one-on-one interview. The group dynamic may also make some people more comfortable. They may be willing to share information because they feel like they are talking to their peers rather than an interviewer. Above all, focus groups provide data at the *group* level: they allow a researcher to understand how a *group* makes sense of a situation. In some settings (e.g., analyzing team functioning in a sports team), the only way to fully understand what is going on is to see how the group as a whole communicates *together* about the setting.

Of course, focus groups also have disadvantages relative to an interview. Can you think of two?

1. ______________________________

2. ______________________________

Some of the "advantages" noted earlier have associated disadvantages. In particular, if people "feed off" each other in an unhelpful direction, a group can end up going on a tangent that the researcher did not desire. And it can be more difficult to refocus a group than an individual! Focus groups can also create challenges if multiple people start talking at once; the researcher may be unable to hear everyone, and even a high-quality audio recorder might not pick up everything that is being said. In other words, you might *lose* important data. Focus groups can also suffer from one dominant person who takes over the group and discourages others from talking. These problems point to the need for a focus group moderator to have certain skills (see the next section).

An additional consideration with focus groups is the number of people you use relative to the amount of data you get. In an hour-long focus group with eight people, each person might talk for only about 5–10 minutes. In eight hour-long interviews, each person would talk for almost an hour. The amount of data *per person* is therefore much higher in interviews. This might be important to you, depending on how hard it is to find the research subjects and how much time you have available. If you have unlimited time, and the research subjects you're interested in are difficult to access, interviews are a better choice. If I were doing research on caregivers for children with disabilities, or transgender people serving in the military, I would do interviews. Recruiting those samples would take time, and I would want to maximize the data I could get from each individual. On the other hand, if I had limited time, and I was studying college students (an easily accessible population for me), I might consider using focus groups so as to get many diverse viewpoints in a short period of time.

There are also logistical disadvantages to focus groups: Getting multiple people to all show up in a certain place at a certain time is a challenge, especially if you are studying people with busy and unpredictable lives (e.g., working parents, emergency medical technicians, undocumented migrants).

Finally, consider whether the topic you are discussing is suitable for a focus group. If you are discussing something very idiosyncratic (e.g., people's feelings about their bosses), there might be few benefits to a focus group: A focus group is not productive if it's just a group of people taking turns sharing their thoughts. Focus groups are also not a good idea for highly sensitive issues. People might open up about drug use or sexual behavior in a one-on-one interview with a trained researcher who can guarantee confidentiality. They are very unlikely to do so in a group of strangers who could walk out and tell all their friends what they heard! The key pros and cons of focus groups are summarized in Table 15.1.

TABLE 15.1 Pros and Cons of Focus Groups

Pros	Cons
More diverse viewpoints in short period of time	Group can go off on tangents
Participants generate ideas from one another	Less data per subject
Group reveals how people collectively make sense of issue	You can't control whether participants share what they heard in the focus group after they leave
	With sensitive or highly idiosyncratic subjects, respondents won't be able to "feed off" one another's experiences or might be reluctant to share any information at all

Facilitating Focus Groups

Facilitating a focus group is a skill, and (as with most skills) people get better at it with practice and by being aware of potential problems, such as those described earlier. In addition, here are four key skills that focus group facilitators should hone.

1. **Listening and attending to the group dynamic.** Part of a facilitator's job is to "sit back" and let the participants talk. However, as outlined in the discussion of "disadvantages," sitting back doesn't mean that the facilitator isn't doing anything. Good facilitators are good listeners who are constantly monitoring what is being said, *who* is saying it, and what is *not* being said. This means attending to language and to nonverbal behaviors (e.g., a subtle nod or shake of the head by one of the people who is not talking). Facilitators who zone out during the discussion aren't doing their job.

2. **Intervening in the group dynamic.** Just attending to the group dynamic isn't enough, of course. Good facilitators intervene when they see problems in how the process is unfolding. If the discussion is getting off topic, the facilitator may need to gently refocus the group: "Thanks everyone for those comments. I'd like you now to return to the earlier discussion of X." If some people are dominating the discussion, the facilitator will need to intervene to involve the quieter participants. "Heather, we haven't heard much from you. How do you feel about X?" This kind of intervention is particularly important if the group appears to be converging on one perspective or opinion, but the facilitator senses that people who hold contrary perspectives aren't talking. Facilitators are also good at getting the participants in a focus group to do part of this job: A facilitator can encourage participants to address one another, to self-monitor so as not to dominate the discussion, and to ask one another questions. On a more basic level, a facilitator may need to ask people to speak one at a time. If a group gets excited, people may all talk at once or separate conversations might break out at different ends of the table ("Hey, everyone, just a quick reminder that our recording won't work if everyone talks at once. So, let's hear from Susan first, and then we'll move down to what Alonso and Sam were talking about.").

3. **Building rapport.** People can be reluctant to contribute in groups of strangers. Good facilitators understand the importance of good icebreakers, while also appreciating that most people don't want to spend excessive time on such exercises. Building rapport with a focus group includes simple things like maintaining a positive and professional style (smiling, being nonverbally open to the group, dressing appropriately), as well as having a repertoire of specific exercises and approaches for making people comfortable. Snacks can also help here!

4. **Creativity.** While many focus groups are organized around a series of questions, an experienced researcher may incorporate other types of activities. Taking a poll on a closed-ended question ("Do you prefer X or Y?") can stimulate lively discussion if participants are then asked to debate with each other (those who prefer X versus those who prefer Y). Having people watch a video or listen to a message can provide impetus for subsequent discussion (e.g., about which types of messages people find persuasive). Giving a group a *task* can reveal a lot of useful information. Imagine asking a focus group to design a message that would persuade students to use the campus rec center. Their discussion while doing the task would tell you a lot about the types of messages they think are effective or ineffective, particularly for a student audience. Analyzing the discussion, therefore, might tell you more about those topics than if you just asked them to talk about "what messages students like" in a more abstract way. A skilled moderator would also know when to ask the group members to reflect on their process (e.g., "Tell me a little more about why you chose that message rather than this other one.").

Focus groups in the private sector

The emphasis in this book is on social science research—learning about how the world works. Focus groups are also heavily used in commercial research, however. For instance, in considering how to market products, it is very common for marketing firms to hold focus groups in which they generate ideas for advertising, for instance, or show a focus group some mock-ups of commercials to see which ones they respond to more positively. Focus groups are among the most commonly used research techniques in marketing and advertising.

Recording

Obviously, just *doing* an interview (or a focus group) isn't enough. Aaliyah will need to record what happens during her interviews so she can analyze the data. This recording happens in two main stages.

First, during the interview itself, Aaliyah (with the interviewee's permission, of course) should audio record what is being said; in some circumstances, she might also want to record video, although that is less common. High-quality digital audio recorders are increasingly inexpensive and provide better sound quality than just recording on a cellphone, for instance. This is particularly important with focus groups, where high-quality recording can help Aaliyah understand what's being said when multiple people are talking. Whenever using a recording device, it is important to practice with it so you are absolutely comfortable with how it works and with what the recordings will sound like in the actual environment where you are doing the recording.

Second, immediately following the interview, Aaliyah should record her own observations and thoughts. These **memos** might include noting things such as the following:

a) Nonverbal behaviors by the interviewee (especially if the interview is not video recorded)

b) Aaliyah's reflections on broader themes in the interview (e.g., if the interviewee seemed particularly uncomfortable at certain moments)

c) Reflections on the interview *process* itself—particularly in terms of planning for future interviews (e.g., deciding to ask more or different questions on a certain topic, eliminating the questions on a topic, or even notes to herself like "don't forget to smile!")

Depending on the context, Aaliyah might be able to take notes on some of these things *during* the interview, which would also be helpful. Taking the time to reflect during and immediately afterward is important to improving the quality of subsequent interviews and memorializing details of the interview that just happened. The audio recording and Aaliyah's memory won't be enough to capture everything that occurred.

The final "record" of the interview is often a typed **transcript** of the audio recording. The written version is important because it is virtually impossible to analyze audio data systematically—as will become clear in the next chapter. Analysis involves reading and rereading what was said, and that is much quicker and more efficient using a written text rather than having to "listen and relisten." The sidebar contains more details on the **transcribing** process.

Transcribing spoken language

Transcribing is a time-consuming and difficult process. Even for a fast typist, speaking is much faster than typing, and so audio has to be slowed down or repeatedly stopped and started in order to transcribe correctly: A stop-start foot pedal connected to an audio player can aid this process so that hands can stay on the keyboard. Artificial intelligence speech recognition (the tech behind Siri and Alexa) is promising to automate the process, but we are a long way from those systems replacing human transcription. Even for professionals, an hour of audio can take 3+ hours to transcribe. Depending on what analysis you want to do, transcription can take much longer than this. Consider the following two

continues on next page

continues from previous page

transcripts of a short segment of conversation between an older couple and their travel agent (from Ylänne, 2019).

Version 1

Mrs. Morgan:	What we want we as I said we'd like to go to Portugal. We want to go with people
Mary:	Do you want something like a Young at Heart type of holiday? Something like that?
Mrs. Morgan:	Well uh
Mary:	Is do you want do you want to be categorized as one of one of the over fifty-fives or
Mrs. Morgan:	Oh yeah
Mr. Morgan:	Yeah
Mrs. Morgan:	We're over one definitely over the fifty-fives

Version 2

1 Mrs. Morgan:	what we want we as I said we'd like to go to Portugal ...
2	we want to go with people
3 Mary:	do you want something like a Young at Heart type of holiday?
4	something like that
5 Mrs. Morgan:	(very hesitantly) well uh (1.0)
6 Mary:	is do you want do you want to be categorized (.) as one of [(.) one of
7 Mrs. Morgan:	[(laughs)
8 Mary:	the over fifty-fives [or
9 Mrs. Morgan:	[oh yeah
10 Mr. Morgan:	yeah
11 Mrs. Morgan:	we're over one definitely over the fifty-fives (laughs)
12 Mr. Morgan:	(laughs)

continues on next page

continues from previous page

Version 1 just contains the words that were said. Version 2 includes some non-verbal behaviors (e.g., laughter), and tracks when speech overlaps (the square brackets). It notes verbal stress on certain words (underlines) and includes pauses: (.) indicates a brief pause, and a number in parentheses indicates a pause length in seconds (e.g., (1.0) indicates a 1-second pause). The second type of transcription is very useful for people who are examining the detailed mechanics of how conversations proceed; sometimes to explain why somebody says something specific you need to know that there was a long (and awkward?!) pause right beforehand! As you can imagine, transcriptions like the second one take a lot longer to produce than the first. For a very high level of detail, it might take 6–8 hours to transcribe 1 hour of audio. It is important to check the quality of transcripts against the original audio by reading through the final transcript while listening to the audio.

One final point: Notice that the transcripts include grammatical "errors," hesitations, and the like. It might be tempting to try to clean up people's speech when you write it down, but you shouldn't do that. Errors, hesitations, and points where people start a sentence and then change what they were going to say might be really important to understanding their feelings. A long pause or repeated hesitations might indicate reluctance about making a certain point or that the person feels that it is important to express the point in a very precise way, for instance. Qualitative researchers are interested in how people actually talk and write, not a "cleaned up" version of communication.

The Data

Obviously, qualitative data are quite different from anything we've examined thus far in this book. To keep things relatively straightforward, we are going to look at a very limited set of data here. The following link contains a file demonstrating what Aaliyah's data might look like if she just examined short answers to one question from 199 interviewees: http://bit.ly/2Mlfug1.

These data are from responses to Aaliyah's final main question—the one about music overcoming barriers between people. This is an unusually large number of respondents for an interview study—imagine the time and effort involved in doing 199 interviews! I'm including so many responses here to give you an idea of the *diversity* that sometimes exists in open-ended responses and to illustrate the scale of the data analysis challenges in this sort of research. A 1-hour interview might take up 25 pages of single-spaced text. That is a lot of material to read and analyze! In the next chapter, we'll look at one way to analyze these data.

A brief side note here: These are *real* data from research respondents; they were collected as part of a larger study on music and communication. The data are actually from *questionnaires*, not interviews, and so in places, they may sound like they were written rather than spoken. This also explains the large sample:

It is easier to gather 199 questionnaires than 199 interviews! Nonetheless, these are similar to the kinds of responses that might emerge from an interview. Some information in the responses has been redacted to protect respondent confidentiality (a point described in more detail in Chapter 16). There is, of course, nothing wrong with using written responses to generate data for qualitative analysis. Sometimes people will share things in writing that they would be unwilling to share in a conversation, and in such cases, a qualitative researcher might actively solicit written narratives.

Writing the Report

Writing a report of the method for a qualitative study is not that different from writing one for a quantitative study. Aaliyah's readers still want to know the details of her sample and the methods she employed. Typically, she should include her full interview protocol if space is available or at least list examples of the questions she asked if there isn't space for the whole thing. In Aaliyah's case (see Report 15.1), she reports all the key questions and prompts but does not list the general introductory comments. She also needs to be specific on details like how long the interviews lasted, how they were recorded, and (if relevant) whether research assistants were trained. Finally, it is important to respect the confidentiality of participants; therefore, Aaliyah should note that she has changed any names in the transcripts and removed other information that might identify the speaker.

REPORT 15.1 Methods for Qualitative Interview

Sample. Students ($N = 199$) were recruited from introductory communication classes in a large midwestern US university. The sample was 62% female, 38% male, and ethnically diverse (49% white, 26% black/African American, 12% Hispanic, 8% Asian American, 2% Native American, 12% other; numbers do not sum to 100% because respondents could select more than one category). Recruitment of subjects continued until data saturation was achieved.

Procedures. Semi-structured qualitative interviews ranging from 25 minutes to 55 minutes were held individually with each respondent. The interviewer, a trained qualitative researcher, provided general background on the study, explaining the general interest in young people's musical experiences. The interview protocol is provided in Figure 1. During the interview, respondentswere free to answer questions at length; the interviewer prompted as necessary with follow-up questions to get more detail on specific topics. The interviews were audio recorded and transcribed, resulting in approximately 16 pages of transcript per respondent. A second researcher double-checked the transcripts for accuracy. The interviewer recorded process and analytic memos during and immediately after the interviews. This analysis focuses on

continues on next page

continues from previous page

responses to the final question in the protocol—a total of 12,738 words of transcript. Prior to analysis, all names and identifying information in the responses were changed to protect respondent confidentiality.

Main Question	*Potential Follow-Up Probes*
Tell me about the importance of music in your life	If you could no longer listen to music, how would that make you feel? Are there times when music seems particularly important?
What music do you listen to most often?	Any other types? When do you typically listen to_______?
Can you remember a time when you had a particularly intense reaction to a piece of music or a musical event?	Who was with you when that happened? What music were you listening to? Tell me more about how you felt. What made you feel that way—was it just the music, or other things in the moment? What about the music made you feel that way?
Sometimes when people are listening to music or watching a musical performance, they have experiences such as the following: • **"Feeling one with all humanity"** • **"Feeling a bond with people of all cultures"** • **"Feeling like the music overcomes barriers between people"** **Please try to think of a time when you felt this way because of music. Please describe the experience.**	What music were you listening to? Who were you with? How did it make you feel? Why do you think you still remember this experience?
Is there anything else you would like to say about this topic: anything we haven't covered but that you think might be important?	

FIGURE 1 Interview protocol

Other Applications

Qualitative methods, including focus groups and interviews, can be used to explore any topic or subarea in the field of communication. If you are interested in how people react to new technology, interviews might ask people about their feelings when their friends check their phones during face-to-face conversations. If you are interested in organizational communication, you might have focus groups asking people to discuss the challenges or benefits of workplace romances. An intergroup communication scholar might use interviews to ask people when they feel comfortable (or uncomfortable) talking to someone from a different social group. In all these cases, the idea would be to allow interesting ideas to emerge from what people say in the interviews; this is in contrast to quantitative research where the goal is often to test the validity of an idea that the *researcher* generated.

Of course, you can use *both* qualitative and quantitative research to explore a particular topic. Interviews might yield ideas that could be tested with a quantitative study. Or a quantitative study might throw up an unexpected result that could be understood more deeply using focus groups. However, mastering quantitative *and* qualitative methods is not easy: The best work that combines both involves teams of researchers who have specific skills in the different methods. Table 15.2 provides some examples of the kinds of questions a qualitative versus quantitative research project might investigate on a similar topic.

TABLE 15.2 Example Research Questions for Qualitative and Quantitative Research

Topic	Qualitative Research Question	Quantitative Research Question
Political participation	*What kinds of political conversations encourage people to vote?*	*Do negative campaign ads make people more or less likely to vote?*
Video games	*In what ways do people justify game playing as a "worthwhile" activity?*	*Does playing violent video games cause aggressive behavior?*
Intercultural communication	*What aspects of communication between cultural groups do people see as rewarding?*	*What personality traits predict actively seeking out intercultural contact?*
PR	*What are people's responses to a specific PR message? What dimensions do they use to evaluate the message?*	*Are PR messages more effective when they use statistics or when they use personal narratives?*

Varieties of qualitative data. This chapter has focused on interviews and focus groups. These are very common sources of qualitative data, but certainly not the only ones. Data are all around us, and qualitative researchers take a wide variety of approaches to gathering and analyzing those data. Qualitative data can come from **observations** of everyday behavior in the world (e.g., communication between people riding the subway during rush hour). Qualitative data are also available in our media environment (e.g., TV shows, comments on internet news sites, Amazon product reviews). Almost all forms of written communication yield interesting qualitative data: ancient ships' logs, the congressional record, marketing brochures from Fortune 500 companies, and so on. In some of these cases (as with Aaliyah's case), the data need to be *generated*. If a researcher thinks that focus groups will yield the most useful data, then she must design an interview guide, recruit participants, and perform and record the interviews. In some cases, the data need to be recorded. If you were interested in communication on the subway, you would need to ride the subway and engage in detailed observation of the behavior. In other cases, the data already exist (e.g., the old ships' logs, the Amazon product reviews). The researcher's task is just to locate the data (which museum has the logs?) and take a sample (from the billions of product reviews). One final note: This chapter has been focused on analyzing these types of data qualitatively. It is, of course, possible to analyze naturally occurring data quantitatively as well (e.g., by doing a quantitative content analysis of ancient ships' logs). Qualitative and quantitative refer to the form of *analysis;* while it's hard to do qualitative analysis on a bunch of numbers, most forms of data can be analyzed quantitatively or qualitatively (or both!).

Your Turn

Return to one of your earlier "Your Turn" sections. Remind yourself of the question you were investigating. Then complete the following:

a) Write a version of the research question that is suited to qualitative investigation: This might be a question that involves a "how" rather than a "what" type question. How does a communication process happen, or in what different ways do people respond to a particular form of communication?

b) Develop an interview protocol to investigate that question qualitatively. When writing your interview protocol, be sure to include at least three main questions, each with at least two potential follow-up prompts. Make sure the questions invite open-ended responses from the interviewees (avoid "yes/no" type answers, for instance). Make sure the follow-up prompts are designed to elicit more details. Finally, make sure to organize the questions in a sensible order, typically moving from more specific to more general, or vice versa.

Wrap Up

In this chapter, you have learned some of the basics of qualitative research and, particularly, how to do a qualitative interview study. The chapter has discussed how to build rapport with interviewees and how to present yourself as a professional. It has discussed the development of an interview protocol, including follow-up prompts and the process of sampling in qualitative research. It has also provided some hints for how to organize an effective focus group.

If you get nothing else from this chapter, remember the following:

1. Qualitative research typically involves smaller samples than quantitative research. Decisions about the right sample size are made as the research progresses rather than defined beforehand: Data collection stops when new data aren't producing new information (**saturation**).

2. An effective interview protocol will be *structured* carefully, moving the respondent from more specific to more general questions or vice versa, depending on the sensitivity of the topic and what sequence is likely to draw out the most useful responses.

3. Focus groups provide the opportunity for respondents to feed off one another and hence elicit responses that an interview might not be able to get; however, focus groups are less efficient than interviews in terms of the amount of data provided by each individual respondent. Moderating focus groups and interviewing are skills that take time and practice to develop.

Key Chapter Concepts

Building rapport: When performing interviews or other forms of qualitative research (e.g., observing people's natural behavior), it is essential to develop a friendly and *trusting* relationship with the research participants. Building this rapport is helped by investing in the participants (e.g., having some service to offer them), being a long-term participant in their environment, and behaving in a friendly and professional manner.

Debriefing: An explanation about a study given to research participants after the study has been completed. A debriefing often includes an explanation of any deception that occurred in the study. If a study might have caused any distress for research subjects, a debriefing will also include information about where to seek assistance for that distress (e.g., information about the campus counseling center).

Focus groups: Small groups of people gathered together to discuss a particular topic. The researcher (facilitator) guides the discussion but allows and encourages the participants to interact with one another and build off each other's ideas.

Interview protocol: The set of questions that the researcher will address in an interview (or focus group). Good interview protocols are sequenced to provide a logical flow to the interview, often moving from more general topics to more specific ones, or from less sensitive topics to more sensitive ones, for instance.

Interviews: Typically, one-on-one encounters where the researcher asks questions using an **interview protocol** and the research participant provides answers. Depending on the goals of an interview, it may be highly structured, **semi-structured**, or unstructured.

Memos: Memos are a researcher's reflections on the research process, often recorded immediately after interviews, for instance, but also during analysis (see Chapter 16). Memos are sometimes subdivided into process memos (reflecting on the interview process, e.g., whether the order of questioning should be changed) and analytic memos (reflecting on the content of responses—the preliminary stages of data analysis).

Observation: Any situation where the researcher examines people engaged in natural behavior, typically taking notes and attempting to understand what is "going on" through detailed and extended observation.

Rapport: see **Building rapport**

Sampling: Sampling in qualitative research is designed to achieve **saturation:** the point where gathering new cases does not provide additional information. Qualitative researchers seek breadth and diversity in samples and may purposively seek out specific important individuals, but they typically are not concerned with issues of "random" or "representative" sampling.

Saturation: The point at which additional data collection is not yielding any new information from respondents.

Semi-structured interview: A semi-structured interview will have some questions that the interviewer will ask all participants, but the interviewer will also be free to ask follow-ups or clarify/elaborate on interesting responses by going "off script."

Transcribing: To save time and make coding more systematic, **interviews** and **focus groups** are almost always transcribed—the audio converted to written form. Transcribing must be done carefully and checked for accuracy against the original audio. Transcription may be at different levels of detail, depending on the goals of the research: sometimes it's important to note details like the length of pauses or nonverbal behavior, and sometimes it is not.

■ CHAPTER 16

Reporting the Research: Qualitative Thematic Analysis

Aaliyah is now ready to analyze her data, although in a sense, she's been analyzing her data from the moment she started interviewing. As her interviewees talked, she was thinking about what they said and asking them follow-up questions to get more details. She was also assessing whether interviewees were providing her with new information in order to judge whether she had done "enough" interviews. She has already been writing memos noting important themes and ideas that will contribute to her analysis. So, she has been analyzing the data already. Some qualitative researchers do a "complete" analysis on a subset of their interviews and then do more interviews to test the conclusions they drew from the first set. Data *collection* and data *analysis* are hence much more intertwined in qualitative analysis than quantitative analysis. With that in mind, this chapter will describe Aaliyah's data analysis process.

The chapter describes one widely used form of qualitative analysis: thematic analysis of text. "Thematic" here means that the researcher is focused on identifying important themes or topics in the data. Often, researchers do this with a goal of developing a theory to explain the data. That approach—allowing the data to drive the theoretical development—is often called "**grounded theory**." The theory is *grounded* in the data (Strauss & Corbin, 1990). Central to a qualitative thematic analysis of text is the idea of coding.

Coding

You are already familiar with the idea of coding from Chapter 13's discussion of quantitative content analysis. Coding in qualitative analysis is similar in that it collects groups of objects that are alike in some way by putting them into the same coding category. As noted earlier, when you tag somebody or something on social media, you are doing coding, albeit less systematically than coding in scientific research. Qualitative coding is different from coding in quantitative content analysis in three important ways.

1. **There is no requirement for qualitative codes to be mutually exclusive.** Remember that in quantitative content analysis, for any given variable, a case could only be coded with one "level" of that variable; for example, a TV character might be coded as a hero, *or* a villain, *or* neither. Unless you

create an additional category, a character can't be coded as *both* a hero and a villain. In qualitative coding, any given part of an interview might be coded using any code or set of codes.

2. **There is no fixed unit of analysis.** In quantitative content analysis, if you are coding television characters, then the coding and analysis needs to occur at the level of the character. If you are coding shows, then the coding and analysis has to happen at the level of the show. With qualitative coding, some codes might apply to specific words or sentences, while others might apply to much larger sections of an interview or the entire interview. There's no problem in switching between different levels of analysis.

3. **Qualitative coding is bottom-up, flexible, and designed to evolve.** In a quantitative content analysis, codes are determined before the analysis begins, and once they are decided, they have to remain unchanged for the entire coding process. In qualitative coding, it is acceptable (even desirable) for codes to evolve and change as the analysis proceeds, reflecting the researcher's growing understanding of the data and the development of her theory. As described next, the development of new and higher level codes reflects the development of theory. A different way to think of this is that qualitative coding is typically bottom-up; the researcher determines the codes based on the data. Coding in quantitative analysis is typically top-down; the researcher decides what she wants to code. In some cases, a qualitative researcher may code something without even having a category to put it into. A particular comment might simply be tagged as "interesting" and relevant to the research question, with the task of assigning it more meaning or putting it in a specific category being postponed to a later stage in the analysis process.

Aaliyah's coding proceeds in three stages. First, she begins reading the data carefully and noting any ideas or thoughts she sees as important and relevant to her research question. She records these as she sees them. As this process develops, she also begins to organize all of the identified units into groups based on similarity. This process is often called **open coding**—developing codes based on whatever is in the data. Many of these codes are at a fairly low level of abstraction—they *describe* concrete aspects of the data. For example, Aaliyah codes when she sees references to specific songs occurring repeatedly: The Macklemore song "One Love" comes up more than once in her data, so she creates a code for that. Sometimes these codes can be generated automatically by searching text (e.g., telling a computer to search for the word "Macklemore" in the transcripts).

As she becomes more familiar with the data, Aaliyah also codes some broader ideas that she notices—more abstract and *interpretive* codes (i.e., codes that involve her *interpreting* what she is reading). For instance, a number of the interviewees describe situations in which they feel music bridges barriers between groups: playing or listening together makes people feel like the differences between them have been transcended. Aaliyah creates a single code for these types of experience: She calls it "music transcends cultural difference." Similarly, she develops a "music as joint activity" code to reflect any situation in which interviewees report singing or dancing together with other people (whether with a few people in a car, or thousands of people at a concert). Note that *naming* the categories is important: When a theme is named in a way that accurately and vividly reflects its content, it is more likely that readers of the work will pay attention and remember the message.

Hence, she ends up with a set of open *descriptive* codes, as well as a set of open *interpretive* codes. If you look at her data analysis (see the section on software), you'll see that Aaliyah's coding system is organized into these two types of open codes. **Open coding** is like brainstorming: If something looks interesting, tag it, and then as you become more familiar with the data, start grouping those items that are similar. Some of those codes might turn into something interesting, while others might get dropped as her ideas become more focused.

Aspects of the data that Aaliyah will be looking for to suggest open codes include the following:

a) **Relevance to the research question:** Sometimes, the research participants might say things that sound really cool or interesting but that aren't relevant to the research question. Aaliyah might make a memo to pursue those ideas separately, but she needs to resist getting sidetracked too much!

b) **Repetition:** Topics, themes, words, or ideas that come up repeatedly are good candidates for coding.

c) **Emotional salience:** Statements that reflect strong emotions suggest areas worthy of deeper investigation—these things are *important* to the people who are saying them.

d) **Contrasts:** Places where one person says something that is the opposite of what someone else said are points for further exploration and hence worth coding.

e) **In vivo codes:** These are places where people are using specific words or phrases that are specific to their context. If Aaliyah heard people repeatedly talking about a "drop" in music, that would suggest an important topic for her to explore (surprisingly, she didn't!). When people develop a specific vocabulary for phenomena, that suggests that those phenomena are important.

Take a quick look at Aaliyah's data (http://bit.ly/2Mlfug1) and see if you can spot two broad themes or ideas that ***you*** would code based on the aspects described earlier. Write a name or a short sentence that describes your open codes.

Open code 1: ____________________

Open code 2: ____________________

As Aaliyah's coding moves from a lower to a higher level of abstraction, she will begin to notice certain trends or contrasts in the data that she feels are important across the entire data set: a limited number of codes that account for almost everything that is going on in the data relevant to her research question. This is the ultimate goal of this sort of analysis: to account for important variation in the qualitative responses using a limited number of concepts. This, of course, means using concepts that are at a higher level of abstraction—broader and more general ideas that can act as umbrellas for a lot of individual responses. This doesn't happen quickly. It requires a lot of time spent reading and rereading the responses and looking at different combinations of open codes before the broader codes emerge. These broader descriptors that tie together open codes are called **axial codes.**

Aaliyah develops three **axial codes** that provide deeper understanding of the reports of musical experiences. These axial codes aren't just brainstorming; they are organizing and synthesizing tools: They *are* theory. Whereas the earlier codes described or interpreted some fairly specific elements in the responses, these codes *explain*. Aaliyah can explain something about music's power in social and communicative contexts using these concepts. Here are Aaliyah's axial codes.

- **Intrapersonal—Music as peak psychological experience:** The first axial code involves intrapersonal (individual) experiences. Various of the lower-level codes relate to the personal experience of being emotionally moved or otherwise changed by the music in ways that don't involve other people (e.g., "Religious music lifts my heart and makes my whole body feel light. I felt a powerful spirit within me." "There is one particular song that I hear every year for Christmas time that really gets to me when I hear it ... hearing, "O Holy Night" by MercyMe is one song that makes me feel very emotional.").
- **Interpersonal—Music as peak relational experience:** The second is a set of interpersonal experiences: cases where listening to music brings you closer to a friend, a romantic partner, or a family member, or where the musical experience is enhanced by the presence of a loved one (e.g., "The experience I most remember was a December 31 before the new year come. My dad started playing an old rock song that he likes, and we were near the ocean it was literally one of the most wonderful experiences of my life ... I think it was so especial this experience because was with my family and

because of that I still remember it until today."). These experiences reflect the interactive power of relationships to enhance music's effects and music to reinforce the relationship. Not all of these are positive, however. Music might also have the power to remind people of a negative relationship experience (e.g., "I was listening to a song by [artist]. In it, it said one of my ex- [boy/girl] friend's birthday, made me remind of [him/her], made me feel angry at [him/her]."

- **Transcending the personal—Music connecting to collective humanity:** Third, some of the experiences described in the data are at a broad collective level (e.g., "I became friends with the people around me as we danced together. Everyone was from different states and even from different countries around the world, but I felt a bond with people of all cultures"). Aaliyah creates an axial code for these experiences of shared human experience that go beyond interpersonal relationships. A lot of these experiences occur in festival settings (one of her open codes), but there are descriptions of experiences at festivals that don't involve "joint activity" (e.g., "I still vividly remember the festival because of the happiness I felt along with the amazing DJs that I got to see"—the setting is a large collective group, but this comment does *not* describe an experience that fits the "transcending the personal" category).

These three higher level codes capture the most important aspects of the lower level (open) codes that Aaliyah developed—they summarize the data from her theoretical perspective. You can easily imagine (and in a lengthier presentation she might describe) connections between lower level codes and these higher level codes. A lot of festival experiences would fall into the "transcending the personal" category, as whole crowds of people move together and feel like they are unified. And the "solitary peak experiences" almost all end up in the intrapersonal category.

These higher level codes also lead her toward *new* ideas to pursue in the data. For example, how do these categories intersect? Does the large-scale activity sometimes occur with friends, and how does that interpersonal level intersect with the mass experience? Are "individual" experiences that happen at large public events like festivals different from individual experiences that occur alone? Aaliyah might also start trying to connect the type of musical experience (e.g., emotional responses versus physical responses) to the nature of the context. Are the *mass* events largely driven by coordinated physical responses to music (e.g., dancing), whereas the private events are emotional but not physical? She can answer those interesting questions by returning to the data and examining when certain codes *co-occur* (e.g., individual experiences and emotional responses), and from that, she could start to develop a very sophisticated theory of transcendent social and musical experiences. One fascinating (and sometimes frustrating) aspect of qualitative analysis is that there is always "more" to say about the data.

Software for Qualitative Analysis

Keeping track on all those codes can be a mammoth task. Fortunately, there is software that can help: **computer-assisted qualitative data analysis software (CAQDAS)**. Some are free (e.g., http://www.aquad.de/en/) and some you have to pay for. Aaliyah used a "lite" version of a widely used package called QDA Miner. The "lite" version is free and is powerful enough to help her keep track of her codes. If you want to play around with Aaliyah's data, you can download the software (http://bit.ly/2yISRM1—or just google "QDA Miner Lite") and then download Aaliyah's data file here: http://bit.ly/2RAZSdj. Note: If you use a Mac, you will need to use Boot Camp or Virtual Machine for this PC software to work. Some hints for exploring QDA Miner are in the sidebar.

Much like you can do statistics with hand calculation, it's possible to do qualitative analysis using index cards and Post-it notes. But software for qualitative data analysis is incredibly helpful. It doesn't just help keep Aaliyah organized, it can also do things that simply aren't possible (or would be prohibitively time-consuming) manually. With full versions of this software (the kind you have to pay for!), it's possible to extract all the cases that are coded with one code but not coded with a second code and that feature a specific word or set of words in the text. That ability allows deep exploration of the data that would be virtually impossible in a manual analysis.

Exploring QDA Miner Lite

If you are not exploring the software, you can skip this sidebar. However, if you want to explore, here are a few hints to help you understand Aaliyah's data and analysis. See Figure 16.1 for a screenshot of the software to orient you to what it looks like.

First, a reminder that you can download the QDA data analysis file (http://bit.ly/2RAZSdj) and open it in QDA Miner Lite. Playing around is a good way to learn the software. Each "case" (i.e., each person who was interviewed) in the data set is listed in the top left, and you can scroll down and select any case to see their responses in the center part of the screen. To the right of the screen is a list of codes that have been applied to that particular case. In the case that's visible in Figure 16.1, you can see that it was coded into the categories "music transcends cultural difference," "experiences at festivals," "music as joint activity," and "transcending the personal."

continues on next page

continues from previous page

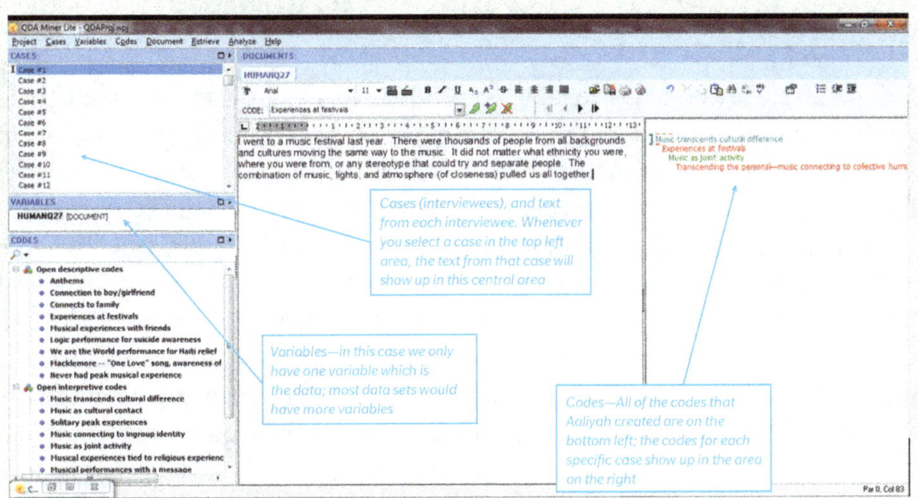

FIGURE 16.1 Using QDA Miner Lite

Here are a few things you can do with the data:

To apply a code to a case, you first click the code in the bottom left window and then right-click anywhere in the text (or highlight a portion of the text) in the middle window and select "Code as _____" (whichever code you selected will be present).

If you need to remind yourself what a code means, right-click on the code in the bottom left and click on "Edit Code." A window will appear that includes a description of the code. To create a new code, select "Codes" in the top menu and then click on "Add."

To automatically code based on specific words, go to "Retrieve—Text Retrieval" and search for any word in the "Search for Text" box. When the cases appear that feature that word, click on the blue plus sign, type a name for the new code, and click "OK." Then click the yellow and green "highlighter" to code all of the retrieved cases with the new code.

To look at just a subset of the coded cases (e.g., only the ones tagged with a specific code), go to "Retrieve" in the top menu, select "Coding Retrieval," and then under "Codes" select whichever codes you are interested in.

To create your own project from a set of documents (e.g., if you had a bunch of text files of Amazon product reviews or some old ships' logs!), go to "File—New Project" and select "Create a Project From a List of Documents/Images." Locate all the relevant documents on your computer, highlight them, and click "Add." Click "Create" and give your project a name.

Judging the Quality of Qualitative Analysis: Reliability and Validity

Good qualitative research is reliable (reproducible, consistent) and valid (true). Reliability and validity in qualitative research are *gauged* differently from quantitative research, but the same underlying principles still concern Aaliyah as she does her work. Not all qualitative researchers agree on using principles of reliability and validity in assessing qualitative work—and some researchers agree with the specific processes I describe next but call them different things. I'm using **reliability** and **validity** because they are familiar terms from earlier sections in the book. The "Going Further" part of this chapter describes a different qualitative approach and should make it clear that there is great diversity among qualitative scholars. A single approach to judging quality is unlikely to gain support from all of those perspectives, but most of the ideas that follow will be endorsed by most qualitative researchers.

Reliability

Aaliyah needs to make sure that her work is consistent and that other people examining her data might reach similar conclusions. This is a concern with reliability. We dealt with reliability issues in quantitative work both when talking about coding in content analysis and measurement using questionnaires. Briefly remind yourself of those by writing a description of reliability in one of those contexts:

In content analysis, we discussed intercoder reliability. This is the type of reliability obtained when two people (operating independently without talking to one another) can code a set of objects into a set of categories with a high level of agreement. In questionnaire research, we talked about computing measures of test-retest reliability: checking whether someone's scores on a questionnaire at one point in time were consistent with their scores at another point in time. If someone's intelligence score one week is really high, we'd expect that person to score similarly high in a subsequent week. If across a group of people their intelligence scores varied dramatically from 1 week to the next, we might suspect a problem with our intelligence measure—that is a reliability problem.

Reliability in qualitative research has many parallels to these forms of reliability, but because qualitative research isn't dealing with measurement in the same way, indicators of reliability are different. Aaliyah needs to focus on providing evidence to readers that her work was careful, systematic, and paid attention to the details. This is often accomplished by reporting research in concrete ways: using the words of participants, describing the analysis process in great detail, and being transparent about the research procedures. These techniques are sometimes collectively called the use of **low-inference descriptors**. Low-inference means that someone reading about the research doesn't need to do a lot of inferring (or guessing) about what went on—the person doesn't need to use his or her imagination. The researcher has laid everything out in a way that is vivid and clear. Specific aspects of a research project that reflect low inference include the following. Note that a number of these were already mentioned in the previous chapter, again reflecting the fuzzy boundaries between method and analysis in qualitative research.

- Audio or (even better) video recording, reliable and detailed **transcribing**: To analyze human communication, it's essential to have a record of it. We cannot do effective analysis just from listening to something once, because analysis involves thought and reflection. Hence, it is critical to have recordings wherever that is possible. Most qualitative analysis of interviews or conversations is done on transcripts, not the audio or video recordings themselves. Give two reasons why you think analysts mostly prefer using written transcripts instead of audio recordings?

Because transcripts exist "on paper" (or more likely in digital files), they can be highlighted and coded easily. It's much more difficult and time-consuming to tag little bits of audio files, and it is incredibly time-consuming to listen and relisten to audio. We read text much quicker than we can listen to audio, so the repeated reading is easier when transcripts are available. And computers can search the content of text files much easier than they can search the content of audio files. It is, of course, critical that transcripts are accurate. Accuracy can be gauged by having two people transcribe and comparing their two transcriptions, or by having a second person listen to (or view) the recordings while simultaneously reading the transcript to check for errors (you might remember from the previous chapter that Aaliyah did this; see "Writing the Report" in Chapter 15).

- Having detailed **field notes** or **memos** and providing the reader with details about how those notes were constructed. For Aaliyah's project, you might remember that she took detailed memos about the participants' responses immediately after each interview (e.g., noting nonverbal behaviors—something that is particularly important if the interviews were only audio recorded). She also referred to those notes while she was doing her analysis to help her understand deeper meanings in respondents' comments. The process of memo writing continues through data analysis, as Aaliyah writes notes about possible interpretations or additional lines of analysis to pursue. Field notes are, of course, particularly critical in situations where recording is not possible, or where a recording can't capture everything that is going on. An anthropologist observing a complex cultural ritual might have a video camera pointing at one aspect of a ceremony but would need to be watching and observing things outside of the camera's range, and that would require note-taking to preserve a full record of the events.
- Research is also more credible when the researcher keeps an audit trail—a record of all the important decisions that were made throughout the process that can be referred back to. When a researcher decides to combine two open codes into a single category, that moment in time and the reasons for combining the two codes can be recorded in a memo. Keeping track of all those decision points and being able to refer back to them helps a researcher keep track of the whole research process rather than just the outcome.
- Presentation of **extracts** of data in the report also adds to the credibility of the writing. While qualitative researchers are expected to provide summaries of important themes, topics, and the like in their data, it is also common for them to provide examples of their interviewees' exact words. These examples can bring a report "alive" for the reader, but they also help demonstrate the reliability of the research. Seeing a particular category described and then seeing a response that clearly fits into that category can help the reader get a feel for how much the researcher's coding corresponds with the reader's instincts. This is like a form of intercoder reliability, but between the researcher and reader. In vivo codes are a useful example here.

Remember that in vivo codes are examples of specific language or terminology used by respondents in explaining their situation. When you use in vivo codes, you are effectively having the research participants themselves generate the terminology for their categories.

- Intercoder reliability (or intercoder discussion) enhances a sense that the research is providing reliable information. While intercoder reliability is typically associated with quantitative research, it is not "wrong" for qualitative researchers to also use the technique. In particular, when qualitative researchers are working in a team, it can be very helpful for multiple members of the team to independently code part of the data and then examine their consistency. Such a strategy can reveal variation in how members of the team understand the categories (hence allowing clarification and clearer definition), and in a final report, providing information on intercoder reliability reinforces the idea that the work was done carefully and systematically. This is sometimes called **confirmability.**

Of course, it is not merely a question of Aaliyah *doing* these things. It's also important that she describe them in her research report so that her readers *know* that she did them; in the "Writing the Report" section, you'll see some ways that Aaliyah incorporates these details in her reporting.

Public availability of entire data sets

Increasingly quantitative scholars are making their entire data sets public to allow others to verify their analysis. This is occurring less often with qualitative studies—for some very good reasons. In a quantitative data set, except under unusual situations, it is virtually impossible to identify an individual's responses: Any individual's data is simply a string of numbers, and an individual person's data would only be identifiable if the data includes extensive demographic information. If the quantitative data reveal an individual who is a resident of Topeka, Kansas, who has been divorced three times, is 35 years old, has eight children, and is currently employed as a high school principal ... there's probably only one person who fits that profile! But this would be a rare occurrence. On the other hand, qualitative data will often include a large amount of identifying information. The "point" of qualitative data gathering is typically to understand people's personal experiences, and those will all be laid out in detail in their responses in an interview.

continues on next page

continues from previous page

As a result, qualitative researchers have significant challenges to protect their research respondents' confidentiality. They will obviously need to make sure materials are anonymized, but they may also need to look carefully for any identifying facts in their data. People in bad relationship breakups, for instance, might describe specific things that occurred in the breakup that would make them identifiable to others who knew about the situation. Tsai et al. (2016) provide some nice examples of the kind of work that might need to be done to data to remove such identifying information. Before making a data set public, the researcher would need to redact identifying information or replace it with "generic" information. Instead of "she broke up with me in a Safeway parking lot in South Tucson, right after we'd bought stuff for a St. Patrick's Day party," the researcher might make publicly available something like, "She broke up with me in a [redacted] parking lot in [city], right after we had [gone shopping]." In a large study, the work involved to do this for the entire data set could be substantial. You might notice that in the data for the current chapter, any potentially identifying information has been replaced. For instance, in most cases, references to specific cities where events took place have been replaced with [city name].

Validity

Aaliyah needs to make sure that her work reflects the reality of the situation—that it tells us something meaningful about the *truth* of her respondents' experiences. This is a validity concern. Validity in qualitative research can be supported by the following procedures.

- **Triangulation**: Using multiple data sources and methods is a way of strengthening qualitative work. Aaliyah only has her interviews, which is one limitation of her project. Combining interviews with focus groups or perhaps some observations of people experiencing music (at clubs, at festivals) would have strengthened the validity of her research. She could also triangulate by asking different groups of people: If the same broad ideas emerge from a sample of professional musicians and a sample of retirement community residents, then the validity of the analysis is supported.
- **Constant comparative** analysis: The constant comparative method is a technique involving developing coding systems and (as the name implies) constantly comparing them to the data as new data are analyzed or collected. This involves diverse approaches, such as (a) adapting interview protocols for later interviews based on what is observed and analyzed in

earlier interviews and (b) analyzing one part of the data set, and then "checking" those analyses based on a second part of the data set. In Aaliyah's case, she could have developed her coding scheme based on half of her sample and then gone to the remaining cases to check that the coding system accounted for everything in that second half. More broadly, constant comparison means that the analysis process is cyclical. In quantitative research, the researcher collects the data and then analyzes the data. In constant comparative qualitative analysis, data collection and data analysis occur simultaneously, and mutually influence one another. Aaliyah reads her data multiple times, and each "pass" through the data provides additional insights, new codes, and new ideas for future interviews.

- Sampling: It is important that researchers have sufficient data. While Aaliyah is not concerned about having a random sample, she is nonetheless concerned about having a diverse sample and having responses from enough people so that she can be confident that she has captured the breadth of possible musical experiences. This, of course, reflects the notion of **saturation** described in the previous chapter: Aaliyah must convince her readers that she didn't miss anything crucial.
- Engagement in setting: For many types of qualitative research, it is important that the researcher remain engaged in the setting being studied for a prolonged period of time. You probably wouldn't "trust" a study of an Amazon tribe done by a researcher who flew in by helicopter on a Tuesday afternoon and left early Thursday. That's not long enough to gain any sort of understanding of how a culture operates or for the culture to get used to having a stranger in its midst. Time is important. Among other things, spending time in a particular setting allows the researcher to describe the situation in great detail for the reader: This is called **thick description.** Aaliyah can claim some degree of engagement simply through the very large number of interviews she performed.
- Deviant case analysis: To ensure the validity of her work, Aaliyah should actively seek out cases that don't fit in her category system. Quantitative work deals with "averages," allowing unusual cases to just "disappear" in the crowd. But for qualitative researchers, unusual cases represent opportunities for new understandings of the data. Computer software can be very helpful here, as it makes it easy to systematically look at all the cases *not* coded in a particular way. So-called **deviant case analysis** can be very helpful in theory building. Imagine you were trying to build a theory about how questions and answers are related in conversation. Examining cases where questions are *not* followed by answers would be very informative about this process; you'd probably find that questions about embarrassing or highly personal

issues are typically *not* followed by answers but instead by other questions ("Why do you want to know that?") or by other communication querying the validity of the question ("Mind your own business!").

- Member validation: Once Aaliyah's analysis is almost complete, another validity check she can do is to return to her research subjects (or other similar people) and solicit their input on her analysis. This is called **member validation.** "Member" here refers to members of the group that is being studied. Aaliyah can present a small group of people with the categories from her analysis and check with them that the categories make sense, as well as checking that there are not any additional categories that she might have missed.

KEY POINT

Variation in qualitative analysis. Aaliyah's project has approached the data with the goal of understanding people's experiences. She believes she is getting at something *real* about those experiences—something approaching or resembling the truth. In this regard, her work is similar to many types of quantitative research. While she is using different methods, the underlying approach to research is similar: uncovering truth. Other research paradigms exist whose goals (and methods of analysis) vary. For some qualitative researchers, the idea of "truth" is very problematic; they view their task as uncovering a *version* of the world but by no means the only true version. For some researchers, the potential for a particular analysis to make the world a better place might be more important than whether it is "truthful" in the traditional sense of that term.

Writing the Report

Qualitative researchers need to describe the nitty-gritty of their analyses and results. As should be clear by now, the boundaries between "method" and "results" are less clear for qualitative scholars because the processes of data collection and analysis are more intertwined and interdependent. As you read Aaliyah's report (Report 16.1), notice how she includes information relating to the validity and reliability of her work in the description of her procedures.

The report presents the analysis as "complete," but as noted earlier, there are probably additional steps to be done with this analysis for a full examination of these data. Indeed, all qualitative analysis could be seen as potentially incomplete given the infinite variety of ways to analyze qualitative data. One final note: You will see that this report of a qualitative study is much longer than the earlier reports of quantitative data. This is often the case. It requires more space to provide a summary and examples of text data than it does to report a few numbers. However, a typical report from a *quantitative* study might involve more details than the examples in this book suggest. Our examples have typically provided one or two statistics, but a full quantitative report might include many times that number.

REPORT 16.1 Results for Qualitative Thematic Analysis

Data were analyzed using the constant comparative method. In an initial open-coding phase, individual responses were examined for recurring themes, with a particular focus on the circumstances surrounding a transcendent or profound experience with music. After multiple passes through the data, 10 open descriptive codes were identified. Subsequent passes through the data revealed interpretive codes that incorporated broader aspects of the data, including themes crossing multiple open descriptive codes. The researcher uncovered seven interpretive codes. Finally, she derived three axial codes from the earlier descriptive and interpretive coding, capturing fundamental patterns of profound musical experiences.

The primary researcher coded all of the transcripts. At three points during the coding process, a trained research assistant coded portions of transcripts, checking for consistency between her codes and those of the primary researcher. Discrepancies were discussed and the coding scheme adjusted. The primary researcher engaged in multiple passes through the data, focusing particularly on cases that were difficult to categorize. In all cases, interpretation of the transcripts was assisted by reference to memos taken during and immediately after each interview.

All the codes are presented briefly in Figure 1 and described in more detail next. Coding was managed using QDA Miner Lite. Any potentially personally identifying material in the data is replaced by generic text in square brackets.

continues on next page

continues from previous page

Open Descriptive Codes

- **Anthems:** All comments containing references to national anthems.
- **Connection to boy/girlfriend:** Mention of romantic relationships—generated from text search of boyfriend/girlfriend, and additional manual coding of other similar terms, includes experiences *with* partner, or where music reminded person of partner.
- **Music connects to family:** Reference to musical experiences *with* family members, or music reminding person of family member.
- **Experiences at festivals:** Any reference to experiences at a music festival—includes references to specific festivals derived from text searches (e.g., Coachella).
- **Friend:** References to experiences with friends, or music reminding person of friends/friendship. Includes text search for "friend."
- **Logic performance for suicide awareness:** References to suicide—these codes largely occurred in the context of a specific award show performance by artist Logic related to suicide prevention awareness.
- **"We are the world" performance for Haiti relief:** Mentions of Haiti or "We Are the World"—relates to a specific award show performance raising funds and awareness for aid to Haiti in which the song was performed.
- **Macklemore—"One Love" song, awareness of diverse sexualities:** References to artist Macklemore—all in the context of his "One Love" song promoting understanding of people identifying with different sexualities.
- **Never had peak musical experience:** Indications of never having had the experience in the question.

Open Interpretive Codes

- **Music transcends cultural difference:** The power of music to bridge barriers between groups; includes references to events where people from different groups came together around music and experiences when music reminded person of groups coming together.
- **Music as cultural contact:** References to experiencing music with people from different cultures, or directly experiencing other groups' music (e.g., when traveling or at cultural festivals).
- **Solitary peak experiences:** Describes an individual experience, not necessarily shared with others (e.g., the influence of music on individual mood or thought). Sometimes part of a joint experience, but the emphasis is individual.
- **Music connecting to ingroup identity:** Music enhancing in group identity—e.g., when a song makes you aware of your gender, ethnicity, etc. and enhances your feelings of belonging to that group, or where an event causes awareness of music's value to another group.
- **Music as joint activity:** Situations in which a transcendent musical experience is driven by joint movement—typically dancing, singing, or swaying together with a very large group of people (often in a festival or concert environment).
- **Musical experiences tied to religious experiences:** References to experiences grounded in religious ideas or experiences—e.g., music in church.
- **Musical performances with a message:** Performances with a concrete (typically prosocial) message—includes "We Are the World", Macklemore, and Suicide-logic, as well as national anthems.

Axial/Theoretical Codes

- **Intrapersonal—music as peak psychological experience:** Describes intense individual emotional or physical responses. Includes "individual experience" codes, as well as other experiences marked by individual level response (e.g., crying).
- **Interpersonal—music as peak relational experience:** Instances featuring music enhancing relationships or increasing reflection on personal relationships. Also includes situations where being surrounded by friends enhancing musical experiences.
- **Transcending the personal—music connecting to collective humanity:** Describes collective experiences transcending the individual or interpersonal. Often coincides with coordinated group physical activity—collective dancing or singing in festival environments in particular—or observations of collective emotional experiences (all feeling united, as one).

FIGURE 1 Open and Axial Codes

continues on next page

continues from previous page

OPEN DESCRIPTIVE CODES

Eight descriptive codes emerged from open coding, as well as one code for nonresponses or indications of never having had the experience (the latter is not described further).

Music connects to family. Responses in this category included references to singing or listening to with family (e.g., "listening to Christmas music during the holidays with friends and families creates a feeling of happiness and relaxation"). As is clear from this example, the comments often included associated affective responses, such as happiness. This theme also encompassed situations in which music reminds someone of his or her family:

I felt this way when watching the Pixar movie, Coco. *The music made me think of my family and looking around, it seemed it had the same reaction with others. The music and the words were powerful that people either teared up or cried.*

In addition to references concerning family in general, responses also described being reminded of a specific family member ("the chorus of the song called "Fight Song" by Rachel Platten makes me feel stronger and connected to the song because it makes me think of my mom fighting through her [type of] cancer"), as well as experiences that occurred *with* specific family members ("The music was [artist and title]. I recall listening with my brothers and feeling like the song could overcome barriers between people, because the song dealt with the theme of the passage of time.").

[similar descriptions of the other open descriptive codes would also be included]

OPEN INTERPRETIVE CODES

Eight interpretive codes emerged after additional readings of the analysis and consideration of the descriptive codes. These interpretive codes involved more abstract conceptual issues and were less driven by text-based searches of the data. In many cases, they involve overlap with the descriptive codes, but they emerged in later passes through the data.

Music as joint activity. These codes involved situations in which a transcendent musical experience is driven by coordinated physical movement in a large group—often (though not always) dancing, singing, or swaying together with other people in a concert environment. A large number of the descriptions in the "festival" descriptive code appeared here, as in the following example:

continues on next page

continues from previous page

I was at Summers End music festival this fall and when I was listening to Kanye West. The whole crowd around me was screaming and yelling the words to the songs and the connectedness between the people was overwhelming and the intensity felt was enormous.

These descriptions frequently involved references to groups joining together across cultural or other boundaries:

There were thousands of people from all backgrounds and cultures moving the same way to the music. It did not matter what ethnicity you were, where you were from, or any stereotype that could try and separate people. The combination of music, lights, and atmosphere (of closeness) pulled us all together.

Smaller, more intimate gatherings also involved descriptions of coordinated or joint activity and again these themes of bridging group boundaries were present:

When I was traveling abroad in [country]*, we spent a day camel trekking ... to spend a night at [camp]. The men who led the camels ... sat down and played drums and sang in Arabic. Some students joined in, learned the chants, and then after a while one of them offered to play an American song. They taught it to the camel drivers and were eventually all singing the same song around the fire.*

[similar descriptions of the other open interpretive codes]

AXIAL CODES: THREE LEVELS OF ANALYSIS

The researcher examined the open codes, looking particularly for themes that crossed those codes and that were theoretically distinct from one another. Three key areas of profound musical experiences were identified.

1. Intrapersonal—music as peak psychological experience: These comments describe intense individual emotional or physical responses that are framed by the respondent as *not* shared with others. It is primarily represented by the "individual experience" open codes, as well as other experiences marked by strong intrapersonal responses to music (e.g., "Religious music lifts my heart and makes my whole body feel light. I felt a powerful spirit within me."). Many of these responses relate to individual songs or very specific moments of listening, as in the following examples:

One song that I connect with is the song "No Rain" by Blind Melon. This song reminds me of the summer time and being on the beach and having no worries in the world. This song just makes me forget about everything.

continues on next page

continues from previous page

I remember when I first transferred to the university from my hometown [city name]. I hardly knew anyone on campus and that was sort of intimidating on my first day of class. While walking from my dorm to the student union for my first class of the semester, I was understandably nervous. However, I had my music playing in my earbuds, and every time I listen to certain songs, I get a wave of confidence and happiness that comes over me.

The latter of these two extracts illustrates the use of music for managing mood and coping individually with difficult experiences—a relatively common theme in the data set.

Intrapersonal experiences connect to the two subsequent axial codes in interesting ways, as will be described in the next two sections.

2. Interpersonal—music as peak relational experience: The second axial code involves a set of *inter*personal experiences: cases where the experience of music is shaped by the presence of other people or where music reminds you of an interpersonal relationship in some way. For example:

The experience I most remember was a December 31 before the new year come. My dad started playing an old rock song that he likes and we were near *the ocean it was literally one of the most wonderful experiences of my life ... I think it was so especial this experience because was with my family and because of that I still remember it until today.*

These experiences often reflect the interactive power of relationships to enhance music's effects and music to reinforce the relationship, as in the following example.

When I was in high school at prom my freshman year I had my first kiss and listening to the slow R&B song with my girlfriend at the time it explained everything that we were feeling towards each other in terms of our love for each other at the time.

Open codes relating to family and friends were relevant to this axial code. Some of these interpersonal experiences have *intra*personal components, thus tying these responses to the first broad axial code. This includes cases where music reminded someone of a family member or a romantic relationship. While these are predominantly positive, that is not always the case (e.g., "I was listening to a song by [artist]. In it, it said one of my ex- [boy/girl] friend's birthday, made me remind of [him/her], made me feel angry at [him/her]"). In some instances, the musical experience has mixed emotional components, such as when it reminds someone of a loss while also providing comfort. See the following for example:

continues on next page

continues from previous page

Over the summer my [close relative] passed away and a week later I went to a [artist] concert. His music spoke to me and made me feel happy in a time where I was emotionally not ok. For those couple hours he performed I felt as though I was meant to be there and that everything will be ok because there are so many other things going on in the world, and that everyone was there together for the love of music. It was as if everyone there was there for me and there to cheer me up and let me know that everything will be ok.

3. Transcending the personal—music connecting to collective humanity: Third, some of the experiences described in the data are at a broad collective level (e.g., attending a concert where everyone is shouting the words of a song together), and those collective experiences translate to a transcendent sense of shared humanity. Many of these experiences occur in festival settings.

When the music came on and I was standing in the middle of the crowd, nothing else mattered anymore and everything seemed harmonious. I became friends with the people around me as we danced together. Everyone was from different states and even from different countries around the world, but I felt a bond with people of all cultures.

One respondent elaborated on this notion, describing how a popular type of festival (electronic dance music) operates under an informal code specifying "peace, love, unity, and respect" among the attendees. The respondent elaborated on respect:

This is where the Respect aspect comes in. Another example that I love is that people are generally very accepting of other peoples' beliefs, whether that be sexual preference, religion, or even just your worldview.

Joint activity was not always described as part of the process of bridging boundaries; at times, the collective experience was simply provided by "being there" or even just by listening and having a sense of connectedness to others, as in the second example below, which describes an experience that occurred while the interviewee was alone but nonetheless felt a connection with others.

I experienced this at country music festival I went to this past summer. During the concert portion, everyone was connected through this music. That it didn't matter who you were or where you're from, each person was connected with each other.

When I listened to "We Are the World," I felt a bond with people of all cultures. There was about 25 artists that came together in order to sing this song that was made to recognize and help the people of Haiti. I thought it was inspiring how all the different music cultures came together for a greater cause.

continues on next page

continues from previous page

Intrapersonal experiences also connect to this "transcending the personal" theme. Group events are sometimes simultaneously individual psychological experiences. The feeling of being connected to others or of shared humanity can, interestingly, be presented as *not* experienced collectively. The following examples illustrate this, especially the second, which contrasts the group ("we") that attended the event and yet frames the experience in the first-person singular:

"Where Is the Love?" by Black Eyed Peas is a kind of song that makes me feel like there is hope and a sense of equality. It makes you think about the world and the poverty in the world as well as equality. It sends a message that people need to look out for one another.

Last year we attended ... Coachella ... As I stood there watching and listening, I was overwhelmed by euphoria.

Similarly, and as already illustrated in a number of the examples provided earlier, there are strong connections to interpersonal experiences here. The sensation being described in many cases is a combination of personal transcendence, but also a deep connection to others present—often people who are complete strangers but are experienced as friends, but also sometimes including people who are friends.

These axial codes lead us toward a theoretical approach wherein profound experiences of music involve strong psychological and emotional responses to the music that are reinforced by connections between music and interpersonal relationships, which at times culminate in large-scale group activity and feelings of closeness and identity with all of humanity. These axial codes also reveal detailed intersections between two complementary aspects of musical experience: a physical coordination that can be experienced jointly with large groups of people, and an emotional resonance that is largely (although not exclusively) individual.

Other Applications

Qualitative research and analysis in communication can be applied to any of the typical contexts and areas of study in our discipline, as discussed in the previous chapter. The following represent just a few more examples of possible qualitative research studies in communication.

- Analysis of interactions between parents and children while watching television together. Qualitative analysis could uncover multiple ways in which parents encourage media literacy in their children by commenting on shows and advertising.

- Interviews about responses to health messages (e.g., persuasive health campaigns to encourage people to stop smoking). Qualitative analysis could uncover complex ways in which people process the messages, including perhaps revealing ways people resist the behaviors the messages are trying to encourage.
- Observation of behaviors in a student union cafeteria. Careful qualitative observation and analysis could uncover the processes by which people choose where to sit, who to sit with, and the like.
- Focus groups with migrant workers. Qualitative analysis of their interactions could yield insight into how they manage being away from their families and how their interactions with their fellow workers might substitute for the family connections.
- Examination of user reviews on Amazon products. A qualitative analysis of these texts might provide some perspective on why people "volunteer" their time to write the reviews, themes in the reviews (quality of product, value), or surprising aspects in the content (e.g., humor, responses to other reviews, comments on delivery issues rather than the product).

As is clear from these examples, qualitative research has infinite scope: Almost any aspect of human communication could be subject to qualitative analysis. As noted elsewhere, there is also a wide array of qualitative methods and approaches. Quantitative data have a fairly restricted set of options for how the data can be analyzed. On the other hand, a qualitative data set could be analyzed in many ways, depending on the researcher's interests. Recordings of romantic partners' phone conversations could be analyzed to find out something about how romantic partners talk to one another, or to see how phone conversations unfold, or to see how self-disclosure works, or just to understand how people have conversations. The list of plausible approaches and foci in the same set of data is huge.

Your Turn

You can do this alone or in pairs: If working in pairs, use the same data, but analyze it separately and then share your analysis at the end. Find a product type that interests you on Amazon—music from a band you like, clothing from your favorite brand, or whatever. Copy at least 20 customer reviews of those products into a separate document. Following the procedures described in the chapter, identify what you see as important themes or topics in the reviews. Starting with just the data rather than any preconceptions, look for what you think is interesting and make notes of the types of things you see (open coding). Remember, this is brainstorming; if in doubt, code it! Read and reread to make sure you're not missing interesting stuff. Once you are satisfied with your set of open codes, think about higher level themes or issues underlying those codes (axial coding). Are there a small number of key critical issues that capture most of the important factors in the open coding? Those are the axial codes. Write your analysis following the same organization as in the example for this chapter.

Wrap Up

In this chapter, you have learned the basics of doing a qualitative analysis of text. The process of coding involves spending a lot of time reading and rereading, looking for important issues in the data, and keeping track of them. Coding typically moves from examining fairly "obvious" things to developing deeper insights into the data: a move from descriptive to interpretive analysis. Axial coding is the theory-building aspect of this type of qualitative analysis: It is where researchers move from describing and cataloging data to making inferences about deeper meanings, intentions, or interpretations of the text. The reliability of qualitative work is assessed by examining the quality of the data record (e.g., was it recorded and transcribed) and whether the researcher provides detailed examples from the data. Validity is assessed by factors such as the comprehensiveness of the data (is it large enough?), the depth of the research and analysis (e.g., spending a lot of time on the work, analyzing using constant comparison), and, in some cases, member validation (having research subjects look over the analysis once it is in draft form).

If you get nothing else from this chapter, remember the following:

1. Open codes are brainstorming and axial codes are theory building.
2. Coding requires reading text multiple times, thinking about it from lots of different angles, and paying attention to themes, topics, and contrasts across an entire data set.
3. The quality of qualitative research can be gauged with reliability and validity, but those terms are used differently in qualitative as compared to quantitative research.

Key Chapter Concepts

Axial coding: A stage of coding following open coding. Axial codes are higher level codes that resemble theoretically important concepts and ideas; often axial codes will subsume multiple open codes. See also **Open coding.**

Confirmability: The qualitative equivalent of intercoder reliability: an analysis in which multiple researchers agree on coding and analysis is a confirmable analysis.

Computer-assisted qualitative data analysis software (CAQDAS): Software designed to assist qualitative researchers in managing and analyzing data. The software keeps track of codes, allows running of reports (e.g., of all the bits of the data coded in certain ways), and helps to keep memos and field notes associated with other relevant materials (e.g., the specific interview that a particular memo came from).

Constant comparative method: A method of analysis involving continuous comparison between data and results. For example, developing codes and then applying them to new data to see if they are sufficient would be one technique demonstrating constant comparison.

Deviant case analysis: Exploration for, and careful analysis of, cases in the data that do not "fit" a specific analysis.

Extracts: Extracts from a qualitative data set designed to provide rich and helpful examples of a particular theme or idea. Qualitative analysis doesn't allow for the presentation of "averages" among respondents.

Low-inference descriptors: Descriptions of the research process that don't require the reader to make guesses about what was done or what was found. Precise transcripts and recording of research (e.g., video recording) provide low-inference descriptors. Low-inference descriptors are associated with **reliability.**

Member validation: Asking respondents to review the major themes or conclusions of an analysis and offer additional insights; if study participants do not agree with your analysis, that is one indication that the analysis might lack **validity.**

Open coding: The initial stages of qualitative coding, typically driven by coding anything that appears relevant to the research question and creating new codes whenever something new appears. Coding might be driven by themes in the data that are repeated or that appear emotionally important.

Reliability: Qualitative analyses are reliable to the extent that they are grounded in accurate representations of the data (e.g., accurate recordings, detailed transcription) and provide the reader with extracts and examples from the raw data that illustrate specific themes or codes. See also **Low-inference descriptors.**

Saturation: The point at which gathering additional data does not yield any additional insight.

Thick description: Descriptions of a data set that provide the reader with a full and vivid sense of the data as a whole.

Triangulation: Using multiple sources of data (e.g., interviews and observations) or substantively different samples (e.g., working professionals and retirees) to draw conclusions.

Validity: Qualitative research is valid to the extent that researchers engage in constant comparative analysis, engage in **deviant case analysis**, and **member validation**, and to the extent that they can triangulate their findings (reach similar conclusions from different forms of data).

Section Wrap

Section Summary

This section has introduced qualitative analysis, with a particular focus on thematic coding of interview data. Interviews provide an excellent way to get people's insights on their own social and communicative lives. They provide a high level of confidence that responses obtained are "real" because people are less likely to lie, zone out, or respond randomly in an interview as compared to an online questionnaire, for instance. Interviews also allow for asking follow-up questions to clarify or get more detail. All kinds of text (including responses from interviews) can be analyzed using the techniques described in Chapter 16.

Going Further

As already mentioned, qualitative research can involve a lot more than just the text-based analysis described in this chapter. In this "Going Further" section, I'm going to briefly describe one additional form of qualitative research: ethnography. An ethnographer's goal is to understand a social situation: What is going on in a particular situation, and how to the people within that situation know how to behave? This typically involves uncovering the underlying informal (and implicit) rules and norms of the setting. What do people know to do or not do in this social context, and how do they learn what is appropriate? Ethnography often requires multiple types of data collection and analysis. For the purpose of this section, imagine that you are a researcher interested in understanding communication norms in a prison. To get a full sense of what was going on, you might do some of the following; all of these could be part of an ethnography:

1. **Observation:** Observing naturally occurring behavior is one of the most powerful ways to understand a social situation. A qualitative researcher will be trained to observe carefully and to take detailed notes (see sidebar). In the prison setting, you might try to observe at different times of day and in different contexts—meal times, roll call, free time in the yard, etc. And you would want to observe communication among prisoners, between guards and prisoners, and among guards and other prison staff. How do people's behaviors change in different settings, and what is the meaning of those behaviors in terms of their social and organizational relationships?

2. **Interviews:** We have already discussed interviews, and sometimes interviews can make up an entire study. For an ethnographer, though, interviews are just one tool. In the prison setting, interviews with prisoners and with prison staff would help clarify interpretations of the observations described earlier. An ethnographer would probably ask a lot of questions, like "I've seen people doing X; can you help me understand why they are doing that?" As already discussed, focus groups would also provide a useful complement to one-on-one interviews, allowing you to observe where prisoners, for instance, disagree about certain formal or informal norms. Interviews would also help you understand the local language used by prisoners and staff. If you don't understand what people mean when they talk about a "kite," an interview will help you find out.

3. **Document (archival) analysis:** Many settings—especially organizations like prisons—have a lot of written materials and other kinds of archival records (websites, news coverage, letters, promotional brochures). All of these are data for an ethnographer. For instance, prisons will have detailed rules and guidelines for visitors to the prison: how they can behave, what they need to wear, what they can bring in and out, and the like. An ethnographer would be interested in how the reality of visitors' behavior reflects (and especially where it deviated from) those rules.

Observing social behavior

Making good observations and keeping notes about them is a skill that requires practice and training. Here are some basic elements of the process that will give you an idea of how it is done.

Orientation

You should always remember your research question when you enter the environment. As with a semi-structured interview, you should be open to seeing things you don't expect that might be relevant to your study, but you should be cautious about getting side tracked into detailed observations of things that are "interesting" but not relevant. You should also be aware of your own feelings. If you feel uncomfortable in the setting, what does that tell you about the setting, and how might that influence other aspects of your observations?

continues on next page

continues from previous page

What to Write Down

- Basic information: The date, time, location, who is present.
- A description of the physical environment: A picture can be useful if you can take it or even a sketch drawing/"map" of the physical space. Remember to include yourself in the sketch so you can recall your (literal) perspective. If you observe the same setting multiple times, it is useful to place yourself in different locations to get a different perspective.
- The behaviors people are engaged in: As specifically as possible, write down what people are doing and saying (actual words where possible), who they are talking to, their tone of voice, how close people are to one another, whether they are facing each other, whether they are standing or sitting, and the like. If you are recording exactly what people are saying, use quotation marks so you can later know what was verbatim and what was summarized/paraphrased.
- Analysis: Even in the earliest stages of observation, write down ideas or simple "theories" about the setting that you are observing. Remember, data collection and data analysis are simultaneous processes with most qualitative work.

How to Organize

- Number each page of your notes (if taking by hand): If considerable time passes, put time markers in the notes so you can later reconstruct how long different phases of observation were.
- Organize your field notes into two columns: The left column is used for strict observation ("just the facts"); the right column is used for analysis/interpretation as well as for questions that emerge during your observation (similar to the analytic memos described earlier). This division of note taking is important so that you don't mistake your *interpretation* for something that you actually *saw*.

Afterward

As soon as possible after any observation, spend some time reflecting on the experience, revisiting questions that emerged, and writing a summary of the important elements from that observation. This helps you begin analysis while the observation is fresh in your mind and provides useful leads for the next observation. Again, these reflections are memos and will be useful for you when you come back to your notes in the future.

Ethnographers will typically do interviews, observations, and analysis of documents. **Triangulation** is critical to ethnography; to understand a context fully, it's essential to have multiple forms of data to draw on. Part of the constant comparative process for an ethnographer would be going back and forth between these different data sources. Does what you are hearing in interviews reflect what is written in the formal prison procedures? Does what you hear from prisoners in interviews match with what you hear from prison staff? Does the interview data match your observations of natural behavior? When there is consistency across all the forms of data, then you can be very confident that you have a good handle on a particular rule or norm for that setting. When there is inconsistency, then you are probably on your way to an interesting insight. For instance, the prison procedures documents might list a fairly rigid timetable for the day. In reality, you might observe that events often supersede that timetable: A disruption in the yard, a staffing shortage, or a special event of some sort might mean that the formal schedule is rarely followed precisely. This could lead you to understand that the documents in the prison provide an important sense of structure—almost an "illusion" of regulation. But in fact, everyone in the prison (staff, prisoners, etc.) maintains a constant readiness to improvise and shift away from the rules depending on moment-to-moment contingencies. The tension between formal, apparently inflexible rules and informal, flexible daily practices might be something to explore further in interviews.

Ethnography is a complex example of qualitative research that requires a wide skill set, as should be clear from the very brief example earlier. A written ethnography might be considerably longer than even the written report earlier in this section. A good ethnography of a prison might involve long-term observation of the environment, and the volume of data might eventually need a book to cover the various facets of the analysis. The book could be organized around the important themes emerging from the analysis. There might be

- a section on improvisation, following from the idea earlier that everyone has to be flexible;
- a section on hierarchy—prisons are places where power is important, both formal (e.g., guards over prisoners) and informal (e.g., subtle ways prisoners might control their own environments, or have control over one-another); and
- a section on roles (expectations for being a "good" prisoner or guard and the consequences when people deviate from those roles).

These are just my guesses for themes that might emerge from research in a prison: A good qualitative researcher will, of course, allow their observations to guide their conclusions for what is important in the particular context.

Two types of ethnography particularly relevant to communication researchers are the ethnography of communication and ethnographic studies of technology use. The ethnography of communication is focused on understanding how specific uses of language (and other forms of communication) function in certain social contexts. A researcher might examine how obscenities function in certain cultures to mark dominance or masculinity, for instance. What happens in those cultures when you drop an F-bomb, and are there specific skills involved in knowing precisely when and where to do it? Ethnographic studies of technology examine how our uses of technology fit into our social lives. Both academic researchers and technology companies do ethnography with this purpose: Organizations like Microsoft and Facebook want to know when and where technology fits well within our lives and when it causes frustrations. One way to do this is by hiring social scientists who carefully observe how people use technology in their everyday lives, understand the implicit rules in such use, and observe when either their use of technology breaks down or where their social lives get disrupted.

Credit

SECTION 9

Bringing It All Together

By the end of this section, you will be able to:

- ✔ Describe how to assess whether something is a good social science research question
- ✔ Articulate the important considerations in deciding which research question to use
- ✔ Use a decision-making tool to select the right statistical test for a problem
- ✔ Describe at least one way in which theory is important in the research process
- ✔ Describe what a meta-analysis is and why it might be important
- ✔ Explain how research might be important in your own career plans, even if you don't want to be a researcher

CHAPTER 17

Communication Research From 30,000 Feet

This final chapter presents some bigger picture discussions about the research methods the book has studied. Previous chapters have presented some very specific studies; now you should be equipped to think about the research enterprise more broadly. What are some general rules for doing good research? Why does theory matter in the research enterprise? Why is it important to replicate studies, and how can we integrate findings from a large number of studies? By now, you should be ready to think about doing a study to answer a question. But you should also be ready to think about the reasons why no single study will ever fully answer a question. We develop strong scientific knowledge through programs of multiple studies, often performed by different investigators and done over the course of years, decades, or even centuries. Let's begin with a critical moment in the research enterprise: asking the right questions.

Asking Good Questions

When making judgments about good research, people will often focus on the methods—the focus of this book. If measurement is bad, then the research is bad. If sampling is bad, then the conclusions you can draw are limited. However, good research doesn't just have good methods. It needs to begin with a good question. Without a good question, you could end up doing a perfectly designed study that reaches trivial conclusions.

The best researchers have a knack for asking the right questions. There is an art to this, and there aren't many shortcuts to developing a good question. But there are some ways to focus your thinking on so that you are asking questions that matter.

- **Think about your friends or your parents.** If you were going to tell them what your research study is about, would they be interested? Every research study doesn't have to have "real-world interest"; there are purely theoretical questions that are important for communication scholars to answer but might not be immediately interesting to an "average Jane or Joe." But for the most part, if you can't express your research ideas in ways that make them interesting to a layperson, you might want to rethink your question.

- **Think about the results.** What is the most exciting pattern of results you could find? Imagine you got the "best" data you can imagine. What would the results actually say? Sometimes a question sounds interesting, but when you describe the hypothetical results, it seems obvious or boring. Perhaps you think it would be cool to find out whether men or women are more persuaded by Facebook ads. Before investing a lot of time and energy in the research, think about finding in the end that "men are more persuaded than women." Is that exciting enough to justify all the time you're going to invest? Maybe not.
- **How likely are you to find what you hope to find?** Some of the most exciting sounding research studies are also ones that are least likely to get the exciting results. For instance, it might be really cool to show that people who are interviewed in a room with a single houseplant express more proenvironmental views than people interviewed in a room without a plant. But if you were to talk to experienced researchers, they'd probably say that finding that effect is a long shot. You'll need a lot of research subjects, and even then, the manipulation (houseplant versus no houseplant) is so weak that you might not find anything. Unless you have lots of time and don't mind finding null results, you might want to reconsider the project and do something that is more likely to get significant (publishable) results. The following discussion about using **strong manipulations** is relevant here. Perhaps using 10 plants instead of one would make the plants a more salient part of the room's layout and increase the chances of finding effects.
- **Is it about communication?** Communication researchers tend to be a pretty broad-minded group. They are interested in lots of things, and their work often involves psychological and sociological issues. However, as someone in the communication discipline, it is important to remind yourself that the question should be about communication in some important way. Does the houseplant example from the previous question count? Perhaps not. If you are just examining whether a plant influences attitudes, that sounds like a pure psychology study. If you are looking at how *communication* is influenced by having plants in the room, then maybe.
- **Have a theoretical point.** Theory sometimes sounds like a scary word. But good questions (and good research studies) almost always have a theoretical component. And that doesn't need to be anything scary. Knowing that watching a violent movie causes kids to behave aggressively is a fact. Understanding that the children are *imitating* the behaviors they see on the screen and that they are more likely to imitate characters they admire than characters they dislike, that's a theory. A later section in this chapter elaborates on why theory matters.

- **Don't think about the method.** Beginning a research study with "I want to do a content analysis/experiment/survey" is rarely a productive approach. Decide on the *question* that you want to answer and then select the right method for that question. The next section will help you with selecting the right method.
- **Read.** A lot of the intuitively interesting questions have already been answered. To make sure you're asking a good question, you need to read the scientific literature and check that someone hasn't already answered your question. If they have, don't despair! Most interesting questions have equally interesting follow-ups. If someone has already found that women self-disclose more than men overall, that's OK. Perhaps you can develop hypotheses about the situations in which the reverse happens (e.g., perhaps men only disclose about certain *topics*).
- **Sweat the small stuff.** In a research question, every word is important. You should read and edit your question carefully and repeatedly to make sure it is expressing exactly what you want to study. Very subtle differences in wording can change the meaning of a question, so you need to make sure that what you are asking is absolutely clear to your reader (which involves making sure that it is absolutely clear to you first!).

Selecting a Method

Once you have decided on the question you want to ask, you need to decide on the most appropriate method to answer the question. You might remember something like Figure 17.1 from earlier in the book. Here it has been expanded to incorporate qualitative methods. Typically, if you have written a research question that is clear and precise, then the range of methods for testing that question will also be clear; sometimes a single method will clearly be the best approach, but other times, a couple of different methods might be appropriate. Using Figure 17.1 will help with this decision-making process.

Hypothesis/Research Question specifies causal relationship

- IV can ethically and logistically be manipulated → Experiment
- IV cannot ethically or logistically be manipulated → Survey (ideally longitudinal)

H/RQ asks about population characteristics

- Population is humans → Survey
- Population is messages → Content analysis

H/RQ asks about correlations (associations between variables)

- Variables relate to humans → Survey
- Variables relate to messages → Content analysis

RQ asks about behavior more broadly, as it occurs in social contexts

- Research aims to uncover important concepts in communication behavior → Qualitative grounded theory / thematic analysis
- Research aims to understand how things "get done" in a social situation → Ethnography

FIGURE 17.1 Selecting a method for communication research

If your question concerns whether some sort of message influences something about people's attitudes or behaviors, what method would be most appropriate?

Typically, any question involving "influence" (i.e., effects) would be best answered using an experiment. However, there are limits to this. Exposing people to most types of messages is OK, but certain types of messages (e.g., extreme graphic violence) may be inappropriate, especially with **vulnerable populations** (e.g., children, see Chapter 9). If you are interested in the effects of those sorts of messages, you might be better off using survey methods.

How about if you were interested in how college freshmen adjusted to living in a dorm during their first year, with a particular interest in how they learn the *rules* for dorm life?

This is quite a broad question and might be suited to a variety of methods, but an ethnographic approach would certainly provide a lot of useful information in answering the question. An ethnography could uncover how rules get transmitted (e.g., observing residents joking about people who use the elevator to travel just a single floor) and how friendship groups form and dissolve (e.g., via interviews it might be possible to see a shift from having mostly friends from the nearest few rooms to having friends from a wider variety of locations).

Selecting an inappropriate method to answer a question will cause many problems: This is among the most important questions a researcher will face.

Selecting the Statistical Test

The chapters in this book have presented a wide variety of statistical tests. This section provides a final version of the statistical decision tree (Figures 17.2 and 17.3).

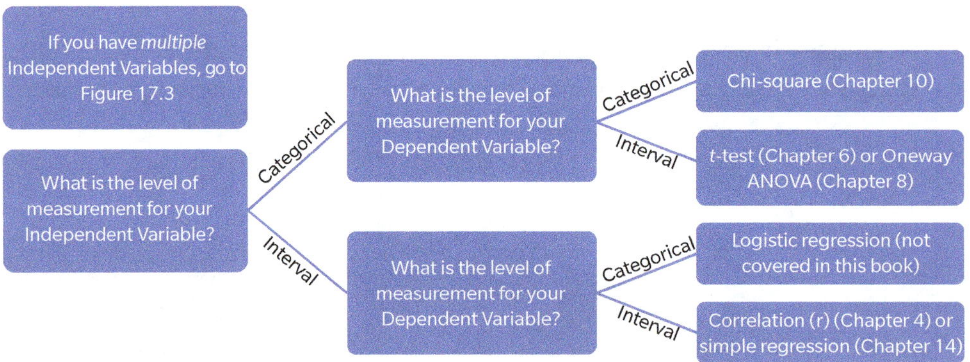

FIGURE 17.2 Statistical tests with one independent variable

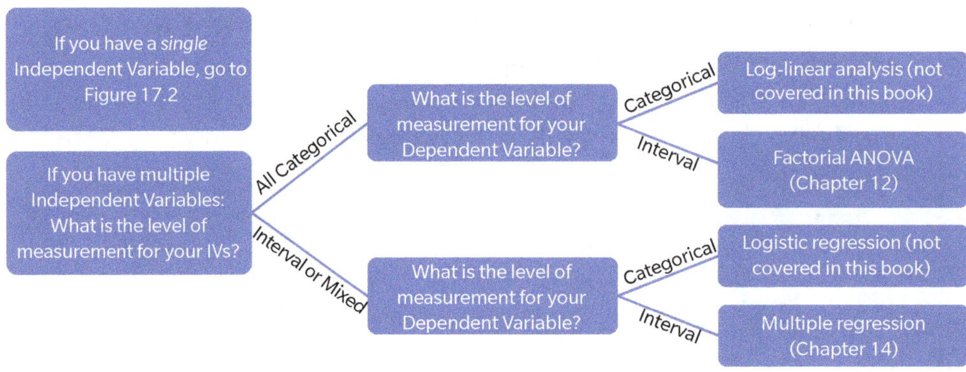

FIGURE 17.3 Statistical tests with multiple independent variables

As with selecting the right method to examine a question, it is also critical to select the right statistical test. The most perfectly designed study examining a tremendously interesting question can be wrecked by an inappropriate analysis. Perhaps you conclude that there are no effects and file the study away, whereas the correct analysis would have uncovered really interesting findings. Or maybe you conclude that there are effects and publish the study, only to be embarrassed by people pointing out that you did all the analysis wrong! Selecting the right analysis begins with making sure you understand what your independent and dependent variables are, and their level of measurement. Chapter 3 is your friend. If you were examining the effects of room temperature (measured in Fahrenheit) and extraversion (scored from 1 to 10) on people's level of argumentativeness in conversation (measured by counting how many times they disagree with a conversational partner), what statistical test would you use?

In this situation, you have three variables (room temperature, extraversion, and argumentativeness). All three variables are measured at the interval level (they are scores measured on some sort of continuous scale). Two of them (temperature and extraversion) are independent variables; these are the ones you think have some effect on something else (the dependent variable: argumentativeness). Once you have carefully gone through that process of identifying the variables, it's relatively straightforward to know that you're using Figure 17.3 (because you have multiple independent variables) and that you are using multiple regression (because all the variables are interval level).

Doing Research Right

Once you decide on a method, it is (as this book has made clear) important to use the method in the most effective manner. Figure 17.4 illustrates a few of the central concepts you should have learned in the course of reading this book. If these look unfamiliar, or you are unclear about what they mean, the glossary can help. Good research studies are designed with the concepts in Figure 17.4 in mind. In the preliminary stages of imagining a study, researchers who think about maximizing reliability and validity, the best forms of sampling, and the most effective strategies for coding will end up doing good research. People who just pick the first idea that comes into their heads without considering these concepts will design flawed research.

Experiments Internal Validity • Random assignment • Manipulation of independent variable • Control of everything else External Validity • Realistic conditions • Representative samples	**Content Analysis** Representative samples (of messages) Coding objects into categories that represent variables and are • Mutually exclusive • Exhaustive Inter-coder reliability
Survey Research Measurement • Reliability • Validity Using existing intruments where available Good questionaire design Appropriate administration method (e.g., questionaire versus interview) Sampling—Representative vs. Non-representative	**Qualitative Methods** Sampling • Using diverse samples • Sampling to saturation Coding • Open coding • Axial coding Reliability Validity

FIGURE 17.4 Important concepts organized by research type

Beyond the technical concepts in Figure 17.4, the following are some hints for producing high-quality research.

In experiments, use strong manipulations: In an experiment, you know that a basic task is to manipulate an independent variable. In most settings, you have a lot of choices as to how to exactly implement those manipulations. If you are manipulating exposure to rap music, you could play people 30 seconds of music or 30 minutes. If you are studying the effects of restricting people's phone access, you could just disable a few apps, or you could take the whole phone away. For those two examples, which do you think would be best? Why?

In each of these examples, the first idea (30 seconds, a few apps disabled) is a relatively weak manipulation; it probably won't have large effects. The second idea (30 minutes, taking away the phone) is much stronger and likely to have bigger effects. Especially when you are just starting research in a particular area, strong manipulations make it more likely that you will find effects and hence have a platform for subsequent studies. If you find nothing with a weak manipulation, you don't know whether you had a bad theory, or your manipulation just isn't strong enough to find your predicted effects. If you find nothing with a *strong* manipulation, then you can be much more confident that your theory is just plain wrong!

Have a big enough sample: This has already been discussed quite a bit. But briefly, can you remember one reason for having a large enough sample in qualitative research and quantitative research?

For quantitative research, larger samples are more accurate; if you are trying to generalize from a sample to a population, your estimates about the population will be more accurate if you have a larger sample. Related to this, larger samples provide more **statistical power** (see Chapter 10). If you are going to the trouble of doing a study, it's a shame in quantitative research to not have enough people to find statistical significance. In qualitative research, you want to have enough qualitative data to reach saturation. Without a large enough sample, you will miss important ideas that would have emerged with a larger sample. Your research will lose credibility in those circumstances—a reader will sense that *three* interviews weren't enough to get at the complexity of the issue!

Don't overanalyze: By "overanalyze" I mean analyzing your data every way you possibly can to see what you can find. It is hard to get research published without significant ($p < .05$) results, so there is a temptation to keep running different kinds of analysis until something (anything!) is statistically significant. Why do you think this might be a bad idea?

This is a poor approach to research for a couple of reasons. First, it violates the basic idea of statistical analysis. You should begin with a hypothesis and then examine the data to see if they support the hypothesis beyond "chance" levels. The more analyses you run, the less the "chance" bit means: If you keep going until you find something, chances are you found that "by chance," but the statistical test doesn't know that. In the language of Chapter 10, you become more likely to make a **Type 1 error** the more analyses you run. This can lead you (or worse, some other unsuspecting researcher) to do more research on an inaccurate "finding." Of course, you'll eventually find out that the particular finding can't be replicated, but by then, a lot of time will have been wasted.

Replicate your work. Replication just means doing the study again. Why is it important to replicate your research studies?

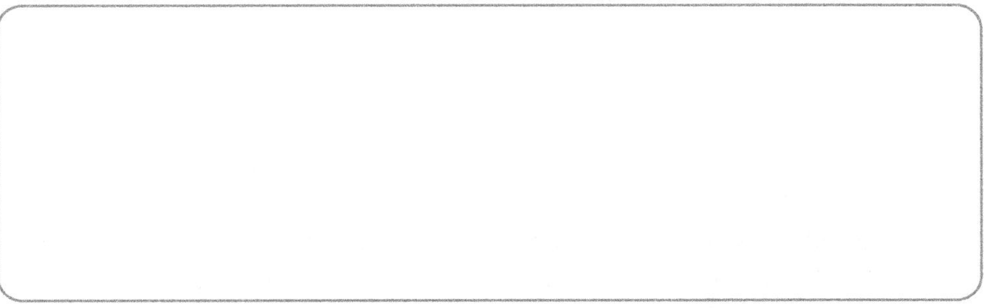

The previous paragraph has already described one important reason. Statistical tests have error associated with them, and replication is the single best way to find out if you committed, for instance, a Type 1 error. If we assume that the null hypothesis is actually true, there is a 5% (1 in 20) chance of rejecting it (incorrectly). However, if you do *two* studies, there is just a 0.25% (1 in 400) chance of incorrectly rejecting the null hypothesis in both of those studies. Replication is a great way to identify Type 1 errors.

Replication also allows extension of research ideas and theory. A replication doesn't need to be *exactly* the same study done again; it can be the same study done on a different subject population, or the same study but with an additional experimental manipulation included, for instance. This approach is sometimes called "replication and extension." By replicating and extending your work and adding a new element, you will get a better idea of whether your ideas work in new contexts, with new subject populations, or using different methodological approaches. This same broad idea applies to quantitative and qualitative work. If you do a qualitative study of communication in one type of organization (e.g., a hospital), it would be very interesting to examine the same types of communication in another organization (e.g., a child day-care center) to see which phenomena were similar in both environments and which changed.

A final point to remember about replication: It can be very *easy*. Once you have done a study, you have done a lot of the hard work. Particularly with quantitative work, the hard work is in creating the manipulations, developing the measurement, and the like. Once that is accomplished, collecting the data is relatively easy, and so replicating a study that you've already done once can be very straightforward. Communication researchers (me included!) don't always do a great job of replicating their work, but it is a critically important part of the scientific process.

Balance internal and external validity. Earlier chapters of the book described how **internal validity** is your confidence that an independent variable caused a dependent variable and **external validity** is your confidence in generalizing from the results of a particular study to other people or places. These are both important concepts in the research process, but they are often in conflict with one another. A carefully designed and tightly controlled experiment will have excellent internal validity but will often require some sacrifice of external validity.

Imagine you are interested in the effects of "overdisclosure" on physical health. You might do a study to see whether receiving embarrassing or intimate information from another person in a conversation increases blood pressure. This could involve (a) creating a situation in a lab where college student research subjects have conversations with someone (actually an experimental confederate) who either discloses something very personal or doesn't, and (b) having the research subject hooked up to a blood pressure gauge. You would then look for differences in blood pressure between the situations where there was an embarrassing disclosure and the ones where there wasn't. Can you think of two problems with external validity in this study?

There are numerous external validity problems here. The subject population is just college students (a convenience sample), and they are having conversations with complete strangers who are actually trained research assistants. The research assistants may not behave naturally (they are, after all, trying to insert random embarrassing disclosures into the conversation—something they might not normally do!). Perhaps most importantly, the subjects are hooked up to a medical device during the conversation. Pretty much the only time we talk to someone while hooked up to a blood pressure monitor is when we are talking to a medical professional or are hospitalized. There are *lots* of ways in which this study doesn't reflect normal everyday interaction.

There might be ways to examine this question in a way that has higher external validity. If you had lots of money, you could recruit a more representative sample. If you could persuade a hospital to agree, you could try doing the study with people who were already hooked up to blood pressure monitoring equipment for a medical condition. Doing that would have its own limitations, of course: people in hospitals probably are not a representative sample! A survey study simply asking people how they feel when others disclose personal information won't directly assess the blood pressure issue but could provide broader (and more externally valid) information about a range of physiological and psychological sensations that people have when they hear "too much information." Such a study would, of course, have much lower internal validity than the experiment.

Such trade-offs are common in research: Work that is high on external validity is often weaker on internal validity, and vice versa. As a researcher interested in a particular topic, the goal should be to (a) maximize each within any individual study while recognizing the trade-off and (b) to do multiple studies on a topic, where the different studies have different strengths and weaknesses.

Triangulate. As you now know, one study rarely answers a question completely. It can take multiple studies to understand a particular communication question fully. While it is useful to replicate studies using very similar methods and measures, it is also helpful to use a variety of methods to understand a particular problem. As hinted at in the previous section, different methods have different strengths and weaknesses. An experiment might be best for demonstrating a causal relationship between two specific variables, but an ethnography is best for understanding the rules by which a particular social situation operates. Most questions benefit from being examined using a variety of techniques.

Relatively few people are experts in experimentation *and* ethnography, but most researchers have expertise in more than one method. People who do experiments also understand survey techniques. People who use qualitative interviews will also be knowledgeable about using focus groups. When a particular question is examined from multiple methodological perspectives, the depth of our knowledge grows stronger. This is called **triangulation**. When you are early in your research career, it is good to try lots of methodological approaches to find out which one fits with your personal mind-set and skills. If you pursue research as a career, you'll find that you need to specialize to become an expert in one or two techniques, and at times, you might need to collaborate with another researcher whose expertise complements your own.

The Importance of Theory

Imagine you are studying whether college student romantic relationships are helped or hurt by "meeting the parents." This is probably an interesting question to a lot of college students (and you are probably a college student). But how can you make that question interesting to other communication scholars? And how can you make it interesting to people who aren't college students? By making it theoretically interesting! Move up a level of abstraction and you have a question about how people's personal relationships are influenced by either partner's *other* relationships. The question about college students' parents then becomes a question about relationship *systems*—the intersections between the multiple relationships that we all have.

The question then becomes relevant to married couples where the partners have different friendship networks, or to siblings where one sib wants to introduce a friend to the other sib, or to organizational settings when a worker wants to introduce a colleague from another department to his/her boss. The question just got much bigger and much more interesting, right?

When people talk about using **theory**, they are not necessarily talking about using a specific theory with a fancy name ("uncertainty reduction theory," "cultivation theory"). All they mean is that the research has implications beyond the specific finding in the specific context and that the researcher should be able to articulate those potential points of interest.

Reading and Reviewing the Literature

Published research papers typically start with a **literature review** in which the authors of the paper summarize what has been found previously, as part of building a justification for what they are going to do in their study. It might seem weird, then, that this book is *ending* by talking about this process. In part, I wanted you to get you straight to "doing" research. If the first chapter of this book had been about *reading* research studies, I was concerned you wouldn't read any further in the book! But I also think you can only appreciate the value of reading after you have worked through some examples of actually doing research.

The reading process is critical to doing good research. Can you think of three reasons why it is good to read previous research before doing your study?

First, there are lots of interesting questions that have *already been answered.* You don't know they've been answered until you read the previous research and find out what we already know. Reading previous research can save you from doing a study that someone else has already done.

Second, reading previous research can give you a theoretical context for your work. Previous researchers will have used certain theories, and their ideas will give you broader and more interesting ideas for framing *your* work theoretically.

Third, reading previous research can give you methodological ideas. Other researchers will have come up with interesting ways to manipulate or measure the relevant variables, and you can use those ideas. Remember, **science is cumulative**; each research study builds on previous studies, and those previous studies will often provide a lot of the raw materials for constructing new research.

Fourth, reading previous research (and citing it when you write your own work) is how scientists do social networking. By citing other work, you are building connections in a scientific network and making it clear where you see your work fitting in the much larger scientific enterprise. And when you do that, the people whose work you are citing are more likely to read your study. Personally, I get an e-mail every time Google Scholar (www.scholar.google.com) logs a new piece of research that cites my own work. Those e-mails nudge me to read the new research, which helps me keep track of the most current findings in my area. It's the scientific equivalent of a re-tweet!

Meta-analysis: A Quantitative Review of the Literature

Reviewing the literature before doing a study is essential. Some people take this idea further and do systematic and detailed *quantitative* reviews of the literature—this is called **meta-analysis**. The basic idea behind meta-analysis is very simple: Take a bunch of published studies on a given topic and calculate the *average effect size* in those studies. Imagine, for instance, that you were interested in the association between children's television viewing and their consumption of junk food. There are probably already a number of studies on that issue that you could read. If you are lucky, each of those studies will report a correlation (r) between the two variables. If you extracted those correlations from the studies, you could generate a table a bit like Table 17.1.

TABLE 17.1 Example Data for a Meta-analysis

Study	Author	Date of Publication	Age of Children	Number of Subjects (*N*)	Correlation Between TV Viewing and Junk Food Consumption (*r*)
1	Gonzales	2015	6–8	50	*.26*
2	Wilson	2017	6–8	50	*.01*
3	Brinks	1998	6–8	100	**.13**
4	Bolsan	1994	6–8	100	**.12**
5	Traore	2002	6–8	100	**.15**
6	Jenkins	1973	10–12	50	*.34*
7	Bradbury	2019	10–12	50	*.09*
8	O'Neal	2003	10–12	50	*.56*
9	Rooney	1983	10–12	100	**.22**
10	Bowles	1994	10–12	100	**.19**
				AVERAGE:	.21

Each row in the table represents a single study, and the far-right column tells you the correlation (in that study) between how much TV kids watched and how much junk food they ate. If you average those correlations, you get a score of **.21**. This is the average association between television viewing and junk food consumption across all of the studies. Why do this? Each of the studies has some error associated with it (e.g., sampling error, measurement error, an experimenter doing something goofy). By averaging across the studies, you will average out some of that error. You are also taking advantage of all of the samples, so this correlation reflects observations of 750 children—a much larger sample than in any of the individual studies. Guess what? You just did a meta-analysis!

Meta-analysis can provide information beyond just the average association. Take a look at the correlations from the samples with 50 children (italics) versus those with 100 children (bold). What do you see? Hint: Think about *variation* among the correlations.

Hopefully, you noticed that the correlations from the studies with larger samples are fairly consistent in size. They range from .12 to .22. On the other hand, the correlations from the studies with only 50 subjects are *all over the place!* They range from .01 to .56. That's not unexpected: We know that sampling error is higher with smaller samples, and so seeing more variation in results is expected. A true meta-analysis would take this variation into account and would use statistical techniques to "pay more attention to" (weight more heavily) results from the larger samples.

Now take a look at the correlations for 6- to 8-year-old children (the top half) versus the correlations for 10- to 12-year-olds (the bottom half). What do you see?

The correlations are bigger for the older children, right? If you just look at the larger samples (the ones we know to pay more attention to), correlations for the younger children range from .12 to .15, whereas for the older kids, they range from .19 to .22. A meta-analysis of the data could explore this and would be able to tell you if there is a statistically significant difference between the correlations for younger versus older children. If there is, you could start considering *why* this might be. For example, younger kids might have more parental supervision while watching television, and hence they can't sit there eating a whole box of Cap'n Crunch. Older kids might have more freedom to raid the pantry, and their parents might be less likely to monitor. You can see that a meta-analysis can suggest new lines for research by revealing these kinds of patterns in studies that have already been done.

Careers in Communication Research

As you go further in your life beyond a single course in research methods, you might be wondering whether you will ever run into these research methods again. You will. We live in an information-based world, and the information is generated by researchers. Jobs in research (including social science and communication research) are growing, and even nonresearch jobs often involve some research component—either being able to read and understand research or actually doing it. Here are a few examples.

- An advertising agency needs to assess the relative effectiveness of two proposed campaigns. They employ researchers to perform an experiment, randomly assign participants to messages from one campaign or the other (manipulated independent variable), and measure responses (how much they liked the message, how well they remembered it afterward, etc.: dependent variables). Using the data, they identify that one of the campaigns is much more effective than the other. Most large advertising firms have their own in-house research departments. Others might hire independent research consultants.

- A political campaign is interested in perceptions of their candidate among voters. Their research staff call a random sample of registered voters in the candidate's district and ask how much they agree that the candidate represents a number of desirable and undesirable characteristics ("tough on crime," "likable," "a flip-flopper," etc.). They use the survey to develop messages that capitalize on the positive perceptions and try to counter the negative perceptions. Most large campaigns have their own research staff; others hire political consultants with research expertise.
- A PR firm is tasked with increasing visibility for a local STD-testing nonprofit. The communication researcher on their team does a survey to identify places where the target population for the organization (teens and young adults) congregate and the activities that engage them. The PR firm designs an "escape room" style intervention to appeal to that group. The intervention travels to music festivals, college campuses, malls, and bars. Client visits to the STD clinics double.
- A soda company is trying to come up with a good name for a new product. They bring the product to a focus group of the targeted demographic. The participants in the group generate ideas for names based on tasting the product. The company also presents the group with some of its own ideas for names to see how they respond. The focus group helps the company avoid one name (the group called that name "patronizing"), and the participants generate additional options for the product name that are better than what they originally had.
- A hospital is interested in why people who have visited the emergency room often come down with new infections a few days later. They hire a qualitative researcher to observe people's behaviors in the waiting room carefully. The researcher identifies surfaces that multiple people are touching and notes that the furniture arrangement is causing people to move closer to other patients than necessary. By rearranging the furniture and cleaning key surfaces more frequently, infection rates are reduced.
- An attorney's office wants to understand community attitudes about marijuana use as part of defending a client accused of growing and distributing

marijuana illegally. They hire researchers to run focus groups with people from the local community. The focus group moderator asks questions about actual use and attitudes about using and distributing marijuana. They find that most people have liberal attitudes about marijuana use but are quite opposed to "unofficial" growing and distributing. Knowing a jury is likely to be unsympathetic to their client, the attorneys take a plea bargain rather than going to trial. Legal consulting firms typically have researchers on staff who do this sort of work.

- A clothing retailer is losing customers to other local stores. The store owner hires a communication researcher to examine the marketing campaigns of other clothing retailers in the community. The researcher's content analysis shows that the most successful stores are marketing brands endorsed by online fashion "influencers." The store owner increases the stock of those brands and develops new marketing messages emphasizing this.
- A campus fitness center is trying to increase activity levels among students to increase student satisfaction and retention (not dropping out). Researchers in the campus student affairs team do semi-structured interviews with students to find out why they don't work out on campus. A common theme in the interviews is students saying things like, "I'd probably go more if my friends went," and "I feel weird going on my own." The fitness center develops a marketing campaign with the tagline "Drag your friend to the gym!" and uses social media tools to encourage people to bring a friend along when they work out. Attendance increases.

These examples, and the others from all the chapters in the book, illustrate a fundamental point. We can make decisions in life based on many things: our "gut" instincts, our political or religious views, or what our best friends tell us. Sometimes using those methods will be fine. But in many situations, the best decisions are made with the help of data. Genuine, systematic, and carefully gathered information about the world will result in better decisions than guessing. I hope this book has illustrated the value of research and empowered you to believe that you can do good research to answer questions that interest you.

Your Turn

Imagine your dream job. It can be as far-fetched as you like. Now, can you imagine one way in which you might need to either do or at least understand social science research as part of that job? Write a few sentences describing a specific question in that job that might be answered using one of the techniques you've learned in this book.

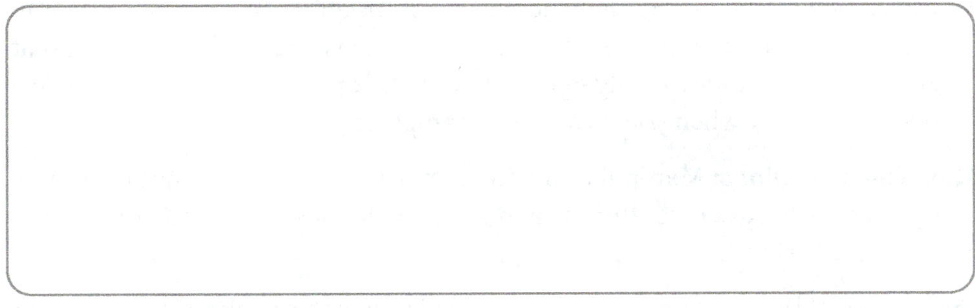

When you are actually in your dream job (I *know* you're going to get it!), don't forget the ways in which research might help you do that job better. Go forth and gather data.

Key Chapter Concepts

Internal validity: Confidence that the independent variable caused the observed changes in the dependent variable, or, more generally, confidence that claims made within a particular study are accurate. Often involves trade-offs with **external validity**.

External validity: Confidence that findings of a particular study extend to other people, places, or phenomena. Often enhanced by using representative samples, doing research in the "real world," and using realistic materials and unobtrusive measures. Often involves trade-offs with **internal validity.**

Literature review: The action of reading previous research prior to doing a study. "Literature review" is also a name for the section of a research report in which that previous research is discussed. Good literature reviews build an argument for the research being done rather than simply summarizing the previous work.

Meta-analysis: A technique to quantitatively summarize previous research by, for instance, calculating the average effect size of previous work. Can also be used to uncover patterns in that previous research (e.g., by showing that an effect is stronger in a certain type of research study than a different type).

Replication: Doing a study more than once (sometimes with variations) to confirm that the findings from a single study were not due to chance.

Science is cumulative: The idea that individual research studies build on previous studies and that our knowledge as a whole accumulates by people developing ideas across multiple studies.

Statistical power: Assuming that there really is an effect (e.g., a correlation in the population that is not zero), statistical power is your ability to detect that effect (e.g., find a statistically significant correlation in your sample). Statistical power is greater when you have a large sample size.

Strong manipulations: Manipulations in an experimental study that maximize differences between conditions and have the highest likelihood of yielding statistically significant results.

Theory: General statements of knowledge, broader than the results of a single study.

Triangulation: Developing knowledge of a concept by examining it from different perspectives. Triangulation often refers to studying the same concept using different methods (experiment and survey, quantitative and qualitative, etc.).

Section Wrap

Section Summary

This final chapter has provided some hints on doing quality research. Taking a step back from the rest of the book, it provides guidelines for incorporating theory in research, the importance of reviewing past research, and an overview of how to select an appropriate method for a particular research study.

If you get nothing else from this chapter, remember the following:

- It takes multiple studies to answer most questions. Triangulation (examining the same question from different methodological perspectives) and replication (repeating studies, sometimes with variations) are both essential to scientific advances.
- Good research begins with good questions: questions that have theoretical importance, relevance to the real world, and that are likely to yield interesting results.
- Good research involves carefully reading previous research before beginning; ideas generated without reading previous research are almost always ideas that someone else has already studied. Meta-analysis is a quantitative technique for summarizing previous studies, allowing you to know the average effect size of prior work on a topic.

Glossary

Alpha level: The probability level at which you are confident in rejecting the null hypothesis. In the social sciences, the norm is to set alpha at .05. This means that to reject a null hypothesis, you need to find $p < .05$, indicating less than a 5% chance of the null hypothesis being true based on your data. But alpha can be set at other levels. This is discussed more later in the book. See also ***p***.

Analysis of variance (ANOVA): A family of statistical tools used for comparing means (averages) between groups of people.

Archival research: Yes, "archives" sounds like some dusty library in the basement of a museum, but an archive is just any existing set of resources (information, data) that you might use to answer a question.

Axial coding: In qualitative coding, this is a stage of coding following open coding. Axial codes are higher level codes that resemble theoretically important concepts and ideas; often axial codes will subsume multiple open codes. See also **Open coding**.

Beta coefficients: These are *standardized* regression coefficients in regression analysis. Beta tells you the strength of the association between any individual predictor variable and the outcome variable. In a simple regression, beta is the same as the correlation coefficient (r). One beta coefficient can be compared against another one—bigger beta means bigger effect. Google Sheets does not report betas (see also **Unstandardized regression coefficients**).

Between groups differences: Differences between the average score (mean) in different groups. Often considered relative to **within groups differences**. Many statistical calculations, including the t-test, involve a ratio of between and within group differences. When between group differences are large and within group differences are small, statistics like t are large and the null hypothesis is typically rejected.

Between subjects variables: Independent variables for which participants in the study only participate in one condition or "cell" of the design. See also **Within subjects variables**.

Bias (in sampling): Systematic (regular, predictable) ways in which a sample doesn't represent a population. A sample of Olympic athletes taken from right outside the swimming pool will include a lot more swimmers than the entire population of Olympic athletes. See also **Error (in sampling)**.

Building rapport: When performing interviews or other forms of qualitative research (e.g., observing people's natural behavior), it is essential to develop a friendly and trusting relationship with the research participants. Building this rapport is helped by investing in the participants (e.g., having some service to offer them), being a long-term participant in their environment, and behaving in a friendly and professional manner. Incidentally, rapport is also useful in quantitative research: being nice rarely hurts.

Categorical measurement: Measurement where scores represent membership in categories, with no order assigned to the categories. Examples include religious denomination membership or preferred flavor of ice cream.

Causality: The idea that changes in one variable are the reason for changes in another variable. Regression and correlation measure associations between variables, but an association doesn't mean that one variable *causes* another. Methods like experiments are how causality is demonstrated. **Multiple regression** can help in the search for causal relationships by incorporating **control variables.**

Cell: A cell in a factorial design is a unique combination of levels of the independent variables. For example, in a study of the effects of medium (television or radio) and volume (loud versus quiet) on understanding of news, "loud television" would be one cell in the design.

Central tendency: The "central tendency" of a distribution is another way of saying the "middle" of that distribution. The book discusses three measures of central tendency—the mean, median, and mode.

Chi-square (χ^2) analysis: The most basic method for analyzing associations between categorical variables. The chi-square statistic gets bigger as differences between **observed values** and **expected values** get larger.

Closed-ended questions: Questions with a limited and predetermined set of response options from which respondents much pick. Responses involving picking a single number (e.g., on a 1–10 scale) or category (e.g., the religious group you identify with the most) are closed-ended questions. See also **Open-ended questions.**

Coders: The people who do the coding in a content analysis or other research that involves coding. In quantitative content analysis, we want these people to be **independent**, and typically we want more than one coder, so we can calculate **intercoder reliability.**

Coding definitions: In order to code variables, it is important to have clear conceptual and operational definitions of those variables.

Conceptual definition: A verbal "dictionary" definition of a variable. The verbal description of what the variable represents. See also **Operational definition.**

Confidence interval: A statement of the range within which the researcher is confident that the population value of a statistic lies. See also **Confidence level.**

Confidence level: The degree of confidence that a researcher has in the confidence interval (typically 95%). See also **Confidence interval.**

Confirmability: The qualitative equivalent of intercoder reliability: An analysis in which multiple researchers agree on coding and analysis is a confirmable analysis.

Confounded variable: If an experimental manipulation involves two independent variables in a way that makes it impossible to distinguish the effects of each, the two variables are said to be confounded. If one group sees a super-scary antismoking *video*, while another group sees a *not-very-scary* antismoking *print* ad, the scariness of the message (scary versus not) and the medium it's presented in (video versus print) are confounded, and so it would be impossible to know whether any effects were because of the scariness or the medium. Scariness and medium are confounded.

Constant comparative method: A method of qualitative analysis involving continuous comparison between data and results. For example, developing codes and then applying them to new data to see if they are sufficient would be one technique demonstrating constant comparison.

Content analysis: The systematic analysis of messages to reveal patterns in their content.

Content validity: The extent to which a measurement scale assesses the full breadth of a concept. If you were measuring *communication competence*, a scale that only assessed your public speaking skills would have weak content validity. A scale that assessed your communication abilities in public settings (e.g., giving a speech, asking a question in a group setting) and private settings (e.g., having a conversation with a stranger) would have stronger content validity.

Control group: A control group is a group of people in an experiment who either receive no **treatment** at all or who receive a "default" treatment; the control group provides the relevant comparison for an experimental treatment. If you were studying the effects of a public health campaign message, the control group would be people who you don't show the message to. If you were looking at the effects of a new fourth-grade math curriculum, you couldn't have a group of kids who got zero math instruction for a year, however. So, in this case, your control group would be a group of children who get the "regular" or default math curriculum.

Control variables: A control variable is included in a statistical analysis to control for potential alternative explanations and hence increase the strength of an argument that **predictor (or independent) variables** cause changes in the **outcome (or dependent) variable**. Control variables are common in regression analysis but can be used in most forms of statistical hypothesis testing.

Convenience sample: A type of **nonrepresentative sample**. A convenience sample is any group of people (or other objects) that is easily accessible to the researcher. For college professors, college students are often the convenience sample of choice.

Correlation: A statistical measure of association between two variables. Correlations range from −1 to +1; their absolute size indicates their strength. A positive correlation indicates that as one variable increases, so does the other. A negative correlation indicates that as one variable increases, the other decreases.

Criterion variable: In regression analysis, researchers sometimes use this term to mean the same thing as **dependent variable** or **outcome variable**. This book uses the term "outcome variable." It's the variable you are trying to predict.

Criterion-related validity: The extent to which a measure is associated with other measures that it "should" be related to (the criterion measures). A measure of communication competence should be related to your success in persuading other people, or ratings of your public speaking performance, or your ability to maintain successful interpersonal relationships. If it is unrelated to any of those things, it's probably not a valid measure of communication competence.

Cross-sectional research design: In cross-sectional research designs, variables are measured in a group of people at the same point in time. Cross-sectional studies are useful for understanding whether certain variables are correlated; they are not good for uncovering *causal* relationships. See also **Longitudinal design**.

***d*:** A measure of effect size for *t*-tests, also called Cohen's *d*.

Data: Recorded information about the world that can be analyzed to answer scientific questions. Data are often numbers, but they can be many other things—videos, texts, audio recordings, etc. The word "recorded" is important here. All the texts you sent in 2014 would count as data, but only if you have some way of recovering them!

Debriefing: An explanation about a study given to research participants after the study has been completed. A debriefing often includes the explanation of any deception that occurred in the study. If a study might have caused any distress for research subjects, a debriefing will also include information about where to seek assistance for that distress (e.g., information about the campus counseling center).

Degrees of freedom: Most statistical tests have degrees of freedom associated with them. Typically, degrees of freedom reflect the number of data points (e.g., research subjects) in a test, as well as the number of groups or subsets of people being compared. For instance, in the one-way ANOVA, the two degrees of freedom numbers indicate (a) the number of groups being compared minus 1 and (b) the number of subjects in the analysis minus the number of groups. A study with four groups and 100 subjects total would have 3 (= 4 – 1) and 96 (= 100 – 4) degrees of freedom.

Dependent samples: Separate samples of data where observations in one sample are *connected to* observations in another sample. This can be because of relationships between people in the samples (e.g., brothers and sisters) or because the two sets of data are from the *same* people (e.g., with repeated measurement over time). Data from dependent samples are analyzed using different statistical tests (e.g., the **paired** or **dependent samples t-test**).

Dependent samples t-test: A *t*-test for comparing **dependent samples**—for instance, the same people measured twice or both people in a romantic couple. The same thing as a **paired t-test.**

Dependent variable: The outcome variable in a **hypothesis** or analysis. The dependent variable is also called a criterion variable in regression analysis. See **Independent and dependent variables.**

Deviant case analysis: Exploration for, and careful analysis of, cases in the data that do not "fit" a specific analysis. Usually a part of qualitative analysis.

Dichotomous variables: Categorical variables with only two categories (e.g., living vs. dead, U.S. citizen vs. non-U.S. citizen, full-time student vs. part-time student). Regression analysis can incorporate predictor variables that are dichotomous, but you should not include other categorical variables as predictors (e.g., ones with three or more categories).

Distribution: An arrangement of a set of numerical scores arranged in order, more generally a name for quantitative data that are to be examined and analyzed.

Double-barreled items: Items in a questionnaire that ask two things at once. "How much do you like your home and family?" is double-barreled: You might love your family but dislike your home (or vice versa). Double-barreled items should be avoided.

Effect size: A measure of how large a statistical effect is, independent of sample size. Some statistics (e.g., *t*) can appear large just due to a large sample size; in such cases, a separate measure of effect size is required. For the *t*-test, ***d*** is a commonly used measure of effect size. Larger effect sizes indicate that one variable is more closely tied to another one and that you can more accurately predict scores on one variable from scores on the other variable.

Empirical questions: Questions that can be answered using observations of the world, including questions that can be answered using scientific research. A question like "What color is Julie's shirt?" is an empirical question but doesn't really require scientific research!

Error (sampling error): Haphazard ways in which a sample doesn't perfectly represent a population. A random sample of Olympic athletes might include a few more swimmers than the entire population of Olympic athletes, just due to chance. That is called sampling error. See also **Sampling bias.**

Eta-squared (η^2): A measure of effect size for ANOVA, typically calculated by dividing the Sum of Squares (SS) for the particular effect under consideration by the SS_{total}. In the one-way ANOVA, this means dividing $SS_{between\ groups}$ by SS_{total}. Eta-squared ranges from 0 to 1, and larger eta-squareds indicate a bigger effect. The number represents how much variance in the dependent variable is being explained by the independent variable (e.g., an eta-squared of .25 indicates that 25% of the variance has been explained).

Ethics in visual representations: Scientists have an obligation to represent the truth, and not use clever graphical manipulations to exaggerate or overemphasize effects. One simple way to do this is to include the full range of the dependent variable on the y-axis or at least to alert your reader when you are not doing so.

Exemplars: Extracts from a qualitative data set designed to provide rich and helpful examples of a particular theme or idea.

Existing instrument: A measurement tool that has been used in published research. Typically, using an existing instrument (assuming it has good **reliability** and **validity**) is better than making up your own instrument—don't reinvent the wheel.

Expected values: A term most commonly used in **chi-square** analysis. The frequencies you would see in any particular "cell" in a research design *if the null hypothesis was true*. Imagine studying a potential association between subscribing to Netflix and subscribing to cable. If there is no association between those two variables, then you would *expect* to see that the proportion of Netflix subscribers among cable subscribers is roughly the same as the proportion of Netflix subscribers among those who don't have cable TV. See also **Observed values, chi-square statistic**.

Experimental control: In an experiment, you need to hold everything constant *except* for your manipulation.

External validity: Confidence that findings of a particular study extend to other people, places, or phenomena. Often enhanced by using representative samples, doing research in the "real world," and using realistic materials and unobtrusive measures. Often involves trade-offs with **internal validity**.

Face validity: The impression that a scale measures what it is supposed to measure, based on a close examination of the items.

Factorial design: A situation in which you have multiple categorical independent variables and are able to examine **main effects** and **interaction effects**.

Focus groups: Small groups of people gathered together to discuss a particular topic. The researcher (facilitator) guides the discussion but allows and encourages the participants to interact with one another and build off each other's ideas.

F-statistic: The statistic used by **analysis of variance** to test hypotheses. The F-statistic gets bigger when **variation between groups** is large and **variation within groups** is small.

F-table: The portion of the statistical output from a factorial ANOVA that reports the F-statistics, p-values, and related information.

Histogram: A chart that illustrates the frequency of specific values (or sets of values) in a distribution. High bars in a histogram indicate that there are a lot of scores of that value.

Hypothesis: A hypothesis is a statement of the expected association between variables. An example might be, "People with stronger social skills will be less lonely than those with weaker social skills." Hypotheses are often numbered in a study (H1, H2, etc.).

Independent and dependent variables: These variables are defined by their (either real or hypothesized) causal relationships. An independent variable is expected or shown to cause changes in a dependent variable. In the relationship between exercise and physical health, exercise is typically the independent variable in that it causes changes in physical health (the dependent variable).

Independent coders: Independent **coders** are coders who (a) are largely unaware of the specific goals or hypotheses of the research project (and hence, obviously, are not the actual researchers) and (b) do not consult with one another or attempt to influence one another while doing the coding. Independent coders are used extensively in **content analysis**.

Independent samples: Samples of data where the observations in one sample are completely unrelated to the observations in the other sample. See also **Dependent samples**.

Independent samples t-test: A *t*-test for comparing **independent samples**, contrast with the **dependent samples t-test**.

Independent variable: A variable that is seen as predicting, causing, or influencing a dependent variable. In regression, the term **predictor variable** is often used instead of the term **independent variable,** but they essentially mean the same thing. See also **Dependent variable**.

Interaction effects: In a **factorial design**, when the effect of one independent variable varies depending on the level of the other independent variable. Potential interaction effects are identifiable in graphs of means by the presence of *non*parallel lines. Descriptions of interaction effects often involve statements of how the effect of one independent variable *depends on* the levels of the other independent variable.

Intercoder reliability: The level of agreement between at least two **independent coders** on a particular coded variable. Intercoder reliability is best assessed using a statistical measure such as Krippendorff's alpha; typically, values of alpha above .70 are viewed as acceptable. Low reliability between coders should be investigated during coder training, and further training or adjustment of the coding system should be attempted to improve reliability. If a variable cannot be coded reliably after repeated attempts, it should probably be dropped from the content analysis.

Internal validity: A global assessment of the quality of a research study in terms of its ability to conclude that the independent variable caused changes in the dependent variable. Experiments with good internal validity include random assignment, a clear and nonconfounded manipulation of the independent variable, and control of all other factors in the environment and procedure. Often involves trade-offs with **external validity**.

Interpreting and graphing cell means: In **factorial ANOVA**, interaction effects can take many forms—properly interpreting them requires thinking about the pattern of means. Often graphing the means in the form illustrated in the chapter can help with interpretation.

Interval measurement: Measurement where the scores represent values on a continuous scale, with even intervals between numbers. Examples would include scores on an intelligence test or the frequency with which someone discloses personal information (measured in number of times in a week). See also **Ordinal measurement**, **categorical measurement**.

Interview protocol: The specific sequence of questions that a researcher will ask in an interview. Good interview protocols are sequenced to provide a logical flow to the interview, often moving from more general topics to more specific ones or from less sensitive topics to more sensitive ones, for instance.

Interviews: Typically, one-on-one encounters in which the researcher asks questions using an **interview protocol** and the research participant provides answers. Depending on the goals of an interview, it may be highly structured, or **semi-structured**.

IRB: Stands for "Institutional Review Board." An oversight committee charged with checking that research in a university or other research institution follows appropriate ethical procedures. Researchers planning a research project need to have it approved by an IRB before proceeding with the work.

Latent content: A term used in content analysis to describe content in a message that is below the surface—not immediately obvious. Coding a movie as expressing optimistic or pessimistic themes would involve coding latent content. It requires deep understanding of the narrative of the movie and probably a weighing of different elements in the story to reach an overall conclusion about the movie's pessimism or optimism. Contrast with **manifest content**.

Leading questions: Items on a questionnaire that "push" the respondent toward responding in a particular way (e.g., "Don't you think that there should be stricter controls on buying lethal weapons?"). These should be avoided.

Likert scales: A format for a questionnaire. Respondents are given a statement (or series of statements) on some topic and asked how much they agree with each statement, often on a 1–5 or 1–7 scale ranging from "strongly disagree" to "strongly agree."

Line of best fit: A line on a **scatterplot** indicating the trend in the points. Typically, a best fit line minimizes the vertical distances between points in the scatterplot and the line. See also **Scatterplot**.

Literature review: The action of reading previous research prior to doing a study. "Literature review" is also a name for the section of a research report in which that previous research is discussed. Good literature reviews build an argument for the research being done rather than simply summarizing the previous work.

Longitudinal design: A research design in which variables are measured at multiple points in time. Useful for examining causality when experiments are not possible.

Low-inference descriptors: A term often used with qualitative research. Descriptions of the research process that don't require the reader to make guesses about what was done or what was found. Precise transcripts and recording of research (e.g., video recording) provide low-inference descriptors. Low-inference descriptors are associated with **reliability**.

Main effects: In a **factorial design**, when there is a difference in the levels of one independent variable, averaging across the levels of the other independent variable. You should be cautious in interpreting main effects when you also have **interaction effects**: Interaction effects indicate that the pattern of a main effect changes under certain circumstances or for certain people.

Manifest content: The content of a message that is on the surface—easy and obvious to see. Coding whether a movie is animated or live action is coding manifest content (although there are movies that involve elements of both, which would require careful operational definitions).

Manipulation: When a researcher controls the values of a variable, rather than letting them vary naturally. If I expose one group of people to a video of a couple having a positive conversation, and another group of people to a video of the same couple having a fight, I have manipulated the positivity/negativity of the video that people saw. Manipulation of the **independent variable** is a defining feature of an experiment. The researcher must be able to change some aspect of the independent variable to create different "conditions" or "levels" of that variable.

Manipulation check: A test to make sure your manipulation operated in the intended way. If I expose people to a video that (I think) is positive or one I think is negative, and then ask them how positive or negative they thought the videos were, I am using a manipulation check. If they rate both videos as equally positive, then I know my manipulation didn't work.

Mean: The arithmetic average of a set of scores. Add all the scores and divide by how many scores there are.

Measurement reliability: The consistency or stability of a measurement tool. Reliability is often measured by assessing whether scores on a measure are stable over time (**test-retest reliability**). Together with **measurement validity**, measurement reliability is an indicator of the quality of a measurement tool.

Measurement validity: The degree to which a measurement tool *accurately* measures the underlying concept. A questionnaire to measure public speaking confidence is valid if it genuinely assesses how much (or little) confidence someone has when they are going to give a speech. Together with **measurement reliability**, measurement validity is an indicator of the quality of a measurement tool. **Face validity**, **content validity**, and **criterion-related validity** are all types of measurement validity.

Median: The middle score in a **distribution**, the 50th percentile. The point in a distribution where half the scores are above that number and half are below.

Member validation: Often used in qualitative analysis. Asking respondents to review the major themes or conclusions of an analysis and offer additional insights; if study participants do not agree with your analysis, that is one indication the analysis might lack **validity**.

Meta-analysis: A technique to quantitatively summarize previous research by, for instance, calculating the average effect size of previous work. Can also be used to uncover patterns in that previous research (e.g., by showing that an effect is stronger in a certain type of research study than a different type).

Mode: The most frequent or common value in a data set. More people have this score than any other score. White is the most common color for cars, so white is the mode for car colors.

Multi-item scale: A questionnaire that measures a concept with more than one question or item; typically, the responses to all of the items are averaged (after **reverse-scoring**) to result in a single score.

Multiple regression: Regression analysis with more than one **predictor variable**.

Multi-stage cluster sampling: A form of **representative sampling** in which larger units are randomly sampled, and then smaller units from within the larger units are sampled to provide the final sample. To obtain a multi-stage cluster sample of zoo animals, you might first randomly sample zoos, and then randomly sample animals from within the sampled zoos.

Negative wording: Questions containing a "not" or similar. Can be useful in generating items for **reverse-scoring** but should be used carefully to avoid respondent confusion over double-negatives.

Nonrepresentative sample: A sample that does not represent a larger population (for example, a **convenience sample**). If you are trying to predict the results of a presidential election, a group of students is a nonrepresentative sample. Students vote differently from the population as a whole, and so their voting plans won't help you in predicting the election outcome. Students differ in *systematic ways* from the rest of the population. Research done with nonrepresentative samples has less **external validity** than work done with **representative samples**, but many scientific questions can still be answered with nonrepresentative samples. See also **Representative sample**.

Normal distribution: See **Shapes of distributions**.

Null hypothesis: A statement that two variables are ***not*** related to one another; that there is no statistical effect. Typically, researchers try to *disprove* the null hypothesis in order to show that there *is* an association.

Observation: Any situation where the researcher examines people engaged in natural behavior, typically taking notes and attempting to understand what is "going on" through detailed and extended observation. Observation is a common part of qualitative research but can also be used in quantitative work. If you want to find out whether certain types of people drink Pepsi versus Coke, you could hang out near a vending machine and see who buys what.

Observed values: The frequencies in any particular "cell" in a research design—particularly one involving **categorical variables**. Imagine studying a potential association between subscribing to Netflix (yes/no) and subscribing to cable TV (yes/no). If your data included 52 people who subscribe to Netflix but don't subscribe to cable, then 52 is the observed value in that cell. See also **Expected values, chi-square statistic**.

Observer effects: Effects that occur simply because researchers are observing a situation. Also sometimes called Hawthorne effects.

One-way ANOVA: A type of **analysis of variance** that examines the effects of a single categorical independent variable on an interval-level dependent variable.

Open coding: The initial stages of qualitative coding, typically driven by coding anything that appears relevant, and creating new codes whenever something new appears. Coding might be driven by themes in the data that are repeated, or that appear emotionally important.

Open-ended questions: Questions without fixed response choices. If you can speak or write freely in response to a question, it is an open-ended question. If you have to pick from a predetermined set of choices, it is a **closed-ended question**. Most measurement tools use closed-ended questions, but open-ended questions are useful if you are seeking feedback on a questionnaire, for instance. Qualitative research relies on open-ended responses most of the time.

Operational definition: The precise method you will use to measure a variable—how do you get numbers that represent a given person's "score." The operational definition must be consistent with the **conceptual definition**. In questionnaire research, an operational definition might be a set of questions in a **multi-item scale**. In content analysis, the operational definition of the variable is the set of instructions for how to **code** the message. This would involve clear definitions, procedures for coding (including how to record codes), and instructions for dealing with ambiguous or unclear cases.

Ordinal measurement: Measurement in which scores represent membership in categories that are arranged in order; distances between categories may not be equal. An example might be an airline frequent flyer program which categorizes members as "regular" "gold" or "platinum" based on how many miles they have flown (the actual number of miles flown would be an **interval**-level measure). See also **Categorical measurement**, **interval measurement**.

Outcome variable: In regression analysis, researchers use this term to mean the same thing as **dependent variable**. Sometimes the term "criterion variable" is also used to mean the same thing.

p: Shorthand used in reports of statistical hypothesis testing. "*p*" can be read as short for "the probability that the null hypothesis is true." When p is small (less than .05), researchers can reject the null hypothesis, and conclude that whatever association they are observing between variables is "real." This is the same thing as statistical significance and is typically reported as $p < .05$. If an effect is *not* statistically significant, it is reported as $p > .05$.

p < .05: The most common way **statistical significance** is referenced. If you see this phrase, it means that your data would be very unlikely (occur less than 5% of the time) if the null hypothesis was actually true in the population. Saying "$p < .05$" is the same as saying "statistically significant."

Paired t-test: See **Dependent samples t-test.**

Path models: Visual models representing the predictor and criterion variables in a multiple regression, typically including the regression coefficients for the paths between the variables and some indication of which paths are statistically significant.

Population: The entire group of people that a researcher wants to understand. If you were studying attitudes toward gay marriage in America, then all Americans would be your population of interest. If you are studying the impact of a breast cancer detection program among low-income women in Minneapolis, then the population would be all low-income women in Minneapolis. See also **Populations of messages.**

Populations of messages: Just like people, messages exist in populations. All issues of Sports Illustrated, or every Disney animated movie, or the entire congressional record all count as populations of messages. Often, **content analysis** can't examine an entire population of messages, so it is necessary to **sample** from that population to achieve a manageable set of messages to code.

Predictor variable: In regression, this term is typically used to mean the same thing as **independent variable**—a variable that is predicting the **outcome variable**.

Purposive sample: A sampling strategy aiming to get a specific sort of person. If you need to study birders over the age of 65, you might go to the local "Retired ornithologist" society meeting to obtain this sample. Typically purposive samples are

nonrepresentative. Obtaining a **random sample** from the entire population of retired ornithologists is logistically close to impossible!

Quasi-experiment: A study that appears to be an **experiment** but is lacking **random assignment** to conditions.

R^2: A common measure of variance explained by a **regression** analysis. The statistic ranges from 0 to 1, and a score of zero indicates 0% of the variance is explained (no effect), while a score of 1 indicates that 100% of the variance is explained (perfect prediction). Perfect prediction is very rare in social science research; a lot of social science research explains 2%–5% of the variance in a given outcome. Humans are complicated.

Random: In science, random means doing something in a *completely* unsystematic and unbiased manner. Being random does not mean being haphazard, but rather it means being *completely* unpredictable. With **random sampling**, there is no way to predict who will be selected for a sample. With **random assignment**, there is no way to predict whether someone will be assigned to group A or group B. Flipping a fair coin is truly, scientifically random. Asking a friend to choose "heads or tails" is not truly scientifically random (people pick "heads" more than they pick "tails").

Random assignment: The process of putting research subjects into two or more experimental conditions without any bias. The process of assigning respondents to conditions purely by chance (e.g., a coin flip) reduces the possibility that the groups will be different from one another. Works well with relatively large samples (i.e., more than 40 per condition).

Random sample: Same thing as a **representative sample**.

Range: The difference between the lowest and highest score in a **distribution**, a measure of **variability**.

Regression analysis: A set of statistical techniques for predicting scores on an **outcome variable** from one or more **predictor variables**. In the regression analysis covered in this book, the predictor variables must be either interval-level variables or dichotomous variables, and the outcome variable must be interval-level.

Reliability (in qualitative analysis): Qualitative analyses are reliable to the extent that they are grounded in accurate representations of the data (e.g., accurate recordings, detailed transcription) and provide the reader with extracts and examples from the raw data that illustrate specific themes or codes. See also **Low-inference descriptors**.

Reliability (in quantitative analysis): See **Measurement reliability**.

Replication: Doing a study more than once (sometimes with variations) to confirm that the findings from a single study were not due to chance.

Representative sample: A smaller group of people (the sample) that is treated as representing an entire population. A representative sample is not biased—it does not deviate in *systematic* ways from the characteristics of the population. The average of a random sample will probably be different from the population average, but it will not be predictably different: it might be higher, or lower. If a sampling method is *biased*, then samples you take using that method will differ from the population in predictable ways (e.g., every sample you take in the student library will yield a set of students who are more studious than your average student). Biased samples are not representative. See also **Nonrepresentative sample**, **random**.

Research question: A question that can be answered by gathering data.

Response rate: The percentage of people (or other units, e.g., schools) that actually generate usable data for a study, relative to the total number that was sampled. If you ask 70 professors to answer your questionnaire and only 35 provide responses, your response rate is 50%.

Reverse-scoring: In a **multi-item scale**, some items may be worded in an opposite manner from other items. For instance, in a scale to measure public speaking anxiety you might include an item like "I feel very comfortable talking to a large group of people." These are reverse-scored items, and before calculating the final score for the multi-item scale, scores on those items must be re-ordered so that high scores on all items mean the same thing. Low scores on the example item would indicate public speaking anxiety (i.e., that you do *not* feel comfortable talking to a large group).

Sampling error: The natural difference between a sample and the population. A **representative sample** will probably not have exactly the same mean as the population from which it was drawn. This difference is sampling error. The more a sample differs from the population, the greater the sampling error. Larger samples have less sampling error (they are more accurate) than smaller samples. **Multi-stage cluster samples** have more sampling error than **simple random samples**.

Sampling (in qualitative research): Sampling in qualitative research is designed to achieve **saturation**—the point where gathering new cases does not provide additional information. Qualitative researchers seek breadth and diversity in samples but typically are not concerned with issues of "random" or "representative" sampling.

Sampling (in quantitative research): Taking a smaller group of units to study from a larger population. A sample can be **representative** or **nonrepresentative.** You can sample from populations of people, but also from populations of organizations or messages, depending on what you are studying.

Saturation: In qualitative analysis, the point at which gathering additional data does not yield any additional insight.

Scatterplot: A visual representation of the association between two variables, with one variable represented on the x-axis and the other on the y-axis. A **line of best fit** is often overlaid on a scatterplot.

Science is cumulative: The idea that individual research studies build on previous studies, and that our knowledge as a whole accumulates by people developing ideas across multiple studies.

Self-report measurement: Measurement where the respondent provides data about him or herself. An easy way for you to find out if I prefer Pepsi or Coke is to ask me.

Semantic differential: A type of response scale where the extremes on a dimension are indicated by antonyms: Happy-Sad, Good-Bad, Strong-Weak, and the like.

Semi-structured interview: A semi-structured interview will have some questions that the interviewer will ask all participants, but the interviewer will also be free to ask follow-ups or pursue interesting responses by going "off script."

Shapes of distributions (normal, skewed): A normal distribution is symmetrical—scores below the middle of the distribution are arranged similarly to those above the middle, and there is an equal number of scores below and above the middle. The mean, median, and mode are all in the same place and the distribution has a bell shape. In a skewed distribution, more scores are bunched together at one end of the distribution than the other—the distribution is not symmetrical. Positively skewed distributions have more scores on the left side of the distribution (low scores) and a tail to the right; negatively skewed distributions have more scores toward the right-hand end. See also **Distribution.**

Simple random sampling: A form of representative sampling in which the sample is drawn at **random** from a list of all the people (or other objects) in the population.

Simple regression: A regression analysis with only one **predictor variable**.

Skewed distribution: See **Shapes of distributions**.

Standard deviation: A measure of **variation within groups** of people; the square root of the **variance**.

Standardized regression coefficients (β): See beta.

Statistical power: Assuming that there really is an effect (e.g., a correlation in the population that is not zero), statistical power is your ability to detect that effect (e.g., find a statistically significant correlation in your sample). Statistical power is greater when you have a large sample size. Power is also the opposite of **Type 2 error:** it is the chance of *correctly rejecting* a null hypothesis.

Statistical significance: A statement of confidence that the effect being examined is not zero. The statement "$p < .05$" indicates statistical significance; it literally means that there is less than a 5% chance that the null hypothesis is true.

Strong manipulations: Manipulations in an experimental study that maximize differences between conditions and have the highest likelihood of yielding statistically significant results.

Test-retest reliability: The correlation between scores on a measurement tool at two points in time (T1 and T2). Measurement tools with strong T1–T2 correlations have good test-retest reliability. See also **Measurement reliability**.

Theory: General statements of knowledge, broader than the results of a single study.

Thick description: Descriptions of a data set that provides the reader with a full and vivid sense of the data as a whole; a term from qualitative research.

Training: In content analysis, it is essential to carefully train coders so they can code a sample of messages with acceptable levels of intercoder reliability. Training typically involves presentation of the coding scheme by the researcher, some practice coding of messages not in the actual sample, discussion of disagreements between coders in the practice coding. It may also involve some revision of the coding scheme. Training is also important in interviewing and running **focus groups** so that the moderator/interviewer behaves in ways that generate the most useful data.

Transcribing: To save time and make coding more systematic, **interviews** and **focus groups** are almost always transcribed—the audio converted to written form. Transcribing must be done carefully and checked for accuracy against the original audio. Transcription may be at different levels of detail, depending on the goals of the research: sometimes it's important to note details like the length of pauses or non-verbal behavior, and sometimes it is not.

Treatment: An experimental treatment is what gets "done" to participants in an experiment to manipulate the independent variable. A treatment might be exposure to a video, or giving people a set of instructions ("disclose a lot to your partner"), or intervening in a situation (e.g., changing a thermostat setting in a room).

Triangulation: Developing knowledge of a concept by examining it from different perspectives. Triangulation often refers to studying the same concept using different methods (experiment and survey, quantitative and qualitative, etc.).

Type 1 error: Incorrectly rejecting the null hypothesis. A researcher's data indicate an association between reading romance novels and having a good sex life. In the population as a whole, however, there's *no* association between those two things. This researcher has committed a Type 1 error. See also **Type 2 error**.

Type 2 error: Incorrectly *accepting* the null hypothesis. A researcher's data indicate *no* association between reading romance novels and having a good sex life. In the population as a whole, however, there *is* an association between those two things. This researcher has committed a Type 2 error. See also **Statistical power**, **Type 1 error**.

Unitizing: For some type of messages it isn't absolutely clear where one message ends and another begins. For instance, in a conversation, you might not be certain what counts as a single speaking "turn." If someone tries but fails to interrupt, does that count as a turn? If someone says "mm-hmm" just to indicate that they are listening, is that a turn? Unitizing is the process of taking a stream of messages and identifying what are the discrete units to be coded.

Unobtrusive measurement: Measurement performed when the person is unaware that they are being measured. A researcher who measures exercise use by checking your entrance and exit times on the gym's computer system is using unobtrusive measurement. A researcher who asks you how often you exercise is not. Unobtrusive measurement has high external validity because it doesn't rely on someone's memory or self-presentation (which might be biased).

Unstandardized regression coefficients (*B*): Regression coefficients that are reported in the units of the original variables. These coefficients allow computation of the regression equation (to predict scores on the outcome from scores of the predictor variables). However, these coefficients cannot be compared against one another: A bigger unstandardized regression coefficient does *not* mean a bigger effect. See also **Beta coefficients**.

Validity (in qualitative research): Qualitative research is valid to the extent that researchers engage in constant comparative analysis, engage in **deviant case analysis**, and **member validation**, and to the extent that they can triangulate their findings (reach similar conclusions from different forms of data).

Validity (in quantitative research): See **Measurement validity**, **internal validity**.

Variability: How much heterogeneity there is among scores in a distribution. In distributions with low variability, most people have quite similar scores; in high variability distributions, people have dramatically different scores from one another. See also **Standard deviation**, **variance**.

Variance: A measure of variation within a group of people; can be obtained by squaring the **standard deviation**.

Variance explained: A measure of effect size. The variance explained in the outcome/dependent variable by the predictor/independent variable(s) tells us how accurate our predictions will be. If 100% of the variance is explained, then if we know someone's scores on the predictor variables, we will be able to perfectly predict their scores on the outcome variable. If 0% of the variance is explained, then our predictor variable(s) are literally useless: They don't help us predict at all. In **regression**, variance explained is reported as $\mathbf{R^2}$.

Variation between groups: The extent to which the mean of one group of people differs from the mean of another group of people. **Analysis of variance** tests whether such differences are statistically significant by using the **F-statistic**.

Variation within groups: It is rare that a group of people will all score the same on any measure. Within any group of people, the within group variation is the extent to which they differ from one another. Sometimes most people score fairly similarly to one another (small variation within groups) and sometimes they differ wildly (large variation within groups). Variation within groups is measured with statistics like the **standard deviation** or **variance** (see Chapter 2). This is the same thing as **within groups differences**.

Vulnerable populations: Populations that receive additional protection from university IRBs—children, prisoners, and people with cognitive impairments among others. Any group of people whose decision-making ability is seen to be impaired or restricted is treated as a vulnerable population.

Within groups differences: Differences between individual observations *within* groups of people (e.g., within an experimental condition, or among people of the same sex, religion, etc.). The most commonly used measure of within group differences is the **standard deviation**. Measures of within group differences are typically in the denominator in the calculation of statistical tests like the ***t*-test**. This is the same thing as **variation within groups**.

Within subjects variables: Independent variables for which participants in the study participate in more than one condition or "cell" of the design (e.g., being measured at more than one point in time, or receiving more than one experimental treatment). See also **Between subjects variables**.

z-score: A measure of how much a score deviates from the mean, expressed in **standard deviation** units. A *z*-score of +3 means that a score is three standard deviation units above the mean.

Annotated Bibliography

Balfanz, R., & Byrnes, V. (2012). *Chronic absenteeism: Summarizing what we know from nationally available data*. Baltimore, MD: Johns Hopkins University Center for Social Organization of Schools.

A report on school absenteeism, used in Chapter 9's discussion of sampling from schools. The report describes how absenteeism—and especially chronic absenteeism—is higher among children from low-income households.

Carney, D. R., Jost, J. T., Gosling, S. D., & Potter, J. (2008). The secret lives of liberals and conservatives: Personality profiles, interaction styles, and the things they leave behind. *Political Psychology, 29*(6), 807–840. https://doi.org/10.1111/j.1467-9221.2008.00668.x

A research article that's the basis of the political orientation measure in Chapter 3. It's an interesting study, showing that "in general, liberals are more open-minded, creative, curious, and novelty seeking, whereas conservatives are more orderly, conventional, and better organized" (p. 807).

Chang, M. K. (1998). Predicting unethical behavior: A comparison of the theory of reasoned action and the theory of planned behavior. *Journal of Business Ethics, 17*(16), 1825–1834.

The study uses the "behavioral intention" measure described in Chapter 7. The study tests two theories of persuasion and examines their efficacy in predicting whether students will engage in unethical behavior (copying software illegally). The study nicely illustrates links between theory and very practical concerns (illegal behavior), as well as the ability of measures to apply across disciplines (this measure is widely used in communication, but here it is used in a journal of business ethics).

Jones, J. M. (2018, April). *Trump's re-elect figures similar to those of Obama, Clinton*. Washington, DC: Gallup. Retrieved from https://news.gallup.com/poll/233000/trump-elect-figures-similar-obama-clinton.aspx

A report of a Gallup poll conducted in 2018 on people's opinions about whether President Donald Trump should be reelected. The poll presents some detailed statistics and is used in Chapter 10's discussion of constructing confidence intervals. It is a nice example of a nonacademic research report.

Mastro, D., & Figueroa-Caballero, A. (2018). Measuring extremes: A quantitative content analysis of prime-time TV depictions of body type. *Journal of Broadcasting & Electronic Media, 62*(2), 320–336. https://doi.org/10.1080/08838151.2018.1451853

A research article discussed during Chapter 13. The study reports a content analysis of body type on television. It shows that women on TV have become thinner over time and that overweight characters (of which there weren't many) are portrayed as less intelligent and articulate than thinner characters.

McConahay, J. B., Hardee, B. B., & Batts, V. (1981). Has racism declined in America? It depends on who is asking and what is asked. *Journal of Conflict Resolution, 25*(4), 563–579. https://doi.org/10.1177%2F002200278102500401

A research article discussed during Chapter 7. The authors present a questionnaire developed to measure "modern" racism. What counted as modern racism in 1981 now seems, of course, quite old-fashioned. The study demonstrates the need to keep updating measures of concepts that change with the times.

McCroskey, J. C., & Teven, J. J. (1999). Goodwill: A reexamination of the construct and its measurement. *Communications Monographs, 66*(1), 90–103. https://doi.org/10.1080/03637759909376464

A research article that is the basis for the source credibility measure in Chapter 5. The article focuses on different ways of measuring source credibility, arguing that "goodwill" should be part of such measures.

Neuendorf, K. A. (2016). *The content analysis guidebook.* Los Angeles, CA: SAGE Publications Inc.

A key resource for people planning on using quantitative content analysis in their research. Covers all the basics in great detail and includes specialized sections on important new areas, such as computer-assisted text analysis.

Rubin, R. B., Rubin, A. M., Graham, E., Perse, E. M., & Seibold, D. (2010). *Communication research measures II: A sourcebook.* New York, NY: Routledge.

A book of research measures (questionnaires) commonly used in the field of communication. A critical research resource for scholars wanting to use an existing measure (normally the best approach) rather than creating a new measure. It includes information on reliability and validity for all the measures included.

Strauss, A. L., & Corbin, J. (1990). *Basics of qualitative research: Grounded theory procedures and techniques.* Thousand Oaks, CA: SAGE Publications Inc.

A detailed introduction to what grounded theory is and how to do it. This is one of the classic texts in qualitative analysis.

Tracy, S. J. (2013). *Qualitative research methods: Collecting evidence, crafting analysis, communicating impact.* Malden, MA: Wiley-Blackwell.

An excellent and up-to-date introduction to the uses of qualitative research in the field of communication. It includes numerous detailed examples that bring qualitative analysis "to life."

Tsai, A. C., Kohrt, B. A., Matthews, L. T., Betancourt, T. S., Lee, J. K., Papachristos, A. V., ... & Dworkin, S. L. (2016). Promises and pitfalls of data sharing in qualitative research. *Social Science & Medicine, 169,* 191–198. https://doi.org/10.1016/j.socscimed.2016.08.004

A detailed and interesting discussion of making qualitative data sets public, including the unique ethical implications with qualitative (versus quantitative) data. It includes concrete guidance for those wishing to share qualitative data.

Ylänne, V. (2019). "Do you want to be categorized as one of the over fifty-fives"? Intergenerational relations in a public context. In J. Harwood, J. Gasiorek, H. Pierson, J. F. NussBaum, & C. Gallois (Eds.), *Language, communication, and intergroup relations: A celebration of the scholarship of Howard Giles* (pp. 182–186). New York, NY: Routledge.

An article that is mentioned in the discussion of transcribing in Chapter 15. The author describes how in casual service encounters (in this case in a travel agency), various meanings of what it is to grow old (and call yourself "old") get negotiated on a moment-by-moment basis.

Index

G

H

I

J

L

T

CPSIA information can be obtained
at www.ICGtesting.com
Printed in the USA
LVHW060715140223
739394LV00009B/97